Llamas beyond the Andes

THE WILLIAM & BETTYE NOWLIN SERIES
in Art, History, and Culture of the Western Hemisphere

Llamas beyond the Andes

Untold Histories
of Camelids
in the Modern World

Marcia Stephenson

University of Texas Press *Austin*

A portion of chapter 1 was previously published as "From Marvelous Antidote to the Poison of Idolatry: The Transatlantic Role of Andean Bezoar Stones during the Late Sixteenth and Early Seventeenth Centuries," *Hispanic American Historical Review* 90.1: 3–39 (Duke University Press, 2010). All rights reserved. Republished by permission of the publisher. A portion of chapter 2 was published as "Colonial Intersections: The Dissection of Andean Camelids and Knowledge Production," in *Animals and Science: From Colonial Encounters to the Biotech Industry*, edited by Maggie Bolton and Cathrine Degnen, 30–60 (Newcastle upon Tyne: Cambridge Scholars Press, 2010).

All translations are by the author unless otherwise noted.

Copyright © 2023 by the University of Texas Press
All rights reserved
Printed in the United States of America
First edition, 2023

Requests for permission to reproduce material from this work should be sent to:
Permissions
University of Texas Press
P.O. Box 7819
Austin, TX 78713-7819
utpress.utexas.edu

♾ The paper used in this book meets the minimum requirements of ANSI/NISO Z39.48-1992 (R1997) (Permanence of Paper).

Library of Congress Cataloging-in-Publication Data

Names: Stephenson, Marcia, 1955– author.
Title: Llamas beyond the Andes: Untold histories of camelids in the modern world / Marcia Stephenson.
Other titles: William & Bettye Nowlin series in art, history, and culture of the Western Hemisphere.
Description: First edition. | Austin : University of Texas Press, 2023. | Series: William and Bettye Nowlin series in art, history, and culture of the Western Hemisphere | Includes bibliographical references and index.
Identifiers: LCCN 2023005956 (print) | LCCN 2023005957 (ebook)
    ISBN 978-1-4773-2840-8 (hardcover)
    ISBN 978-1-4773-2841-5 (pdf)
    ISBN 978-1-4773-2842-2 (epub)
Subjects: LCSH: Camelidae—Social aspects—History. | Camelidae—Andes—History. | Andes—Relations—Europe—History. | Andes—Relations—Australia—History. | Andes—Relations—United States—History.
Classification: LCC QL737.U54 S737 2023 (print) | LCC QL737.U54 (ebook) | DDC 599.63/6—dc23/eng/20230425
LC record available at https://lccn.loc.gov/2023005956
LC ebook record available at https://lccn.loc.gov/2023005957

doi:10.7560/328408

Contents

List of Abbreviations   *vii*

INTRODUCTION. "The Most Interesting Animals in the World": Reconstructing Histories of Andean Camelids in Transoceanic Contact Zones   *1*

CHAPTER 1. From Marvelous Antidote to the Poison of Idolatry: The Transatlantic Significance of Andean Bezoar Stones during the Late Sixteenth and Early Seventeenth Centuries   *25*

CHAPTER 2. Exploring the Body-Interior: Autopsy in Colonial Camelid Contact Zones   *57*

CHAPTER 3. From Curiosity to Commodity: Early Efforts to Ship Living Camelids to Europe   *89*

CHAPTER 4. The Science of Acclimatization: Llamas and Alpacas in Nineteenth-Century France   *125*

CHAPTER 5. Andean Itineraries of Nineteenth-Century Camelid Science: The Case of Charles Ledger   *165*

CHAPTER 6. Camelids in Australia: The Rise and Fall of Charles Ledger's Alpaca Ambitions   *207*

CHAPTER 7. US Camelid Contact Zones in the Twentieth Century: Authenticity, Exoticism, and Celebrity   *257*

CONCLUSION. The Afterlives of Camelid Contact Zones   *285*

Acknowledgments   *291*

Notes   *297*

Works Cited   *335*

Index   *363*

List of Abbreviations

AAM/AMS Archives of the Australian Museum (Sydney)

ACCLIMATIZATION SOCIETY Société Zoologique d'Acclimatation (Paris)

ADMM Archives Départementales de Meurthe et Moselle (Nancy)

AGI Archivo General de Indias (Seville)

AGN Archivo General de la Nación (Lima)

AGP Archivo General de Palacio (Madrid)

AHBCE/JJC Archivo Histórico Banco Central del Ecuador/(Fondo) Jacinto Jijón y Caamaño (Quito)

AHCNM Archivo Histórico de la Casa Nacional de Moneda (Potosí)

AHMRE/F: CRLEF Archivo Histórico Ministerio de Relaciones Exteriores/Fondo: Comunicaciones Recibidas de la Legación del Ecuador en Francia (Quito)

AHN Archivo Histórico Nacional de España (Madrid)

AMC Archivo Municipal de Cádiz (Cádiz)

AMM Archives du Musée de Malmaison (Malmaison)

AMN Archivo del Museo Naval (Madrid)

ANB Archivo y Biblioteca Nacionales de Bolivia (Sucre)

ANC/ACG Archivo Nacional de Chile/Archivo de la Capitanía General (Santiago)

ANF Archives Nationales de France (Paris)

ARP Archivo Regional de Puno (Puno)

BNP Biblioteca Nacional del Perú (Lima)

DGL SMP DeGolyer Library, Stanley Marcus Papers (digitized collection), Southern Methodist University (Dallas)

DMAA JNWP Dallas Museum of Art Archives, John and Nora Wise Papers

DPLA Dallas Public Library Archives

HM-RCS Archives, Hunterian Museum—Royal College of Surgeons (London)

KEW National Archives, United Kingdom (Kew)

LAV Legislative Assembly of Victoria (Melbourne)

MALMMM Maritime Archives and Library, Merseyside Maritime Museum (Liverpool)

viii | *List of Abbreviations*

MEAE Ministère de l'Europe et des Affaires Étrangères, Archives Diplomatiques, Affaires Diverses Politiques (La Courneuve)

ML Mitchell Library, State Library of New South Wales (Sydney)

ML MSS 630/1 Mitchell Library Archives, MS 630/1, Series 01: "Annotated watercolour sketches by Santiago Savage, 1857–1858, being a record of Charles Ledger's journeys in Peru and Chile; with maps and notes" (Sydney)

MNHN Muséum National d'Histoire Naturelle (Paris)

NHS Newburgh (New York) Historical Society

NLM HMC National Library of Medicine, History of Medicine Collection (Bethesda, Maryland)

NSW New South Wales

NSW, VPLA New South Wales, *Votes and Proceedings of the Legislative Assembly, during the Session of 1861–62, with the Various Documents Connected Therewith*, vol. 2, doc. 58-A, "Flock of Alpacas, and Claims of Mr. Ledger. (Return in Reference to)" (Sydney)

PROV, VPRS Public Record Office, Victoria (Melbourne)

SRNSW NRS8362 (9/2659) State Records Archives, New South Wales, Lands Dept., Miscellaneous Papers Re: Introduction of Alpacas to NSW, 1860–1864 (Kingswood, Western Sydney)

UOR H-FCP University of Rochester River Campus Libraries, Rare Books, Special Collections, Preservation, Hickey-Freeman Company Papers (1899–present) (Rochester, New York)

VH *Victorian Hansard Containing the Votes and Proceedings of the Legislative Council & Assembly of the Colony of Victoria* (Melbourne)

VPLA-S *Votes and Proceedings of the Legislative Assembly, with the Various Documents Connected Therewith* (Sydney)

VPPHP *Victoria: Papers Presented to Both Houses of Parliament by Command of His Excellency the Governor* (Melbourne)

VVPLA *Victoria: Votes and Proceedings of the Legislative Assembly* (Melbourne)

VVPLC *Victoria: Votes and Proceedings of the Legislative Council* (Melbourne)

VVPLC, RSCLCA *Victoria: Votes and Proceedings of the Legislative Council, Victoria: Report from the Select Committee of the Legislative Council on the Alpaca*

YBL IMC (GEN MSS 996) Yale Beinecke Library, Inge Morath Collection (New Haven, Connecticut)

Llamas beyond the Andes

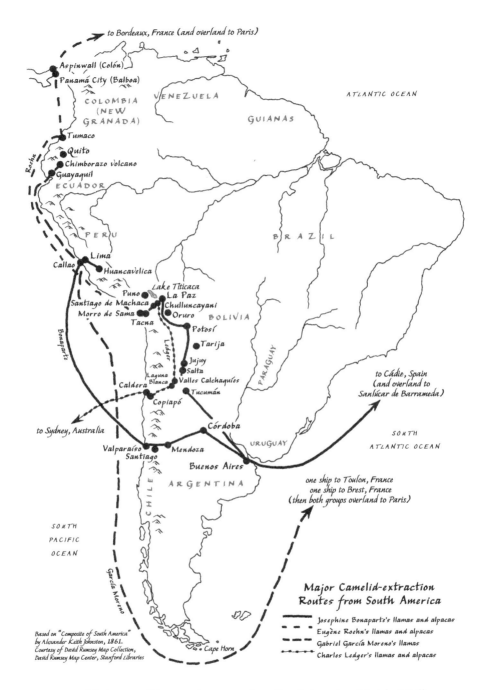

MAP 0.1. *Major camelid-extraction routes from South America. Map by Molly O'Halloran, Inc.*

INTRODUCTION

"The Most Interesting Animals in the World"

Reconstructing Histories of Andean Camelids in Transoceanic Contact Zones

Many years ago, after wrapping up some research at the Arsenal Library in Paris in 2003, I idly flipped through a book of nineteenth-century French circus posters.[1] One bold headline caught my eye: "LIONS!! TIGERS!! JUMPING LLAMAS FROM PERU!!!" I was unaware at the time that living specimens of Andean camelids could be found in Europe during the nineteenth century, much less in numbers sufficient to form trained troupes in circuses. Over the next few months, as I began to research the topic, I discovered that the incidence of camelids in nineteenth-century spectacles was only a small part of a much larger story of llamas, alpacas, vicuñas, and guanacos in global arenas that began significantly earlier. I could not anticipate how that story would bring to light endlessly generative histories and heretofore unexamined contact zones formed around the animals' living and dead bodies and involve myriad participants from across a socioeconomic and ethnic spectrum.

According to my preliminary findings, the Andean camelids captured the imagination of the Spanish who came to the New World perhaps more than any other fauna they encountered. And the more the Europeans learned, the more their fascination grew. The first chroniclers of the conquest of Peru expressed astonishment upon seeing these strange "sheep." It was not long before they discovered that camelids constitute a uniquely valuable resource, providing practical benefits such as transport for cargo, meat, fiber, fertilizer, and exotic, mysterious objects like bezoar stones.

Later on, as I scheduled trips to archives and spent one year studying llama anatomy at Purdue University's College of Veterinary Medicine, I would uncover more about the camelids' international presence and trajectory, which began soon after first contact between Europeans and

2 | Llamas beyond the Andes

Andean pastoral peoples. Word spread quickly overseas about the rare and highly coveted bezoar stones found inside these unfamiliar creatures, which were believed to be powerful antidotes and cure-alls for a range of illnesses. The discovery led to increased hunting of the wild species, with the goal of harvesting the stones from inside them for medicinal and commercial purposes. The camelids themselves drew attention, and Europeans began shipping living specimens overseas as singular examples of New World exotica. When larger numbers of the animals eventually did reach Europe and elsewhere in the nineteenth century, they met with a mixed reaction. Some scientists eagerly anticipated that camelids would help to solve the problems of rural poverty by providing a new source of protein and fiber; others feared that they would compete with the sheep industry. By the early twentieth century, camelid fiber was gaining greater commercial prominence in places like the United States. Products made with vicuña, alpaca, and llama represented the heights of luxury fashion, while the animals themselves (as stuffed or living specimens) featured prominently in ads as exotic symbols of wealth and status. Thanks to such powerful rival scientific, commercial, and cultural interests, the camelids have played an unprecedented role across the centuries as a central meeting point for diverse groups from the North and South.

Those who live in Europe, North America, and elsewhere today may be familiar with llamas and alpacas, which both can now commonly be seen on farms and in zoos and parks around the world. There are four species of Andean camelids: the llama (*Lama glama*) and alpaca (*Vicugna pacos*), both of which are domesticated, and the wild guanaco (*Lama guanicoe*) and vicuña (*Vicugna vicugna*).[2] All four species can be crossed, and their offspring are fertile. The llama and alpaca were domesticated in the Andes 6,000 to 7,000 years ago and are found in regions of high elevation there. The alpaca's present-day natural habitat is generally limited to Peru and Bolivia, whereas the llama can be found as far north as Ecuador and south into northern Chile and Argentina. As for the wild camelids, the guanaco's range extends the farthest, from southern Ecuador to Tierra del Fuego, while the vicuña's habitat encompasses southern Peru and Bolivia and extends into northern Chile and Argentina.[3]

The importance of the camelids for Andean biotic communities historically and in the present cannot be overestimated. The animals have always been a primary source of protein, fat, and bones (which can be used as tools for weaving and household and agricultural work). Camelid manure provides essential fertilizer for crops grown in fragile, high-altitude

Andean ecosystems where the soil is poorly developed, the topography is rugged, frosts and freezes are common, and precipitation is light (Browman 1990, 396–397). Llamas have traditionally played a critical role as carriers, transporting foodstuffs, textiles, and other goods throughout the Andean region and west to the Pacific coast and east into the Amazon basin, thereby facilitating trade among communities of different ecosystems. All of the camelids produce fiber, which can be used for creating textiles and cords. The fleece of the vicuña and alpaca is especially prized due to its lower micron count. Although llama fiber today is coarser than alpaca fiber, recent archaeological research shows that pre-Inca Chiribaya herds at El Yaral (Peru, AD 700–1300) were carefully managed to create alpacas and llamas with extra-fine and fine fleece (Wheeler 2005a). The Incas selectively bred large herds of both animals for high-quality fiber and for color, especially pure black, brown, and white animals for ritual sacrifice. The Incas reserved the use of the wild vicuña's precious fiber primarily for themselves, harvesting it sustainably every five years when they carried out large hunts known as *chacos*. During these events, hunters live-captured vicuñas, shearing and releasing most, while slaughtering others for later consumption.[4]

A significant body of research has focused on understanding the Andean camelids in the context of Spanish conquest and colonization and the devastating ecological and environmental consequences it created, including the overhunting of the wild vicuña and guanaco populations and the mismanagement of llama and alpaca flocks. For example, the Spanish did not distinguish between llamas and alpacas and placed both species together indiscriminately, thereby ending centuries-long selective breeding practices (Wheeler, Russel, and Redden 1995, 833). During the early colonial period, camelid populations were further decimated by deadly outbreaks of contagious scabies (*Sarcoptes scabiei/Psoroptes communis*) (Flores Ochoa and MacQuarrie 1994b, 130). Finally, large numbers of alpacas and llamas were diverted to Potosí and other mining centers, where they were slaughtered for their meat or used as transporters of minerals, mercury, and supplies. Under the colonial *mita* system of forced labor, Indigenous peoples removed to mining centers suffered injuries, illness, and death due to harsh working conditions. The lifespan of llamas used in the mining industry was also very short (Flores Ochoa and MacQuarrie 1994b, 130). Along with the disappearance of 80 percent of Indigenous peoples during this early colonial period, Wheeler, Russel, and Redden (1995, 834) estimate that nearly 90 percent of llamas and

4 | *Llamas beyond the Andes*

alpacas were lost, creating "catastrophic mortality upon camelid genetic diversity and breeding."

Despite the large losses of population, the camelids have continued to play an integral role in the survival of Andean peoples and epistemologies. Our appreciation of the significance of llamas and alpacas in the persistence of Andean cultural practices and "social memory" (Abercrombie 1998, 21–25) under colonial rule, for example, has been enriched by scholars who have studied the animals' function within pastoral communities as symbols in Indigenous rituals of exchange and sacrifice and as key interspecies metaphors for theorizing human development and political hierarchy (Abercrombie 1998; Arnold and Yapita 1998; Caro 1994; Dedenbach-Salazar Sáenz 1990; Flores Ochoa 1977, 1988; Flores Ochoa and Kobayashi 2000; Portús 1994). Ethnographic approaches have examined recent herding technologies, care of the animals, and the transformation of fleece into yarn, while historical studies of herding communities in the context of colonial economic and geographic expansion illuminate the role the camelids played in strengthening Indigenous communities against Spanish encroachment (Dransart 1996, 2002; Medinaceli G. 2010).

Although such scholarship has significantly advanced our understanding of the broad impact that the camelids have had on Andean ecologies, communities, and lives of Indigenous pastoral peoples, my research showed that key aspects regarding the animals and their significance beyond the Andes remained largely overlooked. Chief among these are the untold histories of the animals that were removed from their native habitat and transported overseas, beginning with the colonial period and extending into the late nineteenth century. My book is about these ongoing and concerted efforts over the centuries, primarily on the part of Europeans and European settlers, to transform the living camelids and/or camelid fragments into valuable commodities for introduction elsewhere. The focus on extraction stories signals the importance of investigating the animals' geographic and historical trajectories, their routes and roots (Clifford 1997), as well as the narratives generated throughout their lives and afterlives, what Patchett, Foster, and Lorimer (2011, 112) refer to as a specimen's "biogeographies."[5] Here these biogeographies encompass the histories that emerge from human-camelid encounters in new global arenas.[6]

By centering attention on narratives of camelid extraction over several centuries, my book joins a growing body of scholarship that examines the roles played by animals in the histories of the Americas (for example, Asúa and French 2005; Cowie 2017a, 2017b; Few and Tortorici 2013; Medinaceli G. 2010; Melville 1994). As affirmed by Few and Tortorici (2013, 5), animals in Latin American history have been neglected, but their study brings new ways of understanding animal-human relationships that "complicate and go beyond recent work on the critical examinations of difference through the analytic lenses of race, ethnicity, gender, and sexuality." One key goal of my research is to show how the study of the camelids reveals heretofore overlooked interactions among a diversity of human and nonhuman animals in the context of imperial extraction projects.

Material remains, like a skeleton or taxidermy specimen found in a European museum of natural history, can be a valuable starting point for investigating the histories of an animal's transoceanic life, death, and afterlife. At the center of figure 0.1 stands a nineteenth-century taxidermy llama, accompanied by five stuffed vicuñas and piles of skins. These specimens are housed in the storage facility of Paris's Muséum National d'Histoire Naturelle (National Museum of Natural History). Despite their somewhat musty appearance, these creatures still manifest what Poliquin (2012, 139–140) describes as the taxidermy animal's "alarming magnetism," which provokes "the compelling fascination to look, and the worry about what made that looking possible." Taxidermy achieves this paradoxical effect of attraction and alarm and discomfort because, as a practice, its underlying objective is to re-create a sense of "liveness," to "imput[e] life back into the dead" (Patchett and Foster 2008, 98). Recent critical work has sought to reinvigorate interest in taxidermy collections, with the goal of recovering the histories of their making and maintenance (Patchett and Foster 2008; Swinney 2011). The taxidermic process requires the dead animal's dismemberment and reconstruction; therefore, its method is first and foremost one of re-creation or reenlivening (Desmond 2002, 166). As such, taxidermy serves as an apt metaphor for one of this book's primary concerns: to reconstruct or reanimate, to the extent possible, the biogeographies of camelids in new transoceanic arenas, from first contact through the mid-twentieth century. The process of reanimation brings a certain agency to artifacts like the stuffed llama. My book seeks to recover some of the material and documentary artifacts that help enliven histories of camelids in the global world, to claim, along with Swinney (2011, 229), that "the postmortem reanimation of once biologically living objects as material culture is a process of narration. Afterlives are created through their telling—lives told, lives no longer (biologically) lived."

The taxidermy llama featured in figure 0.1 can serve as an example

6 | *Llamas beyond the Andes*

FIGURE 0.1. *"Lama femelle. 23 mai 1851, mort à la Ménagerie. Vien de Hollande" (Female llama, May 23, 1851, died at the Menagerie. Came from Holland). Photograph taken by the author in the storage facility of the Muséum National d'Histoire Naturelle, Paris.*

of how such specimens provide clues for the narrative re-creation of the animal's life and journeys. The natural history museum's official record identifies the llama as female, her provenance as Holland, and the logged date of her death as May 23, 1851. Further investigation of textual sources prepared by prominent natural historians of the time brought to light additional fragments of information. I was able to ascertain that she belonged to a small flock of llamas, alpacas, and vicuñas brought out of the Andes and shipped to England around 1845. Although the archival record is incomplete, it is possible to hypothesize that the animals may have been gathered by Englishman Charles Ledger, a long-time resident of Peru and supplier of small numbers of camelids to interested parties abroad in the 1840s. His work in the 1850s smuggling a large group of llamas and alpacas out of Bolivia and across the Andes for shipment to Australia is the

Introduction | 7

subject of two chapters. After the 1845 flock reached Britain, King William II of the Netherlands purchased several of the animals and had them brought to Holland. Four years later, his successor William III offered to sell the animals to the French government, which had been trying to obtain llama and alpaca stock for acclimatization and naturalization. The animals arrived in Paris in 1849. Placed with other llamas at the Museum of Natural History's menagerie, the female in the picture lived there for two more years before she died while giving birth. This assertion is possible because that was the only camelid death recorded at the menagerie in 1851 (Bonafous 1847; Geoffroy Saint-Hilaire [1861] 1986, 331).

The llama's taxidermy body, still preserved at the Paris Museum of Natural History, becomes a starting point for reconstructing the multiple itineraries she survived (from the Andes to Great Britain, the Netherlands, and France) and her death and continuing afterlife as a storage and study specimen. As such, this one constructed afterlife provides a glimpse of the kinds of historical, geopolitical, and cultural convergences that formed in and around camelid bodies. Yet, while it was possible to discover certain details about her particular journeys, such reenlivening is not always achievable. Her remains thus represent more than the trajectories of one individual llama. In the case studies in this book, the reanimation of specific camelid narratives evokes the histories of other animals and flocks, most of whose stories have been lost.

Rather than attempting a comprehensive review of camelid extraction over the centuries, my book engages representative case studies, each of which recovers narratives that emerge from distinct camelid-human junctures. Importantly, it also calls attention to the silences or gaps that remain as part of the afterlives of these case histories. My claim is that, once recovered, at least partially, these multilayered stories show how encounters with camelids had an impact on at least three fronts. First, by following the traces and trajectories of living camelids and camelid artifacts as they were moved out of the New World, these histories illuminate the animals' increasingly important role as global commodities in the wider transatlantic context of commercial and scientific networks. Moreover, by incorporating new research from Australia, they expand the field of investigation from the transatlantic to the transpacific arena, bringing to light understudied mercantile relationships between South America and the Pacific world.

Second, I maintain that camelid extraction carried important implications for understanding colonial legacies and confrontations between

8 | *Llamas beyond the Andes*

urban and rural sectors in local contact zones in the Andes, where the animals were found, and in Europe, Australia, and the United States, where they were introduced. Unlike sheep and other imported livestock, which were typically kept in large numbers on mestizo haciendas, llamas and alpacas were raised by Andean pastoral peoples. Anyone attempting to extract the animals usually had to interact with the Indigenous communities, personally or through local intermediaries. Especially in the eighteenth and nineteenth centuries, some creoles from cities such as Lima, La Paz, or Valparaíso and even more remote centers like Puno were willing to collaborate with European scientific societies and/or governments in the extraction of small numbers of camelids.[7] In contrast, most rural Andean pastoral communities refused to part with their camelids willingly. Camelid extraction projects were entangled with modern forms of imperialism and played a decisive role in the "marginalization and alteration of indigenous ecosystems and peoples," as Osborne (2000, 135) has more generally argued. Finally, just as colonialism included the collection and transfer of flora and fauna by Western metropolitan centers, histories of camelids in transoceanic arenas make it evident that local knowledge too was extracted, appropriated, transformed, and redistributed through new global scientific networks.

One of my primary aims in this book is to show how these intercultural sites of encounter or contact zones are productive areas of inquiry for the recovery of camelid histories because they have generated singular integrations of instrumental science, commerce, and visual aesthetics. As such, they provide novel mechanisms through which we can assess the convergence of different knowledges and actors and commercial and political interests. In developing a second central paradigm of the book, I draw on Pratt (1992, 4), who conceptualizes contact zones as those "social spaces where disparate cultures meet, clash, and grapple with each other, often in highly asymmetrical relations of domination and subordination." Following Pratt, the model of the contact zone is fundamental to my study because it emphasizes what she refers to as a "'contact' perspective," which elucidates how colonizers and colonized, as well as other communities, have come together and become connected through their interactions and "interlocking understandings and practices, often within radically asymmetrical relations of power" (7). The value of Pratt's now classic conceptual model can be seen across my study, which gives emphasis to the significance and impact of ever-widening circles of protagonists gathering around camelid bodies. These participatory communities include Andean

Introduction | 9

pastoral peoples, women, and other marginalized actors, even when they are only present as an absence in more monolithic, masculine grand narratives of empire.

My study also extends Pratt's work when it focuses on camelid contact zones as multilateral sites, where Indigenous peoples become active subjects of study rather than mere backdrops to European discovery narratives. I offer as an example a second artifact that illustrates these key themes. The engraving in figure 0.2 comes from the Brawern-Herckemann Dutch military expedition to southern Chile during the 1640s. This early illustration brings to light some of the many participants and issues that historically have converged around the camelid body and are taken up in subsequent chapters, while demonstrating the importance of the visual archive as well as written documents and material specimens in piecing together these case studies. Depicting two groups that stand at opposite ends of the animal, identified as a "camel-sheep," the engraving provides one dramatic example of how Andean camelids functioned as a significant meeting point for different cultures and interactions involving knowledge-making, the commodification of exotica, and commercial exchange. At its head, a curious European soldier points toward the creature as if requesting information about it; the Mapuche couple remains proprietarily close to the animal's hindquarters. Their neutral expressions do not disclose whether they are offering the animal or ensuring that it will not be taken from them.

Bleichmar (2017) has described how early visual representations of European encounters with the New World typically construct such meetings in oppositional terms. She refers specifically to the familiar images by Johannes Stradanus and Theodoor Galle of Vespucci landing in the Americas, which depict a naked Indigenous woman in a hammock greeting the armored Amerigo Vespucci, who wears his sword and carries a Southern Cross flag and an astrolabe. As Bleichmar (2017, 13) observes, "The explorer shows the female powerful technological and cultural symbols representing navigation, exploration, military might, and religion. She counters with curiosities and nature," including exotic implements, plants, and animals. On the one hand, the Brawern-Herckemann engraving follows this visual convention. Although the Europeans are not wearing armor, the principal soldier's sword hangs visibly at his side, while the Indigenous couple's barbarism is identifiable through the familiar tropes of the woman's scantily clad body and bare breasts and the man's bow and arrow and hat with devil-like horns.

10 | Llamas beyond the Andes

FIGURE 0.2. *Engraving of a "camel-sheep" from Brawern and Herckemann (1649, 8). Courtesy of the John Carter Brown Library.*

Nonetheless, there are also significant differences, pointing to further complexities of camelid contact zones. Here the Indigenous man claims equal status with the two European soldiers. With one foot forward and a direct, level gaze, he assumes a stance that Europeans would have deemed imposing, even regal, demonstrating strength and confidence. Furthermore, both he and the European who gestures toward the animal wear plumes in their hats, suggesting their parallel status. Meanwhile, the third figure from the left, standing at the picture's center and next to the camel-sheep, appears to be captured in the middle of speech and gesture, implying his role as interpreter. This scene of exchange prefigures intercultural encounters examined throughout the book, marking out a contact zone where different groups congregated around the living camelid body or carcass, frequently with competing desires attached to it.

Also key in this engraving of a mid-seventeenth century camelid contact zone is the central object of curiosity: the "camel-sheep" and its anthropomorphized, welcoming facial expression. The animal's exotic anatomy calls attention to itself as an object of contemplation and wonder.

Introduction | 11

In particular, with its four-toed front feet and hind hooves, it exemplifies the concept of a "jigsaw-puzzle" beast (Asúa and French 2005, 14), whereby European authors and artists attempted to convey to readers what an unfamiliar animal looked like by comparing different sections of its body to those of familiar animals, in the end creating a sort of composite monstrous beast.[8]

Brawern and Herckemann's "camel-sheep" typifies the classificatory confusion of the camelids for Europeans, beginning with first contact. Although these animals were portrayed early on as a composite of multiple beasts, the sheep, ewe, or ram persisted as the primary point of comparison that Europeans referenced to describe the exotic Andean creatures, beginning with the sixteenth century and continuing through much of the nineteenth century. This rendered the four species of camelids generally indistinguishable from one another, with the appellation of "Peruvian" or "Indian sheep."[9] The question of animal identification and classification figures in the following case studies in at least two strategic ways. First, Europeans tried to develop a growing understanding of these animals and their overall health, especially when there was an urgent need to find effective treatments for contagious diseases capable of eradicating entire flocks extracted to new environments. Second, a deeper knowledge of the animals and the differences among them became necessary once Europeans and South Americans began experimenting with new breeding and hybridization programs in the effort to create what they hoped would be stronger and more tractable fine-wooled animals for national and international fiber markets.

Beyond highlighting the exotic camel-sheep as an object of curiosity and wonder, the Brawern-Herckemann engraving illustrates how these two factors function as drivers of knowledge-construction and collection in the camelid contact zone. Wonder and curiosity operated as an epistemic method in the seventeenth century, triggering inquiry and deliberation by evidencing the border between "the known and the unknown" (Daston and Park 2001, 13).[10] This dynamic plays out in the Brawern-Herckemann image, as it depicts how curiosity impels the collection of knowledge and commodities in a colonial context, while simultaneously making visible the fraught nature of intercultural communication in the knowledge-making process. Here each party plays a role of importance in the exchange of information. On the right-hand side of the image, the curious Dutch soldier signals his interest in the intriguing animal, presumably setting the communicative process into motion or continuing one begun previously

12 | *Llamas beyond the Andes*

outside of the image's frame. Placed at the center, behind the camelid, the interpreter-translator appears to mediate between the two parties situated at either end of the animal's body. His actions imply that knowledge here is generated collectively as it moves from the Mapuche couple through the middleman to the inquiring newcomers.[11]

The importance of the Indigenous couple for knowledge construction is underscored by the way they physically occupy a similar amount of space as the Europeans. Although fewer in number than the strangers, their slightly larger build creates a sense of balance and proportion in the image. All the protagonists except for the figure on the right, including the camel-sheep, share the same ocular plane. This suggests parity of vision and intelligence and highlights the importance of eyewitnessing (autopsia) and the credibility of the experience being depicted.[12]

The representation of the different protagonists' eyes brings attention to the importance of firsthand experience for the reliability of the larger travel narrative. The camel-sheep takes the initiative to communicate with the Europeans by making direct eye contact and appearing to smile.[13] The creature's wide-open eyes match those of the two Indians and translator, underscoring the visual significance of this scene of encounter for the local residents. In contrast, the details of the Europeans' facial expressions remain less evident because they are turned more toward the animal than toward the viewer. The eyes of the rightmost person appear partially lowered and wary, with his body turned slightly away from the scene of encounter. Both he and the Indigenous woman come across as potentially marginal to the scene. Nevertheless, even though we know little about them or their role in this negotiation, the engraving is unusual insofar as it marks their presence, which is generally muted or elided by the prevailing colonial narrative. Throughout this book I address the significance of the many people who materialize on the fringes of camelid contact zones, whose appearance in the scene of knowledge construction points to further stories even though they may not impact directly on the primary scene of narration.

The illustration clarifies that curiosity did not solely entail collecting knowledge about strange and wondrous objects. It also highlights the connections between wonder and the collection and contemplation of exotica and the desire to transform these extraordinary elements of the natural world into commodities (Daston and Park 2001, 23, 67). The discernible presence of the ship in the distance suggests that the Europeans' curiosity regarding the animal was not disinterested. It alludes to another theme of the book, which traces how gestures of appreciation extended by

Europeans toward the camelids quickly became gestures of appropriation when they attempted to obtain the animals for shipment overseas, often by any means possible. Greenblatt (1991, 24–25) describes this process as "the colonizing of the marvelous." Camelid contact zones thus also bring significant attention to colonial ecological relations and the devastations wrought, especially as European nations began to direct efforts toward transferring living animals overseas. Appropriative gestures moved from collecting smaller numbers of camelids during the sixteenth through the eighteenth centuries to more comprehensive extraction projects during the mid-nineteenth century, when France and England especially sought to obtain sizable flocks of these useful animals as fiber and meat stock. Indigenous pastoral peoples were key to the process of Andean camelids becoming global commodities because they had the knowledge and expertise Europeans believed necessary for extracting greater numbers of the animals successfully abroad.

The agency of Indigenous pastoral peoples in the transfer of camelids and knowledge is a central concern of this book. Often resistant to European efforts to obtain the animals, but sometimes participating in them, Indigenous shepherds displayed a range of attitudes and played a variety of important roles in these projects because they were the ones who raised alpacas and llamas and had direct access to them. The case studies taken up here reveal ways in which Indigenous shepherds actively shaped the process of knowledge-making, sometimes by energetically refusing to negotiate with European outsiders and at other times by agreeing to knowledge-sharing. During the nineteenth century, these histories document how the topic of bringing Indigenous shepherds along on the transport ships became a subject of debate among European scientists. With few exceptions, merchants and ship captains relied on Indigenous expertise regarding the animals' health and welfare during the transoceanic crossing. So, too, Indigenous caretakers could be blamed when large numbers of animal casualties inevitably occurred. My attempt to recover and reconstruct these relationships and narratives has sometimes been curtailed because of insufficient documentary evidence. Most of the stories involving the Indigenous shepherds can be characterized as conspicuously incomplete or present only through allusion. As a rule, they leave unanswered questions as a legacy. Nonetheless, I have looked for any openings to call attention to the (missing) presence of Indigenous peoples and knowledges throughout this project, because a full understanding of camelid encounters requires such analysis.

14 | *Llamas beyond the Andes*

Transformations in Nineteenth- and Twentieth-Century Camelid Contact Zones

Although the language of exoticism and wonder was never fully abandoned in Western commentary on Andean camelids, the period of the mid- to late eighteenth and early nineteenth centuries marks a rhetorical shift when promoters of camelid extraction intensified their scrutiny of the animals' utilitarian benefits. By the mid-nineteenth century, French and English scientists and merchants identified the Andean camelids as the single most important livestock for international acclimatization and naturalization projects. The challenge to be resolved was how to obtain the animals in sufficient numbers to make their acclimatization successful from both a scientific and an economic standpoint. In France, for example, the Paris Acclimatization Society had to rely on individuals willing to take the risk of collecting the animals on-site, bringing them out of the Andes, and transporting them overseas. Economic incentives resulted in some undertakings being conducted by individual collectors without the permission of the Andean governments of the places where the animals were gathered.

My book follows the exploits of two such figures, Frenchman Eugène Roehn and Englishman Charles Ledger, both of whom brought one or more flocks out of the Andes on behalf of their homelands and other nations. Each wrote dramatic accounts casting themselves as intrepid protagonists who faced countless adventures and dangers in the local camelid contact zone from hostile Indians and governments. They heightened the emotional impact of their extraction narratives through the use of tropes from the classic heroic quest that linked travel, risk, hunting, and collection with national honor, scientific progress, and economic recompense.[14] Following these two men's stories to their conclusion reveals important variations in the heroic paradigm each developed, including its eventual breakdown in Ledger's case when his project ultimately failed. In the end, his account exposed how heroes can be made and unmade by empire.

One value of reading these extraction accounts through the lens of the intercultural camelid contact zone, I argue, can be found in the discovery that the contact perspective destabilizes the heroic narrative, keeping it from subsuming all other stories. Instead, as already claimed, the analytical paradigm of the contact zone never loses sight of how camelid histories are closely interwoven with multiple narratives, protagonists, and participatory communities. Although they bring to light imperial extractive enterprises such as those carried out by Ledger and Roehn, they also make visible other accounts, such as the story of the Andean shepherds who accompanied these two adventurers; the history of Ecuadorian president Gabriel García Moreno and his gift of a small flock of llamas to the French government; and the narrative about a llama brought to the Vosges mountains in France, where it lived for a few years and became a local celebrity.

When taken as a whole and read together across the centuries, the histories and narratives emerging from camelid contact zones reveal further stories, notably about the devastating physical consequences these extraction ventures had on the animals themselves. Beginning with European first contact in the New World and continuing through the nineteenth century, projects related to the global transfer of living camelids inevitably produced high numbers of animal casualties and impacted negatively on all camelid populations and the local biotic relationships of which they formed an intrinsic part. The search for bezoar stones, for example, led to the slaughter of hundreds of wild camelids. With regard to the commerce of living camelids, while it was not possible to track down complete or always accurate data measuring animal survival rates, the records clearly confirm that these shipments resulted in high rates of camelid deaths, despite the precautions taken to protect the animals during transit overland and overseas.

The leading causes of animal fatalities were believed to be insufficient or inappropriate food and water, contagious outbreaks of pernicious skin diseases, gastrointestinal problems, complications related to pregnancy and parturition, injuries and accidents, and depression and homesickness. Furthermore, the small percentages of animals that did manage to survive the journey through the Andes to the port of embarkation and across the ocean generally had a low life expectancy after reaching their new permanent locations. Given the high costs involved in moving large numbers of animals overseas and the low rate of survival for the flocks in transit and upon arrival, most camelid acclimatization experiments came to an end by the 1870s.

Although the majority of the case studies examined here focus on camelid contact zones formed prior to the twentieth century, changes and transformations taking place in the fiber industry during the 1930s to the 1950s warrant consideration. In the United States, for example, the years between the two world wars witnessed a new interest in camelid fiber on the part of the high-end fashion industry. The New York–based textile mill S. Stroock & Co. specialized in the production of costly llama,

16 | Llamas beyond the Andes

vicuña, and alpaca fabrics and utilized advertising methods that drew on the now-familiar tropes of wonder and curiosity as well as travel and adventure to market its choice products. At the same time, Andean shepherds, like those who gained a certain prominence for their knowledge and skill in nineteenth-century camelid-extraction narratives, were only rarely pictured alongside the animals in ads. Nor were they represented in the company's newly developed marketing strategies created to attract customers. Their presence and expertise no longer figured as a selling point for a modern textile industry uninterested in attempting the hugely expensive and historically unsuccessful project of importing live animals for fiber. Instead, manufacturers like S. Stroock & Co. sourced the still relatively unknown camelid fleeces directly from Peru's fiber-exporting companies.[15]

Textile mills like S. Stroock & Co. did not have to extract live camelids to obtain the fiber needed. Small numbers of llamas did exist in the United States at the time, primarily in zoos and on game farms. Contemporary llama breeders and enthusiasts recognize as the most prominent of these the flock introduced in the 1930s owned by the famous newspaper magnate William Randolph Hearst.[16] Following Hearst's death in 1951, Roland Lindemann of the Catskill Game Farm purchased the remaining flock and had the animals brought to upstate New York. He mixed Hearst's llamas with his own, eventually creating a flock of more than three hundred animals and becoming known as the "llama king" (Lindemann quoted in Hoffman 2001–2002, 11; see also Patterson 1994, 6). For several decades, Lindemann's animals stocked zoos and game farms across the country.

Two of Lindemann's young llamas went on to become media celebrities in the 1950s after they were purchased by New York City animal trainers Bernard and Lorrain D'Essen. Lorrain D'Essen taught the attractive white llamas, Llucky and Llinda Llee, to stand quietly as models for advertisements and appearances on television shows. Llinda Llee and D'Essen flew to Dallas in October 1959 to participate in Neiman Marcus's international South America Fortnight celebrations. For two weeks, Llinda Llee entertained shoppers, diplomats, and artists as an official greeter for the event. As figure 0.3 shows, she posed elegantly for photographs in her capacity as "cultural ambassador," bringing South American authenticity to all events that she attended. This figure captures the excitement and fascination of the Fortnight visitors as they gathered around the exotic "Peruvian" llama to have their picture taken alongside her. The photograph draws surprising parallels with the Brawern-Herckemann engraving already examined. The

FIGURE 0.3. *"Llinda Llee Llama." Lorrain D'Essen can be seen in the back left. MA82-5, Neiman Marcus Archives Collection, Dallas History and Archives Division, Dallas Public Library.*

mid-twentieth-century photograph presents us similarly with a camelid-human juncture that highlights an intriguing animal standing at its center, partly surrounded by curious admirers; the sailing ship has been replaced by the modern car. Llinda Llee Llama comes across here as friendly and docile, like the camel-sheep, and unperturbed by the group of people clustered around her.

The photograph of Llinda Llee includes substitutions other than the car for the ship. The translator-mediator and Mapuche couple from the earlier engraving have been replaced by D'Essen herself, who stands behind Llinda Llee to the far left, recognizable by the folkloric hat she modeled throughout the festivities. From her vantage point, D'Essen can inconspicuously serve as the "native expert" and answer the girls' questions about the pretty llama. The external signs of a (potentially dangerous) Indigenous authenticity in the Brawern-Herckemann engraving,

18 | *Llamas beyond the Andes*

manifested through the Indigenous man and woman's attire (or lack thereof) and style of weaponry, also play out differently in the photograph. D'Essen, with her expertise and traditional hat, and Llinda Llee, with her exotic anatomy and colorful blanket, perform a pleasurable, nonthreatening Andean authenticity even though trainer and llama were both native New Yorkers. For the duration of Neiman Marcus's Fortnight, Llinda Llee represented Andean indigeneity at many of the event's planned activities, including the formal banquet.

Although separated by more than three hundred years, both the Brawern-Herckemann engraving and the twentieth-century photograph direct the viewer's attention to the ongoing relevance of the intercultural camelid contact zone, where the animals straddle the North and the South, culture and commerce. Taken together, they point to the range of themes and participants appearing in these case studies and evoke the thick substrate of histories on which both animals stand.

The Methods and Itineraries of Camelid Extraction Histories, 1568–1960

One goal of my research was to provide insights into the various ways in which new knowledge of llamas and alpacas was generated and sometimes transformed from the standpoint of intercultural camelid contact zones. This approach required an interdisciplinary methodology that would enable me to identify the various perspectives regarding the living animals and animal fragments in a variety of scenes of encounter. The book examines three general arenas: the Andes, where the animals and their remains were originally acquired; on transport ships, where caretakers could include Andean shepherds or European crew members; and in Europe, Australia, and the United States, where the camelids were initially introduced. A second goal was to identify and analyze methods of inquiry utilized to produce scientific and cultural knowledge about the animals and their husbandry over time, including dissection, cross-species hybridization, exhibition and display, and artistic renderings through engraving, painting, sketching, and photography. Finally, I wanted to ascertain the major debates about the camelids that arose over time and in new ecologies and global contexts. Documentary works analyzed included Renaissance treatises on poisons and antidotes, pharmaceutical manuals, bilingual Spanish/Quechua and Spanish/Aymara dictionaries,

Introduction | 19

colonial chronicles, natural history archives, travelogues, scientific reports and drawings, camelid necropsies and field guides to dissection, ship captains' logs, travel accounts, and newspaper articles. The material artifacts I examined included skeletons and skulls, bezoar stones, fiber samples and fabric swatch books, and watercolors and photographs. A critical reading of these varied sources and materials uncovered the multilayered facets of the intercultural camelid contact zones and, notably, established a novel way of looking at relations among Europeans, North Americans, Spanish American creoles, and Andean Indigenous peoples.

My findings have led to a chronological and thematic organization for the book. In the first two chapters I examine the early intercultural contact zone formed around camelid bodies, with particular focus on the body-interior. Although Spanish soldiers and colonizers were already exploiting llamas and alpacas for their fiber and meat, they discovered that wild camelids possessed a priceless secret hidden in their gut: bezoar stones. Chapter 1 introduces the Asian bezoar stone, the medicinal properties it was believed to possess, the large sums of money it brought in, and its reintroduction to European audiences by a renowned sixteenth-century physician from Seville, Nicolás Monardes. Monardes's writings subsequently led to the discovery of the stones in Peru by a Spanish soldier. I consider the conflicting political, economic, and cultural roles the Peruvian bezoar would go on to play in rural Indigenous communities and colonial urban sectors for the next two hundred years. A major finding is the environmental impact of this discovery on the wild camelid populations.

Chapter 2 begins with a discussion of the term "autopsy" and its two definitions, meaning direct observation and anatomization (of a body), after which the analysis takes a more sustained look at the camelid body-interior during the colonial period. First, it considers the significance of the llamas and alpacas for Andean pastoral communities as expressed through ritual sacrifices of the animals and postmortem scrutiny of their internal structures. Sacrifice was intimately linked to environmental sustainability: healthy organs meant a healthy animal, which, in turn, meant a healthy community. The chapter next considers two camelid contact zones from the colonial Andes where study of the camelid body-interior took on very different significance. In each case, a European dissected a camelid gut in search of bezoar stones: the first during the late sixteenth century and the second in the early eighteenth century. The analysis of these two examples brings to light an understudied link between early commodification of the camelid carcass and economic imperialism. Because both anatomizations

20 | Llamas beyond the Andes

were published and circulated in scientific, medical, and popular circles, they helped make the three-dimensional camelid interior better understood and more accessible, thereby facilitating future bioprospecting of the valuable stones. The third and final example comes from the Alfort Veterinary School, located outside Paris in the late eighteenth century, where the body of a female llama was first dissected, preserved, and publicly displayed in a European museum.

Read together, these three dissections by Europeans are significant because they enable us to trace one version of the history of knowledge-as-possession as it pertains to the camelids. Just as soldiers and colonizers mapped the newly conquered lands and catalogued their natural resources, these examples provide evidence as to how the increasingly detailed mapping of the camelid body enabled this valuable resource to be more easily commodified.

Chapter 3 focuses on the eighteenth and early nineteenth centuries and serves as a transition between the colonial encounters with the camelids examined in the first two chapters and the large-scale nineteenth-century extraction ventures of the following chapters. In the Andes, through the sponsoring of numerous scientific expeditions, the Bourbon monarchy promoted a more detailed cataloguing and classification of the region's diverse natural resources and the systematization of relevant information about their utility and value. Attention focused on the usefulness of the whole camelid, with the goal of turning these creatures into global economic benefit. The first portion of the chapter examines writings by Spanish and French scientists who called for bringing the animals to Europe for naturalization. They examined the challenges presented by the animals' extraction and transportation from a theoretical perspective, exploring questions such as how to obtain the animals in large numbers, how to transport them safely, and how to ensure that a new environment and climate would satisfy their dietary needs and ensure their ability to reproduce.

The second half of the chapter looks at Empress Josephine Bonaparte's request to the Spanish monarchy for a dozen alpacas and vicuñas for her Malmaison menagerie. It reconstructs the history of the flock's journey from Peru to Buenos Aires under the management of a Lima postal worker, across the Atlantic, and on to its final destination. Given changing international political relations, the animals ended up at the Sanlúcar de Barrameda botanical gardens in southern Spain, rather than Malmaison. The two halves of the chapter provide a contrast between scientific studies conducted from abroad and the complexities and challenges of their local implementation.

Chapters 4, 5, and 6 constitute the heart of the book. They cover the major nineteenth-century projects to extract camelids in larger numbers from the Andes to France and England and their colonies. Both nations listed the camelids among their top priorities of nonnative animals for naturalization. France, for example, wanted to import camelids into its poorer rural areas. The Paris Acclimatization Society developed projects and created incentives to do so, drawing in part on the theoretical studies and the on-the-ground experience gained with Josephine's camelid project discussed in chapter 3. Britain hoped to introduce the animals into its colony Australia. The analysis of these ambitious and costly extraction projects brings new perspectives to our understanding of the diversity of camelid contact zones, their participants, and neo-ecological consequences.

Chapter 4 examines three case studies from the mid-nineteenth century centered on the science of acclimatization and the extraction of llamas and alpacas into France. The stories in this chapter are unique insofar as each project was supported by state-run institutions, a critical element absent from Englishman Charles Ledger's story covered in the next two chapters. The first section of the chapter takes up the work of French traveler Eugène Roehn and his 1858–1859 expedition to collect alpacas and llamas in the Andes on behalf of the Paris Acclimatization Society. The story follows Roehn, the resistance he met from Indigenous communities who refused to sell their animals, and the difficult return voyage to France (aided by two Bolivian shepherds) with the small number of llamas and alpacas that he did manage to acquire. Roehn's story is significant because it highlights the many difficulties involved in extracting the animals from their native habitat and documents the camelids' low rate of survival as a result of removal and relocation.

The second case history begins with the gift of a flock of llamas that Ecuadorian president Gabriel García Moreno offered the French government in 1862. It brings out the significant impact of geopolitical relations on international acclimatization projects such as this and follows the transportation of the animals on board two French navy ships, where the captains and crew dedicated themselves to safeguarding the animals while in transit. Their records documenting the animals' care during the voyage were hailed as a model for future extraction projects.

The final case history follows the route of one llama from Peru to the French Vosges mountains and documents how the animal became

22 | *Llamas beyond the Andes*

a local celebrity. It describes the arrival of the llama from the perspective of his caretaker and other residents and documents their collective project to integrate the animal culturally and linguistically into the alpine community.

Chapters 5 and 6 focus on the mid-nineteenth century and international camelid acclimatization projects from the perspective of English settler Charles Ledger. Chapter 5 analyzes the exploits of Ledger and a group of Bolivian shepherds who collaborated on the project in the 1850s to smuggle a large flock of llamas and alpacas out of Bolivia, with plans to export the animals to Australia. The chapter shows how Ledger and this unique group of shepherds eluded Bolivian authorities and irate Indigenous communities as they made their way to northern Argentina. There, combining Indigenous and Western knowledge technologies, Ledger and the Bolivians trained llama wet nurses to adopt young vicuñas and implemented the controlled hybridization of llamas and alpacas. Working together, they prepared the large flock of camelids for the difficult journey to Australia, where they hoped ultimately to introduce the animals into the local agrarian culture for profit. Ledger's story stands as an iconic example of neo-ecological imperialism that had as its goal the improvement of the British colony's economy at the direct expense of the Andean nation and its pastoral communities.[17]

Chapter 6 charts the rise and fall of Ledger's experiment in Australia as well as the imperial adventure myths that underpinned such ventures. The chapter signals the end of large-scale nineteenth-century camelid extraction projects more generally, due to their enormous costs, high casualty figures, and low rate of success.

Chapter 7 concludes the study by reflecting on the shifts and transformations in camelid contact zones and their histories as these unique animals took on new significance as symbols of modernity in the US textile industry during the 1930s–1950s and as model ambassadors for Latin America during the important South America Fortnight sponsored by Neiman Marcus of Dallas in 1958.

Altogether, the book addresses the international trajectory of Andean camelids, which has scarcely been examined until now.[18] Quite deliberately, my study does not examine the presence of the camelids in nineteenth-century England. The important flock that belonged to Edward Smith Stanley, 13th Earl of Derby, has been comprehensively researched and studied by now emeritus senior curator of vertebrate zoology (National Museums, Liverpool) Clemency Fisher (2002a, 2002b; Fisher and Jackson

Introduction | 23

2002). As a whole, the case studies document the historical progression of the animals' transformation into global commodities. The studies bring to light the many difficulties faced by scientists and merchants attempting, first, to acquire the animals in the face of organized Indigenous resistance to these advances and, second, to safely transport the animals overseas and acclimatize them to new habitats. They show how ever-changing political relations within and between nations impacted directly and indirectly on extraction projects. The reconstruction of these biogeographical histories sheds new light on the environmental impact of colonialism and the intercultural approaches to camelid science in Andean and transoceanic contexts.

CHAPTER 1

From Marvelous Antidote to the Poison of Idolatry

The Transatlantic Significance of Andean Bezoar Stones during the Late Sixteenth and Early Seventeenth Centuries

All of this is due to you, because your book showed us how to locate and discover [bezoar stones] and how to take them out of the secret place inside the animal where they are hidden. And indeed, we owe you a great deal because you discovered for us such a great treasure, *the greatest that has been found in these parts.*

1571 letter from Pedro de Osma y de Xara y Zejo, announcing the discovery of bezoar stones in Peru (quoted in Monardes 1574, 74v; emphasis added)

On October 12, 1598, one month after the death of Spain's powerful monarch Felipe II, officials commenced the royal accounting of his vast estate. The detailed inventories of books, paintings, jewels, statues, medals, unicorn horns, coral, and other exotic items attest that Felipe II had assembled one of the most important collections in Europe of the sixteenth century (Checa Cremades 1997; Gómez López 2005; Jiménez Díaz 2001; Sánchez Cantón 1958). Among the king's diverse belongings were curiosities and marvelous objects that he had received from America. The Peruvian viceroy, don Francisco de Toledo, sent the king a variety of gifts during his time in office (1569–1581), including stone idols, a 23-carat gold llama with white enameling, and, most intriguingly, a number of bezoar stones. The inventory indicated that the largest of these stones were designated as gifts to the Archduchess Margarete of Austria, wife of Felipe III, and to various members of the royal family in Spain and Germany, while others became the property of the celebrated San Lorenzo pharmacy at the royal palace, El Escorial (Julien 1999; Sánchez Cantón 1958, 1:275, 2:136–140).

26 | Llamas beyond the Andes

How did bezoars come to be such a highly prized possession? The bezoar stone is basically a calcinated concretion found in the digestive tract of many animals, including the four species of Andean camelids. For several reasons, in spite of its less than glamorous physiological genesis, the bezoar stone played a dramatic yet surprisingly neglected role in shaping the social and economic history of early modern Europe and Spanish America.

First of all, it was widely held throughout Europe that these uncommon and difficult-to-obtain stones constituted an excellent remedy for all kinds of poisons. Physicians and apothecaries lauded the powerful curative virtues of bezoars when used as an antidote and claimed that they were equally effective in combating other serious illnesses of the time, such as the plague, typhus, malignant fevers, melancholy, fainting, palpitations of the heart, vertigo, and intestinal worms.[1]

Second, due to their famed medicinal attributes, bezoar stones were frequently exchanged among kings, princes, religious elites, and other members of the nobility. For example, in 1587 Duchess Marie Eleanore wrote to Emperor Rudolph II to request his assistance in acquiring Turkish bezoar stones because she was deeply concerned about the ongoing bouts of melancholy of her husband, Duke Albrecht Friedrich of Prussia (Midelfort 1994, 90).[2]

Third, bezoar stones were so highly regarded during the sixteenth and seventeenth centuries that catalogues of royal treasuries grouped them with diamonds, pearls, emeralds, and other precious gems.[3] It was not uncommon to have a bezoar stone mounted in exquisite gold or silver settings inlaid with colorful stones and costly gems to be presented as a sumptuous gift.[4] Indeed, many of the bezoar stones that Viceroy Toledo and others sent to Felipe II were embellished with detailed gold or silver ornamentation, and some were even encased in delicate gold boxes. These marvelous treasures constituted one of the most sought-after objects for the cabinets of curiosities and chambers of wonders that were in fashion among kings and princes and the incipient European bourgeoisie of the north. The bezoar stone produced further surprises in America when its wondrous qualities became tinged with the threat of danger. The Spanish discovered that bezoars were esteemed by Indigenous peoples in Andean pastoral communities. Colonial religious authorities consequently argued that the stones figured prominently in idolatrous practices. They began to include bezoars among the dangerous objects that should be hunted down

From Marvelous Antidote to the Poison of Idolatry | 27

and publicly destroyed. Thus the bezoar stone played an unexpected role in the colonial drama of competing epistemologies.

This chapter explores the discovery of the bezoar stone in Peru by Spanish soldiers in 1568, a significant event that has received critical attention only recently. The story of the Peruvian bezoar was first told in a medical book, *Historia medicinal de las cosas que se traen de nuestras Indias Occidentales que sirven en medicina*, written and published in three parts during the second half of the sixteenth century by Nicolás Monardes (ca. 1493–1588), a prominent medical doctor from Seville. Monardes's three-part *Historia medicinal* is notable for its scope and complexity, covering (among other things) medicinal plants and animal products sent to him from throughout Latin America over the course of several years. I begin by looking briefly at Monardes's biography in order to situate the publication of the *Historia medicinal* within the double frame of individual and collective colonial economic interests. I also touch on the role of bezoar stones in the history of medicine as described in a treatise on poisons and their antidotes, a work that Monardes included in the first part of his *Historia*. My objective is not to affirm or refute the medical effectiveness of the bezoar stone, however, but rather to consider how it came into being as a salient transatlantic cultural and economic object toward the end of the sixteenth century.[5]

To learn how the stone acquired medical, aesthetic, and commercial value in Europe and America, I consulted archival documents, colonial chronicles, pharmaceutical manuals, books of medical recipes, and inventories of cabinets of curiosities. Finding out how Andean Indigenous peoples treasured and used the stone was more difficult, as the sources were harder to uncover. I looked at Indigenous and colonial chronicles, the early bilingual Spanish/Quechua and Spanish/Aymara dictionaries, accounts of the extirpation of idolatries, and present-day anthropological studies and conversations with herders. I quickly realized that it would take this widespread kind of inquiry to comprehend the many layers of meaning and desire that bezoars accrued. My analysis of these different sources shows the multiple ways in which the bezoar's historical importance resonated materially and metaphorically due to the convergence of competing Spanish and Indigenous interests around it.

Literally embedded in the stomach and viscera of the Andean camelids, the stones were also entangled in a nexus of relationships among commerce, knowledge, and colonial power. For the Spanish, the fortuitous

28 | Llamas beyond the Andes

discovery of bezoar stones in Peru represented an unanticipated economic boon and a chance to compete with Portugal's monopoly on bezoars, which were brought into Europe from its colonies in Asia. As Peruvian bezoars became increasingly visible in the local and international networks of trade and commerce, however, the Spanish discovered that they had a disturbing "dark side." The campaigns of extirpation found the stones secreted away in Indigenous homes and storehouses throughout the area surrounding Lake Titicaca and even openly displayed on "altars" or in shrines and tombs called huacas.[6] The bezoar stone unexpectedly revealed hidden layers of doubled meaning that linked it directly to what Europeans feared as Andean idolatry. While the Peruvian bezoar stone gained fame throughout Europe for its unequaled merits as an antidote for poisonings, Spanish priests participating in the campaigns of extirpation in local communities viewed its presence in Indigenous households as a symbol of the dangerous poison of idolatry that urgently needed an antidote. Ironically, however, the knowledge that Indigenous peoples valued bezoar stones further increased their currency in Europe, because it added a patina of exoticism to their already marvelous origin.

For Andean pastoral communities, the Spanish discovery of the bezoar stone had far-reaching and devastating consequences that went beyond the ransacking of their homes and huacas by extirpators. As noted in the introduction, herds of camelids, including the wild vicuñas and guanacos, were decimated soon after the arrival of the Spanish due to excessive hunting and the spread of disease. The discovery of the bezoar stone would be a third critical factor affecting the population of camelids and, by extension, Indigenous peoples. Their lives depended on the delicate balance of a fragile ecosystem at 4,000 meters above sea level where the camelids played a central role. Following the publication of Monardes's *Historia medicinal*, however, Spanish bounty seekers, soldiers, Indians complicit in this commercial enterprise, and others slaughtered the animals in the search for the stones. The Spanish priest Father Bernabé Cobo, writing in the mid-seventeenth century, clearly indicated the impact that finding these stones must have had for the wild camelids (and deer): "One generally finds in the belly of each of these animals a single stone, and in some, two, three, four and even more. It is also true that bezoar stones will not always be found in all animals of these species because it sometimes happens that *for every hundred killed only one or two will have them*" (Cobo [1653] 1956, 128–129; emphasis added). Cobo's chilling description of the massacre of Andean camelids by the hundreds suggests that the search for bezoar stones played a major role in further reducing the already diminished herds of wild vicuñas and guanacos.[7]

Moreover, the devastation was not limited to these immediate material consequences; indeed, it had symbolic overtones that would resonate throughout herding communities. As I show, bezoar stones were central to the reproduction of Indigenous cultural practices and directly linked to the foundational myths of Andean cosmology. For Andean Indigenous peoples, loss of the stones signified the potential loss of the community's power of regeneration, what Salomon (2004, 116) calls the Andean cultures' "inheritance for continuity." Thus, this chapter situates the bezoar stone as a contact zone, where different meanings are held, created, and contested.

Monardes's *Historia medicinal* and His Treatise on the Bezoar Stone

The second half of the sixteenth century was characterized by a series of discoveries in the New World pharmacopoeia. Due to widespread outbreaks of deadly diseases, epidemics, and plagues that devastated European cities and rural areas, the news of an abundant source of medicinal plants and animal products heretofore unknown to doctors and apothecaries generated as much enthusiastic fervor as would the discovery of penicillin centuries later (Poynter 1963, 3).[8] Information regarding these new products was disseminated throughout Europe and America, due in many ways to the publication of Monardes's *Historia medicinal* in three parts. The initial publication (Monardes 1565) was followed by the second six years later (Monardes 1571). The third and final part (Monardes 1574) incorporated the 1565 and 1571 texts along with new chapters describing the most recent discoveries and experiments.[9] To give an idea of the positive reception that Monardes's work received, during the ensuing four decades more than thirty editions of his books appeared in Spanish, Italian, English, French, Portuguese, German, Dutch, and Latin. As many have noted, the title of Frampton's ([1577] 1925) English translation, *Joyfull Newes Out of the Newe Founde Worlde*, best captured the spirit of excitement rising throughout Europe as word spread about these new medicines.[10]

Monardes himself never traveled to the Americas. He was able to obtain this materia medica, however, because he was well established as

30 | Llamas beyond the Andes

a successful businessman in addition to practicing medicine in Seville. In 1533, years before the publication of his *Historia medicinal*, Monardes formed a mercantile enterprise, sending shiploads of slaves as well as freight such as cloth to be sold in port cities of the New World. On the return run, the ships would be loaded with precious metals, spices and other medicinal products, and additional items purchased with the money made from these sales (Guerra 1961, 24–26; Pardo Tomás 2002, 99–100). Due to a series of familial and financial misfortunes, Monardes was forced to declare bankruptcy in 1567, owing close to 25 million maravedis (1 real = 34 maravedis) to his creditors. To avoid jail, he sought refuge in the Regina Coeli monastery in Seville then set about to regain his former financial standing. The following year the Consejo Real de Indias granted the license permitting the first part of the *Historia medicinal* to be reprinted, while noting that Monardes was still living in asylum at the monastery (Pardo Tomás 2002, 101). Research by Pardo Tomás (2002) has shown that Monardes was finally released precisely so that he could continue his medical writings in the effort to pay off his debts.

During the second half of the sixteenth century, royal officials, bankers, and entrepreneurs not only encouraged but also financed the search for information on new commodities. Therefore it is unsurprising that so prominent a figure as Monardes would have been freed in order to continue his study of New World medicinal products. Indeed, between 1568 and 1588, the year of his death, Monardes paid off more than 16 million maravedis of his debt. Pardo Tomás (2002) has observed that it probably was not coincidental that the publication of the three-part *Historia medicinal* took place during these years of economic crisis and recovery. Consequently, it is still uncertain to what degree Monardes's writings were conditioned by his precarious financial situation. Regardless of the impetus behind the publication of the *Historia medicinal*, Monardes's work clearly was widely received and highly acclaimed throughout Europe precisely because it created connections with all kinds of interests: commercial and scientific as well as collective and individual (Pardo Tomás 2002, 101, 103; see also Guerra 1961, 16–29).

This brief recounting of Monardes's life calls attention to the role that the colonial economic context most likely played in instigating the writing and publishing of the *Historia medicinal*. The discovery and commercialization of new American drugs had become a lucrative enterprise during the sixteenth century (Asúa and French 2005, 91–92, 104–107; Cook 2007). Notable examples were the Fuggers and Welsers, German

From Marvelous Antidote to the Poison of Idolatry | 31

bankers who made a fortune from their monopolies of spices and medicines.[11] Monardes described in detail on the first pages of his book the economic benefits to be obtained from the commercialization of New World medicinal products, which he compared to the fabulous wealth generated by the exploitation of metals, precious stones, and exotic animals and birds already arriving from the New World. His lengthy itemized catalogue of trees, plants, herbs, roots, saps, gums, fruits, seeds, liquors, and stones underscored the diversity and proliferation of an untapped source of wealth, which, he argued, promised an even greater bounty than the fortunes created from the transatlantic flow of silver and gold (Monardes 1574, 1r–1v; see also Bleichmar 2005, 90). There is little doubt that Monardes's *Historia medicinal* stood as a kind of promise or guarantee of economic gain and profit on several levels.

The first part of Monardes's *Historia medicinal* (1565) included his initial study of New World products as well as a separate treatise on the bezoar stone and the *escuerzonera* plant, two antidotes to poisons. Of the many different medicines and remedies that he treated in this inaugural work, the bezoar stone stands out as being one of the most culturally and economically significant. Europeans were somewhat familiar with the medicinal benefits of Asian bezoars even before the sixteenth century (see, for example, Cuba ca. 1499–1502, 135v).

For his treatise, Monardes drew from Pliny's *Natural History* and the medical writings of the great Persian, Arab, and Jewish philosopher-physicians from the ninth through the twelfth centuries to describe the animal that produced the bezoar stone, the formation of the stone inside the animal, its medicinal virtues, and the great danger of counterfeit stones. Monardes also included information on the (folk) etymology of the word itself. He provided the translation used in several different languages while paying special attention to the Hebrew form. His description underscored the stone's widespread dissemination and the magnitude of its healing powers:

> This Bezoar Stone goes by many names: the Arabs call it *Hager*, the Persians *Bezaar*, the Indians *Bezar*, the Hebrews *Belzaar*, the Greeks *Alexipharmicum*, the Latins *Counter-poison*, the Spaniards *the Stone to counteract venom and fainting spells*. . . . Conrad Gesner . . . says that the word *Belzaar* is Hebrew in origin, because *Bel* in Hebrew is *Master* and *Zaar* venom, as if to mean *the Master of venoms*. And for good reason it has that name, because this stone

32 | *Llamas beyond the Andes*

annihilates, kills, and destroys all poisons, as if it were their mistress. And thus all things that are counter-poisons, or that work against venomous things, are called *Bezartics* because of their excellence. (Monardes 1574, 133v–134r)[12]

In Monardes's *Historia medicinal*, the bezoar stone emerged unequaled in the hierarchy of antidotes, esteemed for its occult power as both sovereign lord and lady over all poisons (Monardes 1574, 133v).

Some of the writings that Monardes consulted told of bezoars found in the stomach of a kind of ruminant original to Asia. In other sources, such as travelers' accounts, the animal was described as looking like a wild goat or ram or deer. Additional references presented it as a wild goat-deer (*cervicabra*) found only in the most remote highlands of India and Persia (Monardes 1574, 133v–140r). According to these authors, the bezoar stone was considered to be a very powerful and noble remedy because it served as an antidote to a wide variety of poisons derived from plants and herbs, insects, and serpents. Maimonides ([1198] 1997, 17–18) judged the bezoar to be second only to crushed emeralds for its confirmed effectiveness against poisons. The stone could be placed either whole or in powdered form in food or a beverage in order to counteract the effects of a possible poisoning, a popular method for doing away with enemies or rivals at the time.[13] Beautifully crafted receptacles known as poison cups often had a bezoar attached by a chain so that it could be dipped in the liquid held in the container. Others had a screw or "cage" for securing the stone in the base of the vessel. It was believed that the bezoar could absorb or neutralize toxic substances, thereby rendering the beverage safe. Bezoars could also be set among other jewels in amulets, rings, or pendants for easy access. As Monardes (1574, 134r) noted, due to the perceived potency of this remedy, the word "bezoar" became a generic term used to describe any effective antidote.[14]

Regarding the formation of the bezoar stone in the animal, Eastern and Western sources provided two basic versions. The first account tells of a deerlike animal found in mountainous regions. During a certain time of the year, the animal seeks out caves where poisonous serpents live and devours them all. As the ingested poison heats up its body, the deer takes refuge in a lake or river, submerging itself so that only the head is left showing above water. Large viscous tears form in the corners of its eyes, caused by the heat of the poison. While the sun shines down on the animal's head, these tears draw the poison from its body as they slowly dry

From Marvelous Antidote to the Poison of Idolatry | 33

FIGURE 1.1. *This cross-section of the bezoar, although not drawn to scale, reveals the stone's onion-like layers. From* Histoire générale des drogues *(Pomet 1694): https://www.biusante.parisdescartes.fr/histmed/image?CICL03616.*

and solidify like stone and turn different colors in the process. Once the deer comes out of the water, these hardened tears fall to the ground, so that they can be found along lake shores and riverbanks (Monardes 1574, 134r–135r). Grew (1681, 21) in his catalogue of items contained in the medical collection at Gresham College, England, included:

> A Stag's Tears: A thicken'd Excretion from the inward Angle of his Eye. In colour and consistence almost like to Mirrh; or Ear-wax that has been long harden'd in the Ear. Of a strong stinking smell, like that of the Animal's sweat. They are generally affirmed to be sudorifick, and of an Alexipharmick nature. And if they were as easie to be had, as some Womens, it were worth the trying.

A similar variation of how the stone is formed centers on a wild goat found in the mountains of the East. After eating the serpents and submerging its body in water, the animal eats healing plants that congeal and solidify in its stomach, forming a hard stone made of layers, like an onion (Monardes 1574, 135r; see figure 1.1).[15] The Spanish apothecary Gaspar de Morales (1605, 205v–206r, 207v–208r) explained that precious stones such as bezoars were made up of a mix of different elements, and so their

34 | Llamas beyond the Andes

healing virtues derived from these same substances. Because the animal had eaten poisonous serpents as well as therapeutic plants, true bezoars contained both poison and antidote (Morales 1605, 64r, 203v–205r).[16] This paradoxical combination would have important ramifications for the role that bezoars would play in the Andean campaigns to extirpate idolatries.

The importance that Monardes gave to the Asian bezoar stone can be measured by the fact that he dedicated his treatise to the duchess of Béjar, the woman who introduced him to the stone and its medicinal signifi-cance. Monardes recounted that the duchess had a son who had suffered from fainting spells since he was a young boy. While looking for a cure, she was informed that bezoar stones were used to treat such illnesses at the royal court. The duchess went directly to Monardes, her doctor, to inform him of this discovery. Monardes sent inquiries to Lisbon, the cen-ter of the East Indies spice and drug trade, to try to obtain the stone so that he might treat his friend's son. This inquiry produced two gold-encased bezoars, which, when grains from the stones were mixed with ox-tongue broth and given to the young man on a daily basis, immediately alleviated his blackouts and eventually eliminated them altogether (Monardes 1574, 143v–145v).

By dedicating the treatise to the duchess and presenting the story of her son's illness and cure, Monardes positioned his readers and patients as important witnesses to the effectiveness of these medicines while at the same time creating a niche market and network of potential consumers.[17] The narrative described the incident in detail, thereby underscoring that it was a patient who brought the bezoar stone to the doctor's attention. Monardes could concede this without losing his own authority because ultimately he was the one who made the appropriate inquiries to Portugal, acquired the stones, and successfully treated the ailing young man. Still, his work offered readers, especially those in the New World, a way of inter-acting with his text and with nature, a method that invited them to join him in the quest for new materia medica.[18] The example of the duchess served as a prototype for this scientific method of inquiry and discovery. Like a hunter, the reader would follow clues with the goal of "capturing rare secrets" (Eamon 1994, 271), such as heretofore unknown plant spec-imens or animal products, but their curative benefits would be adminis-tered and confirmed by Monardes, the ultimate author/authority.[19] Due, at least in part, to this kind of professional testimony based on documented experimentation of New and Old World medicinal products, the initial

From Marvelous Antidote to the Poison of Idolatry | 35

publication of the *Historia medicinal* in 1565 was hugely successful: the book circulated widely throughout Europe and America, where merchants, explorers, government officials, and soldiers carried it as a kind of pharmaceutical manual and guide.[20]

The Letter from a Spanish Soldier in Peru to Monardes

It was in Monardes's 1571 publication that readers first learned the exciting news of the discovery of the bezoar stone in Peru. Monardes included a transcription of the letter sent to him by a Spanish soldier, detailing the history of this event. Along with the letter, the soldier, whose name was Pedro de Osma y de Xara y Zejo, sent Monardes sample stones for his experimentation and use, in addition to other herbs and seeds.

In his introductory remarks on the letter, Monardes became increasingly effusive as he praised the wonderful remedies being discovered each day in the West Indies. Illnesses that could not be controlled before were now being treated, thanks to these marvelous new products (Monardes 1574, 71v). He called the reader's attention to his own much-celebrated role in promoting the knowledge and use of these new medicinals. Thanks to these efforts, he received a letter from Peru announcing the discovery there of bezoar stones:

> And so that you can see the fruits of my labor, I include here a letter sent to me two months ago by a gentleman from Peru. In it, you will find that, thanks to what I wrote in the first part [of this *Historia medicinal*], they have discovered bezoar stones in Peru, similar to the esteemed stones brought from Portugal's India. Because of the relation and order of which I wrote, [in Peru] they also came to learn of them. This is a true and invaluable discovery and worthy of consideration. (Monardes 1574, 72r)

Monardes emphasized that this discovery happened only because he had already written about the virtues of the famous bezoars brought from the Portuguese colonies of the East Indies and provided the essential clues regarding the kind of animal that contained the stones.

Monardes's rhetorical strategy here seems to be deliberately calculated. By juxtaposing the Peruvian bezoar stone and the Eastern bezoar in the same sentence, he implicitly drew comparisons of worth between

36 | *Llamas beyond the Andes*

them. Furthermore, he established textually an equivalence between Peru, a Spanish colony, and Portuguese territories in India, noted for their tremendous wealth of spices and other medicinals. After establishing these favorable comparisons, however, Monardes next pointed out crucial differences between the two stones in order to assert the superiority of the new bezoars arriving from the Spanish colonies. He invoked contrasts that played equally to commercial and medical interests when he stressed the marvelous quality of the Peruvian bezoars, their easy accessibility, the enormous price they brought, and, finally, their authenticity. Directly addressing and currying favor with King Felipe II, to whom this second part was dedicated, the doctor declared:

> It is a great event that this marvelous and costly item was found in our Majesty's Indies. [These stones] can be acquired so easily and are certain and authentic, such that we have no need to doubt their effect and virtue. The same cannot be said for those from the East Indies, because for every ten genuine bezoars brought in, there are one hundred counterfeits. Accordingly, those who buy them must do so with care to avoid being cheated. (Monardes 1574, 72r)[21]

By insistently affirming the "marvelous" nature of this news in his introductory observations, Monardes primed his readers so that they would be fully prepared to appreciate the wonders described in Pedro de Osma's letter (see Greenblatt 1991, 73). During this period, the marvelous was associated with the rhetorical and pictorial tradition that described voyages of discovery and encounter: "To affirm the 'marvelous' nature of the discoveries is, even without the lucrative shipments yet on board, to make good on the claim to have reached the fabled realms of gold and spices" (Greenblatt 1991, 74). Monardes (1574, 78r) linked his work with this rhetorical strategy when he established in his narration an explicit relationship between his own leading role in the discovery of this marvelous stone and the promise of economic gain: "Many who were on this Fleet have these stones and they bring them to me, as if I were their first discoverer. They tell such stories of the stones' effect that they seem like miracles." New World nature emerged thus in his writings as a source of wondrous, priceless commodities. In addition to calling the attention of his ideal reader, King Felipe II, to the miraculous properties and abundance of the Peruvian bezoar stone as well as to his own role as "broker,"

From Marvelous Antidote to the Poison of Idolatry | 37

it is even possible to imagine that Monardes, a man pursued by his debts, also was directly addressing his creditors here (see Guerra 1966, 51–52).[22]

The author of the letter, Pedro de Osma, tells how he and a few other soldiers went hunting in the Peruvian high sierra on June 15, 1568, because they had seen some curious animals that looked similar to the bezoar deer-goat that Monardes had described in the first part of his *Historia medicinal* (1574, 73v). Because Monardes's text did not include any engravings of the animal, the soldiers had only a vague written depiction to guide them. They believed that the swift reddish animals they had spotted were identical to the Persian and Indian bezoar goats, with the exception that the Peruvian specimens had no horns.[23]

The soldiers killed several of these animals and, following Monardes's directions, selected the largest and oldest to open. Unfortunately, however, they found not a single bezoar inside it, neither in its abdomen nor anywhere else. Fearing that this animal was not the same as the kind described by the doctor, the soldiers questioned the Indians who accompanied them as their servants, asking them where the animals had their stones. Osma explained that the Indians claimed to know nothing about them because they were enemies of the Spanish and refused to reveal any of their secrets. A young Indian boy around ten years old then came forward and spoke to the men: "seeing that we wanted to learn about this, he showed us the secret of the deal or undertaking, where the stones were located in the animal lying there dead before us" (Monardes 1574, 73v). The Indians, Osma explained, wanted to kill the young boy because he had betrayed them by showing the Spanish soldiers the sacred stones that played a central role in their idol worship and rituals of sacrifice:

> The Indians hold those stones in high regard and offer them to their huacas and shrines where they have their idols. They present their most valuable objects [to the idols], including these stones, an offering as esteemed as gold, silver, precious jewels, animals, and children. (Monardes 1574, 73v–74r)

Pedro de Osma's commentary is of critical significance because it established an unanticipated linkage between bezoar stones and Indigenous idolatry, a relationship taken up in detail in the next section. At this point, however, I wish to call attention to how the initial groundwork for this association was being laid when Osma observed that the Indians, like the Spanish, held the stones in high regard, considering them to be price-less treasure. The difference between the Europeans and the Indigenous peoples, Osma wanted his readers to believe, was the brutal, pagan nature of the Indians, who were prepared to sacrifice the young boy because of his betrayal of their idolatry. Following this assertion, Osma took a small step back from his immediate narrative to offer a more general observation on Indigenous sacrifice, explaining how Indians grouped bezoars with gold, silver, gems, animals, and children, all of which were given as offerings to the idols. For Osma, such perceived savagery on the part of the Indians justified the soldiers' intervention in the protection not only of the small boy but also of these treasured commodities. Predictably, however, Osma and his companions soon forgot about the boy in their excited hunt for more animals: "And later we learned that the Indians had sacrificed the boy, whom we had forgotten about during the hunt. They carried him away, over the mountains, where we never saw him again" (Monardes 1574, 74r). Once the boy had fulfilled his colonial function, he vanished from the text.

Readers of the time might have picked up on a second, more subtle connection linking the stones, idolatrous practices, and commercial ben-efit through Osma's use of the word *negocio* to describe the moment of discovery when the boy showed them where the stones were to be found in the animal: "nos mostro el secreto del negocio" ([he] did show us the secret of the deal or undertaking: Monardes 1574, 73v). Greenblatt (1991) describes how Christopher Columbus's writings achieved a similar associ-ation between religious and commercial enterprises by employing a rhet-oric of conversion for the exchange of precious stones and pearls for gold and for the conversion of idolatrous souls. While this rhetorical slippage might seem unexpected, Greenblatt (1991, 71) reminds us:

> In the Spanish of the Middle Ages and Renaissance, the Crusade to the Holy Land was called not the *cruzada*—that word referred to the special papal concessions granted to the Spanish crown to fight against the infidel within its own territory—but rather the *empresa* or *negocio*, terms in which the mercantile and the religious are intertwined.

Greenblatt (1991, 71) continues: "The rhetorical task of Christian imperialism then is to bring together commodity conversion and spiri-tual conversion." Osma and the other soldiers thus enacted what would

From Marvelous Antidote to the Poison of Idolatry | 39

become standard practice in the campaigns of extirpation when they removed the stones from all of the dead animals, thereby ensuring that the idolaters would not have them to use in their diabolical practices. This action, far from being disinterested, also guaranteed the stones' conversion into treasure or fortune for the soldiers. It bears reiterating, moreover, that the economic value of the stones increased in European markets when word spread of their association with exotic Indigenous rituals. Another irony emerged: from the Indigenous point of view, the soldiers' hunting and butchery of all these animals may well have seemed as barbaric as their sacrifices were to the Spanish. Garcilaso de la Vega ([1609] 1985, 2:188) pointedly observed that, unlike the Indians, the Spanish took bezoar stones from guanacos and vicuñas as well as from deer and other ruminants: "These days they take the stones from all of the wild animals; in my time they never would have imagined doing such a thing."

All of the soldiers present at the hunt that day recognized both the significance of having found a new source of bezoars and what the commercialization of the stones could mean for them. Moreover, it appeared that they had discovered a plentiful supply in these animals. Osma remarked that in total the first animal had nine bezoars and that the others killed also had stones. The soldier thanked Monardes effusively, as already quoted in the chapter epigraph:

> All of this is due to you, because your book showed us how to locate and discover [bezoar stones] and how to take them out of the secret place inside the animal where they are hidden. And indeed, we owe you a great deal because you discovered for us such a great treasure, *the greatest that has been found in these parts*. (Monardes 1574, 74v; emphasis added)

Osma's claim that these stones constituted the greatest treasure yet found in these parts makes an implicit comparison between the stones and the already famous silver mines of Potosí. As early as the publication of the first part of the *Historia medicinal*, Monardes (1574, 1r–1v) had contended that the profits from these New World medicinals would surpass the income generated by the prosperous mining industry. The soldier's discovery of the costly bezoar stone in Peru was further confirmation of this bold assertion. Consequently, just as samples of the silver were sent back to Europe, Osma explained that he was sending Monardes a dozen of the stones in recompense for his work so that the doctor could make

40 | *Llamas beyond the Andes*

good use of them with his patients. He noted that in Peru the stones had already demonstrated amazing medicinal benefits, curing all kinds of illnesses ranging from poisonings and pestilent fevers to malignant humors (74r–74v).

In his commentary following the transcription of Pedro de Osma's letter, Monardes (1574, 78r) indicated to his readers that he would indeed experiment with these wonderful bezoar stones and publish the results, noting that he had already begun to use them with patients. When Monardes published the final part of his *Historia medicinal* (1574), he provided a detailed description of the Peruvian bezoar stone that included the results of the experiments he had conducted, a discussion of the many illnesses it treated, and recipes or formulas for its use. So, from Monardes's *Historia medicinal* onward, the Peruvian bezoar stone—or what would also come to be known as the occidental bezoar stone, in order to differentiate it from the oriental bezoar stone—would take a prominent role in transnational commercial networks as a highly prized pharmaceutical remedy, as an exotic object without peer in collections of marvels, and as a sumptuous gift worthy of a king.[24]

In Pursuit of the Peruvian Bezoar Stone: From Acquisition to Inquisition

Pedro de Osma's letter not only introduced the Peruvian bezoar but also pointed to unforeseen discourses that were already proliferating around the stone, serving to distinguish it further from the stones being brought into Europe by the Portuguese. Unlike its Asian counterpart, which was known solely for its medicinal virtue, the Peruvian bezoar took on more complicated associations because of its significance in Indigenous idolatrous practices as well as medicine. The paradigm of the hunt for treasure is what connects the pursuit of new scientific-medical knowledge and commodities and the search for and eradication of suspicious Andean religious practices.[25] While the hunt served as a literal and metaphorical method of scientific inquiry with its emphasis on the quest for the occult forces of nature (such as bezoars and other novel materia medica), it also encompassed the pursuit and discovery of additional kinds of hidden influences in the context of the New World, such as the demonic power subtending Indigenous idolatry. As Clark (1997, 155) has argued, the epistemological similarities between *magia daemonica* and *magia naturalis*

From Marvelous Antidote to the Poison of Idolatry | 41

meant that both were "philosophical analogues, providing parallel explanations—sometimes in competition, sometimes in alliance—for the same range of phenomena." Both the language of scientific experimentation and the language of the extirpation of idolatries made use of a vocabulary permeated with nouns and adjectives such as "secret," "hidden," and "occult" and verbs such as "discover" and *desentrañar* (to eviscerate or, figuratively, to discover a secret or mystery).

These parallel discourses are observable in Pedro de Osma's letter and in reports by the inspectors of idolatries. For example, Osma referred to how the pursuit of nature's occult secrets led him to the innermost recesses of the animal's body (the stomach and entrails), within which he eventually discovered the treasured stones "secreted away" (Monardes 1574, 74v). The same terminology utilized to describe the hunt for nature's marvelous secrets also played a central role in the centuries-long struggle to overcome and vanquish the Moorish idolaters from the Iberian Peninsula. Not surprisingly, as many have shown, it was deployed again in the New World to distinguish the forces of Christ from those of Satan (MacCormack 1991a, 128).[26] In his inspection report, Hernández Príncipe ([1621] 1923, 25, 64) described Andean idolatry in general as a "deeply hidden secret," while noting that he had discovered so much evidence in his travels of the diabolical hidden rituals and ceremonies that "I thought I was among Moors and Arabs and such was the degree of my affliction, having discovered and revealed this terrible evil that had been hidden until now."

Once the second part of Monardes's *Historia medicinal* was published in 1571 and the account of Pedro de Osma's discovery made public, the Peruvian bezoar stone acquired high intrinsic value not only in European and New World medicine but also in the Andes in the language and struggle over religious conversion and cultural transformation. There it became associated with both divine and demonic power: when it was in the possession of the Spanish, it was lauded for its extraordinary curative virtues; when discovered secreted away in the homes and huacas of Indigenous peoples, it was considered a clear sign of the kind of idolatry so harshly censured by Hernández Príncipe. It is possible to map a shift in the terminology used for bezoar stones if we look at the reports of religious authorities written before the 1571 publication of the second portion of Monardes's *Historia medicinal* (which included the transcribed letter from Pedro de Osma and news of the Peruvian bezoar stone) and those that followed. For example, the report on idolatrous practices in Huamachuco, written by four Augustinian friars in 1560, indicated that they had

42 | Llamas beyond the Andes

discovered bezoar stones but identified them simply as stones or "hardened dung" and not as medicine or as a potential source of wealth in the European sense of the word (Religiosos Agustinos [1560] 1918, 48–49). By the time Cristóbal de Albornoz described idolatrous practices in 1585, these stones were recognized as bezoars (Duviols 1967, 18).

Due to the hidden location of the stone inside the animal's gut, its medical association with occult properties, and the role it appeared to play in Indigenous rituals, the bezoar exemplified both a secret treasure (as a sign of medicinal and economic benefit) and a treasured secret (as a sign of idolatry).[27] Precisely because Iberian colonizers and Andean pastoral peoples alike valued the stone, it became a focal point in the struggle over competing worldviews. As noted earlier, Europeans believed the bezoar to be structured by overlapping layers of poison and healing virtue; hence its symbolic resonance was necessarily ambiguous. We get a sense of the many-layered interests produced around the stone from Pomet's (1694) artistic representation of a cross-section of the bezoar (see figure 1.1). His depiction of the stone from this perspective underscored the bezoar's layers and how much they matter. I unwrap some of the bezoar's layers in the following pages to examine the ambiguity that the Peruvian bezoar stone acquired following the publication of Monardes's *Historia medicinal*, when it took on a salient role in Andean colonial relations as both antidote and poison.[28]

The Poison of Idolatry

Renowned for its wondrous, even miraculous, healing qualities, the bezoar stone shared a certain kinship with religious relics kept in medieval thesauri or treasures belonging to the church or to powerful sovereigns. These relics and marvels of nature "served as objects of meditation" and as a testimony to the power of God (Daston and Park 2001, 76). Acosta ([1590] 1962) dedicated a chapter to the Peruvian bezoar stone, praising the wonderful medicinal benefits it provided while highlighting its particular usefulness for combating poisons and poisonous diseases. Acosta believed that the discovery of the Peruvian bezoar was yet one more indication that the Almighty God had generously distributed his gifts, secrets, and marvels throughout this earth.[29] Recognizing the significance of this stone, the priest called on his readers to glorify and adore the Lord for his magnanimous beneficence ([1590] 1962, 212–214). Cañizares-Esguerra

FIGURE 1.2. San Luis Beltrán by Francisco de Zurbarán. Image courtesy of the Museo de Bellas Artes, Seville, Spain.

(2006b, 146), writing on the perceived influences of Satan on New World nature, has noted that—just as some herbs seemed to embody demonic forces—it also "became clear [to the Iberian colonizers] that there were plants and animals that God had chosen as allies in the struggle to oust the devil from the continent."

Certainly San Luis Beltrán (1526–1581, canonized in 1671), the Dominican priest and later saint, had reason to give thanks for the bezoar stone when divine intervention revealed to him that he had been given a poisoned drink by the Indigenous peoples he was in the process of converting to Christianity (Valdivieso 1998, 138). In his representation of the scene (ca. 1636–1638), the noted Spanish painter Francisco de Zurbarán portrayed the priest at the precise moment of discovery, just as he was about to drink the poisoned beverage (figure 1.2). In Zurbarán's work, San Luis Beltrán looms large, depicted in austere black and white against two exemplary landscapes and contact zones: in the picture's lower right, he is sermonizing to the Indigenous peoples of Colombia; on the lower left, he supervises the burning of Indigenous idols. Holding in his left hand a silver poison cup, also known as a *bernegal*, he makes the sign of the cross with the right hand, causing the poison to reveal itself miraculously by taking

44 | *Llamas beyond the Andes*

the shape of a winged serpent or dragon (Valdivieso 1998, 138). Divine intervention becomes equated here with the bezoardic antidote because it exposes and ultimately conquers the poisonous serpent. Thus the themes of poison, idolatry, and spiritual conversion come together in powerful visual imagery in Zurbarán's painting.[30]

The iconographic representation of poison as a serpent pervaded the pictorial and decorative arts of the sixteenth and seventeenth centuries. Consequently, it was not unusual to find mounted bezoars and poison cups that included figures of dragons or serpents as part of their ornamentation. One well-known example, the gold poison cup recovered in 1973 from the wreck of the *Nuestra Señora de Atocha*, a famous Spanish "treasure ship" that sank in 1622, has striking dragonlike figures as handles (https://store.melfisher.com/blogs/news/the-poison-cup-story). The *Atocha bernegal* is a model of the kind of exquisite craftsmanship being carried out in the Peruvian viceroyalty, where there was great need of precisely this kind of vessel. The Spanish found an astonishing variety of venomous snakes and poisonous plants in Peru. Calancha ([1638] 1974, 2:1171) observed somewhat dryly, "where there are riches there must, perforce, be poisons." Because it could be a life-threatening substance, poison denoted any corrupt influence that overwhelmed the flesh *or* the spirit. Duviols (1971, 21), in his well-known work on the extirpation of idolatries in colonial Peru, observed that idolatry was defined in the Old Testament as a "poison that inevitably pervades all human faculties and pursuits: 'for the worship of idols is the principle, the cause and the end of all evil.'" In the New World it was not long before Indigenous idolatry was broadly defined as a dangerous poison or malignancy in desperate need of therapeutic intervention. Pablo José de Arriaga ([1621] 1968), the famous extirpator of idolatries, deployed a series of medical metaphors to describe idolatry in general while claiming that there was still hope for the Indigenous peoples in the Andes, where it had not yet become a widespread cancer in the same way that it had for the Moriscos in Spain. He played off the double meaning of the word *mal* as illness and evil to argue that the remedy was simple for those who genuinely desired to be cured, punning: "What is needed is a cure or curate" (Arriaga [1621] 1968, 195).

Spanish association of Indigenous peoples with mortal evil and poison extended beyond their religious practices to include very material implications as well. Soldiers like Pedro de Osma and priests like San Luis Beltrán discovered early on that Indigenous Andeans were both very knowledgeable and skilled in the direct application of many different kinds of lethal poisons. In his letter to Monarde (1574, 74r), Osma emphasized how the Indians made frequent use of dreadful poisons to kill each other and especially the Spanish, thereby underscoring a specific and immediate role for the bezoar stone. Murúa ([1611] 2001, 397) similarly cautioned readers that Indigenous weapons such as lances, arrows, and darts were often carefully treated with deadly poisons.[31]

It could be argued that Indigenous expertise in the use of harmful substances was a key factor for the Spanish colonial imaginary: it forged through metonymy an unequivocal correlation between Indigenous peoples and poison itself. Indeed, the bezoar stone's prominence throughout the Andean region helped to make this metaphor literal. For example, the early seventeenth-century bilingual dictionaries provide abundant evidence of the application, function, and even geography of poisons. González Holguín ([1608] 1989, 690), in his Quechua *Vocabulario*, distinguished a "poisoned beverage" from a "natural poison found in plants or animals" and a "natural poisonous thing." Bertonio ([1612] 2006), in his Aymara *Vocabulario*, underscored the ambiguous nature of poison as both remedy and lethal substance, identifying *colla* as "medicinal philter, or poison for killing" and as a "purgative, food item, or drink, or any kind of plaster or curative medicine" (473), whereas *hihua colla* denoted any "food or beverage that is poisonous and kills" (538). *Collatha* was translated as "to cure someone sick," and a *colla camana* was a doctor, while *collani asiro* was a venomous serpent (473). These definitions indicate close etymological ties between the word *colla* of Collasuyo, one of the four territories governed by the Incas, and medicine as well as the accompanying authority, knowledge, and skills of application required by carefully trained specialists.[32]

Indigenous proficiency in administering poisons added further nuance to the association that Europeans made between Indians of the Andes and the dragon or winged serpent. However, the serpent already carried meaning in Andean cosmology beyond its Christian connotations of poison, idolatry, and the devil. Indigenous peoples incorporated the European dragon into their own worldview and systems of representation, associating it with *amaru*, the legendary serpent believed to be found in the Antisuyu region (Esteras Martín 2004, 66). The *amaru* had ties to the Andean concept of *pachacuti*, meaning the established world turned on its head, and both *amaru* and *pachacuti* constituted important elements of the Taqui Onqoy (dance of disease: a large-scale movement determined to overthrow the spiritual and political rule of the Spanish during the late sixteenth

46 | Llamas beyond the Andes

century). "The Taqui Onqoy marked the time when 'the world was turning round.' In terms reminiscent of Andean myths of creation, Andean leaders asserted that the victory of the *huacas* over the Spaniards and their god would shortly inaugurate a 'new world' of 'other people' and that the Spanish would be swallowed up in the sea" (MacCormack 1988, 983). In this paradigm, disease or poison became a symbol of Andean resistance to the cure/curate.

How did bezoar stones figure in the struggle of the huacas to overthrow the Spanish? This question can only be answered once we understand the role bezoars played in Indigenous pastoral communities. Because bezoars came from the camelids, they were embedded in Indigenous cultural practices and directly linked to the foundational myths of Andean cosmology. Pedro de Osma claimed that *indios amigos* (Indian friends) told him that Indigenous peoples also used the stones against poisons, poisoned wounds, and other pestilential illnesses (Monardes 1574, 74r). While there is little evidence to support this claim, it is clear that bezoar stones were highly valued by herding communities and represented a kind of treasure. According to Indigenous foundational narratives, the camelids, especially the llamas and alpacas, had been sent to humankind by the deities but were only *on loan*: their continuing presence depended primarily on the treatment they received. The appropriate care included providing the animals with adequate pasture and water, treating their maladies, protecting them from predators, and carrying out the proper ceremonies to the huacas each year. If the divinities believed that they had been forgotten, they could become angry and take the camelids away (Flores Ochoa 1977, 227). One early story explained that humanity would survive only as long as there were alpacas. Because the camelids were and are so highly valued, Flores Ochoa (1977, 212, 234) argues that it is not surprising that communities of the high puna region would carry out elaborate rituals designed to protect the health and well-being of these animals, whose numbers can be quickly and easily decimated due to predators, thieves, natural disasters, and disease.

Among the traditions that persist through the present are the carefully guarded ritual objects that pastoral families keep wrapped in small bundles of layered woven cloths. These sacred bundles, known as *señalu q'epi*, contain precious objects such as bezoars, small stones shaped like camelids, also referred to as *conopas*, coca leaves, and other ceremonial items (Flores Ochoa 1977, 214–216). Kept private from all but the family, they protect the wealth and livelihood of "their children":

From Marvelous Antidote to the Poison of Idolatry | 47

For the herder, [the bundle] is both a "mother and a father" that provides food and the possibility of survival. It should only be brought out when it is appropriate according to the ritual calendar. Otherwise, one has to perform a full ceremony of propitiation in order to prevent it from becoming angry enough to "eat" someone, or make them sick and perhaps even die, while at the same time no longer protecting the herd. (215)

The value of these bundles for pastoral families is unmistakable. The objects within can never be purchased. Instead, they are passed on to the eldest son of each generation, who protects their contents and makes certain that the rituals are carried out properly (Flores Ochoa 1977, 217, 235).[33] Designated by the term *illa*, the bezoars and stones that are kept in the bundles possess the quality of *enqa*, which is the vital generating force of life and the source of the family's happiness, abundance, and well-being. Like talismans, they protect the herds and consequently the herding families who depend on the health of the animals for their own subsistence (Flores Ochoa 1977, 218–219). As Flores Ochoa (1977, 224) explains, when these *illas* have *enqa*, they are considered to carry masculine or feminine powers of reproduction: "The sex varies in accordance with the context of the prayers or songs being performed or the stage of the ceremony. Like mothers, they conceive and give birth to offspring. Like fathers, they are the powerful machos with the desired nature and qualities to impregnate the females." In part, then, the *illas*' power is actively sexual because through ritual celebration they ensure the reproduction of the herd, which is the family's "silver" and "gold" (226).

The *illas*' *enqa* is nourished and preserved through elaborate rituals and songs in which women play a key role. Arnold (2004) has explored the relationship between gender and the symbolic currency of the bundles for the rituals of reproduction in her analysis of midwife singers from the pastoral community of Qaqachaka, Bolivia. Arnold draws from numerous songs and stories to describe how women symbolically rebirth the herd animals:

In rituals such as the marking of the animals, the women record certain named stone *illas*, said to generate the *ayllu* herds in their vicinity, as a part of this larger cosmic recycling of souls. The women retell the stories woven around these stones and name them in their songs. Each woman herder manages a ritual bundle of miniature *illas* found in such places, wrapped in cloth, and they are taken out and washed on these occasions, so that they gleam as if they were palpating with new life. In songmaking, too, the women draw on these same key elements of stone node and woven wrapping to "envelop their animals in sound and color." Both combinations of stone and wrapping, in ritual and song, appeal to a common corporal matrix, a placental wrapping of a seed element, to effect the necessary transposition of the herd animals toward a cultural rebirth. In rebirthing their animals into human society, the women mid-wife singers seem to drape them in cultural placentas, as woven cloth and fleece in sung wrappings. (Arnold 2004, 156)

The midwife-singers remember the histories of these *illas* through their songs and the ritual act of cleansing and wrapping them, thereby transforming the stones into life-generating seeds that guarantee the reproduction of the herd and the community's future livelihood. Failure to carry out the ceremonial obligations may result in the loss of life, as the stones' generosity can take a dangerous turn. Becoming hungry, the stones satisfy their need by devouring people and animals in the vicinity (Flores Ochoa 1977, 226). Salomon (2004, 115–116) has observed that the priceless wrappings containing the treasured bezoar stones are important because they document a particular *relationship* of the individual, the family and its ancestors, the larger community, and the surrounding natural environment, of which the camelids are an indispensable if not the principal element. This relationship is one of reciprocity, and as a result it must continually be renewed through the proper ceremonies and rituals.[34]

Importantly, however, the gleaming energy of the *illa*'s *enqa* also nurtures a cultural rebirth that goes beyond that of the individual pastoral family and its animals. *Enqa* has played a significant role as a generating life force for recent messianic ideology in the Andes and the persistent belief that the Inca will one day return, as Delgado-P. (2004) has shown. Drawing attention to the meaning of the word in Quechua, he explains how *enqay* refers to the action of stirring up embers and bringing fire back to life in all of its heat, light, and energy. Contemporary Andean social movements are nourished through *enqa*, he argues, as they look to the return of messianic leaders such as Tupak Amaru (*amaru* = serpent, Quechua) or Tupak Katari (*katari* = serpent, Aymara), who were apprehended by the Spanish colonial authorities toward the end of the eighteenth century and publicly drawn and quartered:

From Marvelous Antidote to the Poison of Idolatry | 49

Hope emerges as the driving force of messianic ideology. The idea persists that those severed limbs, representing the divided or quartered body, become a metaphor of the Indigenous peoples lying in wait and regenerating their energy, their *enqa* or *tupaq*, as once again the resplendent, re/membered body newly forms a vital and unified whole. (Delgado-P. 2004, 194)

Enqa's resplendent energy that engenders and nourishes Andean resistance to colonialism is embodied in the bezoar stone or *illa*. For example, González Holguín ([1608] 1989, 367) translated *yllarini* as "to blaze, dazzle, shine, and illuminate" and *yllarik* as "a resplendent thing."[35] Calancha ([1638] 1974, 1:129) wondered at the range of different colors of Peruvian bezoars, including shining gold.[36] The bezoar *illa*'s energy thus regenerates and gives life to the persistence of Andean traditions and ways of knowing that continue to be under siege from colonialism. In this regard, it becomes clearer how the occult nature of the bezoar stone constituted a threat to the Spanish during the late sixteenth and early seventeenth centuries. Precisely because of its ubiquitous presence in the homes and huacas of Indigenous peoples in herding communities, the bezoar stone's *enqa* suggested that the poison of "idolatry" was potentially more powerful than its antidote (colonialism).

Translation and Appropriation

Recognizing the power of bezoar stones in Indigenous Andean communities, the Spanish colonizers attempted to appropriate the bezoar stone first by disentangling it from its Andean cultural context and then by repositioning it as a treasured commodity in the Western sense. It is important to stress from the outset, however, that present-day anthropologists' descriptions of its ongoing symbolic relevance for pastoral communities and Indigenous movements provide ample evidence that these early efforts came up against resistance and met with only partial success. Spanish strategies used to colonize the bezoar stone and dissociate it from its role in the reproduction of Andean epistemologies emerge at the interstices of the early dictionaries, the colonial chronicles, and inquisition reports.[37] For example, as Delgado-P. (2005, 39–40) has argued, Andean concepts translated into Spanish in dictionaries were often manipulated to conform to Spanish categories of knowledge and power in ways that benefited the

50 | *Llamas beyond the Andes*

colonizer (see also Harrison 1995, 3–4). The translations of *illa* into Spanish in the dictionaries and the accounts of them in chronicles become an important case in point.

For instance, Cobo ([1653] 1956, 130) noted how much Indigenous peoples prized bezoars, yet he dismissed as superstition Andean cultural practices associated with them: "The Indians of Peru call the bezoar stone *illa*; as idolaters, they associate it with certain superstitions, one of which was to always carry it around so that they might become rich."[38] Conveying a frame of reference similar to Cobo's, González Holguín ([1608] 1989, 366) wrote that *illa* was a "very large or notable bezoar stone, the size of an egg or larger, one carried around out of superstition for wealth and good fortune."

Both Cobo's description and González Holguín's translation from Quechua worked simultaneously on several levels. First of all, they took *illa*, a very complicated Andean cultural category as we have seen, and simplified it through translation to express meaning primarily related to riches in the Western sense. Drawing from the work of Hiroyasu Tomoeda (1996), Delgado-P. (2005, 39) describes such a process of transformation as a struggle resulting in Spanish translations that "reduced, distorted, generalized or assumed uni-directional ideas in arbitrary fashion." González Holguín's first definition of *illa* as a bezoar the size of an egg or larger transformed the stone into a commodity by reducing its significance to its economic value in the Western sense, since a stone of this size would have brought huge sums of money in Europe. The second part of his translation operated on more subtle levels when he denigrated the importance to Andeans of carrying *illa* around. This dismissal marginalized traditional Andean symbols of power, including *illas*, which authorities carried in bundles for ceremonial purposes and/or for reasons of governance.

González Holguín's ([1608] 1989) subsequent entries added further nuance to the initial translation and transformation of *illa* by recodifying it not only as a valuable commodity but also as a European-style treasure. This definition, as I show later, helped to legalize the seizure of bezoars from homes and especially from huacas. Thus, for example, he rendered *yllayoc runa* as "a very rich and fortunate man, who has and safeguards treasure" (366). Working from Spanish to Quechua, the lexicographer translated the Spanish word for treasure as *illa curi* or *colque*, but again the translation did not carry any of the connotations of treasure in the Andean sense of the word, such as the examples looked at earlier. Salomon (2004, 124) characterizes González Holguín's word choice as "a curious

From Marvelous Antidote to the Poison of Idolatry | 51

Quechua circumlocution: 'Treasure, *ylla* gold or silver, and something made *ylla*; and to treasure something [is] *yllaycuni.*'" I would argue that this rendition was strategic more than curious because it equated *illa* with gold and silver, making *illa* clearly recognizable to the Spanish as a form of treasure. Other variations of *illa* that the dictionary provided similarly associated it with wealth and riches. Thus, *yllayoc* was someone who "gets rich quickly and has good fortune"; *ylla huaci* denoted a "rich and abundant and fortunate house that has *ylla*"; and *ylla* meant "everything that is old and safeguarded for many years" (González Holguín [1608] 1989, 366–367). Word choice such as "safeguarded for many years" formed part of the legal definition of what constituted a treasure.[39]

Although Bertonio's ([1612] 2006) Aymara-Spanish translations similarly indicated the value of bezoars for Europeans, he also provided additional information, specifying which animals had bezoars, where they were located in the animals' general anatomy, and, more ominously, how they were prized by Indian "sorcerers." Thus, under the Spanish entry *Piedra bazaar* one finds: "*Hayntilla.* Large [bezoar] stones: *Illa, Llaullacasu*" (Bertonio ([1612] 2006, 344). Bertonio defined *hayntilla* as "small bezoar stones found in the gut of vicuñas and *carneros*;[40] the large ones are called *Illa*" (535) and *Llaullacasu* as "a small stone that looks like a llama, highly esteemed by sorcerers" (594). These llama-shaped stones were sometimes called *illas-llamas* and *conopas.* All of these terms became part of the vocabulary of the campaigns of extirpation because for the Spanish visitors they denoted the presence of occult demonic practices.[41]

Both González Holguín's and Bertonio's translations helped to position the bezoar as a secret treasure and the *illa* as a treasured secret or sign of idolatry. Describing the many forms of Andean idolatry in his "Instrucción para descubrir todas las guacas del Pirú y sus camayos y haziendas" (ca. 1585), Cristóbal de Albornoz (quoted in Duviols 1967), the famous priest who had been involved in the suppression of the Taqui Onqoy resistance (MacCormack 1991b; Millones 1971), provided detailed accounts of the kinds of huacas for which visitors of idolatry should be on the lookout. Included among them were shrines and tombs where Indians reportedly kept gold, silver, and other minerals and precious stones for worshipping. Albornoz devoted a paragraph to the large caches of bezoar stones he had uncovered:

> Likewise, in the native cattle known as llamas, there can be found some stones that we call bezoars, and some of them are very large

52 | *Llamas beyond the Andes*

and heavy. These have been collected and stored in areas where there are native cattle and [the Indians] worship them in great reverence, calling them *illas llamas*. I have found them in many provinces where these cattle can be found, and have had them burned, because [Indians] make use of them in many of their superstitions and they believe that when they worship this stone, no lamb will abort, nor will anything bad happen to their cattle, nor will they catch the terrible skin disease known as *carache* that afflicts these animals. And ever since they have realized that we are interested in these stones, they have hidden them away, especially the large ones, because since the smaller ones are so easily found they give them to us, not realizing the virtue that they have. I publicly burned many trunkfuls of these stones after I discovered them, in the main squares of numerous provinces of this bishopric. (Albornoz in Duviols 1967, 18)

Albornoz must have caught his reader's attention when he indicated the quantities of bezoar stones to be found in areas where there were camelids. Although claiming that the Indians used them for superstitious purposes, he also gave a sense of their value for the herding communities: the stones protected the animals from abortions and from the highly contagious and devastating skin disease known as *carache*.

In his introduction to Albornoz's *Instrucción*, Duviols (1967, 11) makes the compelling argument that the text reads as if it had been commissioned by a high authority, most likely the viceroy himself. According to Duviols, even though the title announced that the text was a practical guide to the extirpation of idolatries, the document served equally as a vade mecum for the treasure hunter. Given the viceroyalty's perennial financial troubles, it made sense that there would be keen interest in the wealth uncovered from the huacas.[42] Viceroy Francisco de Toledo's *Disposiciones gubernativas* certainly bear out Duviol's hypothesis. Of particular interest is the ordinance outlining the procedures to be followed when a huaca was discovered and dismantled. Toledo ordered that the viceroyalty should collect the tax known as the *quinto real* (royal fifth) for any treasure that once belonged to principal authorities and leaders, including gold, silver, pearls, precious stones, and other items, found in grave sites, mines, tombs, and temples and religious houses of idols and gods. The viceroyalty expected to receive half payment for gold, silver, pearls, precious stones, and so forth discovered in peoples' houses, religious sites, burial grounds,

From Marvelous Antidote to the Poison of Idolatry | 53

and elsewhere (Lohmann Villena and Sarabia Viejo 1986–1989, 1:286). In other words, the huacas should be cleared out to discourage Andean idolatry, but the viceroyalty was to take its economic due. To ensure that this happened, Toledo included specific instructions regarding who was to be present when a huaca was dismantled and who was to write an inventory of the value of the goods found (Lohmann Villena and Sarabia Viejo 1986–1989, 1:286–288).[43]

The viceroy's ordinances clearly challenged Bartolomé de las Casas's earlier writing on the subject. Las Casas ([1563] 1958) had argued against the right of the Spanish to these treasures.[44] His position did not appear to carry much weight with subsequent legislation. Upholding Toledo's laws, Solórzano y Pereira ([1648] 1972) systematized these procedures, arguing that it was perfectly legal to remove treasures found in tombs and huacas so long as any bodies uncovered were treated respectfully and carefully put back in place. He defined what constituted a treasure, who had the right to look for treasure in the huacas, and what percentages of the riches discovered should be handed over to the Crown.[45] As in the case of Toledo, Solórzano y Pereira's concern was to clarify that the riches, even those discovered in the huacas and shrines, belonged to the royal authorities rather than to the church, as some had argued. While it is beyond the scope of this chapter to discuss Solórzano y Pereira's entire commentary regarding the discovery of treasure in huacas, it is important to underscore his argument that the laws did not prohibit the ransacking of huacas if the search for treasure was undertaken so that the wealth might be used to further the public good (as exemplified by the actions of the Crown) rather than for reasons of personal greed. Solórzano y Pereira concluded his chapter by specifying that those treasures discovered in huacas and other temples and shrines should be divided according to the following percentages: the assayer should receive one and a half percent; following this, the *quinto real* should be deducted for the Crown, while the remaining amount should be divided in half, with 50 percent going to the person who discovered the treasure and 50 percent to the *cámara* (tribunal) (Solórzano y Pereira [1648] 1972, 335–344).

In addition to the viceroyalty claiming its share in the wealth, there is also evidence that extirpators and others did not always burn the idolatrous items discovered or seized or turn them over to the royal authorities. Solórzano y Pereira [1648] 1972, 326) had observed the value of bezoar stones while noting that to his knowledge the Crown received little revenue from them: "And so, for as much as these stones are confiscated and collected, I

54 | Llamas beyond the Andes

have never seen any *quinto* or other tax be paid to His Majesty for them." Given the value of bezoar stones for Europeans and the prices they would bring, it is likely that many a bezoar was accidentally slipped into a pocket or two, only to be sold later.[46] The royal inventory specifically mentioned that many of the bezoars that Viceroy Toledo sent to Felipe II for his collection, like the idols, came from people's houses (Sánchez Cantón 1958, 1:275). As suggested earlier, such a story would only enhance the stone's value in Europe by endowing it with an even greater aura of exoticism.

Bezoar stones thus represented a priceless commodity to both Indigenous Andeans and Europeans. For Indigenous peoples, having bezoars seized from their homes during the campaigns of extirpation must indeed have signaled a kind of *pachacuti*, overturning life as they knew it, and the beginning of a new epoch marked by hunger, due to the threat of the disappearance of the camelids that were being reclaimed by the angry huacas.

Paradoxically, then, bezoar stones both gave life and took life away. Some historians of science have dismissed the bezoar stone, claiming that Monardes made a mistake by including it in his books when he had so many more genuine New World medicinals to introduce to early modern Europe.[47] Skepticism regarding the bezoar's medical efficacy actually began with the stone's introduction into Europe. By the mid-nineteenth century, with few exceptions, medical interest in the bezoar had completely waned.[48] The *Dictionnaire encyclopédique des sciences médicales* (1868, 221) dismissed bezoars, mentioning them solely for their historical appeal:

> In the Middle Ages, drugs from Arabic medicine were introduced into Europe along with the superstitious ideas of the Orient. Bezoars were considered to be endowed with marvelous abilities; they expelled venoms, they neutralized poisons, they restored life that was on the verge of expiring, etc., etc. These prodigious attributes existed only in the imagination of those extolling bezoars. Today, these so highly praised medicinals are of historical interest only.

As this entry indicates, by the time the encyclopedia was published, most Europeans considered the bezoar to be solely the stuff of Eastern superstition and Western fantasy, relevant at best as a historical curiosity. The bezoar stone continued to incite curiosity after medical and scientific interest in it had faded, however, appearing occasionally in

From Marvelous Antidote to the Poison of Idolatry | 55

nineteenth-century travelers' accounts.[49] The fascinating and complicated story of the role played by the bezoar as protagonist in the politico-cultural history of European medicine and travel literature must be saved for another time. During the early colonial period, however, the bezoar stone constituted a surprising contact zone for the intertwined themes of violence, wonder, profit, occult forces, and hidden treasure. Indeed, as I argue here, the bezoar stone is a tremendously productive site for reading the complex intersections of sixteenth- and seventeenth-century colonial commercial interests and knowledge production for Europeans and Andeans alike.

CHAPTER 2

Exploring the Body-Interior

Autopsy in Colonial Camelid Contact Zones

AUTOPSY: 1. Seeing with one's own eyes, eye-witnessing; personal observation or inspection; 2. Dissection of a dead body, so as to ascertain by actual inspection its internal structure, and *esp.* to find out the cause or seat of disease; post mortem examination.

The Compact Edition of the Oxford English Dictionary *(1971)*

The preface to the first edition of one of the basic reference tools of veterinary medicine, *Textbook of Veterinary Anatomy*, includes as its epigraph a quotation by Johann Wolfgang von Goethe: "What one does not understand one does not possess" (Dyce, Sack, and Wensing 2002, vii). A statement such as this could well have served as a beacon to the professors and demonstrators of anatomy who worked at the Royal Veterinary School of Alfort (École Nationale Vétérinaire d'Alfort) newly established in 1766 at the Château d'Alfort on the outskirts of Paris. These were the years when the study of comparative anatomy was beginning to flourish, and anatomy and dissection were central practices for acquiring knowledge of the body.

The art of dissection required the cultivation of the senses, emphasizing the importance not only of sight but also of touch, smell, and even taste.[1] Stafford (1991, 47) describes how this multisensorial practice helped shape eighteenth-century methods of scientific investigation and, more broadly, any comprehensive inquiry: "The Galenic conception of anatomy as an 'opening up in order to see deeper or hidden parts' drives to the heart of a master problem for the Enlightenment. How does one attain the interior of things? Anatomy and its inseparable practice of dissection were the eighteenth-century paradigms for any forced, artful, contrived, and violent study of depths." Stafford's observations on dissection as a

58 | Llamas beyond the Andes

mode of three-dimensional investigation also call attention to an inherent violence underlying the method, an association that I point to throughout this chapter. In all its literal and metaphorical implications of dismemberment, discovering, cutting, dividing, separating, and analyzing, dissection has been linked to Western methods of investigation and the acquisition of knowledge in areas ranging from surgery to archaeology, from religion to philosophy (Stafford 1991, 47).

Yet the epigraph by Goethe that would guide readers as their very first axiom in a textbook on veterinary anatomy clearly shows another layer to the series of relationships between dissection and knowledge acquisition. Notably, it underscores how anatomy and dissection became paradigms for the prevailing notion of knowledge *as gain*, whether gain meant the obtainment of wisdom, experience, or wealth.[2] The interconnections linking knowledge, gain, and possession became increasingly salient during the eighteenth-century Enlightenment, especially due to the growing number of natural-history expeditions taking place throughout the Spanish Empire. As Lafuente (2000, 159) has shown, the new Bourbon dynasty's program of political and economic reform sought to exploit more comprehensively Spanish America's many "fiscal, political, and natural resources." In this context, the sponsoring of scientific expeditions served "as a suitable instrument to fulfill imperial ambitions" (159). Through the exploration of coastlines and the mapping of interior lands, plants, animals, and minerals, they played a significant role in the systematization of nature (see Pratt 1992, 18–19). Understanding how the study of anatomy participated in the structuring of these initiatives enables a more nuanced reading of Stafford's comparison of dissection's "violent study of depths" to a "second age of discovery."

This analogy was also seen as early as the Middle Ages and Renaissance, when the body was likened to an unmapped territory, "a location which demanded from its explorers skills which seemed analogous to those displayed by the heroic voyagers across the terrestrial globe" (Sawday 1995, 23). The axiom attributed to Goethe, in other words, helps to clarify how anatomy and dissection in the eighteenth century carried metaphorical, professional, and political implications underlying Western expansion (see MacLeod 1988, 2–4).

In Andean South America, dissection—the violent opening up of interior space—served as an appropriate metaphor for the changing dynamic of Enlightenment colonial relations. During the eighteenth century, increasing numbers of European travelers, naturalists, and collectors made

Exploring the Body-Interior | 59

their way for the first time into the heart of the Peruvian viceroyalty. This distinct movement away from the coastal areas and toward the interior expanses of the Andean altiplano formed part of a "new territorial phase of capitalism," set into motion by the desire to collect and classify raw materials and useful specimens of natural history (Pratt 1992, 9). Among the many items that caught the interest of French travelers and other explorers were the Andean camelids. Like their Spanish counterparts, the French perceived these animals to be a promising source of unexploited riches. As is evident from my analysis, dissection paradigmatically structured "narratives of acquisition" (Adams 1997, 85) of the Andean camelids because, as a practice, it entails a series of "surgical strategies" (Stafford 1991, 64) for the purposes of cutting, extracting, and even transplanting.

It must be argued, of course, that dissection and anatomization and related terms such as "autoptic" and later "autopsy" structured Western colonial epistemologies long before the eighteenth century. Pagden (1993, 51) has identified an "autoptic imagination" in the work of early historians of the New World, driven by the "authority of the eye witness, to the privileged understanding which those present at an event have over all those who have only read or been told about it."[3] As Bleichmar (2005) and Cook (2007) have argued, the colonial logic of the eyewitness account structured early natural histories and medical works such as Nicolás Monardes's *Historia medicinal*. Monardes's style of writing brought together "historia, the narrative description of an experience, with autopsia, direct observation or manipulation" (Bleichmar 2005, 90; cf. Cook 2007, 37). The result was an autoptic *historia* that, as seen in the previous chapter, combined information and efficacy reports of newly discovered materia medica from travelers in American contact zones and the experiments and evaluations of the same medicines carried out in Europe by Monardes and others (Bleichmar 2005, 90).[4] In this study of Andean camelid contact zones, however, I find that emergent autoptic narratives produced in the colonial context also referenced the process of discovery through firsthand accounting in the context of autopsy's later definition: the anatomization of a dead body to scrutinize its internal contents. This investigation of the three-dimensional body plays a part in the *Historia medicinal* as well as in other histories and documents from the colonial period forward and figures as a key trope throughout this chapter.

As suggested, the terms "autopsy" and "anatomization" or "dissection" are redolent with meaning beyond their immediate ocular and medical connotations. For example, Sawday (1995, 1) claims that, in addition to its

60 | *Llamas beyond the Andes*

literal sense of opening and dividing a body for critical investigation, "a dissection might denote not the delicate separation of constituent structures, but a more violent 'reduction' into parts: a brutal dismemberment of people, things, or ideas. This violent act of partition tends to be associated with the related term (speaking conceptually) of 'anatomization.'" Ironically, however, just as dissection constitutes the methodology of partition, anatomization, or fragmentation of the (animal) body, leads to the formation of new bodies of knowledge and insight: "As the physical body is fragmented, so the body of understanding is held to be shaped and formed" (2).[5] Drawing from these observations, I argue in this chapter that anatomization, as a method of separation, reduction, and reshaping, structures a complex, full-fledged colonial logic that seeks to dismantle the agency of local Andean actors in knowledge-making processes while shaping new imperial epistemologies, beginning with the sixteenth century and expanding into the seventeenth and eighteenth centuries.

This chapter analyzes five case studies spanning these three centuries. The focus of each is on a sustained narrative examination of the three-dimensional camelid body, the changing meanings the body accrued over time, and the gradual systematization of knowledge about that body. The first case history investigates basic themes pertaining to the ritual and material significance of camelids for Andean pastoral communities historically, concentrating on the importance of sacrifice and its role in generating knowledge of the internal animal body during the colonial period. It takes as its primary example the illustration of the sacrifice of a llama prepared by the sixteenth-century Andean Quechua nobleman Felipe Guaman Poma de Ayala. This pictorial representation makes visible how a full understanding of the material camelid body at the time (its internal and external anatomy and overall physical condition) fit into a larger ecological context that helped to predict the well-being of the entire Indigenous community.

From there, the chapter returns to Monardes's *Historia medicinal* to discuss the first Western description of the anatomy of the camelid gut as conveyed in Pedro de Osma's 1571 letter from Peru. His observations on the interior body and the placement within of bezoar stones make evident the connections between scientific discovery and imperial economic interests and show how they had already become entangled at the site of the anatomized camelid body. My discussion next moves to the account of a guanaco anatomization near the Ilo valley in southern Peru in the early eighteenth century by the French scientist Louis Feuillée. Feuillée created the earliest known record of a camelid digestive tract from a Western perspective. Although his anatomical description was only produced following a disappointing search for bezoars within the body of the dead animal, Feuillée's study would be the single most important source on the science of the camelid gastrointestinal physiology for many years. The chapter concludes with a transition to late eighteenth-century Europe, specifically the Alfort Veterinary School. The French natural historian Georges-Louis Leclerc, Comte de Buffon, was able to study and describe a living llama and vicuña kept at the school. After its death, a second llama at Alfort was dissected, preserved, and publicly displayed with techniques developed by anatomist Honoré Fragonard. Buffon's textual account of the llama and vicuña in terms of their potential economic utility and Fragonard's carefully preserved llama (*écorché*) resonate today because of the thoroughness with which they mapped the external and internal camelid body. Moreover, the study of their works also brings to light acquisition routes from England to France and testifies to the persistence of an animal's narrative significance into its afterlife.

Read together, the five case histories elucidate how the many cognate meanings of autopsy and dissection, as they pertain to the anatomization of camelid bodies and the creation of new empirical practices and knowledge, resonated throughout the cultural and political context of Andean colonial relations over three centuries. Specifically, they show how the interior body became increasingly visible through dissection. This useful information, in turn, would be vital in laying the groundwork for future large-scale camelid extraction projects.

Epistemologies of Camelid Sacrifice in the Andes

As seen in the introduction to this book, the llama has been described by many as the animal most perfectly suited to the ecology of the Andes. One of the camelid's most valuable assets, its fiber, is a basic resource for pastoral communities as raw material and as processed yarn or thread. It also acquires symbolic resonance as a fundamental signifier in a series of associations linking woven cloth or textile, on the one hand, and skin and tissue, on the other. These intersections have been fruitfully pursued in historical and contemporary anthropological studies.[6] Chapter 1, for example, draws on this scholarship to examine the metaphor of wrapping and unwrapping textiles in the Aymara pastoral community Qaqachaka

62 | Llamas beyond the Andes

and how the tradition is linked ritually to women-centered practices involving the woven bundles used to safeguard *illas*, bezoar stones, and other ceremonial objects. The wrapped bundle can be understood as a symbol of the protected cavity or womb of the animal, where the precious stones are generated, and the woman's womb or placenta that holds the fertile seeds, both of which serve as a guarantee of the community's future (Arnold 2004, 153, 156). Likewise, Abercrombie (1998, 185) analyzes this figurative relationship to demonstrate how Andean rituals incorporating cloth and textiles denote regeneration and sustainability for the herding community by functioning as a form of "social skin."

The Andean social fabric is woven in different ways, but one important manner is through fiestas, rituals, and commemorative events that highlight the associations of people, animals, and the landscape as transmitted through songs, dances, libation rites, and weaving and agricultural practices (Abercrombie 1998, 152, 175–176). In Qaqachaka and other pastoral communities, camelids play a variety of roles in these ceremonial occasions, including the ways in which their physical bodies are ritually inscribed through cutting and marking, such as when their ears are notched or pierced.[7] Camelid ears are made to "flower" when pierced with bits of colored threads that look like vivid blossoms. The selection of the color of the yarn and shape of the flowers is specific to each family and is the responsibility of the Qaqachaka women. They choose yarn in bright shades of reds and carmines for the female llamas and alpacas to ensure that they will reproduce in abundance, while the males' ears are decorated with rose-colored yarn and even tassels and pompoms. In the marking process, the females' ears should bleed profusely because the flowing blood symbolizes fertility and the genealogical persistence of the animal's maternal line (Arnold and Yapita 1998, 131–132). In other communities, year-old animals' ears are marked as a rite of passage, acknowledging sexual maturity and the transition to "animalhood" (Dransart 1997, 90).

Recognizing the camelid's multilayered significance in the life of Andean communities and how the animals' social lives resonate with those of the herding families helps us to understand why "llamas were (and are) the sine qua non of sacrifice" (Abercrombie 1998, 183). For an academic project such as this one, looking back to the precolonial and early colonial periods to comprehend the role of llama sacrifice in the historical context of Andean social memory can be challenging.[8] As seen in the previous chapter, one factor complicating this understanding is that few Spanish chroniclers attempted to document local traditions for their own value and merit. Instead, their efforts to make Andean epistemologies legible to Europeans went hand in hand with objectives such as the conversion of souls, the collection of tribute, and the seizure of property and wealth. In the mind of the Spanish, many Andean practices and ritual objects were linked to idolatry and as a result required eradication (Abercrombie 1998, 130; Dedenbach-Salazar Sáenz 1990, 181; Mills 1997). Most importantly, for the early explorers, chroniclers, and colonists, "there was no possibility for immediate and authoritative knowledge outside the 'structure of norms' provided by the canon [of the Bible and the writings of the Church Fathers]. The world of the American Indians, and of all those other 'others' whose behaviour seemed initially unaccountable, could never therefore be explained . . . 'in their terms' since, for these early writers, 'their terms' could never be detached from 'ours'" (Pagden 1993, 53).

These observations are certainly true regarding sacrifice, a core component of Christian doctrine. For example, in its definition of the term *sacrificio*, the *Diccionario de autoridades* ([1737] 1963, 3:13) links it directly to an offering made to God, and more specifically to the figure of Christ, whose blood was spilled "when he sacrificed himself on the cross, dying for the redemption and salvation of humankind." During Mass, sacrifice also refers to the priest's offering and blessing of the wine and bread, and their transubstantiation into the body and blood of Christ (3:13). Drawing from these same definitions, Dedenbach-Salazar Sáenz (1990, 186) hypothesizes that the colonial chroniclers and campaigns of extirpation would have understood the concept of sacrifice in this Western sense. Thus, the chroniclers' labeling of an Andean ritual as a "sacrifice" underscored its idolatry because it took place outside of Christian doctrine and was not overseen by the proper church authorities. Similarly, the Spanish chroniclers classified Andean protagonists or officiants of sacrifices by means of a variety of terms that underscored the idolatrous nature of the practice.[9] Because many Andean sacrifices were carried out in private spaces, they appeared to the Spanish to be deliberately concealed events. As a case in point, Garcilaso de la Vega ([1609] 1985, 2:51) also described having witnessed clandestine sacrifices of camelids performed by "old Indians who had not yet been baptized."

Specific forms of sacrificing or cutting the animals were expressly forbidden by the campaigns of extirpation. In part, this was because some camelid sacrifices began not with the slitting of the animal's throat, a

64 | *Llamas beyond the Andes*

practice familiar to Europeans, but instead with a cut at the end of the rib cage, on the left side.[10] The officiant could then insert his hand and extract the llama's heart, lungs, and esophagus, preferably in one piece. In some festivals, the veins, arteries, and major organs would be inspected to determine if they augured good or bad fortune for the community. For example, if the pastures had been ample and abundant and the animals were free of life-threatening parasites, the organs would be healthy and strong, indicating prosperity for the entire herd. Similarly, if the community's territorial extension had been encroached upon and pasture lands were insufficient or poor in quality, or if there had been unfavorable climatic conditions, the health of the herd and consequently of the community would be adversely affected. It did not bode well if the organs were damaged during the process of removal from the animal's body. Garcilaso de la Vega ([1609] 1985, 2:50–51) remembered hearing when he was a boy how the officiants present consulted with each other regarding the signs and whether they indicated good or bad fortune. Following this scrutiny and assessment, the organs were generally burned and the animal roasted and eaten.

Llama sacrifice, as described by Garcilaso de la Vega, is visually foregrounded in *Nueva corónica y buen gobierno*, prepared by Quechua chronicler and interpreter Felipe Guaman Poma de Ayala (1615/1616, image 880 [894]). Guaman Poma's representation of the sacrifice of a llama by Andean pastoral peoples (figure 2.1) offers a unique perspective on the important role the ritual played in local knowledge construction. This image depicts a family unit, consisting of a mother, father, and son, gathered closely to sacrifice a llama, with each playing a specific role in the ceremony. The son helps to hold the animal as the father, occupying the central focus of the image beside the animal, carries out the cutting and organ extraction, while the mother stands by, ready with a container. The image could have been categorized as a depiction of Andean idolatrous practices, which the author generally condemned. At the top of the page, he wrote:

> They kill the ram here as in the time of idolatry, by inserting the hand near to the heart. Let them not kill the animal this way, but rather as in the time of Christianity, by cutting the throat. It is idolatrous witchcraft to kill the animal in the old way. Let the Indian man and woman who carry out this practice be punished. (Guaman Poma 1615/1616, 881 [894])

Exploring the Body-Interior | 65

FIGURE 2.1. *Sacrifice of a llama as depicted by Guaman Poma de Ayala. Image courtesy of Det Kgl. Bibliotek/Royal Danish Library.*

The textual exegesis of the image continues the warning against such methods: "The Indians of this kingdom are carrying out the old tradition of idolatry; because, either for eating or for rituals, they killed sheep, they opened it up by the heart, which is the tradition of idolatrous sorcerers" (881 [895]). No longer were such practices to be permitted, and those who did not refrain from eating products made of raw blood or changing their mode of sacrifice were to be shorn and whipped publicly.[11]

Guaman Poma's textual rebuke of the practice appears to be concerned primarily with the idolatrous *method* of killing and the consumption of uncooked meat and blood, rather than with the act of sacrifice itself. While his image focuses attention on the technique of cutting, however, it also highlights the social networks created as a result. Guaman Poma's llama is captured in its final moments of agony, literally at the threshold between life and death: the wide eyes bulge, the gasping mouth exposes incisors and canine teeth. Teetering on tied legs, the animal defecates as the body relaxes its grasp on life and death takes hold. The Western viewer might

66 | Llamas beyond the Andes

comprehend the physical torment the llama appears to undergo as a form of martyrdom, the bloody wound in the animal's side being reminiscent of the passion of Christ, such that the image creates what Sawday (1995, 104) refers to more generally as a "sacred anatomy," because it asserts "the centrality of the body, even in division, to the key articles of the Christian faith." Guaman Poma was certainly familiar with Western Christian pictorial conventions as well as with those depicting savagery and barbarism and was a master at turning negative images of American Indians on their head, as Adorno (1990) has shown. For example, his portrayals of pre-Inca Andean peoples depict them wearing elaborate skins but carrying out actions deemed "civilizing" such as plowing or Christian-like activities such as praying (Adorno 1990). The author's artistic rendition of the camelid sacrifice is similarly complicated because the visual signs generate multiple possible readings.

Guaman Poma's unique illustration of the llama sacrifice is visually striking for the way it captures the ritualized ceremony at the precise moment when the man reaches into the body of the animal, which is balanced at the brink of life and death. With his hand buried inside the llama's body, the concentrated expression of the father's face suggests the detachment of a skilled practitioner: he appears to be deftly navigating his way through the animal's interior by feel rather than by sight, demonstrating both experience and expertise. The hand hidden inside the animal's body does not provide even a glimpse of what he may be about to pull out, thereby maintaining the viewer's attention on the dramatic contest between life and death as the family awaits the signs that will be communicated once the organs have been extracted and interpreted. Despite his stern condemnation of the method of cutting, Guaman Poma nevertheless depicts an intimate scene that underscores not so much the family's shared idolatry but rather the vital social relationship between animals and humans. It may be difficult to perceive this important relationship based on a single image; however, looking at the entire set of images from Guaman Poma's 1615/1616 manuscript, we begin to understand the close affiliation between humans and camelids. Young girls of the age of twelve served their families by watching over the herds of camelids while spinning (225 [227]); boys did the same, while learning how to hunt for birds (204 [206]). Camelids sang or wept in chorus with humans during ritual celebrations (318 [320]) and before being sacrificed (240 [242], 243 [245], 254 [256]). As he emphasized, although he was describing sacrifice to the idols, it was nevertheless also a time of plenty with ample rainfall, which would be good for the lands left to rest, and an abundance of food for people and animals. Together with their animals, herders joyfully sang in what Abercrombie (1998, 183) describes as "llama language": "llamaya llamayayn yalla llamaya" (Guaman Poma 1615/1616, 245 [247]). Taken as a whole, therefore, these images and the accompanying text confirm that Guaman Poma criticized idolatrous practices among Indigenous peoples but admired precolonial Andean traditions, which emphasized the efficient organization of resources and the preservation of sustainable ecologies for the benefit of all (López Baralt 1988, 395; MacCormack 1991b, 139–204). Regarding the image of the llama sacrifice, Guaman Poma may have intended to condemn idolatry, but he also performatively depicted the body so that its signification shifts toward the living and away from idolatry, lifelessness, and decomposition. As portrayed by the colonial chronicler, the ritual emphasizes instead how the culture of sacrifice strengthens the social fabric by rallying the entire community: men and women, young and old; reenacts the interdependence of humans and camelids; and reaffirms the importance of the present condition of the animal for the future survival of the community.

An Early Glimpse into the Camelid Interior

In his third and final part of the *Historia medicinal* (1574), Nicolás Monardes, the prominent doctor from Seville discussed in the previous chapter, provided Western readers a first look at the camelid body-interior. Prior to this time, chroniclers' pictorial and written portrayals of the camelids chiefly described their external physical characteristics and the flat, two-dimensional surface of the body. Monardes's 1574 description of the placement of bezoar stones inside these exotic Andean creatures offered Western readers a first opportunity to catch sight of the heretofore secret interior of the three-dimensional camelid body, ultimately claiming it as a source of hidden wealth. In this way, and even though he had not personally witnessed the anatomization of the animal, Monardes exemplified the early modern scientist whose mandate, according to Sawday (1995, 25), was to explore the body-interior in order to reveal its secrets: "Once uncovered, the body-landscape could be harnessed to the service of its owner. In thus establishing the body as 'useful'—a key term amongst the natural philosophers of the seventeenth century—we are able to perceive the language of colonialism and the language of science as meshing with one

68 | *Llamas beyond the Andes*

another." Monardes's sixteenth-century recounting of the unprecedented search within the camelid body for bezoar stones provides a compelling model showing how the language of Western science and colonialism converged profitably.[12]

We can see how Monardes laid the groundwork for this exploration in his earlier 1571 edition of the *Historia medicinal*, which contained the Spanish soldier Pedro de Osma's letter that described the important discovery of bezoar stones and other materia medica in Peru. In his introductory remarks to the letter, Monardes anticipated for his readers the important discoveries that would emerge in the soldier's narrative by detailing his own scene of encounter with its contents when the soldier's package and letter first reached him. His drawn-out description of this exciting event also foregrounded a series of extended metaphors evoking the association of text, textile, tissue, and skin, although they did so differently from the ways already seen in Andean epistemologies. In Monardes's account, these metaphorical analogies created parallel narratives of discovery by linking the unwrapping and exploring of the package's contents with the "unwrapping" or removal of the concentric wrappings of the animal's tissue-skin to get to its inner recesses. These analogous stories of encounter resonated, in turn, with larger colonial narratives of heroic discovery and conquest and the reward of untold riches.[13] Monardes's introduction to Osma's letter consequently serves as a point of departure for an in-depth reading of Western autoptic histories in the Andes and of how information and wealth were gathered in the camelid contact zone.

These points become salient in Monardes's description of the arrival and opening of the package sent to him by Osma:

> A bundle of the sort used for correspondence showed up, wrapped in a waxed covering that was done up so securely that it could have traveled safely anywhere, no matter how far. After unwrapping the package, I found a small, well-made box from a thick, hollowed-out piece of cork, and there inside were plants and seeds, of which the letter will tell, and all were labeled. And tucked in a corner of the cork there were three carefully packed bezoar stones, wrapped and sealed in parchment. The letter was lying underneath, written in cramped, hard-to-read script. (Monardes 1574, 72v)

In these introductory observations, Monardes lingered in uncharacteristic fashion on the dramatic arrival of the news and samples. By describing

Exploring the Body-Interior | 69

the gradual revelation of the mysterious container and its contents step by step, Monardes created a heightened sense of anticipation and suspense. The reader becomes a participant-observer, peering, as it were, over his shoulder. With its emphasis on the unwrapping of precious contents, we can see how this intimate scene of discovery anticipates a second, parallel moment of encounter in Osma's letter, where the soldier describes the physical act of opening the exotic animal's body-container to uncover its occult secrets. In each case, the unwrapped layers served as a kind of veil, behind which a treasured commodity had been concealed.[14]

Once the animal had been cut open, Osma did not elaborate on the details of the animal's anatomy, noting only that the Indian child revealed to the soldiers the animal's secret, which consisted of what looked like a small purse or pocket (*bolsilla*) located in the inner chest or stomach (*buche*), containing the precious stones,[15] an analogy that clearly emphasized the economic importance of the discovery, as either a purse or a pocket can be used to hold wealth. In this first animal they found nine stones lined in a row (Monardes 1574, 73v–74r).

In the third publication of the *Historia medicinal* in 1574, Monardes returned to this momentous anatomization and elaborated further on the Peruvian bezoars' specific location inside the exotic animal, highlighting the stones' significance and presenting detailed testimony by himself and others of their medicinal use and efficacy in a wide variety of circumstances. Perhaps to focus attention on his own findings, in this final part Monardes did not mention Osma by name, identifying him only as the "first discoverer" of the stones and as a "gentleman" (*gētil hōbre*), while the Indian boy's assistance disappeared completely (Monardes 1574, 110v–111r). According to Monardes, in his initial examination of the animal's interior cavity, the gentleman found the bezoars situated in a sort of "belt" or "girdle, made of bilious flesh" (111r). The girdle, "approximately two hands in length and three fingers in width, and joined to the inside of the stomach," contained stones of different sizes, laid out in a row, placed inside what looked like "the buttonholes of a cloak" (111r). In this 1574 publication, Monardes also included an engraving illustrating the stones' placement inside the animal (figure 2.2). It appears that he drew this image based on Osma's own eyewitness reporting. Such an important image enhanced the utility of Monardes's text, even for those unable to see the stones in situ for themselves, and further consolidated his authority and reputation as an expert in New World medicinals.[16] Being the only such illustration in existence, it would be referenced frequently in later

70 | Llamas beyond the Andes

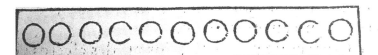

FIGURE 2.2. "The placement [of the stones]." Monardes (1574, 111r).

years to help solve debates, including the number of stones that could be found in a single animal (see, for example, Geoffroy [le Jeune] 1731, 201).

This image thus provided European audiences with one of the first glimpses inside the camelid body. The eyewitness account elucidated an economic anatomy by attempting to map the body-interior and by describing the location and number of bezoar stones within the paunch. Expressing the placement of the stones through the analogy of the buttons lining a cloak helped to make the treasure seem more tangible and accessible and conveniently arranged, as if ready for the taking. For Monardes's many readers, the camelid interior could now be visualized as a three-dimensional receptacle containing untold wealth. This initial appraisal became the starting point for subsequent mappings.

Mapping the Camelid Digestive System

If Pedro de Osma's description of the camelid interior can be considered the first formal account of such an examination undertaken and described by a Westerner, it would take another 139 years before a second detailed commentary was published.[17] One of the earliest French travelers to explore the inner coastal regions of South America was Louis Feuillée (1660–1732), priest, mathematician-astronomer, and correspondent of the Paris Royal Academy of Sciences. Sent by King Louis XIV, Feuillée traveled extensively along South America's west coast in 1709–1710, recording his observations in journal form on a variety of topics related to cartography and the natural history of the region in the pursuit of expanding French commercial and naval interests there. During his travels, he had the unexpected opportunity to anatomize the digestive tract of a camelid, which he identified as a guanaco. Feuillée's commentary is significant in many ways, but of interest here is how his mapping of the guanaco gut elucidates the convergence of science and empire in the camelid contact zone.

The guanaco anatomization can be read on at least two levels. First, it was an unprecedented, comprehensive mapping of the animal's intestinal system that scientists would consider definitive for many years. Second, as the priest documented the removal and examination of the animal's gut, he described another, more subtle kind of extraction. Although his textual record begins by situating the animal within its natural Andean habitat and giving attention to its cultural role in Indigenous ritual practices, these cultural references disappear as the process of anatomization gets underway: the body is gradually claimed by Western science. If knowledge is possession, as discussed earlier in this chapter, then the hope for Enlightenment natural historians and explorers was that greater knowledge and understanding of the body-interior's workings would facilitate the eventual large-scale extraction of living animals via global commercial routes and enable their naturalization in Europe and elsewhere.

Feuillée first encountered what likely were llamas on August 31, 1710, when he caught sight of a caravan of "sheep" accompanied by two or three Indians, approaching from the distance: "I judged by the route they were taking that they would pass close to my tent. I returned quickly, desiring to see them up close so that I could examine them. I knew from the report I had been given that their face was quite extraordinary, and I wanted to do a sketch" (Feuillée 1725, 21). After observing the caravan, he conceded that the drawing of the animals made by his adversary, the French military engineer Amédée Frézier (1682–1773), was true to form (Feuillée 1725, 21). Frézier's representation of the llama, which depicted the animal in the context of its utility to Spanish mining interests, was disseminated widely throughout Europe. Many scientists gained their understanding of the animal's external structure from this image.

Intrigued by this first sighting of the animals, Feuillée turned to early colonial sources such as Garcilaso de la Vega and Blas Valera to give an account of the natural history of camelids and to describe their economic and cultural significance for Andean pastoral peoples, including the close relationship between humans and animals and the role the camelids play as protagonists in Indigenous rituals and the foundational myths of origin. Feuillée concluded that day's journal entry by remarking that Frézier's description of these Peruvian sheep included enough truth that he saw no need to linger on further reflections (Feuillée 1725, 22–24).

The following day, September 1, Feuillée recorded the news that his captain had received a gift of two guanacos and planned to take them back to France. One of the animals died unexpectedly that morning, giving Feuillée the opportunity to take advantage of these unfortunate circumstances to anatomize the gut of the dead animal. He worked quickly

72 | *Llamas beyond the Andes*

because of the fast onset of putrefaction; even so, his plans to finish the dissection on the following day had to be abandoned due to the horrible stench of the body (Feuillée 1725, 25, 32).

The priest's original motive for examining the animal was not science but trade: he was looking for bezoar stones (Feuillée 1725, 25) because they continued to bring large sums of money in the Americas and Europe, even as late as the eighteenth century.[18] When Feuillée opened the guanaco's stomach, however, instead of the treasured bezoar stones he found a sizable quantity of "poorly digested food" (28). The result of an otherwise disappointing experience constituted the first and last written account of the animal's digestive system from the eighteenth century. His extensive description of the esophagus and stomach and the mechanistic, engine-like manner of digestion was not superseded until the mid-nineteenth century. The celebrated French comparative anatomist Georges Cuvier (1835, 72–75) had access to an infant llama while preparing his *Leçons d'anatomie comparée*, but his comments on the camelids were considered incomplete. Consequently, Feuillée's description remained the primary model to which later anatomists would continue to refer. In part, the weight of his anatomical observations could be measured by the detail with which he chronicled them, an accomplishment in this case, given how quickly he had to work.

Cañizares-Esguerra (2001, 16) notes more generally that Feuillée's journalistic record, which includes meticulous descriptions, measurements, and figures, along with pictorial images, enabled specialist and nonspecialist readers alike the opportunity to observe his scenes of discovery and "the making of new 'facts.'" Feuillée's account of the camelid gut provides an excellent example of this kind of reporting. His readers had the opportunity to witness each step of the examination, albeit remotely, and follow along as he generated a textual map of this topography of dissected ventricles, veins, muscles, and membranes and explained the complex processes of digestion.

Feuillée was writing before the discovery of the role of microbial organisms in digestion; therefore, drawing from his observations, he hypothesized that a system of trituration served as the primary basis for the process in ruminants (Feuillée 1725, 26). He utilized a working vocabulary for describing digestion by creating analogies with familiar objects of everyday life and the natural world, much as Osma had done. Accordingly, he commented on how the mixing motion of the first ventricle of the stomach was aided by spike-like protuberances of the internal surface, which worked

Exploring the Body-Interior | 73

like the "files" or "rasps" that a "locksmith would use to smooth metal or shape wood" and how the reticular structure of the second ventricle resembled a "honeycomb" (28–29).

The third ventricle appeared to be filled with numerous leaves or blades, arranged much like "the lamina found inside the head of a poppy," so he referred to it as a "millet" or "livre" (31). As daylight faded and turned to dusk, making his work more difficult, Feuillée observed what he thought were fibers in the third ventricle that enabled the spiky protuberances to move, much in the same way that "hedgehogs move their spines" (32). Although discoveries regarding digestion in the camelids made in later centuries would produce numerous modifications to his narrative, at the time of his writing Feuillée was clearly familiar with existing anatomical concepts and had read the work of important figures such as the Swiss anatomist Johan Conrad Peyer (1685). Based on his own observations of the guanaco digestive tract, Feuillée even suggested corrections to Peyer's description of the tissue structure of the first compartment of the camelid stomach (Feuillée 1725, 28). It is remarkable how Feuillée managed to complete such a detailed study based on the anatomization of one animal over the course of one day, most particularly with regard to his observations on how the ventricles contracted in the digestive process as well as on the peristaltic movement of the esophagus (Feuillée 1725, 27). In his final comments, he justified the lengthy details of his account: these animals were not seen in Europe, so their organs could not be compared with those of more familiar ruminants. Therefore, he had attempted to give anatomists a correct idea of the guanaco's internal structure (32).

As indicated earlier, in addition to the dissection of the guanaco, Feuillée's narrative enacted other kinds of anatomization. His account produced a subtle yet decisive shift in focus regarding the animal's habitat. At the beginning of his writings on the camelids he focused on the animals in relation to Indigenous practices and narratives. During the course of the dissection, however, the presence and agency of Andean Indigenous peoples disappeared as he reframed the animal's importance in a new context of European scientific and commercial enterprises.[19]

More generally, the decontextualization or extraction of animals from their natural habitats and histories through anatomization is also documented in dissection guides and manuals appearing in the late eighteenth and nineteenth centuries. These pocket-sized books provided instructions to scientific travelers and others on how to collect and preserve specimens and how to know which parts of an animal and what kinds of information

74 | Llamas beyond the Andes

should be collected in the field to take back to the natural history museums and zoological gardens of Europe.

For example, the acclaimed Scottish anatomist John Hunter (1728–1793) gave precise instructions to "Travellers of Research and public spirit" on how to prepare to transport mammals that the collector hunted or trapped. "At the time of taking an Animal, it would be proper to collect, on the spot, as many circumstances of its History as possible, relative to Food, Propagation, Locomotion, etc. &c."[20] Even though the animal was dead, valuable information could be gathered that would eventually assist efforts to transport the live animal and ultimately acclimatize it in a new land. As Hunter (1861, 12) recommended elsewhere, "When an Animal is opened, for the Purpose of Separation, it will be proper to take a general View of the Parts in their natural Situation. . . . Animals, whose Food is not exactly known, should have the Contents of the Stomach examined, to learn, if possible, what Aliment they had taken last; and also of the Colon and Rectum, to determine the Kind of Feces they contain." Hunter's instructions to scientific travelers were typical insofar as they too left out of consideration local guides and informants from the collection scene. Instead, Hunter instructed the traveler to rummage through the digestive tract and fecal matter as if all necessary knowledge of the animal were self-contained in its dead body.

Feuillée's narrative follows a format in his scene of dissection similar to those of the manuals and Pedro de Osma's letter. Although he mentioned in passing the presence of Indigenous peoples and how it was an Indian who showed him where in the gut he could find the bezoar stones, Feuillée subsequently dropped him from the storyline altogether, thereby reinscribing the trope of the disappearance of Indigenous peoples and local knowledge. Thus, from his anatomization forward, the detailed mapping of the animal's internal geography would bear his name, and his study would be the go-to reference for comparative anatomists in Europe as well as foreign travelers and hunters.[21]

Buffon's Contributions to Camelid Science

While living examples of the Andean camelids in Europe during the eighteenth century were few and far between, naturalist Georges-Louis Leclerc (1707–1788), Comte de Buffon and director of the Jardin du Roi in Paris from 1739 to 1788, had access to a llama and vicuña while writing

Exploring the Body-Interior | 75

the supplements to his multivolume and encyclopedic *Histoire naturelle, générale et particulière*. Along with his competitor Carl Linnaeus (1707–1778), Buffon defined the direction modern natural history would take. Both men's writings emphasized the discipline's goals of scientifically naming, classifying, and ordering the plants, animals, and minerals of the world (Farber 2000, 22). For Buffon, careful direct observation was key to understanding the particulars of an object, after which it was possible to construct "an overall picture of the order in nature" (15). His formalist approach to the study of plants and animals can be seen in his studies on the camelids.

The French naturalist wrote about the camelids on several occasions. Perhaps the best-known passages come from his essay "Animaux du nouveau monde" (Buffon 1761, 84–85), where he identified two species, the llama and the paco, and noted their inferiority in comparison with Old World camels because of their smaller size and "greater indolence."[22] Four years later, he published "Le lama et le paco" (Buffon 1765) in volume 13 of the original series of the *Histoire naturelle*, which provided a fairly comprehensive review of the information on the animals available to Europeans from existing textual sources, but had not yet had a chance to observe the animals in person. His ideas regarding the camelids had evolved by the time he wrote the supplements to the *Histoire naturelle*. As discussed in chapter 3, he came to be one of the leading proponents for bringing these useful creatures to Europe for naturalization. Given the wide circulation of the many editions and translations of the *Histoire naturelle*, Buffon's contributions on the camelids became a primary source of information on the animals for Europeans during the late eighteenth and nineteenth centuries (see Portús 1994, 77).

For the purposes of this chapter, Buffon's comprehensive observations on the living llama and vicuña that ended up in France in the late eighteenth century can provide a critical point of departure that helps us chart the development of more specialized study of the Andean camelids by Europeans. Buffon examined these animals while they lived at the National Veterinary School of Alfort. He published the results of his analysis in volume 6 of his supplements to the *Histoire naturelle* (Buffon 1782a, 1782b). At the time, the Veterinary School maintained a menagerie of domestic and exotic animals so that students could work on acclimatization projects as well as on the clinical study of diseases that attacked familiar and unfamiliar species (Railliet and Moulé 1908, 378).[23] According to Buffon's record, a young male llama and his mother were sent to

76 | Llamas beyond the Andes

Alfort from England in November 1773. The date of arrival of the male vicuña is less clear, although he may have come along in the same shipment with the llamas.[24] Buffon noted only that the vicuña was drawn while alive in 1774, lived at the veterinary school for fourteen months, and most likely had spent the same amount of time beforehand in England (Buffon 1782a, 208–210). He was fortunate to have these animals in proximity. His observation of the two males enabled him to correct some inaccuracies of his earlier descriptions.

Buffon's account of the young male llama and his vicuña companion—I return to the mother llama below—provides a compelling example of the complex intersections of science and colonialism in the late Enlightenment. The two animals acquired multifaceted significance in his writings as useful study specimens, as singular personalities, and (as shown in the next chapter) as symbols of potential economic benefit.[25] He also identified a number of scientific uncertainties about the Andean camelids that would have continuing relevance in the nineteenth century when efforts intensified to bring large flocks of the animals to Europe for acclimatization. Among the most significant of the questions Buffon considered were the description of the species of Andean camelids, their ability to be hybridized, and the amount of water they required daily. In his earlier writing on the animals, Buffon (1765, 19) had speculated that the llama and vicuña were two species from the same genus (*genre*) but not close enough to be crossed. He later had access only to two males, so there was no way to experiment in this regard.

Creating as accurate and precise a description as possible of the external features of the llama and vicuña as ideal or standard specimens, Buffon (1782b, 204–206) recorded the animals' measurements and provided a detailed profile of their well-proportioned bodies and description of their fiber, coloring, teeth, feet, toenails, and tufted tail, which, he noted, the llama carried upright at all times. He observed how the liveliness of the vicuña's appearance was greatly enhanced by his large and attractive black eyes (1782a, 209). Even though the llama was smaller than the camel, his elegant face and the high carriage of his head created "an air of nobility and lightness" lacking in his Old World relatives (1782b, 204–205). Buffon (1782b, 207) made special note that the llama's penis was small in proportion to the size of its body. In both the llama and vicuña it curved in such a way that the animal urinated in a backward direction, between the hind legs. As also noted in the introduction, this singular feature caught European attention even during the early colonial period precisely because it

Exploring the Body-Interior | 77

distinguished the camelids from sheep and goats, with which they were typically compared.[26]

With regard to the question of how much water they needed, Buffon (1782a, 210) concluded that neither the llama nor the vicuña appeared to require much. The llama had allegedly gone eighteen months without drinking any. The vicuña, which was fed dried bran soaked occasionally in water, had never been seen to drink water or liquids of any kind. Buffon speculated that their need was minimal due to the large amount of saliva they produced (207, 210). Many scientists of the time believed that the stomach of Andean camelids contained water-storage cells, as was also thought to be the case for camels. Therefore, they assumed that the animals could go for long periods without drinking. The subject of how much water these animals required returns in later chapters because it would be of great importance during the nineteenth century when entrepreneurs attempted to ship large flocks from the Andes to Europe and Australia.

After studying the animals, Buffon reaffirmed his theory that the vicuña and llama should be considered two species of the same genus. When writing his earlier history of the camelids (Buffon 1765, 17; 1782a, 210), he had considered the vicuña simply to be a wild paco and the guanaco an undomesticated llama. Although the examination that he conducted on the two animals at Alfort did not change his mind in this regard, Buffon (1782a, 210) recently had been informed by the Marquis de Nesle, an early proponent of the acclimatization of the vicuña, that the alpaca or "paco" was an intermediary species between the llama and the vicuña.[27]

Beyond their role as models for a standard description of the species, the vicuña and the llama also came to life in Buffon's writings as individual creatures, each with his own idiosyncrasies and personality. The llama, he noted, was a pretty brown color mixed with wine-colored red. Kept almost like a pet, the llama was a gentle creature, sweet and cuddly, and permitted his keeper and others to climb on his back. When allowed to move about freely, the llama would frolic and leap in the air and roll in the grass, "often excited by the need for love" (1782b, 205–207). An engraving of the young animal by Jacques de Sève (figure 2.3) soon became accepted as an authentic representation of the species. If the young llama at the Alfort Veterinary School was lovable and friendly, the same could not be said of the male vicuña, which was described as timid, yet vicious and ungovernable, showing no affection for his caretakers. To the contrary, the vicuña constantly tried to bite them and spit repeatedly at the face of anyone who attempted to approach him (Buffon 1782a,

78 | Llamas beyond the Andes

FIGURE 2.3. *"Le lama"* (The llama). Buffon (1782b, 206).

FIGURE 2.4. *"La vigogne"* (The vicuña). Buffon (1782a, 216).

210). Figure 2.4, an image of the vicuña by de Sève, was also referenced universally as true to form.

Both the llama and vicuña can be observed as they were drawn from life in de Sève's two engravings. In each case, the animal was portrayed in "typical" poses that conveyed its natural morphology.[28] The images were intended to communicate accuracy and realism and certainly show none of the more fantastic elements found in the likes of Conrad Gesner's image of the *Allocamelus* (mentioned in the notes to the introduction) or even Amédée Frézier's representation, which depicted the animals as having an uncanny, humanlike face.[29] Nonetheless, de Sève's illustrations give the impression of something unnatural about these creatures, which look almost as if they had been based not on living examples but on stuffed specimens. According to Landes (2012, 32), Buffon's visual records of the animals in his *Histoire naturelle* drew from many different sources, including "anatomized specimens, older natural history illustrations, and verbal descriptions." As already noted, the end result was supposed to represent the "ideal" animal rather than a specific or individual one. Perhaps for this reason, some creatures come across as "incredibly stilted" or "rigidly schematic" (33–34).[30] Further contributing to the artificial composition of the images, in many instances the animals have been set against what Landes (2012, 34) identifies as a "classical or 'foreign' background" or "with certain social accoutrements, attesting to the privileged status of the would-be owner of such an animal . . . or the animal (or animal skeleton) is posed on a plinth, as if in a natural history cabinet, or before a drawn curtain, as in a dramatic or anatomical theater."

In the case of the engravings of the llama and the vicuña, the awkwardness of these idealized images is exacerbated by the vaguely exotic backgrounds included in the lower third of each engraving, especially in the setting framed by the llama's legs: an unusual-looking building or fortress flanked by a palm tree, in an otherwise nondescript landscape devoid of identifiers. The broken-down fence posts in the foreground may reference the animal's domesticity. Palm trees are not usually found in the high Andean altiplano. As a stock signifier of otherness and exoticism in many of the *Histoire naturelle* volumes, their presence reminds the viewer that the animal is not European in origin. In the engraving of the vicuña, which is depicted in two poses, another tropical-like building is situated behind and to the right of the animal resting on the ground, but it is difficult to pinpoint additional geographic features of significance.

The two engravings provide viewers with a hint of the animals'

80 | *Llamas beyond the Andes*

disposition. For example, the llama appears almost to be smiling, and the standing vicuña has a similar expression on his face. Even though the vicuña on the ground sports beautiful long, curled eyelashes, its face offers a suggestion of pensiveness. De Sève's portrayals of the animals, which circulated widely throughout Europe in the many editions and translations of Buffon's work, played a significant role in shaping the imperial processes of "naturalization" of these exotic creatures, making them seem less strange and more "domesticated" and ultimately, it was hoped, easier to acquire.[31] These images, along with the accompanying text, thus helped to lay the groundwork for future large-scale efforts directed toward bringing living camelids to Europe.

The Fragonard Llama

When Buffon was writing his account of the animals in August 1777, the male llama was still alive, but the vicuña had since died and could be seen stuffed and on display in the museum or anatomical cabinet of the school's founder, Claude Bourgelat (Buffon 1782a, 208). Little further information has been ascertained, however, regarding either animal's life or death or their afterlives as part of Bourgelat's collection.[32] As for the mother of the male llama, what we know of her begins at the time of her death and extends into her afterlife as an exotic and singular museum specimen. According to Buffon's record, she survived the trip from England only to die shortly after arriving at the veterinary school. Like the vicuña, she ended up in Bourgelat's anatomical collection, but not as a stuffed creation. Buffon (1782b, 204) noted in his first paragraph on the young male llama that the mother had been skillfully dissected. Her muscles and organs were treated, dried, and varnished, and the veins and arteries were injected with blue and red resins.[33] She can still be found today on display in a glass case at the Alfort Veterinary School in the Fragonard Museum, named for the anatomist responsible for creating most of the collection's eighteenth-century flayed, dissected, and preserved specimens, known as *écorchés*.

All that we know about this llama's life and the journeys undergone before she came to Alfort is that at some point in the previous two years, she had a male llama companion and later gave birth to a male baby. Although the story of her life remains a question, incomplete information does not prevent us from considering how a singular specimen like the

Exploring the Body-Interior | 81

mother llama can still be a valuable resource for examining the stories embodied in her remains.[34]

The man whose techniques were used to preserve the mother llama in her afterlife, Honoré Fragonard (1732–1799), cousin of the famous painter Jean-Honoré Fragonard, was the eccentric director of the Alfort Veterinary School and the principal anatomist and demonstrator beginning in 1766. Bourgelat dismissed him five years later, attributing the decision to the anatomist's madness and claiming that his health had been adversely affected by "a stone in the kidneys and bladder" (quoted in Degueurce 2011, 39). In spite of the controversies surrounding him, Fragonard garnered national and international recognition as a skilled and prolific anatomist. He returned to Alfort in 1783 and, with his former student Pierre Flandrin, drew up an inventory of the anatomical collection, which then amounted to 3,033 items.[35] Unfortunately, only a small number of Fragonard's anatomical creations have survived to the present, but among those that did is the mother llama.[36]

During the eighteenth century, the study of anatomy was comparative in its approach. Students at the Veterinary School examined the human body along with animal bodies to gain a more complete understanding of the subject. Trained in both human and animal morphology, Fragonard was a pioneer in relating the analysis of human anatomy to the interpretation of animal structures and systems (Degueurce 2011, 14).[37] Other anatomists of the time taught their students with the use of illustrations and engravings and wax and plaster models. Fragonard, however, preferred to work with the "original tissue and living skin" (Sournia 1981, 5) of the animal and human cadaver, perfecting the method of wax injection used at the time for the preservation of organs and different parts of the body.[38] Fragonard was not, of course, the only anatomist to use dissection and wax injection for preserving dry specimens. Indeed, these methods had been in use since the previous century. What made Fragonard's work notable was how, in addition to preparing a specific organ or part of the body, he expertly preserved the entire cadaver with his carefully guarded formulas. Although many creations were lost, it was done so well that a significant number have survived to the present (Degueurce 2011, 69–72; Simon 2002, 76).

Most of Fragonard's skillfully formed specimens were used for instructional purposes. Students normally participated in the time-consuming and challenging preparation process, creating complex and delicate pieces that emphasized the study of the muscles, circulatory system, nervous system,

82 | Llamas beyond the Andes

organs, and bones and cartilage (Degueurce 2011, 69). Fragonard's creations provided greater opportunities for students to observe, study, and acquire hands-on experience in addition to consulting the writings of long-established authorities. On those occasions when he and his students had the opportunity to analyze the anatomy of exotic animals such as the mother llama, dissection provided additional pedagogical opportunities. Although the entry on the female llama in Fragonard's 1783 inventory directed attention to the structure and arrangement of the animal's muscles (myology, using the vocabulary of standard anatomical description of the time), the full record documented the following features: "1. the heart; 2. the arteries and pulmonary veins; 3. the aorta and vena cava; 4. the carotid arteries and jugular veins and their distribution to the head; 5. the esophagus and tracheal tube; 6. the arteries and axillary veins, which run as far as the feet; 7. the crural arteries and veins, which run as far as the foot of the posterior extremity; 8. the principal nerves of the head of the neck of the extremities." The description ended with the anatomist's summary reflection: "Beautiful specimen."[39] If Feuillée's account mapped the camelid gut for Europeans and Buffon provided a detailed description of the animal's external features, Fragonard's anatomical report of the llama made visible the entire structure of the three-dimensional body.

While many of Fragonard's dissected and preserved works were prepared for the purpose of teaching, other creations seemed to have been arranged to convey significance beyond their pedagogical importance. *Écorché* dancing monkeys and human fetuses, a standing man holding a jawbone, and Fragonard's famous horse and rider achieve startling effects because they were produced with flayed bodies deliberately arranged in theatrical positions. If nature, for Buffon, was comprehended through measurement and description, for Fragonard, dissection and preservation produced knowledge of the body's physicality and its animated inner essence. Even though these creations cannot be mistaken for living beings, like well-executed taxidermy, Fragonard's artistic and scientific techniques "revived" something of their former vigor, creating the impression that at any moment they might step down and out of their glass case.[40] In contrast to de Sève's somewhat contrived representations of the llama and the vicuña and Fragonard's standard inventory account, there is nothing stilted or dispassionate about the Fragonard llama. To begin with, drawing from Rachel Polinquin's (2012, 107) work on taxidermy and representation, the mother llama is not a *portrayal* of a llama, she *is* a llama, which traveled unknown distances, had at least one offspring, and was reanimated after death through Fragonard's scientific and aesthetic project.

FIGURE 2.5. *The Fragonard llama. Musée Fragonard. Photograph by the author.*

The visceral realism of the llama's dramatic flayed body, wide-eyed facial expression, and flaring nostrils (figure 2.5) captures and holds the viewer's attention. In his biographical remarks on the anatomist, Ellenberger (1981, 8) contends that even today the visitor who first walks into the Fragonard museum experiences somewhat of a shock upon seeing such macabre yet artful spectacles, including the *écorché* llama, which looks as if her skin "had been turned inside out and stretched." The technologies that Fragonard and his students utilized to make the animal's interior world visible highlight the tension between the natural and the manufactured; the llama is neither fully one nor the other. Degueurce (2011, 110) notes how the llama's thin, parchment-like muscles "give the écorché a delicate appearance," while the broken trachea reveals some of the horsehair used to stuff the animal in anticipation of the process of dehydration. A liminal creature, the llama blurs the divide between nature and culture, realism and artifice, and occupies a variety of spaces and ontologies, straddling the line between distant Andean landscapes and the European world of museum nature. The multiple histories and contexts that the llama inhabits along with the processes by which she was transformed into a representative camelid specimen for European audiences suggest that she cannot be easily naturalized and assimilated.[41] Moreover, as I show later, these narratives make visible the structures of colonialism that inextricably entangle such aesthetic and scientific projects.[42]

84 | *Llamas beyond the Andes*

Science, art, and colonialism converge in the aesthetics of the picturesque and, in the case of the mother llama, highlight the camelid body as a promising resource for exploitation in Europe. Using his accomplished techniques of preservation, Fragonard created an artistic approach that shared certain elements with the field of picturesque anatomy, in vogue at the time, and picturesque landscape painting, also coming into fashion during the late eighteenth century. Picturesque or artistic anatomy combined the study of dissected cadavers with the study of living models to give the student of painting, sculpture, or medicine a better working knowledge of the details of the skin, muscles, and skeletal structure as well as of the changes effected when the body is in motion. The famous French anatomist Jean-Joseph Sue (the elder, 1710–1792), in addition to being professor of anatomy at the Collège Royal de Chirurgie, was also professor of anatomy at the Académie Royale de Peinture et de Sculpture, where he offered courses each year on picturesque anatomy. This field of study emphasized close examination of the body's deep, internal structure, which could only be visualized through dissection.[43]

Like Sue, John Hunter's equally famous brother, the anatomist William Hunter, also taught courses in picturesque anatomy in London. He perceived the study of anatomy, like sculpture, wax modeling, and landscape painting, as three dimensional (Jordanova 1985, 395). Hunter's work helps to shed light on Fragonard's aesthetic project and underscores analogies between dissection and mapmaking and knowledge as possession, similar to those seen earlier in the chapter: "Hunter's enterprise was closely akin to that of a cartographer, lovingly recording all the details of terrain—flesh and tissues. There was no smoothing out here but, rather, corrugations depicted in loving detail. When the mapping had been completed, the human [or animal] body would, in some significant sense, be known and understood" (395).

The addition of color to wax injections was key to observing and tracing the contours of the body's geography. For example, Algarotti (1769) suggested that the use of different colors to distinguish muscles and arteries from veins would facilitate the process of memorization for the artist and medical student. Students could thus read the injected bodies much as if they were colored maps delineating the states and provinces belonging to a prince (Algarotti 1769, 22–23). To facilitate the learning process, John Hunter stressed the importance of selecting colors and shades that would catch the observer's eye when preparing to inject the vascular and arterial systems of the anatomical specimens: "To these injections add as much

Exploring the Body-Interior | 85

colour as makes them appear of a proper bright colour to the eye. . . . It would seem that we have not yet any good green colour; but as blue and yellow make a green, blue verditer, added to yellow wax or resin, gives us a fine green" (Hunter 1861, 391).[44] In a manner parallel to the way eighteenth-century European and creole exploration and charting of the Andean hinterland was designed to provide valuable information regarding the region's natural resources, increased knowledge of the animal's body-interior through its detailed mapping enabled it to be more easily claimed for colonial scientific projects.

Like artistic anatomy, picturesque painting emphasized rugged, three-dimensional landscapes, nuance of color, and subtle play of contrast between light and shadow (Gilpin 1792, 20). In her description of the picturesque, Stafford (1984, 6) gives particular attention to its theatrical and exotic elements and how they related to each other, including in areas such as garden theory, which, at the time, emphasized the presence of "an engaging theatrical vocabulary of caves, rocky cliffs, sylvan settings, and inlets—all stressing a wild, untamed environment. . . . It was crucial to the formulation of garden theory that the representation of entangled wilderness depended on the handling of nature in such a way as to produce dramatic, if not spectacular effects." As already seen, Fragonard's aesthetics of preservation also depended on the rough, irregular textures of tissue and muscle and on the contrast of colors. His exotic *écorchés* were dramatic and spectacular, while at the same time "natural." For example, when applying colored wax injections, he deliberately enlarged the arterial and vascular systems in some cases so that they were much more swollen than normal, thereby creating startling images of flayed human and animal faces with almost painfully engorged arteries and veins (Simon 2008, 153).[45] The effect of theatricality was emphasized further in the way the rough and uneven sheets of dried and varnished muscle highlighted the impression of a tortured or martyred body (Simon 2002, 69–70; 2008, 153), in a fashion reminiscent of Guaman Poma's depiction of the camelid sacrifice.

In stark contrast to Buffon's remarks concerning the loveliness of the Alfort vicuña's eyes, some have observed that the most troubling feature of these *écorchés* is their dissected, lidless eyes, which appear to look out onto the world with a sightless, fixed stare (Ellenberger 1981, 8). Fragonard's aesthetics of dissection and preservation thus emphasized both movement and stasis. The play of color and texture of these extraordinary three-dimensional creations, such as the llama, enticed the eye to travel across

86 | Llamas beyond the Andes

the picturesque landscape of the flayed body.[46] So, too, when he examined Fragonard's art, Jean-Joseph Sue spoke of the "'concert' of movement of the fluids in the vessels" (quoted in Sournia 1981, 5). Yet the dissected specimen was also frozen in space and time, on display, as if it had been captured and immobilized by the glass enclosure of the museum cabinet.

It can be argued that picturesque aesthetics helped to structure the processes enabling the colonized body-landscape to be explored, assessed, *and* possessed.[47] Carter's (1988) analysis of the picturesque and Australian colonial history shows how the aesthetic movement participated in the domestication and possession of "wild" nature through the deployment of metaphors of mapping and enclosure. For example, both picturesque travel and gardening reflected an analogous dialectic between movement and rest, travel and settlement. In a colonial context, however, the dynamic took on additional significance as picturesque aesthetics became associated with mapping and possession: "Implicit in both spatial modalities was always the sense of symbolic boundaries defined and rendered eloquent. The screen of vegetation, the trees one would not wish to see cut down, might, in other contexts, be a bar to physical and imaginative progress. To call them picturesque was to attribute to them the observer's own heightened sense of possession, his sensation of suddenly being at home in the world" (Carter 1988, 242–243).

These boundaries could be real as well as symbolic. As Bermingham (2000, 77) maintains, during the years from 1745 to 1825 in Britain "the aesthetic discovery of landscape masked both the economic transformation of rural nature through the parliamentary acts of enclosure and the political agendas that attended it." The act of possession-through-enclosure was heightened when the increasing popularity of landscape drawing overlapped with a rise in surveying and military and civilian mapping (78–80). Like the anatomical mapping taking place at the same time, the combined methods of drawing, surveying, and mapping resulted in a greater awareness of the landscape's natural characteristics and its economic importance (80). With its colorful, mapped anatomy, the Fragonard llama likewise can be understood as a visible or autoptic record testifying to these aesthetic practices whereby colonial knowledge production became inextricably linked to the potential for economic exploitation.

Visually striking in her glass case, the extraordinary female llama stands tall in her uniqueness. A close inspection of the Fragonard llama's ears in figure 2.5 reveals that both have small holes, indicating that they were pierced at some point. Degueurce (personal communication, January

Exploring the Body-Interior | 87

19, 2015) reasons that the holes were likely made during the dehydration process so that the ears could be fastened and held up to prevent them from flopping and becoming permanently misshapen. It is difficult to look at the holes, however, and not be reminded of the Andean tradition of making the one-year-old female llama's ears bloom with crimson "flowers" during the cutting and piercing ceremonies, commemorating the fertility and genealogy of the maternal line. These Andean genealogies, of which the Fragonard mother llama is a direct descendant, haunt us with the persistent agency of their presence, evident in the ambivalent symbol of the holes in the animal's ears.[48]

Writing about how knowledge is generated and preserved, Anke te Heesen has noted that "all knowledge requires a container" (quoted in Brenna 2013, 40). Yet the Fragonard llama represents more than her material remains. As a result, the knowledge and histories conveyed in her flayed body exceed the glass container that encloses her. Her remains overlap multiple spaces and chronologies and map the story of her life and death, the transformations made to preserve her body after death, and the changing ways in which her body has been understood in more than two hundred years of being displayed. Furthermore, we can say that the llama is also metonymic of her species, "redolent of places far away and times long ago" (Alberti 2011a, 8). She makes visible a long history that could well lead back to the Andes, where she might have been purchased, given as a gift, or stolen. In Borgesian fashion, her body tells one version of the story of what might have been the trajectory of Feuillée's guanaco had it survived the journey from the Andes to Europe. As the mother llama's continuing presence reminds us, there is little that is "natural" about the natural histories she incarnates.

This chapter explores key moments in the trajectory of knowledge making at the site of the camelid body when it was anatomized, mapped, classified, and framed. The first case study highlighted how knowledge of the animal and its general well-being has been interpreted within the frame of Andean community welfare and sustainable local ecologies. In contrast, the remaining studies revealed an evolving European model that formalized knowledge-as-possession in the wider economic context of imperial expansion and commodity extraction. Subsequent chapters examine the camelid journey, from acquisition and during transfer across the Atlantic and Pacific, as organized efforts gained momentum to bring large flocks of the animals to Europe and beyond for acclimatization and naturalization.

CHAPTER 3

From Curiosity to Commodity

Early Efforts to Ship Living Camelids to Europe

I imagine that these animals would be an excellent acquisition for Europe and that they would produce greater riches than all the mineral wealth from the New World.

Comte de Buffon's remarks on the vicuña (1765, 31–32)

If only your Excellency could see what a heavy and trying burden this commission is for me; just contemplating the difficulties that come to the imagination is sometimes enough to make me go almost out of my mind. Only because your Majesty wishes to please the Emperor of Gaul for whom these animals have been requested do I put my all into the project.

Julián García on taking vicuñas and alpacas from Lima to Cádiz on behalf of the Queen of Spain (Archivo Nacional de Chile, March 20, 1805)

When Voltaire's eponymous hero Candide and his faithful and clever servant Cacambo stumbled upon the utopian land of Eldorado, located somewhere in a South American valley and surrounded by inaccessible mountains, among the first wonders that caught their eyes were the handsome people and splendid carriages drawn by large red sheep that ran faster than the swiftest horses from Andalucía or North Africa (Voltaire [1759] 1968, 74). Candide reasoned that if he and Cacambo could return to Europe with a number of these exotic animals fully loaded with Eldorado's abundant mineral riches, they not only would be wealthy and therefore free of the Inquisition but would have the resources to locate and rescue his beloved Lady Cunégonde. The benevolent king of the land generously assisted the travelers by providing the animals, supplies, and equipment they would need to be hoisted over the rugged mountains and proceed on their way. They had at their service two red sheep saddled and ready to ride; twenty loaded with provisions; thirty carrying exquisite gifts; and fifty weighed down with gold and precious stones (82–84).

Unfortunately, troubles soon befell the two adventurers and their valuable retinue of animals: two sheep along with the riches they carried sank in a bog; the same number died of fatigue; many starved to death in the desert; yet others perished when they wandered over a cliff. By the time the group reached Surinam's port city, only 2 of the original 102 sheep had survived the perilous journey (Voltaire [1759] 1968, 85). Candide paid a Dutch ship captain to take the animals and himself to Venice, while Cacambo departed for Buenos Aires to rescue Lady Cunégonde. Alas, the wily captain took Candide's money and sheep, stranding the hapless victim on the docks until he found a French ship willing to take him as far as Bordeaux (88–89). While crossing the Atlantic, they came upon a battle underway between two vessels, one of which suffered a fatal broadside hit and sank before their eyes. Shortly afterward, the crew rescued from the wreckage a bright red object spotted swimming in the water. Candide was overjoyed when he discovered that it was one of his own sheep. Now that he had recovered his sole remaining animal, Candide became hopeful that he and Lady Cunégonde would similarly be reunited (93–94).

After landing at Bordeaux, Candide purchased a carriage to continue on to Venice, where he would await Cacambo and his beloved. Unfortunately, due to insufficient space in the vehicle, this plan required leaving his sheep behind. Candide finally decided to donate the exotic creature to the Bordeaux Academy of Sciences, which made the intriguing red color of the animal's fleece the subject of the annual essay competition. The prize was "awarded to a Northern scholar, who demonstrated by a formula, A plus B minus C over Z, that the sheep was necessarily red and ought to die of scab" (Voltaire [1759] 1968, 96–97).

Critics have found that Candide's red sheep embody multiple themes, figuring alternately as a symbol of the fabulous wealth and otherworldliness of Eldorado; as an element of usefulness and scenic realism; as a sign of hope that Candide and Lady Cunégonde would one day be reunited; and as a vehicle for satirizing the powerful French Academy of Sciences (Bottiglia 1958, 343–344). The captivating association of Eldorado's red sheep — or what we now refer to as a camelid — with exoticism, wealth, and good fortune was not limited to the pages of Voltaire. News of these valuable Peruvian creatures was spreading throughout eighteenth-century Europe.

From Curiosity to Commodity | 91

Both the Spanish and French monarchies actively sought out information on the animals with the idea of bringing them to Europe and transforming them into important commodities. The vicuña especially exemplified the idea of the Andean region's untapped resources that might be exploited if natural historians and others could learn more about the animal's habits and its geographic and nutritional needs. As efforts increased to put these imperialist projects into action, it soon became apparent that other aspects of Voltaire's narrative were more prophetic and real than fictitious: notably, as the camelids were brought out of the Andes, they fared little better than Candide's red sheep.

The desire to understand what kind of animals these creatures were and how to transport them safely to Europe for naturalization became the subject of travel memoirs, official reports, and scientific studies. This chapter begins by examining writings by eighteenth-century French and Spanish scientists who promoted the idea of exploiting the camelids in greater numbers and addressed the challenges and obstacles that many perceived would have an impact on initial efforts to acquire and convey them overseas. Juan and Ulloa (1748) and the Comte de Buffon (1782a), among others, discussed how to obtain vicuñas and llamas and debated related matters of concern such as whether it was better to ship the animals around Cape Horn or to walk them across the continent to the port of Buenos Aires for embarkation. Also anticipated were issues that might affect the animals' adjustment and adaptation to new surroundings: notably, how to select a suitable permanent location.

Such discussions on camelid relocation and adaptation formed part of larger scientific discourses of the Enlightenment that included debates on how climate and other factors impacted the acclimatization of people, plants, and animals to new environments. During the eighteenth and early nineteenth centuries, these ideas were only beginning to be understood, as Taylor-Leduc (2019) reminds us specifically in the case of France. Moreover, these areas of study had far-reaching influence: "Debates about climate theory were not limited to the scientific community, but became a political tool to justify . . . imperial control over a country's colonies" (2019, no pagination); this interweaving of science and politics was true not only for France but also for Spain and other European countries. Attention to the calls to bring camelids to Europe highlights these interconnections. The first portion of the chapter examines theoretical discussions on camelid extraction and how they were grounded in eighteenth-century Enlightenment ideas extolling a strengthening of

92 | Llamas beyond the Andes

empire through administrative reform, utilitarian scientific knowledge, and the profitable exploitation of available natural resources in far-flung places like the high Andes. After analyzing these deliberations by European scientists on camelid extraction and the presumed difficulties such an enterprise might entail, the chapter turns to the case study of one of the first large-scale experiments in shipping the animals to Europe for naturalization: the transatlantic story of Empress Josephine Bonaparte's two dozen alpacas and vicuñas. This extraordinary venture stands out today because it makes visible the enormous gulf between a royal request issued from afar (influenced chiefly by academic debates) and the material impact at the local level of such an initiative, including its ever-increasing costs, the severe hardships it caused, and the large numbers of people ultimately required to carry out an order of this kind.

Eighteenth-Century Deliberations on the Extraction of Andean Camelids to Spain

Beginning with the initial days of Spanish exploration of the New World, ship captains and others regularly sent valuable gifts back to Spain, including samples of the land's diverse mineral wealth and newly discovered flora and fauna. As seen in chapter 1, the bezoar stone constituted a prime example of such gestures. Accounts from Peru sometimes told of one or more "Peruvian sheep" included in these shipments.[1] The transportation of live animals generally posed many complications. Efforts to convey them to Europe were largely unsuccessful due to the long and arduous journey over land and across the ocean. Animals could be held for months in the port, waiting for an available ship or the appropriate season of the year. Once a ship set sail, the return voyage might take months and even years if it included numerous stops along the way (Gómez-Centurión Jiménez 2009, 204–206). Loading the animals and securing them safely on board as well as ensuring that they had sufficient food and water for the voyage's duration posed challenges (205). Robbins (2002) notes that exotic animals were particularly difficult to transport: some because they were fragile, others because they could be extremely ferocious. Problems such as rat infestations on ships, along with a lack of knowledge about how to care for unfamiliar animals, could have disastrous consequences. Perilous routes, like the notorious passage around the bottom of Cape Horn, resulted in the death of many living cargos. Finally, animals being transported by ship

From Curiosity to Commodity | 93

also ran the risk of being eaten if the vessel was becalmed overly long and food reserves dwindled (Robbins, 2002, 11).[2]

Despite these difficulties, as highlighted in the Buffon quotation in the chapter epigraph, French and Spanish natural historians of the eighteenth century paid increasing attention to the camelids with the hope of turning them into a large-scale economic resource. Buffon's much-cited remarks, which would eventually become the rallying cry of France's nineteenth-century acclimatization movement, served in the late eighteenth century to generate greater and more sustained interest in the animals, to draw attention to their utility as an untapped resource, and to stimulate new efforts to bring living specimens to Europe. These undertakings did not begin with Buffon, however. Spanish naval officers and mathematicians Jorge Juan and Antonio de Ulloa, who had accompanied Charles-Marie de la Condamine and Louis Godin's French expedition to South America (1735–1743) on behalf of the Spanish government, coauthored a secret report of their observations and findings.[3] Their document warrants attention in this chapter because it includes an early call for large-scale commodification of the vicuña and outlines the challenges the two scientists foresaw as having the greatest impact on the successful transportation and acclimatization of the animal outside the Andean region.

Juan and Ulloa's report has been understood as contributing to "the creation of a 'governing ideology' for the Spanish Bourbon state during the eighteenth century" (Andrien 1998, 177), not least because it compiled information from multiple groups within the Spanish Empire concerning the problems and abuses of government, widespread corruption, and growing unrest. The authors employed a narrative strategy of identifying significant problems faced by the viceroyalty, providing examples to reinforce their claims, and proposing potential solutions (178–186). In this regard, Juan and Ulloa's project of critique and reform worked in tandem "with the efforts of powerful politicians in Spain seeking to reform the colonial regime during the early Bourbon Reform period . . . and fit neatly within the overall effort of Bourbon politicians to reassert royal authority in the Indies and to control colonial resources" (185).

In accordance with their attention to administrative reform, Juan and Ulloa addressed the need for better management of Peru's natural commodities and called for exploiting the region's resources more sustainably and to greater commercial advantage. Their report included a survey of the viceroyalty's abundant natural wealth. As part of this section, they

94 | Llamas beyond the Andes

dedicated several pages to the recommendation that more consideration be given to the potential commercial significance of the vicuña. They reminded their readers that the animal's exquisite fleece exceeded silk in value and had been used with great success to produce fine-quality hats. In order for vicuñas to be exploited successfully, however, changes would have to be made regarding the management of these wild animals and the fiber trade. They called for legislation that would stop the indiscriminate slaughter of the animals: in contrast to the Incas, who had conserved wild camelid populations through carefully regulated collective hunts known as *chacos*, contemporary creoles, mestizos, and Indian hunters killed the animals recklessly, with no thought for the future (Juan and Ulloa 1749, 841–848). They specified that the problem of injudicious carnage was exacerbated by the fact that many wool sellers fraudulently mixed coarser llama and guanaco fiber with the higher-quality vicuña, driving buyers to purchase the entire hide because it was difficult to pass off a guanaco fleece for a vicuña fleece due to their difference in size.

Juan and Ulloa advocated for rigorous penalties being applied to anyone who killed vicuñas and proposed that Indigenous peoples living in provinces where the animals could be found in abundance be encouraged to domesticate as many of them as possible and to carry out live annual shearings instead of hunting them. If these initiatives produced positive results, they suggested that the Indigenous pastoral populations should be excused from a certain percentage of their annual tribute. Juan and Ulloa also anticipated that these policy changes would help to counter the adverse publicity that the Spanish had received internationally because of the aggressive hunting of such a useful animal and the illegal commerce of counterfeit fiber (Juan and Ulloa 1749, 848–850).[4]

In response to the ongoing concerns that the vicuña might be hunted to extinction, King Carlos III of Spain issued a royal order in 1777, giving it protected status, with the goal of better controlling and safeguarding the commercial exploitation of its fleece. He directed the Viceroyalty of Río de la Plata, the Audiencias, and the Captaincy General of Chile to issue the strictest orders to *corregidores* and other local authorities, prohibiting Indians from engaging in independent or commissioned hunts. Instead, the animals' fleece was to be shorn under the watchful eyes of authorized personnel officially designated to ensure that this process took place in a timely fashion. Anyone found disobeying the order should be heavily fined.[5]

The royal directive met with mixed reaction. Pedro Vicente Cañete y Domínguez, eminent creole lawyer and political advisor residing at the time in Potosí, defended local commerce in vicuña fiber, arguing that it provided a living for many. Disputing the concerns that the animals were declining in number, he claimed that vicuña populations flourished in the nearby Lípez region. Furthermore, the Charcas Audiencia had already reported how difficult it was to attempt live shearings of vicuñas because of their wild nature, asserting that one Indian could obtain the fleece from twenty to thirty carcasses in the time that it would take to shear one animal. If stopping all pursuit of vicuñas was impractical, Vicente Cañete y Domínguez suggested that hunting the animals during the birthing season, when tracking and killing could be accomplished more easily, should absolutely be prohibited. As a more workable method for obtaining the fleece, he proposed that young vicuñas be captured and raised with cow's milk, because the animals brought up in captivity were exceedingly tame, as he had witnessed firsthand in Potosí. Once domesticated, these vicuñas could then be gathered into larger herds for more efficient management. Like Ulloa and Juan, he hypothesized that Indigenous pastoral peoples might be motivated to participate in such a plan if offered enough economic incentive. This proposal would additionally ensure that the precious fleece ended up supplying the royal Spanish mills rather than being sold to foreign buyers (Cañete y Domínguez [1787] 1952, 240).

Given the pressures of commerce, however, neither the 1777 royal order nor later legislation put an end to the trafficking in vicuñas (Laker et al. 2006, 40–41; Wakild 2020).[6] We know that Andean Indians actively participated in market relations during the colonial period (Tandeter et al. 1995) and most likely would have engaged in selling and trading valuable vicuña skins and fiber. The onerous annual tribute Indigenous communities had to pay the colonial government played an important role in the ongoing hunting of the wild camelids. Yocabaccio's (2009) research indicates that Indigenous communities located in areas close to vicuña populations paid the majority of their tribute with vicuña skins and fiber, much of which ended up being sent or smuggled to Europe. During the first decade of the eighteenth century, vicuña fiber at the Buenos Aires port was valued at 1.56 pesos per kilogram. Yocabaccio (2009, 14–15) calculates that in the best-case scenario, an individual community would have had to collect 4,404 kilograms of fiber to cover the taxes, which represents at least 17,000 vicuñas.

Because of concerns over the diminishing numbers of wild camelids, during the eighteenth century various perspectives circulated on the best way to exploit vicuñas sustainably for their fleece, including Cañete y

96 | Llamas beyond the Andes

Domínguez's recommendation that young animals be caught and hand-raised. In their 1749 report Juan and Ulloa had proposed an alternative to the mass killing of vicuñas when they recommended that a number of the animals be brought to Spain for naturalization and domestication. Harvesting the fiber of home-grown animals, moreover, had the advantage of ensuring the authenticity and quality of any product marked as vicuña. They warned, however, that such a plan could result in the animals becoming dispersed throughout Europe, in which case Spain risked losing its monopoly, as had already happened with the monarchy's merino sheep population. In addition to this potential problem, they anticipated several uncertainties if naturalization of the animals in Spain became successful. For example, in response to the concern over whether the Spanish climate and pastures would be suitable for vicuñas and their possible impact on Spain's already established wool-bearing livestock, Juan and Ulloa speculated that the animals would get along well in the Pyrenees, the mountains of Granada, and the foothills of any range where there was snow in winter and cooler temperatures in the summer months. The vicuñas would undoubtedly notice a difference from the pasture of their native land. When vicuñas came down out of the mountains seasonally to the plains and ravines of their native region, however, they ate different varieties of grasses and plants, so they should not have difficulty adjusting to Spanish pastures (Juan and Ulloa 1749, 846–847, 851–853).

Juan and Ulloa next addressed the commonly held belief that an animal's fiber could degenerate in quality if moved to a new environment. Drawing from colonial experience, they reasoned that wool from the sheep taken from Spain to the Indies had not undergone any change, so the vicuña's fiber probably would similarly be unaffected by a transfer overseas. The fleece of vicuñas moved within Peru, from the remote mountains to Lima, did not show any transformation, even when the animals were domesticated in peoples' homes and provided a diet of alfalfa and fresh barley rather than native grasses. Furthermore, it was unlikely that vicuñas would impact negatively on Spain's sheep and cattle production because the Peruvian camelids graze at higher altitudes and so would not compete for the same pastures. The animals could even become a viable meat source once their numbers increased (Juan and Ulloa 1749, 853–855). These issues of camelid settlement, diet, fiber quality, and competition with other livestock, as outlined by Juan and Ulloa, were not easily resolved without firsthand experimentation (as discussed in later chapters)

From Curiosity to Commodity | 97

and would remain at the forefront of animal-acclimatization debates throughout the nineteenth century.[7]

Because llamas and alpacas were herded solely by Indigenous pastoral communities rather than by mestizo or creole hacienda owners and vicuñas and guanacos lived primarily in remote mountainous regions, European travelers and merchants generally had little experience with and even less knowledge of these exotic creatures. Learning about them through visual images was one method by which the process of discovery took place. Pictorial collections of New World peoples, plants, and animals, such as Baltasar Jaime Martínez Compañón's late eighteenth-century *Trujillo del Perú* and Luis Thiebaut and José Ignacio Lequanda's *Quadro de historia natural, civil y geográfica del reyno del Perú* (1799), served as mobile encyclopedias and formed part of a "large-scale project to survey, amass, and transport Spanish imperial nature through words, images, and artifacts" (Bleichmar 2011, 69).[8] As documented in part by visual collections, "the culture of the Enlightenment was a two-way process of communications of equal symbolic value" and Peru was an integral participant in scientific knowledge production, which circulated along with its commodities (Meléndez and Stolley 2015, 2).

For Bleichmar (2011, 61), the 214 illustrations and accompanying inscriptions from Thiebaut and Lequanda's *Quadro* form a kind of "book, collection, or box" of local Peruvian nature, which incorporates references and plant and animal terminology and showcases "interconnections among peoples, flora, fauna, history, social order, and territory" (Bleichmar 2012, 184).[9]

Accordingly, and in contrast to de Sève's illustrations from Buffon's supplements to the *Histoire naturelle* that set the animals against exotic yet characterless backgrounds and showcased their anatomy and singular features (such as their long-lashed eyes), the *Quadro*'s illustrations of the camelids reinsert the animals into Andean landscapes and pair each with a native tree or plant of medicinal, economic, or ethnographic significance. Perhaps for these reasons, the camelids come across as livelier and more animated (figure 3.1) than in de Sève's representations. The accompanying text of each camelid image situates the animal within a local yet utilitarian colonial economy. In clockwise order, the llama (top left, pictured next to the *árbol de sangre*) is identified as a carrier animal useful in the mining industry, while the alpaca (top right, alongside the *Lúcumo* tree) is valued for its fiber and meat. If taken as a young animal,

FIGURE 3.1. *Illustration of camelids from* Quadro de historia natural, civil y geográfica del reyno del Perú, *by Luis Thiebaut and José Ignacio Lequanda. Archivo del Museo Nacional de Ciencias Naturales, Madrid.*

the *Quadro* text explains, the guanaco (lower right, standing by the *Pitajaya* or *Gigantón* cactus) can be domesticated. Even in the wild, the guanaco is useful because it assists vicuñas attempting to escape from the *chaco* hunt by breaking through the cordons holding the animals captive. The vicuña under a *Totumo* tree (lower left) is notable for its precious fiber and edible meat.[10] Anyone studying these lovely illustrations and their textual inscriptions would discover that the *Quadro* clearly documents four distinct camelid species, whereas French natural historians such as Buffon reported only two or three. Despite this, the *Quadro* also reinscribes ongoing misconceptions regarding the anatomy of the camelids. In this instance, the vicuña is represented as having horselike hooves rather than toenails.[11]

Regarding the impact that works such as the *Quadro* might have had on viewers back in Spain, Bleichmar (2011, 68–69) has argued that they emphasized linkages between "natural history collections, travel, and trade," making natural history "visible and movable" so that it could be seen by those "who had not experienced the New World themselves. It traveled so that they did not have to." By presenting New World natural history as knowable and transportable, visual collections such as the

Trujillo del Perú and the *Quadro* might also have instilled the idea that the painting and its information could travel, so perhaps the living animals could as well.

Indeed, during the second half of the eighteenth century, the Spanish colonial administration began making more concerted efforts to bring camelids to Spain. Peruvian viceroy Manuel de Amat y Junyent (1761–1776) attempted to dispatch several shipments of vicuñas at the request of Julián de Arriaga, Spain's secretary of the Indies, while acknowledging the challenges involved in such an enterprise. As one explanation for why these endeavors failed, the viceroy observed in a communication to Arriaga that records as far back as the sovereignty of Felipe II indicated that the Spanish had tried to ship specimens of the valuable animals to Spain, but they perished early in the voyage because they could not withstand the intense heat of the tropics.[12]

While shipments of camelids were typically unsuccessful, some animals did survive the journey. For the most part, however, the numbers and histories are difficult to track. For example, twenty animals identified as male and female vicuñas were brought to the royal palace at Aranjuez in 1787 and placed in the Casa de las Vacas, with the hopes that they would reproduce and eventually become established. The camelids were accompanied by a former soldier from Buenos Aires, who planned to remain with the animals as their caretaker.[13] It is not clear how long any of these vicuñas survived after their arrival. Partial stories such as this abound in the archives.

At the time when camelid cargos were on the increase, the Real Fábrica de Guadalajara was engaged in the search for new wools and new wool sources to produce quality fabrics, in part because a large percentage of national wool was earmarked for export. Due to the high international demand for Spanish wool, many sheep farmers preferred to sell their product elsewhere rather than to the Real Hacienda, which offered lower prices and required long-term contracts (González Enciso 1980, 575–576). The Real Fábrica began to experiment with vicuña and produced exquisite cloth used on several occasions as a sumptuous gift for presentation to European royalty. But this project introduced new problems, not the least of which was the difficulty of obtaining the fiber. Bringing vicuñas to Spain was proving impractical, if not impossible, and fiber collected in the Andes entailed high shipping costs. Moreover, vicuña wool did not react to dyes in the same way as sheep wool. Even though the Real Fábrica experimented with new methods for dyeing vicuña, it

100 | *Llamas beyond the Andes*

discovered that the fiber would not take certain colors well without being first whitened. While vicuña made lovely cloth, it was not yet a workable enterprise. Trials with goat and guanaco fiber produced even less favorable results (576).

Research with camelid fiber carried out by the Real Fábrica and other mills drew new European attention to the alpaca, especially white alpacas. Their fleece was also of high quality, was less difficult to acquire, and could be processed and dyed more easily than other colors. Accordingly, by the end of the eighteenth century, in addition to calling for the creation of flocks of domesticated vicuñas, market forces began to pressure Indigenous pastoral communities to form flocks of all-white alpacas. This burden flew in the face of centuries-long Aymara and Quechua breeding practices that had developed what Wheeler (2005a) describes as "elaborate classification systems based on color and conformation characteristics."[14] One article published anonymously in the *Semanario de Agricultura, Industria y Comercio* (Buenos Aires) urged that Indians be persuaded to gather small flocks of white alpacas and give preference to these animals over those of other colors. Once again, the promise of exemption from tribute would be held out as a reward for success ("Sobre la necesidad de domesticar á la vicuña" 1803, 264). This was not the only call for the creation of herds of white alpacas. A second anonymous article the following year similarly argued for the development of all-white flocks, but not to the exclusion of the alpacas' many other colors, which were also necessary for the woolen cloth industry ("Sobre la posibilidad de domesticar á la vicuña" 1804–1805, 311). By the end of the first half of the nineteenth century, however, white alpaca was widely considered to be the most valuable color of fleece and brought the highest prices, a pattern that would persist well into the twenty-first century, with devastating impact on the range and quality of natural alpaca colors.[15]

While debates continued in the Andean region over the practicality of domesticating vicuñas and establishing specialized alpaca flocks, Spanish interest in bringing vicuñas across the Atlantic was on the wane by the end of the eighteenth century. For a time, the Viceroyalty of Río de la Plata tried shipping guanacos instead, hoping they would be more resilient than vicuñas (Figueroa 2012, 135; Mello Pereira 2013, 114–115). In his description of the Real Bosque and the Casa de Aranjuez, Álvarez de Quindos y Baena (1804, 333–334) observed in 1778 that a few guanacos could be found in the Casa de las Vacas along with other exotic creatures. Bourgoing (1797, 68), in his account of Aranjuez, told of having seen a pair of zebras and guanacos leaping about in a field, as much at home as if they were in their native country. Such examples aside, guanacos fared little better than vicuñas on the transatlantic journey and also faded from Spanish shipping records before long.[16] The country would not see sustained efforts to naturalize the animals again until the mid-nineteenth century.

Late Eighteenth-Century French Strategies to Obtain Camelids

The mobilization of political power and science for colonial commercial expansion during the eighteenth century was not unique to Spain, and the exploitation of the camelids stands as a case in point. The *Dictionnaire universel de commerce*, the first encyclopedic dictionary of commerce, prepared by the inspector general of the Customs House in Paris (Savary des Bruslons 1741), included entries on all commercial goods for which duty had to be paid, including the camelids. The *Dictionnaire* directed special attention to the fiber of the vicuña. It referred to the Spanish Crown's attempts over many years to import vicuñas with the hope of naturalizing them, repeating the prevailing scientific belief of the time that these efforts had failed primarily because the animals were not placed in the right kind of pasture or because they could not adjust to the new climate (Savary des Bruslons 1741, 3:624).

Despite the challenges presented by past projects to bring camelids to Europe, the influential naturalist Comte de Buffon expressed confidence that the camelids represented a utilitarian natural resource that he hoped France could profitably exploit. In his essays on the llama and vicuña kept at the Alfort Veterinary School, Buffon (1782a, 1782b) advocated for extracting live camelids from South America, convinced that they could survive the rigors of a difficult sea voyage and adaptation to an unfamiliar environment, so long as the proper precautions were taken. In support of his reasoning, he referred to his earlier publication on the camelids and to Conrad Gesner's report of the *Allocamelus* seen in Holland in 1558, along with accounts of other early successful experiments carried out by the Spanish, as evidence that the animals could thrive in the Pyrenees and Alps as well as in the Andean Cordillera (Buffon 1765, 20–21).

For his commentary on the topic of camelid importation, Buffon (1782a) did not rely solely on his own experience with the animals. He turned to his extensive scientific correspondence network (see Belhoste

102 | Llamas beyond the Andes

2011, 35) to request information on the animals from enlightened individuals with expertise on commerce and some knowledge of camelids. The most important was a report from France's agent general of seas and commerce in Spain, the Abbé Alessandro (Agostino) Beliardy, who was considered to be informed on the subject due to a long sojourn in that country. Buffon published the transcripts of these exchanges in his essay, following Beliardy's observations in 1779 with responses prepared by M. de la Folie, the inspector general of manufacturing, and by Abbé Gabriel-Léopold-Charles-Amé Bexon, one of Buffon's own collaborators on the *Histoire naturelle*.[17] These writings merit attention today because they provide a blueprint for French efforts to bring the animals to Europe and were referenced frequently during the nineteenth century by British and Spanish scientists and travelers as well as by French natural historians.

The primary focus of Beliardy's memoir was to communicate the importance of the vicuña as a valuable resource and to outline the political, economic, and bureaucratic challenges France would need to overcome to acquire a flock of the animals and transport them safely across the Atlantic Ocean. The document emphasized the necessity of strategic negotiation and carefully orchestrated political subterfuge, because the project involved both the Spanish and French monarchies. To set the venture in motion, Beliardy proposed that the French king Louis XVI convey an official request for three to four dozen vicuñas to José de Gálvez, Spain's minister of the Indies, cautioning against revealing the true impetus behind it: the naturalization of the vicuña in France. If the Spanish Crown discovered the real motivation for the enterprise, it would undoubtedly try to protect its monopoly by putting a stop to it. The safer strategy, he advised, was to inform Spain that France sought a few vicuñas in the name of curiosity, as had been done with other exotica, such as monkeys and parrots. As the next section of the chapter shows, Josephine Bonaparte would adopt this same approach years later in her attempt to bring alpacas and vicuñas to her menagerie.

The logistics of the plan were as complicated as the politics. Each step would undoubtedly produce rapidly growing costs. For example, if Spain consented to the idea, the next phase would consist of finding a return ship from Buenos Aires able to accommodate the animals. If no ship was available, Beliardy reasoned that it might be necessary to charter a ship in Europe expressly for this purpose and charge one or two agents with the commission of accompanying and caring for the animals. As to how the camelids would be obtained, he recommended that Indigenous people be dispatched to the mountains of the province of Tucumán, part of the newly created Viceroyalty of Río de la Plata, to collect male and female vicuñas as well as llamas and alpacas. Once the animals were gathered, they could be conducted overland to Buenos Aires for shipment to Europe.[18] This route would avoid the lengthy sea voyage down the west coast of South America and the treacherous passage rounding Cape Horn. Having outlined what he perceived to be an efficient and feasible plan, Beliardy finished this portion of his memoir with a rhetorical flourish, claiming that the "Minister who would contribute to the riches of the realm with such a useful animal could applaud himself just as for an important conquest."[19]

Buffon cited Beliardy at length because both men agreed that it would be a great achievement if they could successfully introduce vicuñas, alpacas, and llamas into France. Although Buffon's essay on the vicuña communicated up-to-date information on the animal gleaned from first-hand observation (as discussed in the previous chapter), the piece clearly was also written with the goal of persuading the French government to support this commercial venture (Buffon 1782a, 210–211). Beliardy's simile likening the acquisition of the animal to a conquest underscored the confluence of these imperial, scientific, and economic enterprises.

In contrast to Beliardy's overall enthusiasm for the project, Folie expressed more caution. While he agreed that the acquisition of the vicuña would indeed represent a "great conquest," he feared that the camelids would fare little better in France than they had in Spain without *ycho*, a native Andean grass and staple of their diet (Buffon 1782a, 216–217). Moreover, he raised concerns about how radical changes in diet and climate might adversely affect the animal's fiber, causing it to degenerate over time, which Juan and Ulloa (1748) had rejected. Given these apprehensions, Folie did not recommend that much money be invested in these initial efforts because the outcome was too risky. Nor did he believe that large-scale commerce in cloth made from vicuña fiber would be feasible. Although the product was beautifully soft, he was less convinced it would wear well over time, leading him to conclude that vicuña cloth would likely remain a luxury item, accessible only to those who could afford costly, if impractical, products (Buffon 1782a, 217).

Buffon also drew upon Abbé Bexon's observations on the camelid importation project and his focus on the alpaca, which Bexon described as a little-known, wild, intermediary species between the llama and the vicuña.[20] He advocated for this animal because it had thicker and finer fleece than the llama and a stronger, more robust constitution than the

104 | Llamas beyond the Andes

vicuña. Those that had been kept as curiosities did not seem dependent on *ycho* and ate a variety of foods, including Peruvian corn, bread, and pasture grasses. Bexon lamented the lack of available information on the vicuña, especially regarding its ability to breed in domesticity. Yet, because the animal manifested character traits similar to sheep, he felt optimistic that it would ultimately thrive and reproduce if maintained in flocks in parks or stables. If this was successful, France could play an important role in saving the vicuña by providing a refuge for this valuable creature that otherwise seemed doomed due to reckless hunting practices (Buffon 1782a, 218).

Buffon (1782a, 220) brought his chapter on the vicuña to an end by reaffirming his belief that llamas, pacos, and vicuñas appeared to be good candidates for domestication and naturalization in France. To his mind, Beliardy and Bexon's plans of action seemed realistic, uncomplicated, and eminently achievable. All that was needed now to take the next step toward implementing this "great conquest" was an individual willing to carry out the venture.[21]

Empress Josephine Bonaparte and the Promotion of Natural History as a Utilitarian Science

One of the first to heed Buffon's call to bring vicuñas to France for naturalization was the Empress Josephine Bonaparte, recognized by many as a notable transition figure in the history of science due to her early nineteenth-century experiments in utilitarian agriculture and horticulture. Her library held a considerable selection of books on natural history, including numerous volumes of Buffon's *Histoire naturelle*, Félix de Azara's natural history of Paraguay, and many others (Grandjean 1964, 232–233). Well-known for her exquisite collections of exotic plants and flowers, Josephine also established a small menagerie of domestic and foreign animals, started when she received a pair of llamas. Her desire to add alpacas and vicuñas to the undertaking adds a distinctive perspective to the study of transoceanic camelids because it presents a unique case study that elucidates the enormous challenges involved in such imperial projects. As illustrated by the juxtaposition of the two epigraphs at the beginning of the chapter, Josephine's camelid venture marks a contrast between the relative ease with which a royal request could be issued and the enormous difficulties entailed in its local implementation, including the huge financial outlay and nearly insurmountable bureaucratic hurdles that had to be overcome. It brings to light the vital importance of local knowledge and practices and the large numbers of people from diverse ethnic, social, and economic sectors drawn into service on behalf of the enterprise. The story of Josephine's alpacas and vicuñas also shows how changing political alliances among imperial powers could have an impact on such a project. In the recounting of this venture, I am particularly indebted to Argentine historian Maud de Ridder de Zemboraín (1998), who reconstructed much of the account of the animals' acquisition and their journey overland from Peru to Buenos Aires. In this chapter I reference portions of her work to bring it under a new lens and to situate the project within larger global commercial and political networks involving the Andean camelids.

Josephine's attention to natural history as a useful and economically beneficial science began in the late eighteenth century. In the spirit of Marie Antoinette's English Park at Trianon, Josephine formed a model agricultural establishment on the grounds of her Malmaison chateau, where she had an important herd of Spanish merino sheep. Her emphasis on "economic zoology" was linked more broadly to the utilitarian understandings of science of the time and the development of research, acclimatization, and the perfection of useful species (Jouanin 1997b, 29; Taylor-Leduc 2013, 46–47). As Taylor-Leduc (2013, 48) observes, Napoleon Bonaparte understood that the development and improvement of agricultural projects would help stimulate the weakened French economy. Josephine's dedication to the study of natural history played a key role in the furtherance of these projects: "Josephine conceived of Malmaison as an estate that could be transformed into an icon of land ownership, a status accessible for the post-revolutionary bourgeoisie whose self-image no longer derived entirely from landed wealth, but who still wanted an association with ancien régime values. Thus Josephine transformed Malmaison into an ornamental farm, coupling a garden with agricultural productivity, so that the estate metaphorically functioned as a symbol of domestic prosperity."

Josephine began learning about merino sheep in 1796 when she moved to Croissy, her place of sojourn during the time of revolutionary turmoil (Taylor-Leduc 2013, 50). Her neighbor and friend Jean Chanorier had a flock of 40 animals, directly derived from the famed 380 Rambouillet merinos brought to France from Spain in 1786, with the intent to better France's sheep stock and textile industry. When Chanorier put some of his animals up for sale, he encouraged Josephine to enhance the value of her property by acquiring a small flock for wool production. She was able to

106 | Llamas beyond the Andes

add to this initial herd just a few years later when the French Agricultural Bureau sent politician Adrien Francastel to Spain to begin the extraction of large numbers of merinos to France as had been agreed upon in one of the secret articles of the 1795 Peace of Basel (Jouanin and Ledoux-Lebard 1993, 48–49, 1997; Taylor-Leduc 2013, 49–51). While in Spain, Francastel offered Josephine his assistance with the enrichment of her collections, ultimately sending her 1,000 merinos for distribution between Malmaison and La Ferte–Beauharnais, the property of her son Eugène de Beauharnais (Jouanin and Ledoux-Lebard 1993, 49–50). Francastel acquired merinos for her directly from the herd of King Fernando VII's favored minister Manuel Godoy. She had 518 sheep by 1807, with numbers reaching their peak in 1812 at 2,167 (Jouanin and Ledoux-Lebard 1993, 50–52). Josephine's burgeoning sheep industry was linked to images of empire, wealth, and pleasure. Her role as a "shepherdess of merinos" by 1808 symbolized France's improved economic well-being (52).

The Science and Politics of the Malmaison Llamas

Josephine's interest in the utilitarian benefits of natural history expanded beyond her experimental farm to include projects dedicated to the collection and acclimatization of exotic plants, birds, and animals. Although her menagerie at Malmaison never attained the status of her extensive gardens and famed greenhouse, the enterprise nonetheless gained recognition for its diversity of rare creatures. The menagerie was defined by two periods. One period of growth at the start of the empire began in 1800 and extended to 1805. The second period was marked by decline, when animals that died or were dispersed were not replaced (Jouanin 1997b, 29–30).

Josephine established her collection of animals in 1800 when she received a gift of two llamas, a male and female.[22] The colonial prefect of Saint Domingue, an important colonial scientific outpost, shipped the llamas to the empress, having received them from the French general Gaëtan Souchet d'Alvimart for this purpose (Lacépède and Cuvier 1801, 1).[23] Before long, the exotic pair was joined by other additions, including kangaroos, a female orangutan, and a pair of Australian black swans, reportedly the first seen in Europe (Chevallier 2005, 88; Chevallier and Pincemaille, 268–269). Josephine's menagerie became a unique institution for the study of exotic animals. Her work there led to fruitful collaborations with other research endeavors, such as those being carried

FIGURE 3.2. Lama femelle/Camelus Llacma, *painted by Léon de Wailly (1803). Collection des Vélins du Muséum National d'Histoire Naturelle, portfolio 73—Zoologie—Mammifères.*

out at the menagerie of the National Museum of Natural History. When an unusual bird or animal from her collection died, she would have the remains sent to the anatomists there for their analysis and use (Lacépède, Cuvier, and Geoffroy Saint-Hilaire 1804, 156).

Lacépède and Cuvier (1801) described the two llamas as always being together and having mated several times. When one was held in their shelter, the other would circle the building continuously, crying out to its companion inside. The animals were known for their exceedingly docile nature, seldom reacting, "even when struck violently" (5), their main weapon of defense being to spit at any tormenter. A description and an illustration of both llamas (figure 3.2) were included in Lacépède and Cuvier's (1801) volume on the National Museum of Natural History's menagerie. The artist posed the two llamas together, with each attentively watching the other's movements, perhaps a reflection of what Lacépède and Cuvier described as the animals' close-knit relationship (Lacépède and Cuvier 1801, 5). The pictorial image of the llamas in quiet stances subtly reinforced the textual description of the animals' desirable traits of

108 | *Llamas beyond the Andes*

tractability, willingness to mate, and ability to reproduce, all qualities of major concern for the success of acclimatization projects. Like many of the illustrations in Lacépède and Cuvier's book, this one highlights a special feature of the animal's anatomy by including an image inset on the rockface below the shy male located on the left. Although the inserted portrayal is drawn on a large scale, it depicts with relative accuracy the structure of the bottom of the camelid foot, showing the pads and toenails. As late as the nineteenth century, as has already been observed, many visual representations of the camelids got the feet wrong, showing them as solid or cloven hooves. This drawing is one of the first to focus solely on the camelid foot and its distinctive features from an anatomical perspective.

The llama pair eventually had at least two offspring. One of them was killed by dogs (Lasteyrie 1834, 59). Its remains were sent to the National Museum of Natural History. On behalf of the institution, Antoine-François Fourcroy wrote to Josephine on April 26, 1804, to acknowledge receipt of the body and to thank the empress for contributing to the development of natural history in France through her donation. He reported that Cuvier was able to take advantage of the young llama's demise to study its internal structure (Fourcroy quoted in Jouanin 1997a, 117–118). This undoubtedly is the infant llama described by Cuvier (1835, 72–75), mentioned in chapter 2. The Malmaison llamas lived for several years, and one still survived in 1814 (Chevallier and Pincemaille 1988, 268; Jouanin 1999, 51–53). Following Josephine's death in 1815 and subsequent dispersal of the menagerie, her son Eugène gifted the remaining llama to the King of Württemberg (Chevallier 1989, 146; Jouanin 1997a, 118).

The different histories of the Malmaison llamas effectively trace the distinctive roles they played in science and politics. Cuvier's study of the infant llama, as discussed in the previous chapter, became an integral part of the debates concerning camelid internal physiology and, more specifically, the digestive tract. In contrast, royal gifts, such as the older llama presented to the Württemberg king, likely enhanced international diplomatic relations and contributed to the global circulation of locally constructed scientific knowledge about exotic creatures like the llamas, as Livingstone (2003, 137–138) has contended more generally, and helped to make the animals more familiar to Europeans. Following the routes of specific Malmaison llamas also brings to light their complex biogeographies. The pair began their journey in Peru, purportedly accompanied by an Indian responsible for the animals' welfare.[24] They were moved first to Cartagena, next to Saint-Domingue, and from there to France (one

From Curiosity to Commodity | 109

finally ended up in Württemberg). The Indian caretaker disappears from the historical record in Cartagena. It is not known whether he returned to Peru after the animals reached the port city, was unable to return to his homeland due insufficient funds, or was taken on to France to care for the animals during transit. The llamas' lives reveal the changing meanings they acquired as they moved beyond their Andean origins, where they formed an integral part of local cultural and agricultural ecologies, to inhabit new European contexts, where they were received as potential stock animals. These shifting environments and perspectives also shaped European understandings of the camelids, demonstrating that knowledge of the Andean animals was becoming increasingly global and local at the same time (see Alberti 2011a, 1–4; Raj 2010).

Josephine's Request for Alpacas and Vicuñas and Its Impact at the Local Level

Josephine's desire to add vicuñas and alpacas to her collection may well have been inspired originally by reading Buffon, although Spanish botanist Simón de Rojas Clemente observed that Francisco Zea, director of Madrid's Royal Botanical Garden, had shared two articles on the camelids from the *Semanario de Agricultura* with the empress and that her curiosity about them developed on the basis of these readings ("Necrología: Simón de Rojas Clemente" 1827, 148).[25] It is not surprising to learn of Josephine's interest in an animal as valuable as the vicuña. The empress was adept at utilizing stylish trends to promote images of affluence, success, and productivity, even as Napoleon employed fashion to invigorate the French textile industry while underscoring his military successes abroad. For example, cashmere accessories became popular in French fashion after Napoleon presented Josephine with an exquisite red cashmere shawl that he brought to her from Egypt, which she wore in several famous portraits. When efforts to acclimatize cashmere goats in France failed, Napoleon urged textile manufacturers to seek new fabrics from other sources (Taylor-Leduc 2013, 44, 53–54). Around this same time, sumptuous vicuña shawls began appearing as embellishments to empire-style dresses in French fashion magazines (figure 3.3).

Josephine's plan to acquire vicuñas and alpacas began gaining momentum in 1803, when word of her interest spread to Spain and Peru through various official and unofficial channels. For example, on December 23,

FIGURE 3.3. *Vicuña shawl.* Journal des Dames et de la Mode *(March 7, 1803), plate 10, 276. Reproduction by permission of the Buffalo & Erie County Public Library, Buffalo, New York.*

1803, a Peruvian creole named José Camacho wrote to the empress, explaining that he had learned of her wish to obtain some of the animals from a Madrid correspondent. He expressed his willingness to gather a small flock of llamas, alpacas, and vicuñas, prepare them for the voyage, and personally accompany them to France as their caretaker.[26] Camacho apparently included documents along with his letter regarding the transaction so that Josephine could decide the best way forward for the project. Camacho's plan never got off the ground, most likely due to disinclination on the part of the Peruvian viceroy for reasons not explained.

Although Camacho's name disappeared from the enterprise, Josephine remained intent on acquiring the animals, as indicated by correspondence that she received from Francastel the following year. While in Spain and working on the extraction of merinos, he contacted the empress in January 1804, to express his regret over not having vicuñas, llamas, and alpacas already gathered and en route to join the convoy of sheep. Although Francastel assured her that everything would be done to obtain the Andean animals successfully,[27] a month later he communicated the disappointing news that no vicuñas could be found in Spain and that there was little chance of acquiring them through regular commercial channels. Nonetheless, he expressed hope that before long she would have not only a flock of merinos established at Malmaison's Swiss chalet but also a flock of the exotic camelids.[28]

Josephine decided to appeal directly to the Spanish monarchy and sent a personal request for the animals to Queen María Luisa. At the time, Spain and France were political allies in the Napoleonic Wars and relations between the two countries were relatively friendly. Josephine's petition received a favorable response, and on February 10, 1804, King Carlos IV issued a royal order to the viceroys of Lima and Río de la Plata for a dozen live vicuñas and the same number of alpacas, "so that the animals might serve as a form of pleasant distraction [for the empress] at her country home where she has gathered other valuable objects of natural history."[29] The wording of the king's order suggests that Josephine's original request made no reference to her intention to make her menagerie, farm, and gardens key sites for naturalizing exotic plants and animals, like the camelids. Perhaps she took inspiration from Beliardy's recommendation years earlier that requests to Spain for the camelids be made in the name of curiosity and without mentioning the true motivation of wanting to naturalize them. Ironically, however, by the time the project came to conclusion, this seemingly trivial request ended up costing the Spanish viceregal treasuries thousands of pesos and demanded enormous feats of strength and ingenuity on the part of many over the course of several years (Ridder de Zemboraín 1998, 38).

Upon receipt of the royal order, Rafael de Sobremonte (viceroy of Río de la Plata) forwarded the charge to the intendants of La Paz, Potosí, Córdoba, and Salta, with the directive that they circulate instructions in their districts for the desired number of animals to be captured or purchased on behalf of the Royal Treasury and sent to Buenos Aires without delay.[30] Responses from regional officials trickled in during subsequent months. Their content demonstrates the many challenges entailed in such a command. Implicit in this correspondence, but never addressed directly, was the potentially fraught relationship between regional authorities expected to carry out the instructions and the local Indigenous communities that would have had to supply the alpacas and likely the vicuñas as well. Although the methods to be used for acquiring the animals were not specified, replies indicated that alpacas were relatively easy to obtain,

112 | *Llamas beyond the Andes*

but they were expensive and prone to injury and disease. The president of the Real Audiencia and governor of Charcas, Ramón García de León y Pizarro, received word in November 1804 that it was not a good season for collecting vicuñas in Poopó (Oruro): the weather had been overly warm, birth rates were down, and the animals were thin and sickly. A priest could supply twelve young alpacas but sought advice as to which route should be used for sending the animals. Informed sources had recommended that it would be more prudent to take the animals by way of the less-populated route of Carangas, which had a lot of alpacas and young vicuñas. They would also be better protected due to the colder temperatures and shorter distances to the ports of Arica and Tacna, from where they could be shipped, rather than walked overland to Buenos Aires.[31]

The general sentiment of the correspondence similarly communicated pessimism about the project being successful. The long hot trip overland to Buenos Aires with alpacas risked exposing them to fatigue and fatal illness. It would be very slow, moreover, because the animals only walk short distances in a day. To ensure a greater chance for a positive outcome transporting the alpacas, others recommended that an Indigenous caretaker be brought along to care for the animals until they reached their final destination, because Indians were the only ones who raised the animals and understood the attention they required. Without their presence, it was unlikely that a single alpaca would survive the journey because of heavy losses due to heat, fraud, and exhaustion as they traveled the long distance to Buenos Aires.[32] All agreed that vicuñas posed even greater difficulties. Unless they were captured while very young, it would be nearly impossible to domesticate them, so they would be unmanageable during transport. Furthermore, many vicuña populations were dispersed due to recent *chaco* hunts, making them virtually inaccessible. A general order to all areas would likely result in people bringing one baby vicuña at a time for purchase and only if they had not already been wounded or killed for their hides.[33]

In January 1805, almost a year from the initial receipt of the royal order, Viceroy Sobremonte responded to the information that García Pizarro had relayed. The viceroy did not appear to put much stock in the concerns raised by local authorities and repeated that transporting the animals by sea, south from the port of Arica and around Cape Horn, was not an option. Ignoring the advice he had received, he instead insisted that the vicuñas and alpacas be taken overland to Buenos Aires as soon as possible, with all precautionary measures necessary.[34]

From Curiosity to Commodity | 113

In the meantime, while the La Plata correspondence traveled back and forth, the Peruvian viceroyalty contracted a man by the name of Julián García to take on the enterprise from that end. The hiring of García, an employee of the Lima Post Office, ended up being a stroke of luck. Despite the herculean nature of the project, he faithfully stayed the course to the end. Archival and published documentation on the subject says little about García himself, who he was, or anything about his personal circumstances, but it does indicate that he dedicated almost five years of his life to conveying the requested animals, from the time he started out to finally reaching Cádiz, Spain. The second epigraph to this chapter communicates García's ordeal in his own words. It gives a sense of the tenacity required to bring the extraordinary commission to completion and the personal toll it took on the modest postal worker. To begin with, García had to oversee countless details in Lima, and the invoices accumulated rapidly. Among other tasks, he had to stock sufficient provisions for the men and animals and prepare them for transportation, hire caretakers, and arrange ocean passage for the first leg of the journey by ship from Callao to Valparaíso.

To complicate matters further, García had to engage constantly with the enormous colonial bureaucracy to obtain funds and additional kinds of support, such as letters of introduction. To get the venture up and running, Lima's Royal Treasury advanced García 300 pesos in January 1805 to cover initial expenses. García used the money to hire eighteen men, plus a foreman named Julián Vega, and two Indians to herd the alpacas and vicuñas to the port of Callao once all arrangements had been made.[35] García contracted Vega and the two Indigenous Andeans with the idea that they would accompany the mission all the way to Spain. He also employed several additional men, minimally described as "negros," to domesticate the vicuñas, which had been stabled at his house before traveling (Escobari de Querejazu 2014, 147; Ridder de Zemboraín 1998, 39). Once all was ready, García and his men brought twenty-four alpacas and thirteen vicuñas to Callao, where they loaded the animals onto the ship *Milagro* for passage to Valparaíso.[36] From there they planned to shepherd the animals overland, across the high Andean Cordillera to Mendoza, and finally to Buenos Aires.

It took the *Milagro* over a month to reach Valparaíso. By the time the ship landed, the animals were in a fragile state and García's funds were depleted. He had now spent the monies authorized in Lima and had even paid several large invoices out of pocket, after facing numerous

114 | *Llamas beyond the Andes*

unanticipated expenses. For example, even before leaving Lima, one Indian fell ill and remained behind. García had to find a replacement for him, along with additional men to care for the animals when some of the Indians later became incapacitated by seasickness.[37] As the men loaded the animals on the ship, two vicuñas managed to escape and run off, so García had to pay four men ten pesos to catch the animals and bring them back. After landing in Valparaíso, García contracted soldiers to unload the animals and escort them to an area on the outskirts of the city known as El Almendral, where five men kept watch over them. The entire first portion of the expedition was marked by escalating costs such as these, for which García had to contact the Royal Treasury for reimbursement.[38]

The anticipated ordeal of the trip over the Andes to Mendoza required new petitions to the Royal Treasury from García. He hired carts to carry the provisions and some of the animals for the first stage of the ascent and contracted twenty men to bring the flock over the Cordillera on foot once they reached the point that use of the carts was no longer feasible. These men eventually would have to carry many of the thin and weakened animals over the high passes when they became unable to advance on their own. While still in Valparaíso, García planned ahead to put together an invoice of expenses that the group would undoubtedly incur between Mendoza and Buenos Aires. For example, he knew that he would again have to hire carts and drivers once they reached Mendoza. Because alpacas and vicuñas travel so slowly, the drivers would be forced to endure longer delays than usual and consequently would expect additional compensation. García calculated that the last leg of the trip would take approximately six months, including two months of winter, which meant that adequate food for the animals had to be loaded to make up for a lack of pasture, including "an abundance of bread because these animals like it so much."[39]

Unsure of how to respond to García's detailed budget request, ministers of the treasury in Santiago forwarded it directly to King Carlos IV in Madrid, explaining what a bizarre story this was and how they could make neither head nor tail of it: "But what can we know about this? Absolutely nothing, we do not understand anything about this subject, nor is there anyone we can consult, because no one ever attempted such an enterprise, one so strange in all its circumstances. Only in Mendoza might there be someone who knows whether the animals will fare better on the journey if they walk or are driven in carts." Despite their uncertainties, they urged that the monies be authorized soon, so that the troop could cross the cordillera before winter set in.[40]

From Curiosity to Commodity | 115

García's request was indeed granted. The Crown also issued a superior decree affording the group protection and authorizing requests for additional funds along the way to Buenos Aires. Furthermore, the alpacas and vicuñas received the official designation of "Imperial Animals," a status that ensured them priority over all those encountered along the route (Ridder de Zemboraín 1998, 39–40). We can only imagine today what the convoy must have looked like as it set out from Valparaíso and how astonishing it would have seemed to anyone who came across it on the road.

At the beginning of the climb into the Andes, the vicuñas traveled in the carts, receiving routine breaks to be unloaded so that they could stretch their legs. Once the group reached the Aconcagua Valley and the village of Santa Rosa de los Andes, however, the carts had to be left behind. In anticipation of having to traverse the cordillera on foot the rest of the way, presumably across the dangerous Uspallata Pass, García contracted a team of sixty-three mules to carry the provisions required for the 41-day journey from the valley of Aconcagua to Mendoza (Ridder de Zemboraín 1998, 39–40).

After reaching Mendoza, García planned for the travelers to remain there for several weeks, allowing the exhausted animals time to recover and for the men to take advantage of any opportunities that might arise to replace alpacas or vicuñas that had died. The preparations in anticipation of the journey to Buenos Aires were also extensive and required time, advance organization, and attention to many details. For example, he again had to contract carts to facilitate the transportation of the animals. In response to problems experienced during the first leg of the journey, García planned to have one man travel in each cart to ensure that the tied animals did not become tangled and strangle themselves. He also had the carts lined with leather to keep the animals from breaking their legs against the sides. Each cart included rope railings to prevent the animals from jumping out and running away. Other equipment included items like a large wooden tub used for bathing the animals when they developed skin eruptions (Ridder de Zemboraín 1998, 40).

These arrangements took García two months to complete, after which the large group finally departed for Buenos Aires. The journey across the hot, arid terrain was long and grueling. The cart owners grew increasingly frustrated by the caravan's slow progress. To help the men recoup some of their losses, García agreed that some space in the carts could be reserved for transporting fruit (Escobari de Querejazu 2014, 148–149). Each day the animals had to be loaded onto the carts and unloaded again at intervals

116 | *Llamas beyond the Andes*

to be allowed time to graze, move around, and drink barreled water. Not surprisingly, the group attracted attention from curious locals they met along the way. At one point, García purchased a shotgun to prevent people with hunting dogs from coming too close to the animals and frightening them. On three occasions, men had to give chase to vicuñas that made a mad dash for freedom. After numerous mishaps and disasters, the convoy finally reached Buenos Aires in late October–November of 1805, the entire trip from Peru having taken almost a year (Ridder de Zemboraín 1998, 41).

In Buenos Aires, García settled the animals first on one estate and then on another so that they had continuous access to fresh pasture. Viceroy Sobremonte took great interest in the Peruvian creatures and visited them regularly (Núñez 1898, 5). He himself had had little success collecting vicuñas and alpacas, as substantiated by the correspondence from Poopó, Lípez, and Carangas. Under increasing pressure from the Crown, however, in late 1805 he dispatched a man named Joaquín Correa Morales to Salta along with an assistant, who had both been instructed by García on how to handle the animals. The men had orders to collect two small herds awaiting them in Salta, one of alpacas and one of vicuñas. Another small number of animals was added by an Indian named Marcos Torres, who had been charged by the intendant governor of La Paz with bringing eighteen alpacas to the governor of Salta. Of these eighteen, ten had died along the route, which Torres confirmed by presenting the Salta governor with eight skins and two heads. He claimed that the missing two skins had been violently stolen from him en route by a traveler who had crossed paths with the caravan. After delivering the remaining animals, Torres ascertained that he did not have enough funds to cover the cost of the return trip to La Paz. Archival records of other camelid shipments indicate that this was a common problem facing Andean shepherds, in particular, who had been charged to transport small numbers of camelids long distances. Torres requested money from Domingo de Iriarte, a military man who originally dispatched Torres to deliver the alpacas on his behalf. Iriarte refused to send any additional money, claiming that Torres should have had enough for the journey home. Torres and the men working with him eventually requested help from the Salta representative of the protector of Indians, who interceded and eventually persuaded the treasury to pay Torres twenty-four pesos so that he and his men would not "die on the way back to La Paz" (Ridder de Zemboraín 1998, 43–44).

In the meantime, the troop led by Correa Morales headed out from

From Curiosity to Commodity | 117

Salta for Buenos Aires on June 26, 1806. In total the caravan had twenty-seven carts, each carrying two animals. The carts were preceded by six herders and a small flock of guanacos and llamas (Ridder de Zemboraín 1998, 44–45).[41] The group was en route to join García's animals when British forces attacked and invaded the port that same month. García rushed to find a secure hiding place for the animals in Buenos Aires, fearing that his precious flock could be in jeopardy. In their haste to move the animals, the men did not have time to prepare the six carts that they collected for the transfer sufficiently; as a result, all the men riding in them to accompany the animals were severely injured by being kicked. Notwithstanding García's efforts to conceal the royal animals, the British troops seized the flock with the intention of shipping it to England. Within six weeks, however, Spanish forces under the command of Santiago Liniers reconquered Buenos Aires. García happily regained possession of the small flock (Ridder de Zemboraín 1998, 41).

Recognized for his heroism in twice forcing the British troops to withdraw, Liniers was made interim viceroy of Río de la Plata after Sobremonte and other Spanish government officials fled into the country's interior following the British attacks (Socolow 2007, 7). Liniers knew of García's animals and made public his plan to fulfill the original request and forward them to Josephine. By doing so he fueled the animosity of his political adversaries, who argued that his loyalties were with France (Arzadún y Zabala 1910, 20–21). His enemies emphasized that he was born Jacques Liniers in France, not Spain, becoming Santiago Liniers only when he joined the Spanish navy (Socolow 2007, 3). Although he had served the Spanish military loyally for many years, rumors repeatedly claimed that he was an agent for the French. These reports grew even more intense after Napoleon invaded Spain (8). Liniers did himself no favors following the liberation of the Andean camelids from the British when he publicly described the satisfaction he felt in knowing that they could finally be shipped to Josephine. Not surprisingly, his political rivals maintained that this decision was infused with treason (Arzadún y Zabala 1910, 20–21). The interim viceroy never had the opportunity to make good on his intentions, so the flock remained in Buenos Aires for another three years while García waited for a decision regarding the animals' fate. The Spanish Royal Treasury continued paying his expenses.

It is difficult to imagine the time, energy, and expense required by the enterprise that García directed over the course of five years from Lima to Buenos Aires. Escobari de Querejazu (2014) estimates that García's

118 | Llamas beyond the Andes

portion of the trip alone—excluding the additional flocks brought from La Paz and elsewhere under Corrales and the subsequent journey by sea to Cádiz—cost the Spanish Royal Treasury 40,000 pesos at a minimum. To give some perspective on this figure, she notes that the cost for building a substantial bridge on the Pilcomayo River in the 1770s was about 15,000 pesos (Escobari de Querejazu 2014, 152). The 40,000-peso figure, while staggering, does not do justice to the extraordinary amount of time the venture required or the hardships it created for the people and animals involved.

The Voyage to Cádiz and Arrival at the Jardín de Aclimatación in Sanlúcar de Barrameda

In July 1809 the new viceroy, Baltasar Hidalgo de Cisneros, arrived in Buenos Aires with great fanfare, more than a year after Napoleon had invaded Spain and only a few months before the French emperor and Josephine would divorce. Hopeful that under this new administration the camelid endeavor might finally move forward, García sent Cisneros a letter recounting his journey from Lima and extended stay in Buenos Aires and describing how the now fully domesticated animals had intermingled and bred mixed offspring (Ridder de Zemboraín 1998, 45–46). Astounded to learn how long the animals had been delayed in Buenos Aires, Cisneros had García load the animals and their provisions immediately on the warship *Prueba*, which was docked in Montevideo and preparing to leave for Cádiz. Thanks to this quick response, García and the imperial animals finally sailed for Spain on August 22, 1809, five years after he left Lima. The number and species of camelids stated to have been loaded on board ship for the transatlantic crossing vary from one source to another.[42] García carried a letter of recommendation provided by Cisneros for Martín de Garay, secretary of state for Spain's governing central junta, located in Cádiz now that the peninsula had come under French occupation. The viceroy praised García in the letter for all that he had done and requested that he be granted recompense for his labors and for the job he lost in Lima as a result of his dedication to the enterprise. Cisneros also recommended that García be awarded further honors for the many services he had rendered in Buenos Aires during the British siege and afterward (Ridder de Zemboraín 1998, 46).

From Curiosity to Commodity | 119

For most sources, the account ends here. However, we know something of the animals' fate after they sailed from South America thanks to information provided by Francisco Terán, who, in addition to being the honorary intendant of Cádiz Province at the time, was also the first director of the acclimatization garden in Sanlúcar de Barrameda, where the camelids were finally delivered. The animals would not be sent on to France from there. International alliances had shifted after García and his flock first reached Buenos Aires. France and Spain had become enemies following the Napoleonic occupation of the peninsula, and Britain and Spain were now politically aligned. Given these changing political tides, Cisneros had been adamant that the camelids should not be taken to their original destination in France, hoping, instead, that they might become naturalized in Spain (Ridder de Zemboraín 1998, 46–47).[43]

During the transatlantic voyage from South America to Cádiz, the crew, García, his associates, and the animals faced more challenges and ordeals. While en route, one of the leading ships of the Spanish fleet was attacked by a British warship, unaware that peace between the two nations had been signed. In the midst of the conflict, the ship carrying the animals had to lighten its load by throwing overboard many of the provisions brought along as fodder, including sweet potatoes and corn. This action resulted in food shortages and created severe health problems for the animals, especially concerning their digestive tracts. As long as the rations of sweet potatoes lasted, the animals' excretory functions worked normally. But once they ran out, the camelids began to suffer from constipation. To soften the animals' stool, enemas had to be administered and wax cylinders inserted into their rectums. These complications caused the deaths of several of the flock (Theran 1821, 18).

By the time the flock finally reached Cádiz in late fall 1809, its numbers had been greatly reduced. As already noted, Terán described an original shipment of thirty-six animals, of which only eleven survived the voyage to the port city. Shortly after landing, two more male llamas died, having disembarked in a weakened condition. This left a total of nine animals: one female llama, pregnant by an alpaca; two female vicuñas, one pregnant by an alpaca; three mestizo females, offspring of an alpaca (male) and vicuña; and three alpaca males (Theran 1821, 19). Although these animals had survived the transatlantic crossing, none was in stable condition when they reached Sanlúcar de Barrameda (Cárdenas et al. 1879, xiv–xv).

Llamas beyond the Andes

Francisco Terán's Contributions to the Science of Camelid Acclimatization

The botanical garden of Sanlúcar de Barrameda was founded in 1805, with the scientific and utilitarian mission to increase industrial and agrarian production, improve public health, and help maintain the Spanish empire (Cabral Chamorro 1995, 167). Under the directorship of a three-man commission that included Francisco Terán, the garden's land was divided into lots for teaching and for the cultivation of useful plants. The commissioners also developed programs dedicated to the improvement and propagation of horses and native wool-bearing animals and implemented experiments crossbreeding different species (173–174). Exotic animals were also of interest: the commission and others hoped that angora goats, which had already been established near Madrid, and vicuñas, alpacas, guanacos, and llamas could be naturalized, with the expectation that they would foment new industries (179–180). Botanist Simón de Rojas Clemente (1777–1827) believed that Sanlúcar de Barrameda was ideally located for such an experimental agricultural school. As he argued before the courts years later, because of Sanlúcar's proximity to the important port of Cádiz, live plants and animals brought from overseas could be transferred quickly to the gardens, enhancing their possibilities of survival. In the case of the Andean camelids, he believed that they would have all perished if they had had to continue their journey beyond Cádiz to Málaga (cited in Gil Albarracín 2002, 62).

During the Spanish War of Independence from French occupation, Spanish royalists attacked and nearly destroyed the botanical garden in 1808 because it had been founded by Carlos IV's prime minister Manuel Godoy, the man accused of facilitating Napoleon's invasion of the peninsula. Godoy (1836, 362) described the national and personal significance of the garden before its ruin: "At the time, the magnificent and prospering acclimatization garden in San Lúcar de Barrameda, one of my favorite achievements, was the site where the best tropical plants, trees, and shrubs were taking root. A lovely garden and the source of a great hope, it was already well established by 1808. The mobs, deceived and confused by my enraged enemies, tore the place down. Our botanical garden was the envy of Europe." Many intellectuals and scientists of the time, including Francisco Terán, were accused of being *afrancesados* (pro-French), and most were forced into exile after the war (Martín Polo 2010, 388). Rojas Clemente, pressured by the royalist patriots to join their forces, managed instead to obtain a commission with the garden that placed him in charge of the alpacas and vicuñas when they reached Cádiz. Based on this unique experience, Rojas Clemente wrote a memoir on the subject of the vicuña, which he hoped would guide future efforts to naturalize the animal ("Necrología: Simón de Rojas Clemente" 1827, 148).[44] Unfortunately, his manuscript was never published and is considered lost.

Although Rojas Clemente's study is unaccounted for, Terán also assessed the camelid venture at Sanlúcar and outlined several important discoveries for Europeans that would contribute to future attempts to acclimatize the animals. First, the enterprise demonstrated that (female) vicuñas taken while very young could be domesticated and subsequently crossed with male alpacas; alpacas and llamas could also be successfully crossed; and baby vicuñas captured in their native land could be raised by alpaca foster mothers. Perhaps even more surprising for European scientific audiences was the discovery that the mestizo offspring were fertile and could reproduce. García had noted this finding as well. As a result, Terán inferred that the three types of Andean camelids were varieties of the same, not different, species of the genus *Camelus*. Even though Terán's observations were framed in the context of natural history as a way to better understand camelid classification, they also carried economic implications. For example, the scientists at the garden claimed that the female vicuña crossed with a male alpaca produced offspring with abundant and exquisite wool, thereby demonstrating that the garden was on the brink of developing new and useful animal varieties. Unfortunately, however, the surviving animals did not include a male llama or vicuña or a female alpaca, which prevented further experimentation with crossing the three animal types (Theran 1821, 19–20).

Not unexpectedly, much of this information was already well known to Andeans of diverse socioeconomic sectors who lived in proximity to or worked directly with the flocks in different capacities. Andean pastoral communities did not generally have a postconquest history of systematically and regularly crossing the domestic and wild camelids; yet, as discussed in later chapters, mestizos, creoles, and Europeans would become interested in the possibility from an economic standpoint, seeing the practice as a method to make the wild species more tractable and easier to extract abroad, while preserving the fine quality of their fiber. For example, Terán described having experimented with the fiber of the alpacavicuña cross and his conclusion that it was as fine as the vicuña fiber and suitable for replacing beaver in hat production (Theran, 1821, 22–23).[45]

122 | Llamas beyond the Andes

Despite the number of animal casualties resulting from the project, Terán concluded his report with a recommendation that the effort be repeated. He expected that the venture would proceed more smoothly the next time, given the knowledge gained from this first experiment, especially if it involved a larger number of animals. Echoing the sentiment of other European natural historians of the time, he asserted that "the domestication of the vicuña would be one of the most interesting human conquests of the animal world" (Theran 1821, 24).

News of the arrival of the llamas and vicuñas in Cádiz spread quickly through Spain and elsewhere. Before long the Sanlúcar gardens were receiving notable guests who traveled there expressly to see the exotic creatures. Although the dates are not clear, it is likely that these visits took place just before or during the French siege of Cádiz (1810–1812), because the visitors included the "intruder King" Joseph Bonaparte, who brought along his ministers, and the marshal general Jean-de-Dieu Soult (Theran 1821, 20). During this time of political upheaval, there was concern that the occupying troops might attempt to seize the valuable animals. The military governor of Cádiz, General Francisco Javier Venegas, played an instrumental role in protecting the camelids from the French, who were well aware that the original plan had been to send them to Josephine (Theran 1821, 18).

Even though the small flock had not ended up in Malmaison for political reasons, members of the French occupying forces nonetheless expressed interest in the Andean camelids from the perspective of natural history. The Cádiz animals, as the Malmaison animals were now referred to, gained prominence as study specimens for those wanting to know more about how they had adapted to a new environment. For example, the French captain and natural historian who served in Soult's army, Baron André de Férussac, observed the animals with great pleasure, making particular note of how they had become entirely domesticated. He speculated that if they could be crossed with each other or, surprisingly, with Spanish goats, their wool would become a valuable new addition to the Spanish economy (Férussac 1823, 25, 25n3, 48). A second natural historian accompanying Soult's army, Jean-Baptiste Bory de Saint-Vincent (1823), included details on the Sanlúcar camelids after dedicating time to their study. Like Férussac, Bory de Saint-Vincent was especially taken with the animals' wool and sent samples from each to the Academy of Sciences at Paris. Several drawings he made of them unfortunately were later lost in the battle of Vittoria (Rennie 1829, 325).[46]

From Curiosity to Commodity | 123

Reports of the Cádiz animals reached Paris's scientific circles from these different sources, the most important, of course, being Terán's (1821) detailed firsthand account in Portuguese. His report appeared in French the following year in *Mémorial Universel: Journal du Cercle des Arts* and became the subject of discussion on the part of scientists interested in the possibility of acclimatizing alpacas and vicuñas in France. For example, Abbé Henri Alexandre Tessier of merino sheep fame discussed Terán's conclusions at a meeting of the Royal Academy of Sciences in March 1822. Alexander von Humboldt was present at the gathering and offered his comments on the subject afterward.[47]

Based on the information provided by this dialogue, the French commission studying the topic expressed concerns about moving forward to bring vicuñas to France. While Terán had advocated for repeating the full experiment, the French concluded that it would be more economically prudent to experiment solely with llamas and alpacas. Although their fleece was not as fine as vicuña fleece, they were more docile animals. The commission members believed that the commercialization of alpaca fiber would be especially profitable. The commission forwarded its report, along with Humboldt's commentary, to the minister of the interior for his feedback on the subject of the utilitarian and commercial benefits of bringing llamas and alpacas into France.[48] As shown in a later chapter, this information would help to pave the way for France's nineteenth-century project to acclimatize alpacas nationally and internationally.

The dramatic events in the story of Josephine's camelids brought to life many elements of Candide's satirical account with which the chapter opened, most notably regarding just how complicated and expensive it could be to move a flock of animals from one continent to another. This narrative also clarifies the importance of local knowledge for the success of the project, especially because few experts outside of the Indigenous pastoral communities were familiar with the Andean camelids and the care they required. From the perspective of the present, the many twists and turns of the saga provide intriguing glimpses into further narratives and diverse protagonists who worked at the margins of the historical record, without whose participation the venture in all likelihood would have failed. For example, little is known of the "negros" who had the task of domesticating the vicuñas in Lima or the two Indians who were supposed to accompany the group all the way to Spain. In contrast to (European) protagonists, like Empress Josephine Bonaparte, who would gain international acclaim and status as heroes for their work bringing large flocks of camelids out of the Andes, García, the modest postal worker, receded completely from the record after the ship set sail from Buenos Aires, despite his dedication for more than five years to seeing the project through to the end. The ever-changing and always fragile international alliances had an obvious impact on the experiment, even as the information gleaned from reports such as Terán's circulated with few impediments across borders. As later chapters explore, this first significant flock that arrived in Europe generated hope that useful animals could be extracted successfully, moved from one place to another, and eventually transformed into objects of commerce, despite the great human, animal, and financial cost such projects entailed.

CHAPTER 4

The Science of Acclimatization

Llamas and Alpacas in Nineteenth-Century France

In our Alps, in our Pyrenees, . . . there are places that approximate the conditions of the llama and alpaca's habitat. There would, therefore, be areas for them, all prepared by nature. But science has the right to go further. From these first locations, man could, if necessary, bring [the animals] down to lower regions, and, over time, to the plains. This is what happened in the past for our sheep and goats, whose ancestors also lived in the high mountains. Like that of those ruminants, the expansion of the llama and the alpaca across the surface of the globe may have, over time, no limits other than those of our needs.

Geoffroy Sainte-Hilaire ([1861] 1986, 27–28)

Although efforts to promote the extraction of Andean camelids prior to the mid-nineteenth century had largely been unsuccessful, European scientists and entrepreneurs refused to give up on the idea that the animals could make an important addition to global economies. Reports about the Cádiz animals and other hybridization projects fueled hopes that the fragile vicuña could successfully be crossed with the alpaca or llama to create a more robust, yet quality hybrid able to withstand a transoceanic voyage.[1] In the 1850s plans dedicated to moving sizable numbers of camelids to areas with climatic and geographic conditions roughly similar to those of the Andes formed the centerpiece of France and England's transoceanic projects to acclimatize "exotic" plants and animals within their national boundaries as well as in their colonies.

In general terms, "acclimatization" described the process whereby these so-called exotic organisms were transferred from one place to another and subsequently "naturalized" or "domesticated" to their new environment

126 | Llamas beyond the Andes

(Osborne 2000, 137). The term, which originated in late eighteenth-century France and found its way into England by the 1820s, highlighted the role played by climate and the social and natural environments in the adaptability of plants and animals to new settings and cultural and economic roles.[2] French zoologist Isidore Geoffroy Saint-Hilaire, the acclaimed director of the menagerie affiliated with Paris's National Museum of Natural History (1838–1861) and first president of the Société Zoologique d'Acclimatation (Acclimatization Society, 1854–1861), outlined the dynamic between the scientific and cultural essentials of acclimatization. A specimen transported to another country and thus "outside its natural harmonies" could be considered successfully acclimatized once it had become accustomed to "the new conditions of existence" and had "fallen into harmony with them" (Geoffroy Saint-Hilaire [1861] 1986, 255).[3]

Acclimatization projects went hand in hand with colonial expansion and neo-ecological imperialism. Kew Gardens outside London and the National Museum of Natural History in Paris were the primary forces or "hubs in the wheels of international scientific exchange and colonial agriculture" (Osborne 2000, 136). Acclimatization societies were formed in both countries and elsewhere by naturalists, members of the aristocracy, colonial authorities, merchants, landowners, and others (135). These organizations promoted a "practical approach to science, one promising economic prosperity, improved diets and health, and aesthetic enjoyment" (136). Indeed, science was supposed to serve economic needs and foster the development of agriculture and commerce (Lever 1992, 7). Within a year after the formation of the Paris Acclimatization Society in 1854, regional societies began to form in Grenoble and Nancy. By the early 1860s France had thirty-nine scientific institutions and five colonial acclimatization societies, while twenty-four foreign scientific institutions also came under the aegis of France (4).

Although Paris was the center of a large interconnecting network and the site of encounter and discussion, the study of acclimatization by its very nature crossed national and continental boundaries (Aragón 2005, 60). And while Paris and London may have been focal points, other European countries as well as scientific elites in Latin America and elsewhere participated in acclimatization projects, developing their own strategies of experimentation that made use of different cultural perspectives and scientific traditions (62).

From the start, the Paris Acclimatization Society enthusiastically promoted the idea of obtaining Andean camelids. As outlined in the chapter epigraph, the society anticipated that they could be domesticated in rural, economically depressed areas such as the more remote mountainous regions of the country and provide a welcome source of meat and fiber. The project generated such excitement that Émile Deville (1854, 3), who had formed part of Francis de Castelnau's 1843 expedition to South America and had seen the animals in their natural habitat, declared that the introduction of the alpaca would usher in a new era, a veritable renaissance for France's agriculture. Nicolas Joly, professor of zoology at the University of Toulouse and the Toulouse delegate to the Paris Acclimatization Society, provocatively suggested that the famous chicken in every pot, which Henry IV envisioned French peasants enjoying on Sundays, might actually be a llama (Joly 1854, 10). Because the llama and its fellow creatures (*congénères*) could provide labor as beasts of burden, fiber, meat, and perhaps even milk, Geoffroy Saint-Hilaire placed the camelids at the top of his list of useful animals that ought to be brought to France, claiming that *"their husbandry is destined to create sources of wealth in places that are completely lacking in this regard today"* ([1861] 1986, 32; emphasis in the original). Based on the successes that Europe had already achieved in acclimatizing sheep and goats, he fully believed that it would not be long before the expansion of the llama and the alpaca reached all across France and even the rest of the globe (27–28).

This chapter examines France's imperial history of acclimatization as it impacted on camelid-related ventures by taking up three case studies that emerge from separate spaces of encounter. The studies elucidate specific facets of the enterprise, such as how projects were funded and animals obtained, and foreground the diversity of individuals and groups that became involved with these imperial exchanges. As with previous chapters, these examples dramatize the challenges entailed in acquiring camelids and keeping them safe and healthy during the shipping process and later on as they adapted to new environments. The first case study looks at how the Paris Acclimatization Society incentivized and sponsored multiple actors to collaborate on transoceanic camelid projects, giving prominence to Frenchman Eugène Roehn, who played an unparalleled part on an international scale in the extraction of four flocks of llamas and alpacas. Although today his name is largely forgotten, Roehn embodied the aspirations and disappointments embedded in the acclimatization process and is exemplary for crafting a unique discourse of heroism around himself and his exploits. Yet, even as he repeatedly highlighted his courageous dedication to bringing camelids out of the Andes in the face of

128 | *Llamas beyond the Andes*

countless difficulties, including hostile Indigenous pastoral communities who refused to sell their animals, Roehn also admitted that the success of the enterprise depended on the collaboration, knowledge, and expertise of a few Indian shepherds, two of whom accompanied him to Paris. Their story, however, remains almost entirely eclipsed by Roehn's personal narrative, only emerging from the archival record in fragments, most notably when official accounts assigned blame to them for the eventual failure of his last project.

The second case history continues the story of camelid acclimatization by turning to Ecuador. President Gabriel García Moreno offered a flock of llamas to Emperor Napoleon III and the Paris Acclimatization Society in 1862. This gift brings attention to the decisive role played by creole actors in global exchange networks and illustrates how such gestures served strategic political as well as scientific objectives. García Moreno's offer breathed new life into France's efforts to acclimatize camelids following the demise of Roehn's flock and helped solidify French protection of Ecuador at a time when the Andean nation was rocked by internal conflict and threats from Peru to the south. The case study follows the animals' journey to France on board two French warships, where they were tended to by crew members. The captains maintained daily logs on the llamas, providing evidence of the captains' and sailor-shepherds' awareness of their instrumental role collecting and recording knowledge about the animals in the context of the transoceanic voyage. This unprecedented account-keeping of the lives of the animals while in transit facilitated the sharing of the information gained with the Paris Acclimatization Society and other national and international scientific communities upon landing.

The third case study follows the archival trail of llamas and alpacas that survived the journey overseas and were subsequently moved into new social, cultural, and physical environments in the Vosges mountains, the French Alps, and the Pyrenees, where they became exotic attractions and even cherished additions to one rural community. It documents how, in the interests of facilitating the llama's full integration into France's pastoral economies, local enthusiasts of one region even proposed a new, more Gallic-sounding vocabulary with which to refer to male and female llamas and their offspring. Finally, to illustrate the varied spaces and roles the llamas inhabited, this case study considers the histories of a few specific animals, including their rise to celebrity status, their deaths, and their subsequent afterlives as museum artifacts.

The three particular cases on camelid acclimatization emerge from nineteenth-century French popular magazines and scientific journals, such as the *Bulletin de la Société Zoologique d'Acclimatation* (Paris), the main serial for the Paris Acclimatization Society; the journals of regional acclimatization societies; and archival documents. Articles by international proponents of acclimatization and observations and reports on the animals by travelers from different countries were translated into French and circulated in this periodical press. These records are significant because they substantiate the colonizing process underlying acclimatization and animal extraction. Making use of scientific, biographical, and travel-adventure genres to circulate new reports and evidence, they invited readers to share from a safe distance the wonder and dangers of camelid extraction and even to feel as if they formed part of the Andean expeditions (see Lightman 2000, 2–10). When examined in combination today, therefore, these articles and manuscripts provide insight into the trajectory of France's camelid acclimatization projects: from the initial enthusiasm and excitement regarding the animals in the early 1840s and the role it was hoped that they would play in the nation's agricultural economy and elsewhere, to the eventual failure and abandonment of the experiment by the early 1870s. Notably, as the chapter shows, the same record verifies the large numbers of camelid fatalities that occurred throughout the extraction and acclimatization process.

Case History 1: The Paris Acclimatization Society and Eugène Roehn's Collaborative Project to Acquire Llamas and Alpacas

From its formation in 1854, the Paris Zoological Acclimatization Society's objectives focused on the naturalization of valuable plants and animals in France and elsewhere. Within two years it had raised nearly 12,000 francs to fund acclimatization projects. Members hoped that these monies would make it possible to prioritize the plan to import alpacas and llamas into France, along with a few other fiber animals and silkworms (*Bulletin de la Société* [1857], 39). To further these goals, the society organized prizes and designed gold and silver medals, such as the one pictured in figure 4.1, worth varying amounts of money, to be awarded to those individuals who played leading roles in acclimatization ventures. As expressed in the image of the medal's face, the society, represented by the figure of a woman, occupies the focal point, highlighting its role as a creator of north/

FIGURE 4.1. *Silver medal awarded to Charles Ledger by the Paris Acclimatization Society in 1860. "Medals awarded to Charles Ledger for his experiments with the alpaca, 1860–1862." Reference code: 888187. Item 01: Société Impériale d'Acclimatation (R332 no. 1). Mitchell Library, State Library of New South Wales (Sydney). Photograph by the author.*

south commercial networks and as a facilitator in the collection of animals, plants, and knowledge. To her left and serving as steadfast support, the medal depicts the successful history of acclimatization of animals like the horse, ox, sheep, and chicken. To her right are the animals to which the society aspires: she beckons to welcome the West African ass, yak, New World partridge, and alpaca. In the background, behind these eagerly anticipated creatures, a ship sails toward the society, underscoring the imperial roots of the new undertaking (*Bulletin de la Société* [1856]: 54–55n1).

The society designated its first prize for the introduction of a flock of pure alpacas into the mountains of Europe or Algeria. Henri Aucapitaine, of the French army in Algeria, outlined useful acclimatization projects for the colony in 1855. He especially hoped to introduce the llama, believing it to be ideal for incursions into Algeria's Atlas Mountains. As a beast of burden, the llama could assist with the extraction of minerals or more generally aid travelers across the difficult terrain, thereby serving as a valuable counterpart to the camel. Although useful on the low plains, camels could not perform well in the mountains, at times even becoming a hindrance there for the French troops (*Bulletin de la Société* [1855], 117–118). The Paris society's award for the introduction of alpacas was an example of the kind of institutional support provided for such colonial endeavors.

The award stipulated that the herd must consist of a minimum of three males and nine females and that the individual who successfully headed the venture would receive a medal worth 2,000 francs (*Bulletin de la Société* [1857], xxii). Carlos III, king of Spain, became the first to be presented the society's gold medal in 1857 for the acclimatization of a

The Science of Acclimatization | 131

small flock of thirteen llamas and alpacas at Aranjuez.[4] In his enthusiastic report to the Rewards Commission, Geoffroy Saint-Hilaire praised Spain for having already carried out the greatest feat of acclimatization that the world had yet seen with the introduction of many animals (including the horse, sheep, cow, pig, and chicken) into the Americas. In the imperial neo-ecological rhetoric of the time, he argued that it was fitting that now Spain, in return, should receive valuable camelids for its mountainous regions (*Bulletin de la Société* [1858], lxxxi). Spain, however, would not have succeeded in this endeavor without several important intervening agents. The llamas and alpacas had been presented to the Crown as a gift from Havana's Sociedad Real de Fomento (Royal Development Society), but they had been brought from the Andes to Cuba and sold to the society by French *voyageur naturaliste* (naturalist-explorer) Eugène Roehn.

Born in Paris in 1806, Roehn commenced his travels soon after completing high school, spending time first in Louisiana and Egypt and later exploring in Europe. He left again for the New World in the early 1830s, where, according to his account, he already had the idea that alpacas should be brought to Europe. After returning from these initial voyages, he began planning in earnest to introduce alpacas into France and elsewhere.[5] In his writings on the subject, Roehn presented himself as the person best qualified to undertake this project because he had studied equine medicine and hygiene at Saumur, the site of France's famed cavalry academy (Roehn and Barthélemy-Lapommeraye 1848a, 13, 1848b, 11), presumably implying that this knowledge could be transferred to camelids. In all, Roehn made several trips to South America bioprospecting for llamas and alpacas on behalf of different individuals and organizations. His accounts of this work help us map the different nineteenth-century commercial routes along which the animals traveled, from the Andes to the Caribbean, to Europe, and to Australia.

Roehn first began collaborating on a project to import llamas and alpacas into the south of France in the 1840s with his colleague Christophe Jérôme Barthélemy-Lapommeraye, then director of Marseille's Museum of Natural History. The two men drafted an ambitious plan to acquire alpacas and llamas by creating an association of the fourteen departments of the south of France, including Algeria and Corsica. According to the proposal's key points, each participating department would pay a hefty subscription to finance the purchase of a flock of 350 animals, composed ideally of one male for every eight females. The money would cover travel expenses for those participating in the expedition, including two Andean shepherds

132 | *Llamas beyond the Andes*

who would care for the animals on the return trip.[6] Back in France, the surviving alpacas and llamas would be divided among the contributing departments (Roehn and Barthélemy-Lapommeraye 1848a, 9–13).

Drawing from his previous explorations of South America, Roehn mapped a northern itinerary, up South America's west coast and across the Isthmus of Panama. While not the first to suggest this route as a possibility for transporting camelids out of South America, Roehn and Barthélemy-Lapommeraye were the first to plan for its implementation. Barthélemy-Lapommeraye cautioned potential subscribers that, although shorter in distance than shipping the animals around Cape Horn, this journey too would be fraught. The Isthmus of Panama, like the Suez, made for difficult crossing, creating "intolerable nightmares" for the modern "spirit of navigation, industry, and commerce" (Barthélemy-Lapommeraye 1847, 213). Roehn likely opted for this route because he had explored the Isthmus of Panama extensively in search of the best passage connecting the Pacific and Atlantic oceans. He wrote a comprehensive description of the entire area as well as of the Chocó region from the perspective of its natural history and resources.[7] Before the construction of the railroad in 1855, crossing the isthmus required a few days of difficult going. Roehn planned for the expedition to travel by land to Cruces, a trip that would take approximately twenty-five to thirty hours. The animals would then be loaded onto canoes or rafts and sent down the Chagres River to the port of the same name. From there, a chartered ship would transport them to France (214).

In one spirited essay on the proposal, Barthélemy-Lapommeraye (1847, 211) urged his compatriots to join the subscription venture, making a number of exaggerated claims no doubt designed to fuel patriotic support for the project. One that stands out was his assertion that Scotland, thanks to a special expedition sent to Peru, allegedly had acquired more than six thousand perfectly acclimatized vicuñas, alpacas, and llamas. France could not remain behind; the moment had come to act on this alpaca project: "Famine, with its hideous procession, has just knocked at our doors" (218–219), he reminded his readers, referring to the disastrous period in much of northern Europe known today as the "hungry forties." Although starvation had been held at bay in France, it continued to threaten from a distance. Moreover, furnishing the country with new and productive animal species that could feed and clothe people cheaply would be the most efficient way to provide jobs and double the country's productive forces.

According to Roehn and Barthélemy-Lapommeraye's calculations, the total cost for the entire undertaking would come to the enormous sum of 112,000–117,600 francs, requiring a contribution of 8,000 francs for each department. While acknowledging its high price, the authors contended that the enterprise was grounded in a patriotic spirit. If enough associates agreed to participate, they felt certain that within the short span of ten years the animals would "conquer" France in its entirety (Roehn and Barthélemy-Lapommeraye 1848a, 5, 11, 13).

In the end, although Roehn and Barthélemy-Lapommeraye's expensive venture received support from many principals of France's scientific community, their initial proposal never got off the ground. Notwithstanding this failure, the project represented a significant example of the relationship between camelid extraction and imperial power. It introduced rhetorical strategies that promoted national collaboration and cautioned against the threat of international competition that Roehn would employ in his later writings on the subject. The successful introduction of camelids required cooperation among different entities—in this case, the fourteen departments. The two entrepreneurs deliberately raised fears that France risked falling behind Britain if it did not take advantage of this unique opportunity that they presented. Finally, the venture correctly predicted some of the complexities that such a project would entail, especially with regard to the large sums of money it would cost.

Undeterred by this setback, Roehn resolved to bring llamas and alpacas out of the Andes and sell small flocks to interested scientific societies. Barthélemy-Lapommeraye reported to the Paris Acclimatization Society in 1858 that his colleague had successfully transported two sets of llamas and alpacas out of the Andes. He deposited the first set in Havana (1856) and the second in New York City (1857).[8] Roehn claimed to have over three hundred animals remaining in the Andes and proposed to bring a flock to France, an offer that the Society's Council took under consideration (*Bulletin de la Société* [1858], 223).

Roehn's Undertaking to Bring Camelids to France

While Roehn worked to transport his first two lots of camelids out of Peru and on to Havana and New York City, the Paris Acclimatization Society's interest in collecting information on the animals' behavior, natural history, and health and welfare intensified, as the members contemplated

134 | Llamas beyond the Andes

bringing a flock to France. The society had followed Roehn's endeavors and in 1859 awarded him the Premiere First Class Silver Medal for introducing camelids to the world. From the beginning, Roehn had offered his assistance and was prepared to deliver a hundred animals to France for the society. Given earlier costly failures attempting to introduce llamas and alpacas into the country, the society had been reticent to risk its funds for such a venture. Now, however, its finances had improved: the project to bring the animals into France once again came under consideration (*Bulletin de la Société* [1859], lxxx–lxxxi, 113–114).

Previous acclimatization projects of llamas and alpacas undertaken at Versailles in 1851 and at the menagerie of Paris's National Museum of Natural History in 1845–1854 (Geoffroy Saint-Hilaire ([1861] 1986, 335–340) aided the understanding of the many challenges involved in obtaining the animals and keeping them healthy in their new surroundings. Familiar with this history, the commission appointed by the Acclimatization Society to study Roehn's latest proposal expressed concern over the amount of money this venture would cost. Nonetheless, convinced of its importance, the commission recommended that the society move forward with the offer but not commit full payment until the animals had reached France safely. The proposal presented to Roehn in 1859 stipulated that he would deliver twenty pure alpacas and ten vicuñas to France within twelve to eighteen months. Hoping that this flock would provide the basis for a growing alpaca-vicuña fiber industry, the commission instructed that the animals should preferably be between the ages of three to four years old, of good conformation, and suitable for reproduction (*Bulletin de la Société* [1859], 115–116). All the camelids were to be branded with the society's mark: a star on the left cheek (Macé 1859, 236). The commission claimed the right to reject any animals that did not meet the requirements; if none were suitable, all could be refused. Any individual or organization wishing to participate and receive animals would have to agree to these same conditions (*Bulletin de la Société* [1859], 116).

As deliberations with the Acclimatization Society continued, Roehn addressed one of its sessions in February 1859 on the subject of the camelids, highlighting his knowledge of the Andes and expertise in the natural history and care of the animals. He described his various travels across the region, recounting how he reconnoitered at the foot of the famous Chimborazo volcano in 1856 with a herd of 117 alpacas, llamas, and guanacos and a second time in 1857 with 103 animals (Roehn 1859, 139). By referencing his exploits in the shadow of the mountain, Roehn created an

The Science of Acclimatization | 135

unmistakable association between himself and other celebrated scientific travelers who had described their journeys to the magnificent volcano. This connection was made even more explicit several months later, when the popular weekly publication *L'Illustration* (Paris) included a story on Roehn's many adventures in the Andes: his proposal to bring alpacas to the Paris Acclimatization Society had been accepted by then, and he had already arrived in South America.[9] The article dedicated as much space to Roehn's frustrated attempt to reach the summit of the volcano and his measurement of distances and comparison of approach routes along the mountain's base as it did to the acquisition of the animals (Macé 1859, 234–236). The tenor of the article undoubtedly encouraged the reader to compare Roehn, until then a figure unknown to the general public, with the famous Prussian traveler and natural historian Alexander von Humboldt.[10]

Chimborazo had reached iconic status in Europe by 1859, thanks in large part to Humboldt's writings and drawings as well as illustrations and articles published in journals with a wide readership.[11] This was also the year that Fredric Church's celebrated landscape painting *Heart of the Andes* created an overnight sensation in Europe and the Americas.[12] The work portrays men, plants, and animals as eclipsed by the sheer power and immensity of the snow-covered volcano but nevertheless emphasizes a general state of harmony between humans and nature. Church's striking image communicated as no other could the perceived ability of landscape painting to capture Humboldt's theory of aesthetics: the unity of scientific knowledge and art, such that a "great landscape painter is the highest servant of both nature and the human mind" (Gould 2000, 33; see also Manthorne 1989, 100–101).

Theodore Winthrop's pamphlet that accompanied Church's painting lauded the Edenic qualities of this luminous Andean landscape: "When our mortal nature is dazzled and wearied with too long gazing on the golden mount, where silence dwells and glory lingers longer than the day, we may descend to the Arcadian levels of the Llano at the *Heart of the Andes*. . . . Perpetual spring reigns. . . . Life here may be a sweet idyll" (quoted in Manthorne 1989, 11). As these examples suggest, by 1859 (the year Roehn was featured in *L'Illustration*) Chimborazo, with its celebrity status, had become an internationally renowned icon of a South American landscape where science and aesthetics came together peacefully, united in their "sweet idyll."

The iconic forms of landscape painting also gave shape to the imperial economy of acclimatization in the camelid contact zone. C. Macé's

136 | Llamas beyond the Andes

FIGURE 4.2. *"Halte de M. Roehn et des Indiens de sa suite au pied du Chimborazo: D'après des dessins de M. Roehn."* L'Illustration: Journal Universel 33 (January–June 1859), 236.

article on Roehn in *L'Illustration* included an image by the French artist and engraver Jules Worms (figure 4.2), which captured the drama of Roehn's enterprise as it unfolded in the shadow of the volcano. Based on a sketch by Roehn, this engraving takes inspiration from the aesthetic discourse of landscape painting but with important transformations. We still find a harmonious scene at the foot of the volcano, but now it is a harmony of utilitarian activity harnessed and set into motion in the name of a practical and applied science. Roehn, the intrepid *voyageur naturaliste*, is depicted as a towering presence in the foreground, taking on a heroic stature that mirrors that of Chimborazo in the background. Claiming center stage, he stands out from the Indigenous shepherds accompanying him, in part because he is fully clad in Western-style clothing and appears to be the only one carrying a rifle. His left foot gently lifts off the ground, symbolically referencing his movement forward with the plan to bring a new industry to France. Lara (1986a) aptly describes Roehn's stance in this

The Science of Acclimatization | 137

engraving as that of a mythological giant or an enigmatic Moses, gesturing with his right hand toward an unknown promised land.

Like a conductor with his arm lifted and finger pointing, Roehn directs the activities taking place around him and carried out by the shepherds, performing the intersection of science and colonialism. The narrative frame of the image celebrates Roehn's work, translates it into a pictorial form that is easily comprehended by a French audience, and thus popularizes empire (see Safier 2010a, 138–139; Sivasundaram 2010, 154). This heroic narrative depicts one way in which science "provided a language of command," offering a visual vocabulary "for othering, racializing, and gendering peoples across imperial realms" (Sivasundaram 2010, 154). At the same time, as Safier (2010a, 138–139) reminds us more generally, a visual document such as this, even while it expresses admiration for Roehn and his exploits, can also be instrumental in bringing to light unanticipated and nontraditional actors. Although relegated to the margins of the image, the seminaked, muscular Indians still maintain a significant presence in the image's visual economy. They carry out a multitude of tasks, including childcare, underscoring how knowledge practices are co-constructed in this Andean camelid contact zone.[13]

This imperial neo-ecological image of a paradisiacal and abundant Andean nature ready for the taking did not remain intact for long. Roehn discovered upon arrival in Peru that the country was at war internally and externally, with Bolivia. The prolonged sojourn of a stranger crossing between the two republics who did not want to explain his activities created an aura of suspicion about him. He was accused on both sides of the border of spying for the other republic. After many difficulties, including being jailed for fourteen days in Peru, he eventually managed to reach La Paz. There, he met with Bolivian president José María Linares, who authorized the extraction of a flock of llamas and alpacas on behalf of the French Acclimatization Society (Roehn 1860, 498–499).

Scientists and the general public who perused Roehn's published letter telling of the dangers and uncertainties involved in seeking camelids (Roehn 1860) could find numerous literary devices borrowed from travel narratives and biography through which he constructed an image of himself as an intrepid and courageous adventurer. By detailing the many misfortunes he faced, he created tension and expectancy in his readers, appealed to their imaginations, and encouraged them to feel like they were co-participants in the venture (see Lightman 2000, 2–13). Like other heroic narratives, his story necessarily involved antagonists, which in this

138 | Llamas beyond the Andes

case included Indigenous pastoral communities. Roehn discovered that in times of conflict the Bolivian military government had the right to confiscate all livestock except for the camelids. Unsurprisingly, pastoral communities and households refused to sell or make any exchanges with him, regardless of the prices he offered (Roehn 1860, 499).

President Linares's permission for the project, granted back in La Paz, held no sway over the Andean communities with which Roehn came in contact. Moreover, at this time, Linares was laying the groundwork for what would later become a full-fledged assault on Indigenous territory. Andean communities around Lake Titicaca were prepared to respond with violence, if necessary, in the effort to stop incursions by large landholders, local authorities, and others (Calderón Jemio 1991).[14] In the political climate where Andean territory and resources were coming under increasing pressure from the government, it could be anticipated that few would be willing to sell valuable resources like the camelids to a stranger. Also, as Roehn (1860, 499) observed, the Indians were fully aware that by letting the animals out of the country they risked losing competitive advantage in the fiber market and could be forced to sell their product at much lower prices to the merchant houses in Tacna and Arica.

After unsuccessfully combing the region around Lake Titicaca, Roehn resolved to move closer to the border to be able to pass quickly from one side to the other and thus acquire the animals that he needed "at any price and by any means possible" (Roehn 1860, 499). Nevertheless, it was not until he met a local priest from Santiago de Machaca that his fortune changed. Learning that Roehn had received the government's permission to extract a small flock of llamas and alpacas, the priest agreed to help him obtain the animals (499–500). Serving as Roehn's intermediary with nearby Indigenous communities with whom he had an established relationship of mutual respect (according to Roehn), the priest somehow acquired a flock of 128 alpacas and llamas for Roehn to purchase. Thanks to this intervention, Roehn was able to hire an unspecified number of men, presumably Bolivian shepherds, to assist him. Without the priest's involvement on his behalf, it is likely that Roehn would have returned to Paris empty-handed.

Prior to his travels to the altiplano, Roehn had contracted with the Pacific Steam Navigation Company for a ship capable of transporting the animals to France. However, after he and his group reached Tacna, he discovered that the agreement made with the prefect of Arica to extract the alpacas and llamas had fallen through. Due to a treaty of commerce

The Science of Acclimatization | 139

between Peru and Bolivia ("Chronique de l'Amérique Latine" 1861, 272), the prefect refused to give permission to let the flock out, simultaneously issuing the order to seize any animals found. Forced to smuggle the animals out of the country, Roehn now had to make new plans in all haste. Moving as rapidly as possible, the men and animals made the journey to the coast in four days across the dry desert, from Tacna to Morro de Sama, with neither water nor food for the animals. With the previous plan canceled and blockades set by Peru along the Bolivian border, which prevented their crossing, Roehn had little time to arrange for a new, appropriately fitted ship to be waiting for them at the mouth of the Sama river. The *Rayo*, a 136-ton brig captained by Édouard Marchand, was ill prepared to receive the animals, in part because it lacked the necessary ballast and therefore had poor stability and was hampered in its movement. Nor did they have enough food and water for the journey to Panama (Roehn 1860, 500–501).

Adding to an already difficult situation, the experience of loading the animals onto the ship was harrowing for all. The animals had not had anything to drink for four days and were exhausted by the rushed trip. The men had to carry the animals on their shoulders through the surf and across sharp and slippery algae-covered rocks, with the swell threatening to knock them over at any moment. They worked as quickly as possible, fearing that they had been followed on their route and at any moment could be shot or detained and imprisoned. Despite the need for an urgent departure, the ship remained for a day off the coast to make needed repairs before taking leave (Roehn 1860, 501).

The journey to Panama was equally desperate because the animals had little food and water and there was no place to put in before the port of Tumaco in New Granada (Colombia). Sailors made further repairs to the ship there and loaded much-needed supplies in preparation for the approach to the large bay of Panama. The animals suffered terribly in the meantime, having to endure five days in the hot sun and torrential downpours of the Chocó region. In one day alone, they lost nine animals (Roehn 1860, 501–502).

Thirty-one days after having left Peru, the ship finally reached Panama. The men unloaded the animals on July 20, 1860, and the next morning placed them in cattle cars for transportation by rail across the sixty-mile isthmus.[15] As soon as the retinue reached the east coast, the flock was loaded immediately onto the steamer *Plantagenet* of Liverpool, which was already heating up to depart. The steamer set out before Roehn could

140 | *Llamas beyond the Andes*

load barley for the animals, the skins of the animals that had died, and cases containing grains and tubers that he had collected on his journey through the Andes and hoped to donate to the Paris Acclimatization Society. Despite the terrible rush to board the animals, Roehn felt certain that not one would have survived if they had remained any longer in the heavy rains and heat of Colón (Roehn 1860, 502–503).

By the time Roehn and his group reached the French port of Bordeaux, the original flock from Bolivia—108 alpacas, 20 llamas, and 2 vicuñas—had been reduced to 35 alpacas, 9 llamas, and 1 vicuña (Roehn 1860, 503). They were received by several representatives of the Acclimatization Society charged with providing a report on the state of the surviving animals and determining whether they met the society's requirements (*Bulletin de la Société* [1860], 474, 509). Frédéric Davin, member of the Alpaca Commission and delegate of the society's Administrative Council, examined the animals and concluded that they appeared to meet the prescribed conditions. He found the surviving flock to be in reasonable health despite the difficulties of the lengthy journey. Six animals, however, showed signs of a skin infection around their heads and tails, owing to their long sojourn at sea. The veterinarian of the village and the municipal stables prescribed a treatment to be administered by the two Bolivian Indians who had accompanied Roehn from the Andes (*Bulletin de la Société* [1860], 509–510).

The alpacas' arrival created a sensation not only in France but also in England and Australia. Their story was followed with great interest, notably because both places were attempting similar camelid acclimatization projects. The *Manchester Times* (October 13, 1860) carried a story written by a Paris correspondent who described his visit to see the new inhabitants of the Bois de Boulogne acclimatization gardens, where the animals were placed after delivery to Paris:

> Before reaching the central building at the extremity of the garden, my attention was attracted by a park containing about fifty alpacas, from Peru. This is the leading novelty of the exhibition. There has never before been seen in Europe such a collection of these animals, whose woollen hair, or hairy wool, has of late assumed such an important place in our manufactures. There was much difficulty in getting them over, and very many of their companions died on the voyage. I can certify, however, that those who fortunately arrived in safety seem to be thoroughly acclimatised; they look in

The Science of Acclimatization | 141

excellent condition, and were browsing away with a healthy appetite on the nice short grass provided for them in the gardens. They are handsome animals, nearly twice as big as an ordinary sheep, and with longer legs; but, speaking as an ordinary observer and with submission to naturalists, they seem to me of the ovine species. The flock of them is a most picturesque object, the variety of colour being as great as in a bed of dahlias or China-asters. There are black, white, grey, red, chocolate colour, and pied varieties of every description. If they can really be acclimatised in Europe for any practical purpose, there is no doubt that a most important addition in manufacturing wealth will have been achieved. There is no time to be lost, if it be true, as I hear, that the breed is fast dying out in South America.

The correspondent's description captured the excitement caused by the animals' arrival and lingered on their "exotic" ovine-like appearance, reminding readers today of the confusion surrounding their classification, which persisted well into the late nineteenth century. Although the correspondent utilized sheep as a recognizable point of reference when describing their shape and size, he resorted to a different sort of comparison when commenting on what really stood out for him: the picturesque quality of their varied colors. More like a bed of exotic flowers than animals, their wide range of colors was stunning to nonspecialist eyes. By associating the animals with China-asters, which had only recently been acclimatized successfully in Europe at the time of the article, the author subtly reinforced the possibility and promise of acclimatization more generally and led the reader to hope that these animals, like the dahlias, might similarly become a fixture of the local landscape.[16] He reframed this point with urgency toward the end of the article by claiming that the animals were "fast dying out in South America." This idea was undoubtedly influenced by European and creole claims that the alpaca was being used indiscriminately for food and that the vicuña was under pressure in its native habitat from overhunting and on the verge of disappearance.[17] Perhaps more to the point, using Roehn's numbers as indicators of the camelids' rate of survival while being transported overseas, it became evident that the animals did not fare well in transoceanic acclimatization efforts.

The animals were to remain at the Bois de Boulogne for a few weeks so that they could recover from the voyage before being sent on to their final destinations. Geoffroy Saint-Hilaire planned to send six alpacas and

142 | *Llamas beyond the Andes*

llamas to the emperor; others were to go to the Acclimatization Society of the Alps and to the banker James de Rothschild, who had agreed to finance some of the costs and risks of the expedition. The remaining few camelids would join a group of animals, mainly yaks and angora goats, kept for reproduction in the Cantal department (*Bulletin de la Société* [1860], 430, 475).

Unfortunately, however, by the end of October all the animals suffered from a contagious skin disease that threatened to decimate the flock. To combat it, the llamas and alpacas had to be sheared so that their skin could be treated, delaying their journey to the mountains, where colder temperatures prevailed. None of the animals were to be dispersed until they had healed completely (*Bulletin de la Société* [1860], 564). The effects of the late-season shearing were disastrous, even though their caretaker protected the animals with double blankets. The camelids became increasingly weak. Due to the advancing season and insufficient personnel and accommodations, all but seven died within a short time, and those seven lingered in a terrible state. The surviving animals were moved to a shelter in early November and furnished with a stove that burned day and night. Their shepherd moved his bed into the same stable so that he could keep watch over them, treating the animals' diarrhea and weakness with laudanum enemas, fortifying drinks (rice water, quinine extract, flax-seed water), a rich diet of hay and alfalfa, small quantities of mixed oats and bran, and eventually carrots (*Bulletin de la Société* [1863], 2–3, 5).

To counter the disease's advance, the llamas and alpacas received regular baths of warm soapy water, followed by treatments with specialized pomades. As the weather improved, the animals were permitted to go outside and graze for short periods. Despite this care, the skin disease did not disappear completely; therefore arsenic baths were added to their regimen in May 1861. These treatments appeared to clear up the skin infections. By the time warmer weather arrived, the llamas and alpacas were allowed to move freely inside and outside of the stables during the day. Given their improved health, one female llama was finally sent to the Vosges; the remaining four females each gave birth to a healthy baby male llama during the summer months. Acclimatization Society member Frédéric Jacquemart declared that the value of these animals and their offspring was much greater than the total cost of their care and that the knowledge gleaned from this experience would be valuable for facilitating future efforts (*Bulletin de la Société* [1863], 3–5).

Despite the high mortality rate of Roehn's animals, the Paris Acclima-

The Science of Acclimatization | 143

tization Society voted to award him the Prix Extraordinaire, a medal worth 2,000 francs, for introducing a flock of alpacas into the country. The society reminded members of Roehn's letters describing his heroic expedition on its behalf and marveled that he had been able to bring a single animal back, given all the dangers that he had had to face (*Bulletin de la Société* [1861], lxvi–lxvii). In the meantime, Geoffroy Saint-Hilaire accompanied Roehn and the two Bolivian Indians who had come along with him from the Andes to France to meet Emperor Napoleon III in 1861. According to Roehn, the emperor received the two Bolivians and himself with great kindness. When asked what could be done to thank the *voyageur naturaliste*, Geoffroy Saint-Hilaire advised Roehn to put together a request for compensation to be presented to him. Unfortunately, the ensuing illness and subsequent death of Geoffroy Saint-Hilaire apparently suspended any further action. The documentation does not clarify whether the two Bolivian Indians received compensation of any kind. The last word concerning them is a brief mention by Roehn, who noted that one of the two was still living in Paris in 1867; the other had presumably returned home.[18]

In the end, Roehn's shipment of camelids to France represented a loss of more than 25,000 francs for the Acclimatization Society. The council nonetheless remained optimistic and assured members that the society's finances continued to be strong. They reminded everyone that setbacks could be expected with acclimatization experiments, even when carried out by those with experience, but the society believed in persevering in the pursuit of its priorities. Moreover, the alpaca experiment had not represented a failure in its totality. Everyone remained convinced that the acclimatization of alpacas in France was ultimately achievable (*Bulletin de la Société* [1861], lxxxvi). Roehn made one last journey to South America to attempt to bring alpacas and llamas back after the news reached France that Peru and Bolivia had both lifted their bans on exporting the animals and had permitted a flock to be shipped to Australia (Viennot 1862, 828). The president of Peru, General Miguel de San Román, had expressed the desire to pay homage to the French emperor and offered the Paris Acclimatization Society a large number of llamas and alpacas, but the agreement was plagued by a long series of delays (*Bulletin de la Société* [1863], 293). The untimely death of the general in April 1863 rendered the agreement problematic (*Bulletin de la Société* [1864], xx), and Roehn eventually returned home without the anticipated animals.[19]

Although Roehn's efforts on behalf of the Paris Acclimatization Society to extract camelids from the Andes for introduction into France had

144 | Llamas beyond the Andes

only mixed success, his story is instructive in understanding some of the challenges such imperial exchanges faced. Even the supportive infrastructure of money and prizes put into place by the French government and the Acclimatization Society was not enough to overcome the problems inherent in the camelid venture's imperial foundations. The camelids were largely acquired without the collaboration of Indigenous pastoral communities or full authorization on the part of Andean governments. This resulted in the animals having to be moved quickly from one place to another, with insufficient food and water, all of which impacted on their well-being and ability to survive the ordeals of transoceanic travel. While Roehn's accounts laud his own heroic feats in the camelid contact zone, they provide little information about the two Indigenous shepherds who accompanied him to Paris, on whose expertise the project relied. Even though we know almost nothing about these men, the story of Roehn's camelids enables us to imagine the kinds of challenges they faced and the pressure from expectations that they would keep the animals healthy in the most difficult conditions.

Case History 2: García Moreno and the Ecuador Shipment of Llamas and Alpacas

While the Paris Acclimatization Society awaited news from Roehn and the second shipment of alpacas from Peru, it learned that Ecuadorian president Gabriel García Moreno had offered to present to the French emperor what would become one of the most important flocks of llamas and alpacas to reach France. The story of the Ecuador camelids marks a contrast with Roehn's venture by providing a unique example of a South American government fully authorizing and taking the lead on the extraction of a small number of llamas. It highlights how such gifts could have personal and political ramifications. Because the project entailed an international collaboration, the entire process could be planned in advance. Two ships and their crews were committed to the animals' safe conveyance overseas. Given the precautions taken, it is unsurprising that in the end the animals' overall survival rate was better than that of Roehn's flock.

Throughout his life, García Moreno had maintained a strong interest in the study of natural history (Pólit Laso, 60–70). Maiguashca (2005, 236) contends that García Moreno's true passion was science: if he had been born in France, England, or the United States, he would in all likelihood

The Science of Acclimatization | 145

have become a scientist rather than a politician (a calling he believed he had a patriotic duty to follow). While president, García Moreno actively fostered interest in sericulture, pisciculture, and apiculture, hiring a French consultant to assist Ecuador in developing these fields of study. This was part of a much broader effort to institutionalize scientific investigation and technological development in the country.[20] He became a member of the Paris Acclimatization Society and arranged for his foreign minister in France and England, Antonio Flores, to pay annual dues on his behalf (Villalba F. 1976, cxxxvi–cxxxvii). Flores also followed the field of natural history. He played a significant role in the circulation of scientific knowledge between Europe and Ecuador, regularly forwarding the latest newspapers and *Bulletins* to the Ecuadorian Office of Foreign Affairs from the French Acclimatization Society and Geographical Society, in which he also was a member.[21]

The García Moreno administration wanted to participate in international debates about natural history and make Ecuador a key protagonist in the global circulation of knowledge, plants, and animals. The president collaborated with European governments by sending them numerous items reportedly of scientific interest. For example, Flores received thanks from the Spanish Embassy in Paris in 1863 for having sent Queen Isabella II the head of an Indian "mummified and shrunken by processes unknown in Europe."[22] Other offerings, such as the llamas, undoubtedly reflected political as well as scientific agendas. Due to ongoing conflicts with Peru and its attempts to annex Guayaquil and the southern coast of the country, in late 1859 García Moreno secretly approached the French government to suggest the idea of Ecuador becoming a protectorate of France. Although this initiative never went very far, two years later France agreed to prevent Peru from establishing further blockades of Guayaquil and sent a warship, "invoking a recent revision of international law that obliged the world's naval powers to intervene on behalf of a fleetless nation unjustly attacked" (Henderson 2008, 95; see also Howe 1936 and Van Aken 1989, 253–257). García Moreno initiated the gift of camelids the following year.

In a letter to Antonio Flores on May 21, 1862, the president asked his foreign minister to contact Édouard Antoine de Thouvenel, then French minister of foreign affairs, and request permission to load fifty llamas designated for the emperor on the next available French warship returning to Europe from the Pacific.[23] In his lukewarm response to García Moreno's offer, Thouvenel stated that he was too busy to follow up on the matter.[24] Flores reiterated the offer in December 1862, this time approaching

146 | *Llamas beyond the Andes*

Thouvenel's successor, Édouard Drouyn de Lhuys.[25] Drouyn de Lhuys, who at the time happened also to be president of the Acclimatization Society, invited Flores to a dinner at his home to express his appreciation for the generous offer.[26] Shortly afterward, France designated a warship in the area to transport the llamas. In a letter to his father, General Juan José Flores, Antonio Flores alluded to Ecuador's troubled relations with Peru, observing that it would be helpful to have a French warship in the Guayaquil port as the llamas were being prepared for embarkation.[27]

It took several months for the arrangements to progress. In early July 1863 García Moreno notified General Flores in Guayaquil that two French corvettes should arrive sometime during the month to take the llamas to Europe. The animals would be brought to the port at that time, after which Flores would be responsible for coordinating their loading with the French commanders (Loor 1954, 149–150, 155; Villalba F. 1976, xxxix). As García Moreno explained to his general, he planned to cover all costs involving the llamas because he considered this a personal gift to the emperor. The National Treasury, however, was responsible for the expenses resulting from the visit of the two ships.[28]

The fear that the llamas would not survive the various stages of the trip concerned everyone, including the French. One of the warship commanders voiced his apprehension that the animals would not endure the five-month navigation to France.[29] García Moreno also worried about their safety. While waiting for the ships to arrive, he wrote to thank General Flores for the care that he had taken with the llamas and to express his hope that further delay would not result in any loss.[30] It would be a misfortune if the llamas died during the voyage, but he noted that in that case he could at least show that he had fulfilled his promise to the emperor (Loor 1954, 164).[31]

If García Moreno used the llamas to serve his personal and political objectives, French scientists wanted the animals to move forward with their experiments in acclimatization. The correspondence between the Paris Acclimatization Society and other entities shows the collective nature of knowledge production and that learning about the camelids and their care was a complex process involving multiple localities. "Only through an elaborate process—both in the field and in the networks where this material circulates—does this contingent and contradictory mass of information become science. Once knowledge becomes official, the markers of its origins often become erased or at the least rewritten" (Musselman 2009, 31–32). Hoping for greater success with the incoming llamas this time,

The Science of Acclimatization | 147

one member of the Paris Acclimatization Society and director of the Jardin d'Acclimatation at the Bois de Boulogne, Étienne Rufz de Lavison, sought advice from those who had experience with all four species of the camelids. He sent a questionnaire to the directors of the zoological gardens of London, Antwerp, Cologne, Amsterdam, Brussels, Ghent, Frankfurt, Marseille, Florence, and Madrid as well as to Grenoble and the Vosges, expressing hope that information gathered from past involvements regarding the camelids' placement, diet, and reproduction would help guide new experiments once the animals arrived from Ecuador (Rufz de Lavison 1864, 331–337).

The Paris Acclimatization Society did not seek information solely from European metropolitan centers. Discovering that Antonio Flores had been called back to Quito to become minister of finance, Albert Geoffroy Saint-Hilaire, son of now deceased Isidore and assistant director of the Jardin d'Acclimatation in the Bois de Boulogne, drafted a set of questions and instructions with the title "Questionnaire et instructions sur les lamas et leur introduction," which he had forwarded to Flores (*Bulletin de la Société* [1863], 71–72, 130; Soubeiran 1864, xx, n4). Flores agreed to look after the matter personally and ensure that the animals were sent to the port of embarkation with trained shepherds who could provide directives for their care during the ocean voyage (*Bulletin de la Société* [1863], 72).

The documentation shows that even local knowledge-gathering about the camelids was a cooperative enterprise involving different groups of people with various expertise or skills. But it also points to noticeable silences or gaps in the record. For this shipment, the animals themselves and the information about their care would presumably have come from rural pastoral communities; nevertheless, their participation in the project (or lack thereof) and expertise are conspicuously absent from this record.

Other gaps in knowledge became salient as well. Upon receipt of the Acclimatization Society's questionnaire and instructions and learning that its preference was for alpacas, Flores consulted with the governor of the province of Chimborazo, the person placed in charge of obtaining the animals for García Moreno, who assured him that no alpacas were to be found in the country.[32] Amédée Fabre, French consul in Quito, followed up on this subject in a letter to Drouyn de Lhuys and the Acclimatization Society's Council, informing them that no distinction was made in Ecuador among the different kinds of camelids, according to García Moreno. In putting the herd together, emphasis instead was placed on the quality of the wool and the size and strength of the animals selected. Even so, Fabre

148 | *Llamas beyond the Andes*

planned to advise the ship commanders to pay particular attention to any alpacas that might be found in the flock: all preference should be given to preserving the alpacas in terms of the care provided at sea or if some animals had to be sacrificed (*Bulletin de la Société* [1863], 373, 518).[33]

The flock of forty-eight camelids finally shipped on the French navy ship *Galatée* in early September and headed directly for its first stop at the Peruvian port of Callao. There seventeen of the animals were transferred to a second warship, the *Cornélie*, which was en route to Toulon, while the *Galatée*'s destination was the port of Brest (*Bulletin de la Société* [1863], 625, 698). At the February 5, 1864, meeting of the Paris Acclimatization Society, the council publicly recognized García Moreno's generous gift of the flock of llamas and alpacas. Even though neither ship had yet arrived and they held little hope that the animals could survive the voyage, the members of the council nonetheless expressed appreciation to the Ecuadorian president and, at a subsequent meeting, made him an honorary member (*Bulletin de la Société* [1864], 149, viii).

Knowledge Making on the High Seas

Happily, the *Galatée* reached port on February 11 with fourteen llamas, which were to be transferred to the Jardin d'Acclimatation as soon as possible. The *Cornélie* arrived a few weeks later at Toulon with twelve animals. Of the forty-eight animals originally boarded at Guayaquil, twenty-six reached France safely, after enduring a seven-month voyage. On behalf of the Acclimatization Society, Drouyn de Lhuys gratefully acknowledged the sailors and their meticulous care of the animals while on board ship (*Bulletin de la Société* [1864], 152, 202).

Following the arrival of the Ecuadorian llamas, official reports were prepared and published in the Paris Acclimatization Society's internationally circulated *Bulletin*: by Albert Geoffroy Saint-Hilaire, describing the animals' overall condition upon disembarkation; and one by each of the two ship captains, René de Cornulier-Lucinière, the commander of the *Galatée*, and A. Lévêque, commander of the *Cornélie*. These are "composite accounts" (Duncan and Gregory 1999, 3), containing information, some of which was originally transmitted orally and later transcribed, and texts embedded within texts, such as medical statements prepared after the animals' arrival included within other reports. To a great extent, the commanders' reports were based on daily journals that the crew of both

The Science of Acclimatization | 149

ships were ordered to keep. Each journal had a separate page dedicated to a single animal on which all instructions regarding care and treatment were recorded, preserving the crew's observations and serving as memory documents (Bourguet 2010; Musselman 2009), like other travel notebooks and natural history journals. This information was subsequently passed on to the captains, who transformed the notes and daily records into the final reports.

These unique documents are among the first to communicate detailed information on the challenges involved in shipping camelids at the time and the captains' measures to forestall accidents and injuries and resolve problems that arose during the journey around Cape Horn and across the Atlantic. They also provide evidence of the high rate of animal casualties, even when the entire crew was dedicated to keeping the animals safe and healthy. Because these three reports were subsequently published in the *Bulletin*, they became public sources of information that could be consulted, annotated, and expanded upon by scientists and acclimatization societies from around the world that had interest in the extraction of camelids from the Andes.[34] These and other documents, along with the correspondence between the Paris Acclimatization Society and other entities, reveal the contingent nature of knowledge production and show that learning about the camelids and their care was a complex, commensurate process involving multiple collectives of people, including regional Ecuadorian governors, the French crew and officers, and international scientific communities. Drawing from the work of Safier (2010b, 359), I contend that the questionnaires, logs, reports, and journal publications blur "the boundaries between Atlantic worlds that are defined along linguistic or imperial lines and demonstrat[e] the importance of alternate forms of correspondence and communication in the establishment of epistemic authority."

Geoffroy Saint-Hilaire's observations included a letter from a doctor named Turrel, the delegate for the Acclimatization Society in Toulon, who had verified firsthand the precautions taken on board the *Cornélie* to ensure the animals' safety and welfare as much as possible. Noting that he did not want to suggest that the animals' circumstances on board ship had been ideal, Geoffroy Saint-Hilaire remarked on how healthy their skin was upon arrival, expressing optimism that the weakness and emaciated state resulting from the long voyage were slowly disappearing with rest, exercise, and a fortifying diet and that it would not be long before they could be sent off to various leaseholders selected by the society's council. He concluded

150 | Llamas beyond the Andes

that it was hard not to compare the state in which these animals arrived with the state of the animals in Roehn's shipment. The *Cornélie* animals showed no sign of the devastating skin disease thought to have been the cause of the decimation of Roehn's flock. A few of the animals unloaded were covered with insects, but these were dispersed with the help of insecticide, ointment, tobacco juice, and the open air (Geoffroy Saint-Hilaire 1864, 321–323).

The two ship captains' reports elucidate in detail the difficulties the crew faced in keeping the llamas out of harm's way throughout the lengthy voyage. Specific problems included identifying the safest way to load the animals, especially pregnant females; keeping track of individual animals once on board; organizing appropriate lodging for the animals; formulating a schedule for daily feeding and hygiene; preparing for adverse weather conditions; and identifying and caring for ill animals. By systemizing this information, the captains and the Paris Acclimatization Society established one model for transporting camelids that could then be shared with the wider international scientific community and consulted and modified in preparation for future shipments.

The captains and crew could also compare differences between shipping the animals as a single flock and dividing them into two smaller lots. Cornulier-Lucinière, captain of the *Galatée*, in Guayaquil was responsible for transporting the entire flock to the Peruvian port of Callao. After the *Cornélie* arrived, the two captains distributed the animals between their ships. Cornulier-Lucinière shared the information his crew had learned about the animals during the first leg of the trip with his counterpart Captain Lévêque in response to the situations and concerns already described and communicated their system of maintenance and record keeping. For example, to protect the animals during the loading process, Cornulier-Lucinière had sailors carry each llama individually in their arms, taking extra precautions with the females because many were pregnant. Once on board, he registered the name of every animal and gave it a number so that daily observations could be recorded consistently. He had been unable to locate any "mountain shepherds" willing to accompany the animals on board ship in Guayaquil. As he explained in the report, however, he did not regret the lack of Indigenous experts because the French sailors willingly accepted responsibility for the animals' care. Many of these men came from rural backgrounds and were accustomed to caring for livestock: they took pride in the collective effort to bring the animals safely to France (Cornulier-Lucinière 1864, 394).

The Science of Acclimatization | 151

Placement on the ship was one significant factor that had an impact on the animals' welfare. Once on board, Cornulier-Lucinière had the llamas separated by sex and divided among three prepared pens. The most valuable animals were kept in a small bamboo-covered structure built for them on the poop deck, while the rest were placed in two pens set up in the artillery battery of the ship. The crew hung canvases around the stable area to safeguard these animals from the noxious air of the battery at night, while cannon openings provided them with fresh air. The sailors followed a daily feeding schedule for the llamas. Unless the sea was terribly rough, the animals were brought out of their stables twice daily. An infirmary was set up to treat any that became ill. Maintaining the stables was also crucial to the animals' well-being. Sailors cleaned them thoroughly each morning and changed the bedding material twice a day. When the weather permitted, they groomed the animals out on the deck, sponging their ears, legs, and abdomens. Notwithstanding these extensive preparations, the trip from Guayaquil to Callao was difficult for the animals, as the ship battled strong southern winds and high waves. Cornulier-Lucinière believed that the llamas had not been carefully selected: many showed signs of their earlier biographies, including "traces of a long servitude," "cracked ears" and "worn knees." For these reasons, he feared that the animals were unlikely to survive the rigors of the journey. In the end, they lost eleven animals during this first leg and a twelfth while at port in Callao (Cornulier-Lucinière 1864, 393–396).

After the animals had been redistributed between the two ships at Callao, the remaining llamas could be lodged on the *Galatée*'s poop deck, which, as Cornulier-Lucinière observed, played a pivotal role in their health and ability to survive the transatlantic voyage. The crew members feared for the llamas' safety during the voyage around Cape Horn due to the very high seas they encountered. Surprisingly, they did not appear to suffer much, although one llama died from a fall that caused a head injury. Other deaths among the animals during the voyage were attributed to "intestinal inflammation," with symptoms including diarrhea, "melancholy, complaints, loss of appetite, abundant discharge of saliva from the mouth, tears and lassitude" (Cornulier-Lucinière 1864, 396). Cornulier-Lucinière believed that their care and attention had been so thorough that he congratulated himself in the end for not having brought shepherds from the Andes (395–396).

While location played a key role in the animals' welfare, other safety measures were also important. Lévêque, captain of the *Cornélie*, instructed

152 | *Llamas beyond the Andes*

the crew to cover the insides of the stables with cushions stuffed with hay to protect the llamas from being banged into the walls when the seas were heavy. The men stabled the males and females together at first but finally separated them with a bamboo partition because the males kept trying to mount the females and many of the pregnant females on board the *Galatée* had aborted and died (Lévêque 1864, 397–398, 400). Based on the information that the captain received from the *Galatée*, they followed a similar dietary regimen for the animals. It was especially evident that the llamas reacted adversely to any changes in their diet. For example, when the crew introduced new forage at Valparaíso and at Sainte-Hélène, they had to do so gradually, to accustom the animals to the change and avoid digestive upset. The water provided had to be fresh each day, otherwise they drank "showing their disgust" (399). According to the captain, it was easy to tell if a llama was indisposed. No longer interested in eating, the animal would cry and display an unmistakable "air of sadness." Trying to find a comfortable position, the animal would alternately stand up and rest on the ground (399–400).

Besides having to withstand the effects of local weather, such as storms and high seas, the animals also had to be prepared for passing from one climate zone to another. Once they reached the southern tropics, Lévêque ordered that the animals be given a partial shearing to prevent ill effects from the extreme heat, but not so short that the cold would harm them when they later reached higher latitudes. While sailing in the tropics, the men hung a canvas over the poop deck area and kept it wet to cool the llamas. Like Cornulier-Lucinière, Lévêque concluded his report by emphasizing that he had done everything in his power to ensure the project's success (Lévêque 1864, 399–401).

In his assessment of the Ecuadorian flock, Geoffroy Saint-Hilaire (1864) described it as composed of alpacas, llamas, and crosses of both. The llamas in particular were small animals, and the quality of their fleece caused him to speculate that they had been crossed with guanacos as well as alpacas. The conformation of the animals and the nature of their fiber suggested that they were of a variety different from any that they had seen before. As a whole, he considered them inferior to the animals Roehn had brought from Bolivia and Peru in 1860 (Geoffroy Saint-Hilaire 1864, 324–325). Despite these observations, the Paris Acclimatization Society hoped that this recent importation would create a better understanding of what the camelids' contribution might be to the nation's agricultural economy (326). Perhaps most importantly, the society now had confidence that

The Science of Acclimatization | 153

live animals could be shipped and landed in good health. As noted, thanks to the care provided during the transatlantic crossing, the animals arrived without any indication of the deadly skin infections that had decimated Roehn's flock (*Bulletin de la Société* [1864], xxx). This was no modest accomplishment, because the French society frequently received animals arriving from overseas and was cognizant of the expense and hard work entailed in landing a healthy animal (Geoffroy Saint-Hilaire 1864, 326). In appreciation of their efforts, the society conferred medals on the two captains, the crew members, and medical personnel who had attended the llamas during the voyage (*Bulletin de la Société* [1864], lxxiv).

Given the successful arrival of healthy animals, French scientists held up the Ecuadorian shipment as a model on which future projects could be based. A comparison of the rates of survival between the Roehn and García Moreno shipments indicates that Roehn had a 5 percent survival rate while the Ecuadorian shipment had a 46 percent survival rate for the animals upon arrival. The greater level of achievement of the second shipment was likely due to the institutional support the venture received from both France and the Andean nation, which allowed crew members to be assigned exclusively to the care of the animals, rather than from having or not having Andean shepherds on board, as some argued. This institutional collaboration resulted in a unique record of imperial knowledge making on the high seas that highlights the significance and impact of the participation and contributions of multiple actors and reveals some of the complex itineraries of its evolution and transformation. The next stage for acclimatization scientists was to place the animals in suitable locations and study their ability to adapt to new surroundings and diet. The chapter's final case study takes up the changing roles and histories of camelids in France as they moved from number to name, by looking at one experiment in their acclimatization.

Case History 3: Celebrity Llamas in the Vosges Mountains

Albert Geoffroy Saint-Hilaire (1864), secretary to the Paris Acclimatization Society's council, observed that the acclimatization of the llama and alpaca in Europe had been at the forefront of the society's priorities from its inception. Now that a few shipments had brought small numbers of the animals to France, the next step was to determine whether and where the llama and the alpaca could be most economically beneficial. The answer

154 | Llamas beyond the Andes

to these questions required experimentation, because experience showed that challenges and successes varied according to each placement of the animals (*Bulletin de la Société* [1864], 323–324).[35] This final portion of the chapter brings forward the collaborative nature of knowledge production and focuses on how learning about the camelids and their care in France was a multifaceted process involving caretakers, scientists, agriculturalists, and local communities.

The Acclimatization Society received several requests for camelids from enthusiasts who wished to assist with the study of the animals and their potential role in the future of France's agricultural economy. To distribute the animals, the society utilized a system called *cheptel* (lease) of llamas and alpacas to an individual or regional acclimatization society. The leaseholder was charged with caring for the animals and acclimatizing them, anticipating that they would eventually be able to reproduce normally and be trained for use. Their offspring would be divided between the Paris society and the leaseholder.

The Paris Acclimatization Society organized three important placements of llamas and alpacas in this way. The first took place in the Vosges mountains under the responsibility of Charles Galmiche and the Société Régionale d'Acclimatation pour la Zône du Nord-Est (Northeast Regional Acclimatization Society), founded in Nancy; the second was located outside of Besançon in the Jura mountains, directed by a man named Pinondel de la Bertoche; and the third was led by Nicolas Joly and the Haute-Garonne Agriculture Society, in the Haute Garonne Pyrenees of France. The analysis of this final section of the chapter focuses primarily on the Vosges animals, although it refers to the two other assignments as well. The Vosges experiment is exemplary in showing how the camelids were integrated into the local community of Remiremont, as they transitioned from being anonymous herd animals to become celebrated, named individuals.

French shipowner Th. Barbey brought four llamas to France in 1858 from Peru, one of which was sent to the Vosges mountains to attempt acclimatization there (*Bulletin de la Société* [1858], 223).[36] A few locations had vied for the animal, but the Paris scientists chose the Northeast Regional Acclimatization Society in Nancy (*Bulletin de la Société* [1859], 462). At the time, Nancy's important textile manufacturers and embroidery workshops were especially interested in the possibility of developing the use of llama and alpaca fiber for commercialization (Osborne 1994, 134), so this was a logical placement.

When the llama first arrived in the Vosges mountains, the Regional Acclimatization Society described it as a "superb" and "magnificent" animal but regarded Barbey's gift as more of an honor than a useful present because he did not have a female companion. Nonetheless, members hoped that the llama would be a prelude to future zoological wealth. The Northeast Regional Society officially charged Charles Galmiche, the Remiremont forest inspector, with the llama's acclimatization and domestication in the Vosges mountains: he was to research all aspects of the animal's potential value (*Bulletin de la Société Régionale* 4 [1859], 298, 441).

From Paris, the llama was sent to Galmiche by train, arriving in Épinal in June 1859. Galmiche met the animal there. After allowing a few hours of rest, he loaded the llama onto a wagon and set off on the 28.7-kilometer trip to Remiremont and then to his farm in Saint-Mont, a further distance of 4.7 kilometers. There Galmiche let the animal settle in for a few days, as he made observations and became used to the llama's habits, character, and needs. One of the first activities he undertook was to shear the animal, removing its heavy fleece.[37]

The llama enjoyed being left outdoors to graze at will and gradually grew stronger over time and gained weight. A small bell around the neck helped the caretaker to locate the llama, which sometimes wandered far away. Within a short period, the llama, now named Pérou, was able to accompany Galmiche on his daily responsibilities, transporting two large loads of fertilizer, tile, firewood, or the bodies of animals caught in Galmiche's traps, traveling two kilometers for each trip. On other occasions, Galmiche proudly promenaded the llama through the woods, carrying young children or slight women on the animal's back. According to the caretaker's report, the llama was exceedingly sure-footed and walked at a gentle pace. Although Pérou was easygoing, Galmiche observed that the llama longed for the companionship of other animals. When the llama came across goats in the village of Saint-Étienne, he would make "little cries," which Galmiche interpreted as an indication of the animal's wish for "love and society." He did not call to the dogs and horses in the same manner, but he appeared to take pleasure in their companionship (Galmiche 1860, 401–403).

After working with Pérou for several months, Galmiche evaluated the llama's contribution as a working animal, comparing his abilities to those of a small donkey, although he required less care; his food needs came to about the same as those of three ordinary sheep. Another advantage of the llama was that he did not require shoeing. Galmiche speculated that

156 | Llamas beyond the Andes

the llama could render important services for that area of the country, especially when the roads and paths were slick or ice-covered: the animal was as agile as a dog. Indeed, the llama seemed more suited to the Vosges mountains than donkeys, because the neighboring houses were far apart, and the farrier to shoe them lived an inconvenient distance away (Galmiche 1860, 403).[38]

Galmiche next introduced experimental trials with llama manure as a fertilizer. He sent the Regional Society a sample of March blue wheat, which he collected from the top of Saint-Mont after using a light application of the manure. According to his report, it yielded a remarkable harvest and took only 140 days from planting to harvest. Following these positive results, he distributed manure samples to local farmers so that they too could put it to use. He planned to expand these experiments during the coming year (*Bulletin de la Société Régionale* 2 [1863], 74).

Within a short period, Galmiche's beloved llama had become such a local celebrity that one anonymous enthusiast argued that a new vocabulary was needed in anticipation of the expected increased presence of camelids in the region, proposing that the word *lama* (the French word for *llama*) be written as *liama*. This spelling, he argued, provided a more accurate rendering of the Spanish *llama* and would differentiate the animal's name (now *liama*) from its homonym, meaning the solitary Buddhist *lama*.[39] While this distinction might not seem important now, given Galmiche's successful work acclimatizing the llama, it would not be long before the "wooly mountain quadruped from the Andes" would be found as far away as "the alpine regions crowned by the high peak of Dhavalaghiri" and beyond, to Kouen-Lun, the towering mountain chain bordering western Tibet ("Expérimentation de l'emploi du liama dans les Vosges" [1859], 440n1). Once this happened, separate words would be necessary to distinguish between "two different sorts of assistants useful to the Tibetan traveler: the gentle ruminant who would be carrying his packages along the edge of the precipices, and the charitable disciples of Buddha who, like the French religious community of Saint-Bernard, settle in the middle of a snowy region and spend a lifetime there of devotion and service to people in need" (439–440).

Galmiche and the members of the Northeast Regional Acclimatization Society experimented using *lâma* for the male, *lâme* for the female, and *lâmet* for the offspring, the circumflex constituting the distinguishing feature so that the new words would be neither homonyms nor

The Science of Acclimatization | 157

homophones with other French terms, like the Buddhist monk or a knife or sword (*lame*) ("Sur les llamas ou liamas" [1859], 332). They later settled on *liama* for the male, *liame* for the female, and *liameau* for the baby (Galmiche 1864a, 456). Even though this terminology was used in the *Bulletin* of the Northeast Regional Acclimatization Society, it did not appear to gain popularity outside of the Vosges.

Galmiche's llama finally received a female companion named Lima in 1861, one of the few survivors of Roehn's shipment from Peru. Lima's arrival to the Vosges had been delayed due to the skin disease that all his animals had suffered (*Bulletin de la Société Régionale* 2–3 [1861], 33).[40] Galmiche experienced some difficulties handling Lima at first because she had never before used a halter or lead line. In addition, she was skittish and easily frightened, especially by machinery and sudden movement. Because Lima still showed signs of the skin disease, Galmiche kept the two llamas separated. He first treated her lesions with potassium sulfide but eventually gave that up in favor of letting her have free access to move around outdoors, where she could graze at will. Within three weeks Lima's skin had cleared up and she had become more tractable (34).

Once the two llamas were put together, they became inseparable companions and thrived under Galmiche's care. Eventually, Lima also cooperated as a carrier and could be found on the mountain trails with Galmiche and Pérou. The animals' fiber showed so much improvement that Galmiche dispatched it to be processed, after which he submitted samples to the Northeast Regional Acclimatization Society for inspection and review (*Bulletin de la Société Régionale* 2–3 [1861], 35–37).

Pérou and Lima received a third llama companion in 1863, a female named Blanchette. Blanchette had suffered multiple injuries during her travels. When she arrived, she had a severe, long-lasting limp and a damaged shoulder. Blanchette was also extremely nervous and uncontrollable, so Galmiche held off training her to caravan with the other two llamas until she had fully recovered (Galmiche 1864a, 458).

The same year that Blanchette arrived, Pérou and Lima welcomed a new male baby, born at the end of May 1863. Lima had given birth the previous year, but the baby only lived for three days.[41] Galmiche named the second baby Mexico and hoped that the young llama would grow into a fine stud animal, because Pérou was beginning to show signs of age. The excellent health of the baby suggested that the animals could reproduce in their new environment with few problems, which led Galmiche to

FIGURE 4.3. *The llama Mexico in front of the Remiremont abbey.* Bulletin de la Société Régionale d'Acclimatation pour la Zône du Nord-Est (Nancy) 2 (1864), insert, 236–237.

conclude that the acclimatization of the llamas in the Vosges should now be considered successful beyond a doubt. He expressed his aspiration that the region of Lorraine could be transformed into a major center for the acclimatization of llamas (Galmiche 1864b, 246). Galmiche forwarded photographs of baby Mexico to the Northeast Regional Acclimatization Society and a drawing of the month-old animal based on one of the photographs (figure 4.3). The illustration was created by an officer of the line regiment whose work had been recognized by the Lorraine Friends of Art Society (Galmiche 1864b, 236). Portraying the llama in front of a prominent local landmark, the Remiremont abbey, the drawing created the impression that the animal was simultaneously exotic and familiar. The handsome baby attracted much attention because it confirmed that the reproduction of llamas was feasible in the Vosges mountains (Galmiche 1864b, 238). In honor of these accomplishments, a tourist penned a short verse on the door of the Saint-Mont chapel:

> Prier, c'est . . .
> C'est doter le pays d'un animal nouveau
> Qui donne sa toison, qui porte le fardeau (239)

(Prayer . . .
Bestows on the country a new beast,
It carries your loads and provides you its wool)

The Northeast Regional Acclimatization Society was clearly pleased with Galmiche's progress with the llamas, and the beautiful baby Mexico represented the culmination of his time and effort. The society's official seal was based on an image of Galmiche's popular animal (*Bulletin de la Société Régionale* 3 [1864], 297).

Galmiche's work with the llamas, along with the efforts of the unnamed caretakers, was key to understanding how new information gained about the animals became science (see Musselman 2009, 31–32). He regularly updated the Northeast Regional Acclimatization Society on his small flock, communicating the activities of each animal in detail. This information, in turn, was summarized or reprinted in the *Bulletin* of the Paris Acclimatization Society. In one report he described the llamas with phrases such as "our family" and "our animals," rendering his account more intimate and depicting the animals as family members or pets rather than livestock (Galmiche 1864a, 457).

Galmiche clearly enjoyed showing the llamas off to the local public, exhibiting them at fairs and festivals, such as the popular fêtes d'Épinal. At the Épinal fair, the llamas became one of the most popular attractions, drawing more than 20,000 curious visitors who inspected the animals up close, petting them, and admiring especially Mexico's soft fleece. Everyone remarked on the animals' health and attractive appearance and congratulated Galmiche for his accomplishments with the unusual creatures. He paraded them about to demonstrate their utility for farms, especially for smaller, more isolated estates, describing the llamas as so sweet-tempered and obedient that children could easily handle them. They were the perfect animals for the local region, he maintained, because they walked with agility, even on precipitous mountainous paths. Although they could not carry a large adult, they were perfect for transporting containers of milk, cheeses, and other market purchases (Galmiche 1864b, 243–246). Galmiche's llamas and his work with them so impressed the local community that the mayor, jury, and commissioner general of the fair informed the public that they planned to request that the president of the Paris Acclimatization Society confer a special gold medal honoring the Northeast Regional Society for its positive results in naturalizing the llama (Galmiche 1865, 409–410).[42]

160 | Llamas beyond the Andes

After the hustle and bustle of the Épinal fair, the animals seemed excited to head home. According to Galmiche, they walked so fast up the mountain trail that their shepherd had difficulty keeping up. Their trip appeared to have gone smoothly: they had not suffered any mishaps from the trip or experienced unusual circumstances or conditions while at the fair. A few weeks after the llamas' return to Saint-Mont, Galmiche received a fifth llama, a young male named Quito, that had been part of the Ecuador shipment. Galmiche described Quito's outward appearance as most expressive but also observed that the animal exhibited a "sweet and sad sickliness." From the beginning, Galmiche explained, he felt uneasy about the introduction of Quito into the flock. The animal often kept to himself and did not mingle with the others. The same age as Quito, Mexico occasionally joined him, ignoring "his mother's cries to return" (Galmiche 1865, 410–411).

Galmiche discovered in early October that Quito and Mexico exhibited similar signs of skin disease, with crusted red scabs on different parts of their bodies. Because both animals were so young, Galmiche hesitated to treat the problem aggressively with overly strong medications. Before long, however, the older animals showed the same indications of the disease. Galmiche reported that he had treated skin infections on dogs and horses but had never seen abrasions such as those that he found on the llamas. Although treatments of potassium sulfide appeared at first to clear up the disease, it reappeared soon after on Quito and Mexico. To prevent its further spread, he brought the llamas down to Remiremont, where he separated the healthy animals from those that were sick. But there seemed to be no stopping the disease's progression: Mexico was the first to die, toward the end of December. Galmiche sent Pérou and Blanchette to Épinal shortly afterward, hoping that they would be better protected that way. Quito and Lima in Remiremont died next. Even with the assistance of the local veterinarian, Pérou and Blanchette died a few weeks following their arrival in Épinal. Within the short space of a month, Galmiche lost all his llamas (Galmiche 1865, 412–413).

Thus ended more than five years of experiments with the Vosges llamas. Speculating on the possible causes of death, Galmiche argued that it could not be related to climatic changes because the llamas who had been in France the longest died last. He hypothesized that Quito carried a disease, which eventually infected the entire small flock. This theory was supported by his observations that Quito kept to himself much of the time and already had skin lesions when he arrived (Galmiche 1865, 413–414; see also Joly 1869, 6–7n2).

The Science of Acclimatization | 161

The unexpected death of Galmiche's flock struck a blow to the optimism felt by the Paris society regarding the successful acclimatization of llamas and alpacas. Hopes declined further with the subsequent demise of similar flocks. This disappointment was increasingly shared by many. The high mortality rate of Roehn's shipment raised serious concerns about extracting camelids, because the journey to Europe weakened them terribly and made them susceptible to skin infections, which were perceived to be the primary cause of death. Animals that did manage to survive the voyage and adjust to their new circumstances and even reproduce still seemed exceedingly vulnerable to skin disease, especially when new (possibly contaminated) animals were introduced, as happened with the Vosges llamas.

The drop in the number of reports on llamas and alpacas in the Paris Acclimatization Society's *Bulletin* beginning in 1867 provides further evidence that enthusiasm over the animals was flagging. Incoming reports on their use-value from different parts of France were also discouraging. Some agriculturalists argued that the llamas did not provide enough services to make up for the cost and difficulties caused by their introduction (*Bulletin de la Société* [1862], 759). Pinondel de la Bertoche, the man who organized a lease of llamas on his property in the Jura mountains, was equally pessimistic. He believed that the acclimatization of llamas was of interest from the perspective of natural history and curiosity. He could not recommend the project as a fruitful or lucrative pursuit from an economic point of view, however, unless concerted efforts were made to bring in larger importations of females to increase the flocks in appreciable numbers. Unlike Galmiche's experience, Pinondel de la Bertoche had no success utilizing the animals as carriers, complaining: "They can only be employed for this purpose to satisfy a fantastic whim. The difficulties [in training them] in this regard, their fearful, insubordinate, and vagabond habits, do not allow us to expect useful results in this direction." Concerning their importance as fiber animals, he believed that their value would increase only if their numbers did the same (*Bulletin de la Société* [1866], 52, 54).

Nicolas Joly, in charge of the Haut-Garonne Agriculture Society's small flock of llamas in the Pyrenees, expressed confidence early on in the experiment, speculating that it would not be long before delicious llama meat would be found in the market stalls alongside beef and lamb, in the same way that yak meat and especially horse meat were making inroads in many markets (Joly 1869, 10; 1870, 9). Some of the llamas already had begun to show symptoms of skin disease the first summer after they arrived,

162 | *Llamas beyond the Andes*

however. It continued to spread to the rest, who all perished by the middle of the summer of 1870 (Joly 1872a, 146). One of the females died in such an advanced state of decomposition that she had to be buried immediately, although they marked the site in case someone later wanted her skeleton for research. Their male died soon after the females. His body was packed up and sent to Montréjeau, but the putrefaction was so bad that the driver complained bitterly. The box had to be dispatched quickly to the Toulouse Cabinet of Natural History (Fouque 1872, 31–32). Despite this devastating loss of the animals, Joly still expressed certainty that, under better circumstances and without the contagious disease, the experiment would have been a success (Joly 1872a, 150).

Pinpointing some of the reasons for the failure, Joly called attention to the way the animals had been shipped from Paris to Toulouse in very small containers and were forced to remain standing. He surmised that this situation alone could have accounted for one premature birth that resulted in the death of the mother and baby. Albert Geoffroy Saint-Hilaire (1870) responded immediately to Joly's report, arguing that the containers in which the animals had been shipped to Toulouse were appropriately sized; experience had shown that the smaller the enclosure, the less susceptible the animals would be to injuries and the more likely that they would arrive safely. Furthermore, he had sent animals of all sizes to many countries and had never received complaints. He willingly admitted that it had been imprudent to send female llamas so close to the date of parturition and also regretted the terrible skin disease. They were aware of the kind of scourge that it created in Paris but had seen no sign of it before dispatching the animals (Geoffroy Saint-Hilaire 1872, 152–153). Joly (1872a, 149) similarly blamed the presence of a contagious animal in the flock for spreading the disease to the others. The treatment prescribed by the University of Toulouse Veterinary School unfortunately was ineffective and the entire flock succumbed to infection.

Albert Geoffroy Saint-Hilaire expressed great disappointment over the death of the Pyrenees animals, the costliest of the experiments and the one on which the Acclimatization Society had placed great hopes. While he could not say what more might have been done to combat the outbreak of the skin disease, he reasoned that one sick llama did not mean that the entire flock had to be lost. In the end, however, Joly (1872b, 35–36) captured the sentiment increasingly shared by the larger scientific community about the llama acclimatization ventures when he lamented that no traces remained of the Pyrenees llama experiment. He corrected himself, however, commenting that this observation was not quite true. The skin of one llama that died at Toulouse, along with her skeleton, had become a valuable addition to the Comparative Anatomy Collection of the University's Faculty of Sciences. And the skeleton of their adult male enriched the collection of Toulouse's Museum of Natural History.

We could conclude that the attempt to acclimatize camelids in France in the nineteenth century was ultimately unsuccessful. Even in the case of the Ecuadorian flock, where greater institutional support resulted in a higher survival rate for the animals during the transatlantic journey, most of the animals died in the months following their arrival. One of the more important debates to come out of the acclimatization movement was the role of Indigenous shepherds, their knowledge of the animals, and their ability to keep them healthy. In the case of Roehn's animals, Geoffroy Saint-Hilaire placed blame squarely on the two Indians who accompanied the *voyageur naturaliste*, stating that they should have had enough experience to do a better job of caring for the animals than the French caretakers. He claimed, moreover, that the health of the animals improved as soon as they came under the care of the French, providing evidence that their well-being did not depend on the presence of Andean shepherds (Geoffroy Saint-Hilaire 1872, 152–153). Despite these reflections, the few surviving llamas from Roehn's and the Ecuadorian shipments did not last for long after reaching France.

Although Albert Geoffroy Saint-Hilaire's father Isidore expressed hope in the chapter's epigraph that the only limits placed on the acclimatization of llamas and alpacas would be demand, the three case histories show that specialists of the time were unable to keep the animals alive. As Osborne (2000, 151) argues, "the checkered history of acclimatization signaled that much in nature, was, in the end, beyond European control. The fact that so many acclimatization projects and societies failed served to mark the limits of European science." Nevertheless, the unsuccessful French efforts in acclimatizing llamas and alpacas did not deter other endeavors, such as the work of Englishman Charles Ledger and his project to smuggle alpacas and llamas out of Bolivia for naturalization in Australia, the focus of the following two chapters.

.

CHAPTER 5

Andean Itineraries of Nineteenth-Century Camelid Science

The Case of Charles Ledger

We have had the great Mr. Charles Ledger with us dining occasionally, and have been greatly diverted by his untiring yarns on his alpaca expeditions. He is Livingstone No. 2, and in other times will be looked upon as a hero of trials that few have known and hardly any equalled, in snows, deserts, and mountain regions; with social, political, and religious difficulties in the work against him; sometimes all but buried in mountain snows, with hungry men and flocks to protect; now chased by the police, and again hunted by the hungry natives in pursuit of the flock, and with all the privations of six years' absence from his home and family, and over a journey of 6,000 leagues with animals and men; sometimes having even to defend themselves from the ferocity of their own mules, lest they should be eaten by them—not a rare event. But enough—Mr. Charles Ledger has nearly 400 alpacas on the coast ready for shipment to Australia, to which place he takes them; and I trust he may arrive safe, and thus confer upon Australia and England one of the greatest boons man could bestow.

Letter from Henry Swinglehurst in Valparaíso, quoted by an anonymous correspondent of the Times *(London), April 3, 1859*

This letter from Henry Swinglehurst, British mining engineer and long-time resident of Chile, painted a dramatic portrait of his fellow countryman Charles Ledger (1818–1905) as a larger-than-life "Livingston No. 2" and captivating raconteur. Using broad brushstrokes, Swinglehurst described highlights from Ledger's extraordinary alpaca venture and the trials and tribulations he endured while on the road from 1853 to 1858, accompanied by a small group of Andean shepherds and a

166 | Llamas beyond the Andes

flock of some 400 llamas and alpacas. Ledger and the Indians smuggled the camelids out of Bolivia and headed for Chile through the Argentine Confederation. While en route, they spent several months in Laguna Blanca (Catamarca) in northern Argentina, preparing the animals for the difficult crossing of the high cordillera into Chile and the subsequent voyage to Australia, where they hoped that the llamas and alpacas could be naturalized. Creole friends and colleagues throughout Peru, Bolivia, and northern Argentina and members of Valparaíso's community of British residents played an important role, providing hospitality, raising financial support, and creating public awareness of Ledger's project. The epigraph to this chapter presents Swinglehurst's version of Ledger's alpaca expedition, focusing on its heroic elements and piquing the curiosity of his readers, who, like himself, were left in suspense regarding the outcome of this tale of encounter and survival on behalf of a patriotic enterprise.

Despite his celebrity status in the mid-nineteenth century as a bold adventurer, Ledger came to the attention of contemporary audiences only in 1953 when the Mitchell Library, State Library of New South Wales, in Sydney, Australia, acquired his medals and journal, which included notes, sketches, a map of his travels throughout the Andes, and watercolors prepared by the artist Santiago Savage, who accompanied Ledger for some months (see Jones 1953).[1] This unique multimedia archive portraying Ledger's narrative of hardship, altruism, and perseverance sets it against a formidable backdrop of ever-present risk and danger on a multitude of fronts. The extraction of a large flock of llamas and alpacas from Bolivia skirted the boundaries of lawful commerce, so many of the preliminary details of the project were never committed to writing and remain uncertain today. In the manner of epic tales, promises of fame and fortune were held out to Ledger if he could successfully complete the journey to Australia. Yet adversaries of all kinds abounded, including local government officials and Indigenous pastoral communities unwilling to have alpacas moved out of the Andean region. Ledger describes how he had to use his wits continually to outmaneuver them.

By the time Ledger's retinue reached the coast of Chile in 1858 and was preparing for departure for New South Wales, the alpaca venture had already created an international impact. Peruvian and Bolivian officials mostly decried the illegality of his actions, while Indigenous herding communities denounced the high mortality rate among the animals being moved. His story also generated enthusiasm and participatory excitement among many others. A mix of financial, scientific, Indigenous,

Andean Itineraries of Nineteenth-Century Camelid Science | 167

political-military, and artistic communities thus emerged at the peripheries of the enterprise, some of which provided much needed economic support. Others materialized in opposition to the project, refusing to acquiesce to his neo-ecological imperialism. Although Ledger himself was not a scientist, natural historians and business leaders in international circles followed the news of his alpaca expedition with great interest. Many of his friends had ties to the sciences, and he became a member of several different societies through them. As Schell (2013, 6) argues more generally, "Historians have recognized the importance of emotion, social relationships, and effective bonds in the natural sciences, with trust and good manners forming the foundation." These social relationships, moreover, "were not a by-product of scientific work but rather an essential part of its practice" (7). Just as Ledger required the adversarial communities for the construction of his narrative of heroism, he needed friends and colleagues in local and international scientific and commercial circles whom he could trust to help spread the word of his work and provide financial support and other opportunities.

Even though Ledger's story fired the imaginations of patrons like Swinglehurst who appeared to live vicariously through his endeavors, the participatory role of these peripheral communities belies the trope of the solitary, romantic hero. This chapter points to the presence of these groups that formed around Ledger and in his wake. Even though he became a hero to Europeans, he stood on the shoulders of many people and depended upon their collaboration. My story of Ledger therefore varies somewhat from the usual accounts of his life, which have emphasized his great courage and decried the lack of gratitude and insufficient reward shown him following years of self-sacrifice and dedicated service to the British government. Instead, this chapter pulls at the tangled threads of Ledger's yarns to explore some of the contradictions and inconsistencies that emerge from his story, including surprising moments and spaces where his narrative of Western-style heroic masculinity breaks down or creates unexpected emotional connections with the Indigenous other.[2] These incongruities make visible the presence of Indigenous pastoral peoples within the story, including women and older men, revealing their agency despite their restrictive positioning within a wider frame of colonial and imperial domination.

The chapter pays special attention to the months that Ledger and the Bolivian shepherds who accompanied him spent in Laguna Blanca, to argue that the intercultural experiments forged there present us with

168 | *Llamas beyond the Andes*

an ethos of trust and collaboration that contrasts with the singular Euro-centric perspective of many travel narratives. For example, Ledger and the shepherds worked collectively in Laguna Blanca to forge a space for developing new breeding practices and forms of animal care. A few Englishmen and a number of Indigenous herders worked together to create a large flock of Andean camelids for export and, it was hoped, for profit. In the end, Laguna Blanca became a complex, plural site where the animals were literally being refashioned or rebred for circulation in new transnational networks of people, places, and economies (see Whatmore [2002] on hybrid geographies).

Initial Stages of the Alpaca Enterprise

Ledger moved to Lima, Peru, in 1836 when he was eighteen years old and began to work for Naylor's, Kendall & Co., a British merchant house involved with wool interests.[3] This opportunity enabled Ledger to learn Spanish and the administrative ins and outs of the fiber trade (Gramiccia 1988, 5). Two years later, Naylor's transferred Ledger to Tacna to work in the merchant house's branch office, where he was in charge of making and collecting wool contracts, sorting the wool by color, and packing it for shipment to Liverpool.[4] Within a short period, Ledger developed a reputation as a hardworking businessman, which facilitated his entry into the city's prominent social circles. He married a young woman in 1842 named Candelaria Ortiz from one of Tacna's most influential families (Gramiccia 1988, 7; Ledger 1859, 154).

Ledger's work took him on frequent travels throughout the highlands and region of Lake Titicaca, including the border area of Peru and Bolivia. He met with Indians on a daily basis (Gramiccia 1988, 5; Ledger 1859, 154) and consequently learned what he described as a "smattering" of the native language, never clarifying whether he learned Aymara or Quechua or a little of both (Ledger 1860b). As he gained more experience and cultural and linguistic fluency, Ledger began undertaking projects independently of the Naylor company. His brother Arthur joined in his ventures in 1842, following him to Peru (Gramiccia 1988, 7). This was around the same time that a large, ill-fated shipment of alpacas was sent to Liverpool along with a cargo of guano on the *Sir Charles Napier*. Ledger recalled the events and protagonists involved in the disastrous incident, giving testimony to the illegal manner in which the animals had been

Andean Itineraries of Nineteenth-Century Camelid Science | 169

obtained and the complicity of local authorities in the process. According to his account, more than four hundred alpacas had been seized forcibly from Indigenous communities by the prefect of Puno, Mariano Escobedo. Escobedo then sold the animals to the Arequipa merchants Moens and Marriott, who shipped them to Liverpool aboard the *Sir Charles Napier* (Ledger 1864a, 96). Of the four hundred animals embarked, only three arrived alive but so weakened from the devastation of the voyage that they died within a few days of landing. Ledger attributed their deaths to having been overdriven to the port of Islay, lack of sufficient food while on board ship, and their fodder becoming permeated with guano (95).[5]

Although Ledger did not comment further on how the animals had been obtained, he described in some detail the Indigenous communities' angry reactions to the reports of the alpacas' demise. Large numbers converged on the city of Puno, demanding that the government prohibit any future exportations of the animals: "Owing to the clamour of the Indians, and to other political reasons by which the 'English' were in a bad 'odour' with the Government and people of Peru at the time, the Congress passed the law of the 9th of April, 1845, prohibiting the exportation, under very severe penalties, of a single Alpaca from Peru" (Ledger 1864a, 95–96).[6] As described by Ledger, the legislation barred the driving of alpacas within a distance of forty leagues of the coast, presumably with the intent to remove the animals from the country. Anyone caught in violation of the law could be sentenced to ten years of hard labor, condemned to join the chain gangs on the Chincha or Guano Islands (Ledger 1859, 155, 194).[7] Despite the severity of punishment called for in the legislation, Ledger felt convinced that the Peruvian government by and large was uninterested in the topic of alpaca exportation, doubtless because most attention at the time was directed to the burgeoning guano industry. Moreover, Ledger believed that local authorities had been involved in the ill-fated deal and would be happy to turn a blind eye to the problem. Yet, "as they can conciliate so easily such a numerous, influential class, as the Indian population, this law was passed without delay" (Ledger 1864a, 96).

As early as 1842, Ledger (1859, 154–155) began receiving queries from Europe for small lots of alpacas (also Ledger 1860–1861, 214).[8] Although he did his best to fill the requests, he had difficulty obtaining alpacas due to the Andeans' refusal to sell their animals. Based on this initial experience, Ledger realized that any project to extract a significant number of alpacas would be difficult and likely have a low rate of success (Ledger 1859, 155). The tragedy of the *Sir Charles Napier* and similar failures undoubtedly

170 | Llamas beyond the Andes

convinced him that a large venture of this kind would require a great deal of planning and preparation to be profitable. "Mr. Ledger began to think that the only way to success was to train the animal before removing it from its native home" (Swinglehurst 1893, 169).

To this end, Ledger rented a hacienda known as Chulluncayani in 1848. Located on the border between Peru and Bolivia, it was well situated for collecting cinchona bark, obtaining copper from the Corocoro mines, and assembling and breeding alpacas.[9] Ledger's initial herd consisted of some two hundred llamas and alpacas, most of which he described as old and in bad condition (Ledger 1859, 155). As he attempted to build a larger, healthier flock, he encountered numerous challenges. To begin with, nearby rural communities employed a variety of strategies to prevent him from obtaining the animals. He described this hostility as originating from Andean shepherds' long-standing superstitions concerning the camelids and was convinced that "had I not employed natives of the country to buy the animals for me, and led them to suppose that I wanted only a few to breed from, further on in the interior of the country itself, and moreover, kept my own counsel until fairly out of Bolivia, and among another race of people without the prejudices for the animal, I should never have got one Alpaca out of the country" (Ledger 1864a, 96).

Ledger (1859, 155) claimed that this resistance on the part of Indigenous peoples to selling or parting with their animals was based on a "superstitious reverence," which included the belief that they and their families would suffer the same fate if any misfortune came to the animals while being taken from their land, such as "hunger, thirst, and foot-soreness" or death. He recounted traditional stories of bearded men appearing who would commit many atrocities, including taking the alpacas and llamas back to their foreign land for breeding.

Seemingly, Ledger missed the irony of the way his own activity connected him to these narratives when he adhered to what Van Dooren (2014, 5) refers to in a different context as an "exceptionalist framework," in which his actions were somehow external to rather than directly implicated in these neo-ecological misfortunes and disappearances. Instead, Ledger cast himself in the role of victim of these beliefs: "It would occupy too much space were I to enter into description of the superstitious veneration with which the alpaca and llama are regarded by the Indian of Peru; it is carried to almost incredible extent, and, to believe it, it is absolutely necessary to see and suffer from it as I and others have done" (Ledger 1860b). Ledger's use of superstition here was misleading, because Indigenous communities had a clear understanding of how easily their monopoly on the camelids could be lost and their better animals seized from them; the recent tragedy of the *Sir Charles Napier* would only have heightened their angry response to further attempts at the animals' removal.

While the documentation indicates that Indigenous peoples occasionally agreed to sell alpacas and llamas to outsiders, international travelers' narratives generally concurred on the barriers to acquiring the animals directly from them.[10] This active refusal led to situations where travelers like Eugène Roehn (as seen in chapter 4) would enlist the aid of local priests, caciques, or other authorities to take the animals by force if necessary. Ledger preferred to employ Indigenous intermediaries to purchase the alpacas rather than attempt to do so himself. Moreover, the opposition already described may also have been rooted in a different kind of use-value attributed to the animals by Indigenous pastoral peoples that was external to the monetary economy. Caro (1994, 36–37) has called attention to a similar dynamic of defiance in the northern Bolivian area of Ulla Ulla toward the end of the nineteenth century. Her work shows how Indigenous possession of the camelids was linked to an alternative way of understanding wealth that fortified a herding family's access to a network of reciprocal labor relations rather than to the accumulation of cash income. When herders sold their animals, they "ran the risk of losing land as well as considerable utility from family labor" (36).[11]

Given this environment, Ledger had to work surreptitiously to build his herd so that the local pastoral communities did not become suspicious and discover his plan for taking the animals overseas. He told the story of Miguel Ibernégaray, a young Frenchman who had served for a while as his clerk. Ibernégaray and a few Indigenous companions were beaten to death in 1856 by nearby Andeans in Andamarca because Ibernégaray had attempted to purchase alpacas and made it publicly known that he planned to take them out of Bolivia (Ledger 1864a, 96). Ledger recalled how he had passed through the same area two years earlier and come up against heavy resistance on the part of Indigenous communities, especially when they discovered that he was driving a flock of female llamas and alpacas. "I was detained four times by them, once for sixteen days. Councils were held by them, and I had to exert all my ingenuity to get the flocks free. Had I not possessed a smattering of their language and knowledge of their customs, which enabled me to conciliate and cover my intentions, I should not have been allowed to pass" (Ledger 1860b). The story of Ibernégaray's sad fate served as a contrast to Ledger's narrative, highlighting his

172 | *Llamas beyond the Andes*

own savoir faire and understanding of regional and local "socio-ecological tensions" (Ross 2017, 15) and how to work around them. Ledger's rhetorical strategies also provided dramatic authentication, enabling his readers to imagine the variety of perils he faced and demonstrate his ability always to outsmart the craftiest of enemies.

Despite these difficulties, Ledger (1859, 155) had gathered several hundred animals by 1851. His first major opportunity to export a sizable number came that same year. Ledger, his brother Arthur, and a Mr. Jackson planned to smuggle a herd of four hundred alpacas out of Peru on board the *Julia*. The captain of the ship, George Duniam, was hired by the Sydney firm Mort and Brown, of New South Wales, to bring the alpacas back to the British colony. Members of the Legislative Council and wool industry there had collected a subscription of £1,500 for the effort (Carter, Vilches, and Santoro 2017, 400; Gramiccia 1988, 27). Although certain conversations appear to have taken place between Ledger and the British consul regarding the project, all parties eventually backed out of the agreement because of the Peruvian government's restrictions and the risks involved in contravening them. Believing the deal to have been terminated, the British consul at Arica was caught unawares when the ship landed at the port of Arica. The entire affair ended in failure: the *Julia* eventually sailed back to Sydney without a single alpaca on board (Gramiccia 1988, 27).[12]

The idea of extracting a large flock of alpacas to the British colony of New South Wales did not end there, however. Further conversations took place the following year, involving Ledger, George Hodges Nugent, the British consul at Arica, and William Pitt Adams, the British chargé d'affaires in Lima. Although at first the British government appears to have refused to become involved in any such proposal, at some point all parties came to an agreement to move forward with the plan. Due to the illegality of the proposition, no part of the arrangement could be put in writing. This lack of a paper trail would later come back to haunt Ledger. His version of the story was that Nugent and Pitt Adams requested his assistance with bringing a large herd of alpacas to Australia for naturalization (Ledger 1859, 156; 1864a, 97).[13] Ledger (1859, 156) described how Pitt Adams appealed to his "spirit of patriotism" in their conversations, declaring that he was the only Englishman who would be able to pull off such a venture. Placing his trust in their word, Ledger did not appear to need much convincing before he accepted Pitt Adams's offer. Shortly afterward, he began plans for a brief trip to Australia to look the place over and determine its suitability (Ledger 1859, 182; 1864a, 97).[14]

Andean Itineraries of Nineteenth-Century Camelid Science | 173

Ledger's flock contained more than eight hundred llamas and alpacas by 1852. He divided them into two separate flocks, left under the charge of his "head drover" (Gramiccia 1988, 44), with instructions to begin moving the animals at a leisurely pace south through Bolivia toward the border with the Argentine provinces.[15] Given the ongoing state of conflict between Peru and Bolivia, Ledger reckoned that the Bolivian government's attention and troops would be focused on the northern border, making it more likely that the animals could be slipped over the southern border with less danger of discovery and capture. The herd could also be replenished along the way, in the province of Lípez, where llama herders especially were in abundance (Gil Montero 2008, 90; Platt 1995).

With his plans for the animals now in place, Ledger and his brother-in-law Major Ortiz set sail from Valparaíso for New South Wales on December 24, 1852.[16] Ortiz traveled with him under a concealed identity: as a Peruvian major in the army, he would have received severe punishment for participating in the extraction of alpacas from the country (Gramiccia 1988, 72). The two men reached New South Wales on March 18, 1853, and began their explorations of the countryside around Sydney, staying within thirty-six miles of the coast, to determine whether the area was appropriate for their purposes. Pleased with what they found, they returned to Sydney and set sail for Valparaíso on May 21, 1853, arriving forty-three days later (Ledger 1859, 182).

In early August Ledger reached Copiapó (Chile), where he purchased mules and supplies in preparation for his journey over the Andean Cordillera into Argentina. He required an experienced guide who could take him over the mountain range, because it was early in the season and the passes were not fully open or free of snow. Ledger described his good fortune in meeting up with Pedro Cabrera, the man he hired as his guide, who would remain in his employ for several years. Ledger also took on Pablo Sosa as his "general servant" and assistant to the guide. He provided no additional information on either man (other than having met them in Copiapó), presumably to protect their identity from the Bolivian authorities. Both would accompany Ledger and the animals to Australia (Ledger 1859, 182–183). The small group of three was joined by Samuel W. De Blois, a fellow passenger on the ship from Australia, who was slowly making his way back to Halifax, Nova Scotia (Ledger, 1860–1861, 215). De Blois wanted to see something of the interior of South America and decided to accompany them on the journey. On September 17, 1853, the four men set out from Copiapó with twelve mules and two horses to cross the cordillera and continue to Salta (Argentina) (Ledger 1859, 183).

174 | Llamas beyond the Andes

Because they were traversing the cordillera so early in the season, their journey was perilous on multiple fronts. One of the horses froze to death during the night. A baggage mule that got caught in a deep snowdrift broke its back in the effort to get free. Another mule had to be left behind at one point when it became so lame it could not continue. All along the route they found crosses and heaps of skeletal remains of people, cattle, donkeys, oxen, and mules. Ledger embellished the narrative of their own adventures with stories of others who perished along the way due to lightning strikes, extreme cold, and heavy snowfalls accompanied by hurricane-style gales. He told of one man whose entire herd of eight hundred cattle perished during a storm. Although his men all survived, each lost a hand, a foot, a nose, or ears from frostbite.[17] Other non-weather-related dangers abounded as well. Ledger and his men had to stay on the lookout for threats from their own animals: hungry mules notoriously exhibited aggressive behavior, approaching the sleeping men at night and causing severe injury by biting them (Ledger 1859, 183). Ledger appeared to relish these embedded stories, which played a critical rhetorical role in his own account. They illustrated the dangers and risks that continually beset the enterprise and showcased the bravery, knowledge, and resourcefulness of himself and the men who accompanied him. He would later have the company of artist Santiago Savage, who brought these stories to life with his whimsical drawings and bright watercolors.

This initial series of adventures and misadventures served as a blueprint for the effort to move the camelids south through Bolivia and into Argentina. Much of the later journey was similarly plagued by hazardous conditions due to storms, extreme cold, and high altitudes, which led to numerous accidents and even fatalities. Difficult travel circumstances, inclement weather, and lack of water and pasture for the animals all contributed to continual heavy losses of alpacas (Ledger 1859, 185). On the human front, Ledger's men drove the alpacas and llamas in three separate herds toward Argentina, each group taking a separate route the better to avoid raising the suspicion of Bolivian authorities. Doubts and concerns on the part of his financial backers forced Ledger to undertake the long and difficult trip back and forth several times from Bolivia, Salta, and across the cordillera to Valparaíso, to seek support for the enterprise. Ledger's frequent comings and goings likely contributed to local rumors, which claimed that he worked as a spy in Argentina for the Bolivian president Manuel Isidoro Belzú, making note of those conspiring against the leader. While claiming he did not appreciate being considered in such a light,

Andean Itineraries of Nineteenth-Century Camelid Science | 175

Ledger did nothing to discourage the stories, because they assured him that his actual plans remained unknown to the authorities (Ledger 1859, 190).

In addition to the harsh conditions that Ledger and his group endured while traveling with the animals, they also experienced a multitude of problems due to difficult encounters with local Indigenous communities. Llamas appear to have been relatively easy to obtain, especially in the Carangas area.[18] In contrast, obtaining alpacas was much more difficult. With so many animal casualties, Ledger made every effort to acquire additional alpacas before leaving Bolivia, the southern point of their natural habitat. Getting new stock was easier said than done and required contact with herding communities. Ledger contracted with the *corregidor* from Vilca Pujio, a man with the name Obando, who was to bring Ledger another 200 alpacas that he had agreed to collect for him. When Obando did not appear on the scheduled date, Ledger went to search for him, finding him in Vilca Pujio in the middle of a predicament of his own making. Obando had obtained 170 animals from nearby herders, who not only refused to sell him the remaining 30 that he requested but also appeared to regret the original sale. They demanded that the animals be returned, throwing the money back at the *corregidor*. Ledger described the scene as volatile, with the potential to turn violent. He portrayed the women in particular as dangerously irrational: "the number of women howling and screaming, the vociferations of the men, were indeed not to be laughed at, seeing that [Obando's] authority would soon be entirely lost" (Ledger 1859, 192).

Ledger enlisted the aid of three of his own men and two soldiers so that they could use their long reins to drive the animals through the crowd and out to the road at a clip fast enough to discourage pursuit: "Not a minute elapsed ere stones from the slings of the Indians were flying about, in all directions, we all got our share, but none of us seriously hurt; for about two miles they followed us, then seeing that we were rapidly gaining on them, they desisted" (Ledger 1859, 192). The group traveled on through most of the night without further incident, and the next morning Ledger sent the two soldiers back home. Pablo Sosa and the two remaining men set out toward the border with the 170 alpacas and 8 donkeys and 3 mules carrying provisions, while Ledger remained behind (192).

Three days later, Obando came looking for Ledger, heavily bandaged from the wounds he had received and accompanied by three Indigenous elders. These men demanded that the alpacas be returned to them, which Ledger refused to do. He quickly paid them the remaining balance owed.

176 | Llamas beyond the Andes

Conversation revealed that Obando had exploited his authority as *corregidor* to take the animals forcibly from the herders, claiming that they were needed by the government. To make matters worse, Obando skimmed off most of the money Ledger gave him for the purchase of the alpacas, paying $5–$6 for each animal, whereas Ledger had given him enough to pay $20 per animal. Satisfied that he had fulfilled his end of the bargain, Ledger left Obando to settle the conflict between himself and the herders. Although he did not know how the *corregidor* resolved the situation, he noted that the men appeared to be satisfied. The group returned together to Vilca Pujio the next day (Ledger 1859, 192–193).

Following this encounter, Ledger set out to catch up with Sosa and the alpacas. As he approached the group, he discovered that the men and animals were being pursued by a large group of thirty-five to forty Indigenous women, vociferously demanding that the alpacas be returned to them. Ledger (1859, 193) described them as "old women that day and night kept up a continual howling, crying, and screaming, calling us all sorts of names." They refused to be placated, so eventually he simply ignored them, until they asked for food: "I gave them provisions and coca, they then begged me to be kind to the animals, stopped behind and we saw them no more; some of these poor creatures had actually travelled more than three hundred miles from their homes, following the Alpacas that their husbands had sold to Obando" (193).[19]

The story of Ledger's procurement of the alpacas starkly illustrates the collision between traditional (nonmonetary) economies and the modernizing tenets of liberalism in the historical conjuncture of mid-nineteenth-century Bolivia. As Larson (2004, 7) has shown, colonial tributary regimes gave Indigenous peoples the right to claim communally held lands and maintain local self-governance. During the mid-nineteenth century, newly imposed forms of liberalism and modernity attempted to convert land and labor (and animals) "into transferable commodities, whose redistribution would be mediated by the play of market forces and secured by individual property rights." This conflict created "an *arena of interpretive struggle* over indigenous political rights, social memory, location, and identity, which reflected the postcolonial predicament of so many native Andean peasants caught between the contradictory legal-political discourses of colonialism, liberalism, and racism" (7–8; emphasis in the original). This particular scene, as narrated by Ledger, makes visible this conflict between individual and communal epistemologies.

The tenets of nineteenth-century liberalism posited that money had

Andean Itineraries of Nineteenth-Century Camelid Science | 177

the power to eradicate preexisting social hierarchies while serving as an index of a culture's advancement. As Harris argues (1995, 303), "For liberal philosophy, the breaking down of any hierarchy that does not arise out of the 'natural' mechanisms of free competition and market forces is progressive, and money is accordingly the signifier of progress." For Ledger (and his readers), the Andeans who literally threw the money back at the *corregidor*, demanding that he return their animals, exhibited irrational, premodern behavior. Drawing from Platt (1982), Harris (1995, 303) explains: "Money according to [liberalism's] view does not merely embody the beneficial effect of destroying unnatural constraints on its own operations, but represents rationality itself. In the language of development and underdevelopment, those who fail, or refuse, to participate fully in the market . . . are seen as irrational." Ledger's endeavor to broker the purchase of Andean camelids was thus constructed in his narrative according to the parameters of liberalism's civilizing principles that depict those who resist unconditional participation in the capitalist market not only as irrational but also as closer to the animal state.[20]

Ledger's narrative account is further complicated by the ways in which ethnicity, liberalism, and colonialism intersect with gender. When Obando showed up to request that the animals be returned, Ledger described the three Indigenous men who accompanied him as "old." He later used a respectful form of address in his narrative, *tatas*, although he retained the epithet "old" ("old *tatas*"). The repeated reference to their age may well have conveyed the idea of their "frailty" or "weakness" to the reader in faraway New South Wales or England, especially in contrast to the strength and sharpness of Ledger's heroic self-depiction. Ledger neglected to explain to his readers that the term of respect *tata* is not used to call attention to age as a sign of defenselessness and fragility in Andean pastoral communities. Rather, the term underscores the wisdom elders acquire, which accrues from an abundance of lived experience and knowledge of the community's trajectory from a mythical and historical past to the present and on into the future.[21] Although he highlighted the weaknesses that he perceived to be inherent in their age, Ledger nevertheless presented these men as reasonable because they ultimately seemed satisfied with what presumably ended up being a monetary resolution to the situation.

In contrast, the "old women" who followed Ledger's men and animals for over three days and hundreds of miles could not be appeased by the money, refusing to give up on their demands for the animals' return (Ledger 1859, 193). Although Ledger somewhat reluctantly admired their

178 | Llamas beyond the Andes

perseverance, he nevertheless characterized them as much more irrational than the men and suggested that their age and agency added to their exaggerated behavior.[22] This incident thus mobilized vexed representations of gender and ethnicity, which for the purposes of his larger heroic narrative underscored the Indigenous peoples' perceived superstitious, antimodern nature. Readers could then easily contrast his calm, rational, and even benevolent demeanor with these unruly women and frail men.

Ledger's troubles were not limited to the difficulties resulting from encounters with Indigenous communities over the need to replenish his flock of alpacas. He also had to dodge increasingly vigilant authorities charged with preventing him from taking the animals out of the country.[23] Official correspondence began circulating on the subject of Ledger in late June 1855 and continued into September of the same year. On June 26, 1855, the Finance Office in the Ministry of the State issued orders from Sucre to the prefect of the department of Potosí. According to this document, President Manuel Isidoro Belzú had learned that Ledger planned to take 400 alpacas out of Potosí to transport them to Australia. Fearing that this action could harm the country's fiber economy, the president ordered that Ledger be stopped by any means possible. If he eluded arrest, "the animals should all be captured and killed [*degollados*]."[24] The prefect of Potosí was also instructed to forward the order to the prefect of Cobija and to the governors of Chorolque and Lípez.

Additional orders for Ledger's apprehension moved through the chain of command, from Sucre to the governors, subprefects, and police intendants in the wake of Ledger's route south toward the border with the Argentine Confederation. Local authorities responded to confirm that they would do all they could to prevent Ledger from carrying through on his mission. They reported that he had been spotted, first in the province of Lípez, later in the Atacama province, in a pasture area (*potrero*) called Susques, and finally across the border, in the small village of Rosario, Argentina.[25] On September 30, 1855, José V. Rivera, the governor of the Atacama province, wrote to Sucre to explain that 170 of Ledger's alpacas had already relocated to the Cachi Valley in Argentina by the time he received the circular. At the time of his letter in September, however, he claimed that only 70 of the original number still survived and reportedly were in a bad state of health due to the intense heat and insufficient pasture. To find any decent grass for grazing they would have to cross the desert with no resources. In his opinion, it was unlikely that any would survive.[26] The prefect of the Departamento del Litoral, Gabriel Moreno,

Andean Itineraries of Nineteenth-Century Camelid Science | 179

expressed concern about the quantity of contraband activities taking place in the region. In addition to his apprehensions regarding the widespread illegal movement of money, Moreno had learned of Ledger's smuggled alpacas, which only increased his alarm (Jemio Arnez 2015, 178).

Ledger had two close scrapes with the law. The first took place early in 1855 when he crossed into Bolivia from Argentina in search of his guide Pedro Cabrera, who had charge of one of the alpaca flocks. The local mayor of the border town San Antonio de Esmoraca, Manuel Alarcón, took Ledger into custody when he discovered that he did not have a passport. The mayor had instructions from the governor of the province to stop anyone coming in from Argentina without proper documents and escort them to Tupiza, then the customs seat for southern Bolivia. Many of the government's political enemies had congregated near the border in the northern Argentina provinces, so officials on the Bolivian side were expected to monitor all activity. The evening before the mayor and eight Indians were to conduct him to Tupiza, Ledger learned that the mayor's wife was seriously ill. Ledger, who had a reputation for curing ailments, examined her, "bled and blistered her, and by the morning she was very much relieved" (Ledger 1859, 191). In appreciation, the mayor sent the Indians away and gave Ledger a signed and sealed passport, allowing him to continue on his way unhindered (191–192).

The second run-in with authorities took place while on the southward march with one of the flocks of alpacas. Ledger and his group were overtaken by an officer and four soldiers with orders to arrest Ledger. Because these directives did not mention the animals, Ledger sent Pablo Sosa on, urging him to keep the flock moving south as quickly as possible, while he went off with the soldiers. They escorted him to Tola Pampa and placed him under guard at the house of the *corregidor*, planning to transport him to Potosí. To give Sosa time and delay the move to Potosí, Ledger feigned illness, claiming that he was unable to get out of bed or travel, thereby managing to postpone the departure for five days. After that, the *corregidor* told him that he could either ride his own mule or be carried on a litter. Ledger protested, insisting that he would not move under such "barbarous proceedings," and demanded that the *corregidor* send to Potosí for orders, figuring that would stall further action for another eight days or so. In the meantime, Ledger discovered that the *corregidor* suffered from ongoing toothache, so he planned his escape by lacing the man's brandy with morphine and laudanum and offering the soldier guarding him the same stiff drink. Ledger and his men slipped outside, saddled their own mules, and

180 | *Llamas beyond the Andes*

rode off, driving the *corregidor*'s and soldier's horses in front of them (Ledger 1859, 193).

Ledger defended his actions in his writings, crediting his linguistic abilities, medicinal skills, and knowledge of local customs for getting himself out of trouble. Claiming this kind of intimate knowledge of Indigenous communities and regional authorities distinguishes his heroic narrative from that of many other European travelers. He emphasized consistently that he had not broken a single law in either Bolivia or Peru because he had not driven the animals to the coast, which is why he had instead headed south into Argentina. Ledger admitted, however, that even though he had not technically violated the law, he realized that the Bolivian government opposed the extraction of the animals from the country. He insisted that officials had done little to implement the legislation: had the Indians been notified of the prohibition, they would have been more effective than the 500 officers placed along the border in ensuring that the law was obeyed to protect their own interests (Ledger 1859, 194).

Soon after crossing the border, Ledger tallied the number of animals that he and his men had successfully brought into the Argentine Confederation from Bolivia as well as the number of losses: 312 alpacas and llamas out of 450 survived the trip in 1852; he added 160 out of 197 in 1854, for a total of 472 animals. From this number 184 perished in snowstorms. The remaining 288 animals gave birth to 113 babies in February 1855. Obando's flock augmented the number with 169 animals out of 171, and Pedro Cabrera's flock added another 158 out of 200, for a grand total of 728 animals surviving out of 1,018. Ledger's total numbers do not include the loss of 200 babies in 1853–1854 (Ledger 1859, 222). By then, however, Ledger's funds were depleted. He had 19 men in his employ in addition to the large flock of alpacas and llamas to care for, resulting in costly monthly expenses.

Ledger's dwindling resources obliged him to return to Valparaíso to meet with potential financial backers. The artist Santiago Savage appears to have joined the group around this time, perhaps accompanying Ledger from Valparaíso or Salta, and he began depicting the groups' adventures. Savage (discussed in more detail later) created a sketch depicting the tragic events that took place during one heavy snowstorm, when the company lost 161 alpacas, 31 llamas, 20 donkeys, 3 mules, and 1 horse (Ledger 1859, 194). During the storm, two Indigenous shepherds were sent out for firewood and never returned. Three days later, while Ledger's group was digging itself out, they saw condors flying in the distance and verified

Andean Itineraries of Nineteenth-Century Camelid Science | 181

afterward that the birds had found the bodies of the missing men. Savage illustrated the scene. This image subsequently was one of four drawings that he and Ledger later presented to Swinglehurst in appreciation for his financial and emotional support. The image provided "a graphic view, more than words can give, to those who have not been in such regions" (Swinglehurst 1893, 171).

Condors figured prominently in Ledger's narratives and Savage's watercolors, as unsettling tropes heralding the proximity of danger and death. This early image and others that Savage prepared call attention to the importance of the visual archive and how Ledger made strategic use of it to construct a heroic representation of his enterprise and draw in a sympathetic audience of potential patrons.

Ledger and the group sometimes found themselves under attack from small Bolivian units that crossed the border looking for him but did not suffer any major injuries as a result, and eventually the Bolivian forces stopped their pursuit.[27] The men and animals headed toward the winter paddocks that Ledger had selected in the Calchaquí Valleys. The 120-mile trip was grueling due to the weakened state of the alpacas; most were unable to stand on their own, let alone walk. With neither water nor pasture available along the way, the animals could not regain their strength, so they had to be carried on the backs of the donkeys or the men's own shoulders. Ledger admitted that he felt discouraged and overwhelmed by self-doubt as the men became increasingly exhausted and the numbers of animal fatalities continued to rise: "Our donkeys and mules being overworked bringing water from a distance, and having but little to eat were dying daily, the men also done up, yet not a murmur did I hear, the immense number of condors that followed our track gave evidence of our losses in Alpacas" (Ledger 1859, 221–222). By the time they finally reached their winter paddocks at La Poma, they had lost 103 out of 409 animals. Their losses continued even after arrival, with 53 more dying over the next two weeks, because many of the alpacas refused to eat dry fodder (222).

Now that the men and animals had reached the Calchaquí Valleys, Ledger hoped that the worst lay behind them. Disaster struck again, however, when the animals drank from the freshwater lakes and became infected with the *unca* parasite.[28] Nothing could be done to help the sick animals, and within a short period, 200 more alpacas died. The men had no choice but to move the animals once more. In October 1856 they gathered the surviving flock and headed slowly toward Laguna Blanca, where they hoped that the herd would fare better.

182 | *Llamas beyond the Andes*

Ledger and his team finally reached Laguna Blanca in March 1857. The entire ordeal of bringing the animals out of Bolivia and into Argentina took a total of three years. Ledger summed up this leg of the venture: "After a journey of nearly 1,700 miles through a country that no description of mine could ever adequately represent, with losses of animals from different causes, passing two of the main and three minor ranges of the Andes" (Ledger 1864a, 97). Ledger's friend, Benjamin Poucel, a French traveler with business interests in Río de la Plata's bourgeoning merino sheep industry, offered explanations for the high number of animal deaths, which Ledger had communicated to him in correspondence. These included a lack of experience with the special needs of the alpaca; negligence on the part of some of the herders; the temperatures of the valleys, which were too warm for the alpacas; the difficulty of training the alpacas to eat hay, alfalfa, and bran; and a lack of funds, "which failed in the most critical emergencies, such as at times when it was found necessary to buy up dry stuff, to be placed in different spots, which were destitute of pasture, both green and dry" (Poucel quoted in Bradshaw 1858). With so much working against Ledger, Poucel marveled that he had managed to keep even one animal alive. Contemporary readers of Ledger's account must have thought much the same. These writings convey the impression that Ledger was at the height of his heroic narrative by the time the group reached Laguna Blanca. He had managed to persevere with the enterprise despite many losses and moments of overwhelming self-doubt. Thanks to his endurance and fortitude, he seemed capable of almost superhuman feats and able to outsmart the most dogged of his adversaries.

Laguna Blanca: 1857–1858

Secluded in a valley at the altitude of 2,600–3,000 meters above sea level and encircled by high, often snow-covered peaks, Laguna Blanca was the perfect place for Ledger, the men accompanying him, and the animals to spend the next months in anticipation of the voyage to Australia. Ledger believed that preparing the animals beforehand would be key to their survival while traveling and afterward as they became acclimatized to a new land. He chose Laguna Blanca as a location well suited for his purposes because the valley area was disease-free, dry, and cold, while offering adequate water and pasture (see Bertrand 1885, 238). It was situated on one of the main routes that crossed the Andes into Chile via the Paso de San

Francisco.[29] Ledger expressed his appreciation of the area in his journal: "We had plenty of wood for fuel & very many blessings that Kind Providence supplied to us in the shape of good water, sufficient pasture for the animals! Blessings indeed after what we had previously passed."[30]

During his time in Laguna Blanca, Ledger kept a multimedia diary that contained the notes and illustrations for a planned memoir of his adventures in the Andes, while transporting the camelids through Bolivia and Argentina to the Chilean coast and on to Australia. His hopes were that upon arrival at the British colony he would be heralded as a benefactor like John Macarthur, the celebrated importer of merino sheep into New South Wales at the turn of the nineteenth century. As he explained on several occasions, Ledger intended to publish his account once he and the animals successfully reached Australia. He referred to his writing project in different lectures that he gave, including one to the Scientific and Literary Society of Valparaíso, Chile, in August 1858, before embarking for Australia.[31] An anonymous author describing the event remarked that "we anticipate a real treat in the perusal of the full account of this remarkable expedition, with his observations on the impressions made on him by the scenes through which he passed" (quoted in Bradshaw 1858).[32]

Another writer shared similar feelings of excitement in anticipation of reading the published narrative, highlighting elements that emphasized the heroic nature of the enterprise: "The details of this remarkable journey, the obstacles, both natural and artificial, which had to be overcome, form the subject of a journal full of incident and hardships of all descriptions, which Mr. Ledger, we are happy to hear, intends to publish at some future period" ("Mr. Charles Ledger" 1859, 173).[33] Ledger brought Savage's sketches and watercolors with him to his public presentations. It is apparent that he planned to supplement his lively narrative to help bring his adventures to life before the reader's eyes (Ledger 1864a, 90).

Unfortunately, following his arrival in Australia with the animals and the ensuing financial disasters that plagued him for the rest of his life, publication of the planned narrative became impossible. Apart from a few talks on the topic of the alpacas, which were subsequently published (some only in incomplete form), a narrative published by his brother George, and two reports by Poucel, the major source we have for understanding what life was like in Laguna Blanca and later while crossing the cordillera into Chile is Ledger's original diary and sketchbook, still held by the Mitchell Library, State Library of New South Wales, in Sydney, Australia.[34]

184 | Llamas beyond the Andes

Ledger's Journal: Constructing Community through Narrative and Visuality

Ledger's journal is a plural or composite archive that includes a variety of media, including textual and pictorial documents, such as watercolors, drawings, and sketches; written accounts; fold-out lists and measurements of distances covered in a day, with accompanying commentary (sometimes in Spanglish) on the accessibility of pasture, alfalfa, water, and fuel; a scribbled chronology of significant dates and encounters; and a map annotated with the dates and routes that he and his travel companion Manuel Incra Mamani had navigated over the years.

The journal, and undoubtedly Ledger's ambitious book project, presumably had at least four purposes. The first was to play up the risks that challenged Ledger and his team in their efforts to collect and extract alpacas from Bolivia. The second purpose was to introduce Laguna Blanca to an international audience and demonstrate the knowledge, skills, and expertise needed there to work with the animals to control their reproduction and gradually prepare them for the overseas voyage. The third was to portray Ledger as the man best able and qualified to direct the heroic enterprise, offset the risks involved, and prevent losses as much as possible so that the goal of bringing the animals safely to Australia could be successfully accomplished. Finally, Ledger wanted to make the case that he deserved to be generously compensated for his epic labors. Read as a whole, however, the journal and its contents reveal that heroic narratives can be difficult to sustain, as their pluralistic perspectives confound the idea of a single, solitary protagonist, laboring alone. Like Laguna Blanca itself, the journal created a sort of textual community that ultimately decentered the imperial heroic subject, enabling us to recognize the complexities of this constructed physical space of encounter and the work of its diverse protagonists.

During Ledger's time and even today, the journal's colorful images have captured the attention of those who examine its contents. The series of watercolors and drawings shows influence from European pictorial traditions of the sublime and the picturesque, natural-history illustrations, and nineteenth-century Andean *costumbrista* drawings (colorful scenes of people and everyday life). Little is known about the artist who prepared these illustrations and signed most with the name "Santiago Savage" or "S. Savage." Like the artists who formed part of scientific expeditions of the time, Savage accompanied Ledger and his men for a portion of the

Andean Itineraries of Nineteenth-Century Camelid Science | 185

journey through the Andes, creating an eye-catching visual archive of the group's endeavors.

Ledger's biographer, Gramiccia (1988, 664) concludes that the artist was likely Manuel Incra Mamani's son Santiago, who accompanied Ledger on many of his travels, including on the trip to Australia. Firsthand examination of the images, however, has led me to speculate that the artist was not Indigenous but rather a fellow British or Canadian traveler, perhaps named "James Savage." First, although Savage signed most of his works as either "Santiago Savage" or "S. Savage," one signature clearly reads "J. Savage." In South America, per convention, non-Hispanic first names are often Hispanicized. For instance, in much of the correspondence from the Bolivian archives, Ledger was referred to as "don Carlos Ledger." Hence my guess is that the artist's name could have been James ("Santiago" in Spanish) Savage. Second, Ledger referred to Savage as "Mr. Savage," as he did with all of his other European and Canadian travel companions, while he referred to the shepherds who accompanied him by their first names (Manuel, Pedro, Pablo, and so forth). Third, the artist wrote the date in English in at least one of the images. Finally, the images themselves confirm Savage's non-Indigenous identity because he sometimes depicted himself in the role as cook and his European features are evident.

I have paused here to reflect briefly on the identity of the artist in hope that the exercise could call attention to the perspectives conveyed in the images examined later: specifically, the ways in which the shepherds are represented physically and spatially in relation to the Europeans; how humor is constructed in some pictures, usually at the expense of the shepherds; and how the artist appears to have had access to certain spaces and not others or at least chose to depict particular spaces over others. Figure 5.1 shows one evening at camp, while the troop of men and animals was en route to Laguna Blanca following the debacle of the Calchaquí Valleys in October 1856. Handwritten on the back of the image is the following description: "The night of 24th Feby. Remarkable by Pepe falling over the dog 'bochorno' & spoiling our anticipated feed after a hard day's work. Mr. Savage officiates as 'cook' whenever we get *something* more savoury than our general meal of boiled bits of meat & maiz meal—the frying pan & sauce being ready, the ducks shot during the day got a roll in the sand & having no water we could not eat them. 1857" (emphasis in the original). Savage, kneeling on the ground with Ledger standing by his side, is recognizable in other images from the same clothing he wears here and also he holds a frying pan in two other instances.

186 | Llamas beyond the Andes

FIGURE 5.1. *"Evening meal on February 24, 1857."* ML MSS 630/1. *Mitchell Library, State Library of New South Wales (Sydney).*

From what little is known about Savage, it appears that he may have joined Ledger's group sometime in late 1856, accompanying him until the men and animals reached the Chilean coast in 1858. Swinglehurst (1893, 170) commented on their friendship, noting how Ledger spoke "kindly of the solace Mr. Savage was to him after November, 1856, making an all but unendurable life bearable, by enlivening the long and dreary nights when all seemed desperate. This gentleman made the sketches which it was his intention to use as illustrations to a book of his travels. But whether any were spared, besides those at [Swinglehurst's] Hincaster House, is very doubtful."

Ledger indeed planned to include the watercolors and drawings in his published narrative, which, as already noted, never materialized. It is less certain how many people during his lifetime actually saw the illustrations. As Bleichmar (2012, 10) persuasively argues more generally for images and their power to influence, "whether in the end images managed to be seen or not, whether they proved themselves useful or not, they had great epistemic and cultural value." Although Ledger saved many illustrations for the planned publication, he utilized others strategically for separate purposes. Some of Savage's drawings were given away to friends and patrons, and Ledger appears to have occasionally presented the remaining images to his audiences when lecturing on the subject of his alpaca venture in Chile and Australia. In Valparaíso, Swinglehurst (1893, 167) received at least four sketches directly from Savage and Ledger: "Mr. Ledger and Mr. Savage who was for some time his companion, gave me certain sketches made during the expedition, and I have four of these made up neatly in water colours, now at Hincaster House." These sketches that Ledger presented to Swinglehurst were likely a gesture of appreciation for his generous financial assistance. As Swinglehurst explained in his memoir, "Mr. Ledger had been supported by Mr. Waddington and one or two very wealthy gentlemen in Chile, and finally I, and another friend or two, put a few pounds sterling into the hands of Mr. Ledger to ease his progress, after he had come near to the end of his great labours" (167).

Although the images are not especially accomplished, they nevertheless played a key role in commanding the attention of the viewer and communicating the goals that Ledger hoped to achieve with his journal-book project. Employing a variety of visual traditions and techniques, Savage's portfolio offers a captivating aesthetic that portrayed the Andean region and especially Laguna Blanca as areas whose serene beauty belies their perils and possibilities. For example, Savage's general depictions of the Andean landscape used parallel planes receding into the distance to create a captivating physical and emotional depth of perspective that draws the viewer into the image and its narrative. By contrast, his descriptive depictions of daily life at Laguna Blanca abandoned the tropes of an awe-producing environment to deploy elements of *costumbrismo*, which Majluf (1997, 879) has characterized as "the Latin American counterpart of the picturesque." Recognizable faces, bodies, and activities enter the foreground in an orderly and methodical fashion in these scenes, creating the sense of place, animals, and community. Images depicting this collective yet hybrid social enterprise also bring out the hard work required for the sake of accomplishing the project's innovations. For instance, successful advancement of the camelid extraction venture in Laguna Blanca depended on Andean-style practices of herd management, corral construction, and animal organization combined with the implementation of new dietary practices for the animals. If they were going to be able to survive the passage across the cordillera and the Pacific Ocean, they would have to be trained to eat dry alfalfa.

Other illustrations bring out lighter moments. In figure 5.2, Thomas

FIGURE 5.2. "1857. Thomas Grey teaching the Indians to slide." ML MSS 630/1. Mitchell Library, State Library of New South Wales (Sydney).

Grey, about whom little is known, teaches the Indians how to "slide" in what is clearly a moment of leisure and relaxation, although it may not have been so much fun for those falling on the ice. Ledger provided the names and significant roles played by a few of the Indigenous men who accompanied him, most notably Manuel Incra Mamani and his son Santiago, his guide Pedro Cabrera, and his servant Pablo Sosa. Figure 5.3 brings in other protagonists and is suggestive for its representation of knowledge construction at Laguna Blanca. Although the caption tells us that orders are being delivered to the scouts, the construction of the scene in the illustration appears to be more complicated.[35] Ledger is depicted here seated at the desk and writing instructions, a note, or a letter. The Indigenous man standing next to the table overshadows Ledger, who is looking down at his paper. While we would not expect to see the man seated, as if he and Ledger enjoyed equal status, he maintains a more active stance, talking and gesturing. The seated scout has exaggerated prognathic features, but the man standing and pointing to another document that may be a map clearly appears to take on a leadership role and occupies the image's focal point.

The rendering of the scene can be read as showing the creation of the collaborative class, with one Indian dictating instructions to the seated subaltern, while Ledger attends to other business. Or, as a possible counternarrative, the image can be understood as the culmination of creating community, underscoring the idea that knowledge at Laguna Blanca was produced through the coming together of written and oral traditions and mobilized through intercultural relationships based on collaboration, interaction, and negotiation. Despite the ambiguity of the image, the depiction of the two Indigenous men in relationship to Ledger nonetheless shows that the layered power relationships among the men have not been erased, regardless of the interpretation.

FIGURE 5.3. *"C.L.—giving orders to scouts."* ML MSS 630/1. Mitchell Library, State Library of New South Wales (Sydney).

Documenting New Experiments with Camelid Husbandry

Once Ledger and his men had settled in Laguna Blanca and turned it into a working space, together they began to create and implement new techniques of camelid husbandry designed to prepare the animals for their voyage to Australia and subsequent acclimatization in a new land. The projects facing the group were demanding, starting with their first task, which was to restore much of the herd that had been decimated from the *unca* catastrophe of the Calchaquí Valleys. A few of Savage's images explore these challenges and the procedures implemented. Alpacas did not naturally inhabit the northern area of the Argentine Confederation; consequently, Ledger was unable to replenish the herd with alpacas purchased locally. Unwilling to take the risk of traveling back into Bolivia to obtain more, he put into action an experimental breeding program whereby he crossed female llamas with pure alpaca herd sires. He then bred the female offspring of the first cross with a pure alpaca sire, following the same procedure for each subsequent generation, eventually hoping to breed the animal back to a full-blood alpaca. Young males born were gelded so that they would not complicate the project.

Ledger may well have conceived this idea after learning about a paco-vicuña hybridization project developed in Macusani, Peru, by the priest

190 | Llamas beyond the Andes

FIGURE 5.4. *"Vicuña hunters taking their 'morning' on starting up."* ML MSS 630/1. Mitchell Library, State Library of New South Wales (Sydney).

Juan Pablo Cabrera during the 1840s, an undertaking with which Ledger was clearly familiar.[36] Through this breeding program, in addition to increasing the number of alpacas, Ledger hoped to create a larger, more robust animal like the llama, better able to withstand the stress of traveling, yet exhibiting the high-quality fiber of the alpaca. Swinglehurst claimed that the second-generation crosses were almost indistinguishable from the alpaca, even though it was a more full-bodied animal. Moreover, it had a less delicate constitution than the alpaca and was able to eat coarser pasture (Swinglehurst 1893, 169). Poucel was slightly more circumspect in his report on the second generation of crossed animals: "Speaking as a practical breeder, I allow that these animals of the second generation do not yet possess in perfection the purity of the noble alpaca blood, but, seeing the surprising change already effected, it is indubitable that, by continually crossing the females of these and successive breeds with none but male alpacas of pure blood, the result must be a race combining superior size with all the perfections of the purest alpaca species." In spite of his uncertainties, Poucel clearly was impressed by Ledger's accomplishments, calling him "a creative genius, who, inspired by the importance of his mission, has torn from nature even the most mysterious secrets of procreation" (Poucel quoted in Bradshaw 1858). Reports of Ledger's work were followed with great interest in Europe because little was known about the fertility of crossbred offspring (Ledger 1860a, 1860b; Poucel 1858). Ledger could now verify from his own experience that the offspring reproduced successfully.

In addition to crossing the llama and alpaca, Ledger worked on domesticating wild vicuñas with the hope that by so doing he could transport them safely to Australia along with the other camelids. A series of four dramatic images documents the work that went into these projects. The first three (figures 5.4, 5.5, and 5.6) graphically portray a local *chaco* hunt for vicuñas, which Ledger made use of to acquire the young animals. The fourth drawing (figure 5.7) stands in contrast to these by showing an experimental approach to developing the vicuña fiber industry.

The first watercolor (figure 5.4) presents the hunters as they prepare to set out in the early morning. From the far right of the image, Ledger plays host to the group, sending the hunters off with a drink. One of the men passes the glass in salutation, while another to the far left enjoys a final smoke. The *costumbrista* scene enables the viewer to observe ethnic and social differences among the hunters. Most of the participants ride beautifully groomed horses, except for the Indigenous man in the foreground tying his sandals. He has a much less elaborate getup than the others and no horse to ride. His clothing and hair once again help the viewer to identify him as an Andean Indian from Bolivia. Four dogs congregate at the bottom center of the image, anxious to be off and running. A fifth dog, lying at Ledger's feet, shows little interest in the preparations and will presumably remain behind. The same men and animals can be followed in the next illustration of the hunt in progress (figure 5.5).

This figure depicts a seemingly chaotic scene where the vicuña hunters and their adventurous dogs chase down and slaughter animals and *ñandús* (rheas). In contrast with much of Ledger's own narrative and many hunting narratives of nineteenth-century travel writing, the visual clues here no longer solely construct the landscape as a testing ground for the production of European imperial masculinities.[37] In addition, it is a scene of carnage. The men expertly use the *boleadora* or sling to immobilize and kill the animals while the dogs close in on them, running pell-mell. In the confusion and turmoil, the Indigenous hunter rushes forward, losing his hat in the excitement.

Figure 5.6 portrays the tired men, who have now returned to their

FIGURE 5.5. *"The Mêlée—scene in 'Aparoma' Apl 1857."* ML MSS 630/1. Mitchell Library, State Library of New South Wales (Sydney).

camp with the spoils from the hunt. As the sun sets, the same protagonists break into smaller groups, some settling in around campfires, amidst the carcasses, roasting meat and relaxing, while others unsaddle their horses or transfer their catch to a spot safe from the dogs. Most appear to have the luxury of tying the animal carcass on the back of their horse, except for the Indigenous man who carries the body on his back. It is possible to see these three drawings as depicting a glorious hunt and its valuable trophies. While the tradition of the *chaco* might bring short-term economic gain to the successful hunters (even the man on foot), the viewer who serves as a witness to the scene of carnage can grasp the long-term costs for the species that these uncontrolled hunts imposed.[38]

The next image (figure 5.7) proposes an alternate scenario by contrasting the male-dominated scenes of tumult and death with an orderly, female-centric portrait of reproduction and sustenance. Ledger experimented with the possibility of domesticating young vicuñas, although the plan was not without its challenges and required negotiating with the local hunters, as he explained years later: "The five Vicunas brought to this colony [New South Wales] were all that remained from 83 that I purchased

FIGURE 5.6. *"Hunters making themselves cosy for the night."* ML MSS 630/1. Mitchell Library, State Library of New South Wales (Sydney).

from the Indian Vicuna hunters in the spring of the years 1856, 57, 58. The men watched the flocks of these animals at that particular season of the year, and immediately a lamb was 'dropped,' they rode it down, and often from a distance of 20, 30, and 40 miles a young Vicuna has been brought to my camp in the middle of the night by a hunter who had caught it during the day" (Ledger 1864a, 92).[39] Out of this scene of chaos thus emerged new methods for managing camelid husbandry, which Ledger and his men developed together with the idea of eventually making a nice profit from their approach. In the words of Poucel, "These nine little animals will form the ground-work of a fortune for Mr. Ledger's children, furnishing himself at the same time with a new title to fame, acquired by the numerous benefits conferred by this enterprise, which practically demonstrates the utility of crossing the llama, and originates the breeding of the vicuña" (Poucel quoted in Bradshaw 1858).

The men's method of saving the baby animals was to train llama "wet nurses" to raise them. Figure 5.7 shows four female llamas that were particularly social and willing to adopt vicuña orphans. Ledger referred to these llamas as the "four famous nurses 'Burra,' 'Sarca,' 'Cacho,' and

194 | Llamas beyond the Andes

FIGURE 5.7. *The four llama foster mothers. ML MSS 630/1. Mitchell Library, State Library of New South Wales (Sydney).*

'Chúcara.'"[40] Some are even shown here to have accepted two vicuñas, an unusual circumstance since twin births are extremely rare with camelids and milk production is relatively low. A young Indigenous boy named Ylaco, who had been with Ledger for three years, holds a vicuña named Luracatao with a lasso so that it will not try to run away because it does not have a nurse like the others. These llama wet nurses became a focal point of experimentation because they were central to the success of the vicuña domestication project, without which the ability to transport large numbers of these fragile animals would not be workable.

Ledger's success with the domestication project was especially noteworthy as camelids, specifically vicuñas, could be notoriously intractable on occasion, refusing to cooperate. As depicted in other illustrations from Savage's collection, the animals had resources to demonstrate their annoyance, including spitting and kicking. The llama nurses' conduct contrasted sharply with the behavior of the more recalcitrant animals. Regarding eighteenth-century wet nurses more generally, Meléndez (2011, 165) has shown how families that employed these women expected them to be "quiet, controlled, submissive, and obedient" because their behavior was

Andean Itineraries of Nineteenth-Century Camelid Science | 195

believed to play a significant role in shaping the "character and education of children everywhere." Similarly, the llama foster mothers are depicted in figure 5.7 as standing peacefully and cooperating in the corral while the vicuñas nurse, thereby aiding the role of domestication by setting a good example of docility in this enclosed space. The llamas appear to have been successful: the young animals continued to nurse or sit quietly on the ground even when Ylaco was present alongside them. Luracatao did not resist the lead line or strain to break away. Ledger explained in his diary that Ylaco needed to keep a tight hand on the vicuña at first, but the animal eventually became quite tame: it would graze alongside the alpacas in the pasture and gave no sign of wanting to escape.[41] Evoking ideas of wildness and domesticity, Savage's rendition juxtaposed the (feminine) corral as the privileged site of a practical science and controlled reproduction against the backdrop of a (masculine) untamed and brutal Andean landscape.

Yet Ledger's description of the domestication project and Savage's illustration of the llama wet nurses concealed the violence behind the training of the foster mothers. First, the baby (male) llama had to be killed, following which its skin would be draped over the baby vicuña like a coat to encourage the mother to accept the new baby (Poucel 1858, 183). If this method proved unsuccessful, they had to resort to rougher measures with the mother llama, which "generally succeeded after a fortnight's tying up, with fore and hind legs hobbled, with kindness or harshness, and by exertion of very great patience in making the Llama adopt the new comer. At one time I had more than 40 Llamas that daily depastured at large, totally unfettered, each with its adopted young Vicuna" (Ledger 1864a, 92).

If this scientific experiment succeeded, Ledger believed that it could become a significant breakthrough in acquiring the fiber from this animal.[42] He was aware of many cases where vicuñas had been raised by hand or by an alpaca, but he thought that he might be the first to use llama wet nurses to raise the young animals in this way. His ultimate goal, as he explained in the journal, was to carry out a project similar to the project of Peruvian Juan Pablo Cabrera and eventually create paco-vicuñas by crossing the vicuñas with the alpaca. Ledger's optimism filled the journal page, where he gave full expression to his hopes for success next to the drawing of the foster mothers: "If my views can be carried out or I live long enough to carry them out myself, New South Wales will be celebrated as the only country providing this 'non plus ultra' in wool. I spare no trouble or expense and I can only hope that parties of enterprise in New South Wales will supply the means to enable me to realize my fond

196 | *Llamas beyond the Andes*

hopes and expectations."[43] Ledger's use of the phrase "non plus ultra" resonates within Spanish and Latin American studies, harking back to the early Renaissance, when "plus ultra" became the maxim for the empire of Charles V, the age when "scientific inquiry was increasingly conceived as the discovery of new things rather than as attempts to demonstrate the known" (Eamon 2014, 240). As Juan Pimentel (1999, 41) observes, "plus ultra," or the widening of all that was known, became the epic formula for the discovery of the New World and hence the foundational act of modern history. By using this phrase, Ledger perhaps hoped to underscore the economic potential of his work, highlight the heroic nature of his imperial enterprise, and secure financial backing for the new discoveries that he saw himself offering (at great personal expense) to New South Wales and to the world, by domesticating the vicuña and creating a valuable hybrid, the "non plus ultra" of the modern fiber world.

As a series, the images of the vicuña hunters and llama nurses foregrounded the triumphal march of scientific knowledge in lockstep with empire that Ledger and his men fostered at Laguna Blanca. In sharp contrast to the violence and chaos of the hunting scene, Ledger represented himself as an explorer-entrepreneur who put into action new techniques dedicated to saving these valuable animals from extinction and enabling their transformation into a valuable commodity. Ironically, however, Ledger rarely discussed the paco-vicuña again after the diary, perhaps because the vicuñas' survival rate in captivity remained dismal despite the collaboration of the llama foster mothers.

The story of Ledger's work would end up being circulated by others to prop up a heroic portrayal of his endeavors. Due to the remoteness of the area, news of his activities in Laguna Blanca spread primarily through reports from visitors, the most well-known being Poucel, who had traveled to Laguna Blanca expressly to meet Ledger and learn more about his alpaca project. Poucel saw himself as instrumental in making Ledger's achievements known to the world at large, having first published a story on the Englishman's work in the Catamarca newspaper *El Ambato* (see Bradshaw 1858 for an excerpt). The article was picked up and published in "every province all the way to the Atlantic, in Buenos Aires, and in Montevideo" (Poucel 1860, 255). This article became the basis for a letter that he wrote to a colleague back in Paris and subsequently published in the Paris Acclimatization Society's *Bulletin* (Poucel 1858). The article reached an even wider audience when it was reprinted in English-speaking newspapers, such as the *Hobart Town Daily Mercury* of Tasmania (March

Andean Itineraries of Nineteenth-Century Camelid Science | 197

8, 1859). In response to a request for more information from the Paris Acclimatization Society, Poucel published a second article in the *Bulletin* (Poucel 1860). At the Regional Exhibition of Marseille Poucel displayed fiber samples from Ledger's animals, which he had collected in Laguna Blanca in September 1857 (Poucel 1861, 14).

Many in France read Poucel's account with interest, including Geoffroy Saint-Hilaire ([1861] 1986, 342–347), who described not only Ledger's but also Roehn's and Poucel's attempts to extract flocks of camelids for transportation overseas in his prominent work on acclimatization and domestication.[44] Ultimately, Poucel played an influential role in circulating information on Ledger's projects to an international audience, at the same time providing important eyewitness testimony confirming his accomplishments. These and other articles on the activities taking place in Laguna Blanca published in scientific journals in France, England, and Australia brought the remote location to South American and European readers' attention.

Victor Martin de Moussy (1860), Poucel's colleague and travel companion, further monumentalized Ledger's achievements when he incorporated Ledger's name into the map he prepared on the provinces of Salta and Jujuy. In the northern sector of the "Vallée de Laguna Blanca" he included the site where Ledger had spent the year, identifying it with the name "Alpacas de Ledgers [*sic*]."[45] His gesture memorialized Ledger's name and project while simultaneously bolstering Argentine national discourses by erasing local peoples and histories. As Mazzitelli Mastricchio (2015, 68–70) observes, even though Martin de Moussy (1860) wrote in French, his book immediately became a key primary source used for the consolidation of the national geographies of the Argentine Confederation and fomented the expansion of international interests and investment. The site "Alpacas de Ledgers" thus gained visibility within transnational scientific networks, international economic expansion, and more local discourses of national unification.

Ledger and his men and animals departed from Laguna Blanca in March 1858 to commence the journey over the main range of the Andean Cordillera and down into Chile. The party consisted of 31 men; 619 alpacas, llamas, and vicuñas; 77 mules loaded with provisions, hay, and fuel; and 38 donkeys and 45 pack llamas all carrying supplies. It would not be an easy crossing for them because it required traveling across rock, shale, and sand at high elevations upward of 18,000 feet above sea level and making their way for miles without pasture of any kind. In places

198 | Llamas beyond the Andes

where they encountered extensive snowfields, the group had to travel at night, when the snow was frozen hard enough that they could progress without sinking. Several of the men had to keep ahead of the flock to deposit fodder for the animals to eat along the way (Ledger 1864a, 98). For much of the journey, the group had to cope with snowfall and high winds, with some gales being so violent that several times Ledger feared all the men and animals would be lost (Ledger 1860a, 260).

Santiago Savage still accompanied Ledger's party. His watercolors provide vivid illustration of the treacherous conditions and numerous difficulties encountered. To document what the party endured and create a visual space that invited the viewer's sense of empathy and co-participation, he divided the dramatic events of one night into two- and four-hour intervals, rendering them in three watercolors (figure 5.8). In the first of the three images, viewers witness directly the dangers of an unmediated nature as men and animals seek protection from the elements in the very early hours of the morning. The observer can sense the freezing wind that leads the alpacas to huddle together for warmth and the mules to turn their heads away. Three men shelter next to a rock while two others move about with difficulty because of the snow and force of the storm. The scene makes it possible to imagine the perils the expedition continually faced, thereby subtly underscoring the courage and tenacity of all involved.

As seen in figure 5.8, a follow-up to the previous image depicts the same spot two hours later, with the wind now having died down. Men and animals huddle together for warmth, attempting to catch a few hours of sleep before moving on at daybreak.

However, at eight the following morning, before the men could get on their way, they had to look for and collect the alpacas that had become dispersed during the gale. Some of the animals had been separated from the rest of the herd, so Ledger sent a few of the shepherds out to search for them. Savage transformed an otherwise exhausting and tense situation into a droll, almost playful moment, by placing the unfortunate Pepe once again at the center of the watercolor's narrative (see figure 5.8). A note penciled on the back of the image reads: "There was one advantage in the snow—Pepe always fell soft." The same Pepe who fell over the dog and dumped the duck dinner on the ground in figure 5.1 can be seen here, sprawled out, headfirst in the snow, his hat tumbling away. Even the alpacas seem more amused by Pepe's misfortune than frightened over being lost. The viewer is so close to the scene that the animals' smiles can

Andean Itineraries of Nineteenth-Century Camelid Science | 199

FIGURE 5.8. *"Passage of cordillera into Chile."* From top to bottom: "1858. Apl. 4. 2 am. Passage of Cordillera into Chile"; "1858. Apl. 4. 4 am. Passage of Cordillera into Chile"; "Apl. 5th 8am. Animals that separated during the march being brought back." ML MSS 630/1. Mitchell Library, State Library of New South Wales (Sydney).

be detected. Despite the sense of immediacy conveyed here, the perception of danger is minimized by the scene's expressed lightheartedness.

Notwithstanding these moments of apparent levity, the passage of the cordillera pushed men and animals to their limits. In one drawing, Savage portrayed Ledger in a moment when he appears to be resting after a long day, assuming the classic contemplative position of the romantic hero. He,

FIGURE 5.9. *"Hardships on the road."* ML MSS 630/1. Mitchell Library, State Library of New South Wales (Sydney).

a tent, and supplies are figured against the harsh, snow-covered landscape, which they dominate in scale. The annotations on the back, however, modify this initial interpretation: "Afternoon, after passing Cordillera with loss of 119 animals in 22 hrs. 176 miles without a blade of grass. Elevation 17/21,000 ft." The text now obliges the viewer to construe the meaning of the portrayal differently. Although the written description relies on the use of numbers and measures in a typical technique of quantification (see Poole 1998, 119) that distances sentiment, the visual image now reveals a man exhausted and devastated by the losses he has had to endure. Notwithstanding Ledger's apparent dominance of the landscape, the viewer comprehends that this harsh place cannot be domesticated by narratives of romance.

A final watercolor (figure 5.9) depicts more clearly some of the ordeals of the road. The image's attention shifts away from a close-up view of Ledger to provide a more panoramic view of one specific incident. The inscription on the back documents the devastating toll on the animals when they had to endure a lack of water and pasture for one segment of the journey. Ledger sent word ahead to a place called Corralitos, which had a small river gully located four leagues from the road. The alpacas were so exhausted by this time that he realized they would not be able to

walk the additional distance to the water: "& when we arrived found that a man living there, named Benito Colque had brought water to the road in every imaginable domestic utensil, himself, wife, & daughters bringing it that distance—our mules and donkeys although all but done up managed to go to the water. —The poor people here cried to see the state in which the flocks were. We here lost 5." While the perspective of the drawing makes it difficult to perceive the stress and anxiety that everyone felt, the panoramic view of the bleak landscape, the animals, and the long line of family members carrying containers dramatically illustrates the distances that Colque, his wife, and daughters had to walk to bring water to the flock. The approaching condors on the horizon help to convey the sense of impending tragedy, while the position of the alpacas lying on the ground at the image's lower left communicates their fatigue and physical distress.

These vivid illustrations testified to the large number of animal casualties resulting from the harsh conditions that the expedition continually suffered. Although Ledger's figures on the total number of animals lost during the passage of the Cordillera varied from report to report, in his diary he recorded upward of 119.[46] In a letter to Poucel he reported 93 deaths (Ledger 1860a, 260). In an address to the Acclimatisation Society (Ledger 1864a, 98) he described losing 198 alpacas and llamas in the

202 | Llamas beyond the Andes

twenty-day crossing, in addition to 18 mules, 27 donkeys, and 34 pack llamas. While the numbers are inconsistent, they convey the significant and devastating impact of loss.

Ledger, his men, and the animals finally reached the valley of Copiapó, Chile, in May 1858. Their arrival was greeted with great enthusiasm: "The city was almost deserted for several days, the people forming an uninterrupted procession between it and Punta Negra (a distance of six miles), where the flocks were at pasture" (Bradshaw 1858). Now that the dangers of the Andean crossing were behind him, Ledger could turn his attention to publicizing his efforts. One strategy he used was to prop up his heroic narrative by publishing glowing articles about himself under the pseudonym Mr. Bradshaw. In a letter to the *Sydney Morning Herald* "Mr. Bradshaw" observed how the British residents of Copiapó especially admired "the indomitable spirit of perseverance which had upheld Mr. Ledger, and the ability and constancy displayed by him for so long a time (six years) in the prosecution of his unparalleled, daring, and most hazardous undertaking" (Bradshaw 1858). In a similar vein, colleagues of Ledger, like Poucel, commented on how the "natives" of Copiapó were equally impressed and astonished "at seeing that a European had accomplished a feat that had hitherto been considered altogether impracticable" (Poucel quoted in Bradshaw 1858). Poucel felt certain that the British inhabitants planned to offer Ledger an award in appreciation of his patriotic service to Britain and in recognition of the important contributions he had made to science, especially his success in crossing the animals.

For George Ledger (1860–1861, 216), his brother's epic labors demonstrated beyond the shadow of a doubt "the fundamental principle of human society, laid down equally by statists and revealed law": that "'the profit of the earth is for all.'" His words constituted a typical expression of the ideologies of improvement underlying the acclimatization movement, which inspired the work and loyalty of colonialists like his brother Charles. Continuing his argument and revealing its reliance on extractivist relations with the natural world, George Ledger (1860–1861) reiterated the now-familiar complaint that Europe had provided the dependent republics of South America with important and useful products, such as horses, pigs, sheep, and oxen, but Peru had responded to this generosity "by the positive prohibition of the export of its most valuable animal product, thus refusing to mankind a participation in the benefits it is calculated to confer." Charles Ledger would willingly have paid an export tax, George Ledger

Andean Itineraries of Nineteenth-Century Camelid Science | 203

continued, but the government refused to compromise, acting illiberally by keeping such an important benefit to itself.

If his brother had not complied fully with the letter of the law by taking the animals out of Peru and Bolivia, George argued that "it is a much smaller breach of the strict law of political or commercial morality to evade or break such a law than it is to make it, and that the obligations of patriotism impelled my brother 'to do a great right by doing a little wrong,' in the evasion of a prohibition contrary to the laws of nature, and inimical to the interests of mankind. I may add, that if my brother's act may be called by some, politically or commercially, not strictly moral, he at least sins in very respectable company" (Ledger 1860–1861, 216). Notwithstanding his actions that violated at the very least the spirit of the Andean countries' laws, these and other encomia indicate that Charles Ledger became an internationally recognized hero almost overnight for many when he reached Chile.

Ledger and his men remained in Copiapó for three months, during which time the animals rested and he charted and readied a 750-ton vessel, the *Salvadora*, for the forthcoming trip to Australia. Over the course of these preparations, the French chargé d'affaires approached Ledger to offer him $100,000 for the flock and the opportunity to take the animals to Algiers for acclimatization on behalf of the French government (Ledger 1864a, 98). Ledger declined this offer but made it public, presumably because it provided concrete evidence of the value not only of the animals but also of himself and his expertise. He used the offer to emphasize the importance of his patriotism and loyalty to the original agreement and to the British Empire, presumably expecting to receive a similar or larger offer from Great Britain.

During the same months, Ledger traveled back and forth between Copiapó and Valparaíso, solidifying his ties with the British communities residing in both areas. In Valparaíso, as noted earlier, he presented his lecture to the Scientific and Literary Society on the extraction of the alpaca from Bolivia for introduction into Australia (Swinglehurst 1893, 167). This small community of British merchants and business leaders provided important financial and moral support to Ledger and the alpaca project, and his presentation helped to sustain their enthusiasm and interest in his affairs.[47]

While in Valparaíso, Ledger approached Waddington, Templeman & Co. for a supplementary loan to cover the final leg of the trip. Although

204 | *Llamas beyond the Andes*

the financial house agreed to advance him an additional £5,000, it obliged Ledger, who was now £15,000 in debt, to mortgage the animals to the company until it could be fully reimbursed (Gramiccia 1988, 73). As Ledger explained to Swinglehurst in a letter that he wrote on board the *Salvadora* just before departure, he was not pleased with the deal Waddington gave him but had no other options (Swinglehurst 1893, 172–173). It is presumably during these months of financial negotiation that Swinglehurst put some money into Ledger's hands for expenses. In appreciation of his support for the project, Ledger gave Swinglehurst four of Savage's sketches. Swinglehurst prized this gift as a tangible souvenir of having crossed paths with such a remarkable man, noting many years later that these drawings were "perhaps the only remains of a most interesting and wonderful adventure" (167).

Once all arrangements had been settled, the flock traveled from Copiapó across a segment of the Atacama Desert to the port of Caldera and was placed on board the *Salvadora* (Ledger 1860a, 459). Ledger found himself having to make difficult choices, because he could not bring to Australia all the men who had accompanied him over the past months and years. A man named Bradish took Savage's place in the group (Swinglehurst 1893, 172). Although Ledger gave no explanation for this change, it appears that Savage planned to remain in Valparaíso. Of the twenty-eight men working for Ledger, he could only take nine but eventually agreed to include three more who had been especially dedicated to the enterprise. He gave testimony to the men's enthusiasm for the project, explaining how several volunteered to go along for no wages. Such loyalty, he believed, was the expedition's most extraordinary accomplishment to date: "It was generally remarked that it was more wonderful to witness the devotion & willingness of the Indians to accompany me to Austa[a] [*sic*] than my having succeeded in getting the Alpacas to the Coast. I had the greatest difficulty in getting those I did not require on board ship to return to their homes. The faithful fellows offered to accompany me without pay & it was really trying to witness the disappointment of those that drew a '*blank*' in the lottery of names."[48] While it is tempting to connect Charles Ledger's comments here to my earlier analysis of his greater openness to Indigenous perspectives than many European travelers of the time, it is hardly surprising that most of the men were eager to accompany Ledger, as any profits to accrue from the venture would presumably be dispensed in Australia.

Men like Swinglehurst were clearly moved by Ledger's story and keenly interested in following the venture to its conclusion. The last news that

Andean Itineraries of Nineteenth-Century Camelid Science | 205

he received from Ledger was in 1860, however, when Ledger informed him of his plans to prepare a book on the topic of the alpaca expedition. Years later, Swinglehurst recounted what he remembered of the adventure for inclusion in his own memoir, extracting information from letters and papers that Ledger had sent him and notes that Swinglehurst had taken during their conversations in Valparaíso. He assumed that the lack of further news indicated that the project ultimately had failed (Swinglehurst 1893, 167). Contemplating Ledger's final correspondence once again, Swinglehurst mused how it all "now seems like a dream; thirty-five years are gone since receiving the above letter" (173).

Ledger bid farewell to his friends and colleagues as the *Salvadora* set sail for Sydney. He, his co-workers, and the animals had been on the road for more than three years, traveling over 1,500 miles and crossing the two highest chains of the Andes and three of the smaller. They had undergone horrific storms, inhospitable landscapes, inadequate pasture and water, and countless natural and humanmade calamities (Ledger 1860c, 458), in what Poucel (1864a, 173) described as a "magnificent albeit grueling transhumance."

By the time he set sail for Australia, Ledger had earned what Livingstone (2003, 152) describes as bodily badges of virtue and trustworthiness from the adversity and suffering sustained by an explorer out in the field. Ledger's narrative makes it clear that this "moral economy of wounds" was not forged in isolation. It required the establishment of peripheral communities, both sympathetic and oppositional, alongside and against which the heroic adventurer could emerge. Yet the contradictions and inconsistencies of Ledger's heroic paradigm created spaces where unexpected local protagonists came to the foreground. Indigenous collaborators became significant actors in the production of knowledge in the intercultural camelid contact zone that Ledger and his men forged in Laguna Blanca and on the road.

CHAPTER 6

Camelids in Australia

The Rise and Fall of Charles Ledger's Alpaca Ambitions

I would commend these animals to the close attention of everyone interested in the progressive expansion of our empire and the
prosperity of our trade; and I think I shall be able to show that in its
present position the alpaca is, perhaps, the most interesting animal
in the world.

Edward Wilson, "Acclimatisation," letter to the editor of the Times
(London), June 26, 1862

On the faith of the promises made me in this country of Peru, I
undertook to run every risk—did succeed—*and am ruined!*

Charles Ledger to Sir Henry Parkes, June 1, 1860
(emphasis in the original)

When Charles Ledger and a select group of Andean shepherds set sail for Australia from the port of Caldera, Chile, with their large flock of llamas and alpacas, the group held high expectations that fame and fortune awaited them in the young British colony. After all, as illustrated in the chapter's first epigraph, many Australians enthusiastically embraced the acclimatization movement of the mid-nineteenth century. Ledger and his antipodean supporters anticipated that the creation of the alpaca industry would be a profitable enterprise that might eventually achieve the same degree of success as the importation of merino sheep. These dreams of scientific achievement and economic prosperity, however, never materialized. Instead, the men's arrival in Sydney marked the beginning of a downward course in the tale of the rise and fall of Charles Ledger as the heroic introducer of alpacas into Australia, "a romance of the most extraordinary adventure."[1] This new trajectory would have implications not only for Ledger, his men, and the alpacas; it would also impact the acclimatization movement as a whole.

208 | *Llamas beyond the Andes*

Ledger's troubles began soon after arrival in Sydney in late 1858, when heavy debt forced him to sell his alpaca flock to the New South Wales (NSW) government at a loss of £7,000 and accept the position of "superintendent of alpacas" at a salary much reduced from his original expectations. As his fortune took a downward turn, the narrative of his heroism that he had deliberately cultivated throughout his South American travels in Australia became a narrative of self-defense in the face of growing accusations that he had mismanaged the alpacas and overspent government funds. The transition can be followed in Ledger's personal letters, newspaper accounts, and correspondence between himself and the NSW government, collected by vote of the Legislative Assembly and included as a supplement to the annual *Votes and Proceedings* for 1861–1862. This official document served as a record against which the NSW Legislative Assembly examined Ledger's petitions for just compensation in the context of his initial claims and subsequent relationship with the government. The document, along with the letters and newspaper articles, shows how public opinion fluctuated in accordance with government support.

The story begins with Ledger being greeted upon arrival as a hero whose daring exploits could be equated with those of the publicly lauded explorer David Livingstone then moves to associations with British wool pioneer John Macarthur, who had introduced the merino sheep into Australia to great political and economic success. In keeping with this positive association, Ledger claimed in a letter to John Robertson, the NSW superintendent for lands and public works, that the deceased former governor, Charles Fitzroy, had promised him a generous monetary reward and a large land grant of 10,000 acres for his service in bringing alpacas to Australia.[2] As Ledger's financial status worsened, however, and it became evident that no further remuneration was forthcoming from the government, he abandoned his heroic narrative and adopted instead a narrative of grievance: a man whose sacrifices made on behalf of the British Empire had led unjustly to his financial demise.

The opening epigraphs thus appear to set up a contrast between two narrative scripts that played out in this new camelid contact zone: on one hand, the fluid alliance between imperial science and economic expansion and the concomitant promises held out by the heroic fantasy; on the other, the government's breach of trust when it refused to honor those promises, which the hero had accepted on faith. This unexpected discrepancy undoubtedly resulted from at least two circumstances. Ledger no longer had Andean Indigenous communities and governments as antagonists, against which he could portray himself as an intrepid and enterprising entrepreneur. He was now up against the apparatus of the NSW government. It became increasingly difficult to depict himself convincingly in heroic opposition to this entity. Instead, in his correspondence with the secretary for lands and others, he portrayed himself as a victim who had been misled and cheated by the government, as evidenced in his lengthy letter to politician and journalist Sir Henry Parkes quoted in the second epigraph to this chapter.

This conclusion to Ledger's story may seem surprising at first, especially because his Andean story of exceptionalism followed closely the model of nineteenth-century imperial adventure myths, which relied on what Freedgood (2000, 94) has characterized as a "risk-reward ideology." Drawing from the writings of Max Horkheimer, Theodor Adorno, and Max Weber, she describes the ideology whereby "adventurers and capitalists alike risk failure, and consequently their successes are earned and deserved. And this 'morality' accrues not only to the individual who risks, but also to a nation and its people. This conception of risk was essential for moralizing the profits of both industrialization and imperialism" (95). In accordance with these observations, classical tales of travel and adventure commonly represented the home or nation space—in Ledger's case England or the British colonies—as a safe space, in contrast to the dangerous and potentially life-threatening perils of (imperial) travel. Following this long-standing narrative paradigm, the adventure traveler who leaves the nation's confines will inevitably have to contend with challenging and painful trials and grapple with fear and suffering, "the agonies of which are rewarded only in the very end when the hero is finally allowed to take possession of the money or character or spiritual fulfillment he (and it is always he) has earned" (95).

From Ledger's perspective, he had faithfully complied with this narrative contract, risking life and limb in his travels to land a large number of valuable alpacas in Australia. Indeed, he was the only person in the nineteenth century able to acquire, transport, and successfully introduce a substantial flock of these animals into a European country or colony. And yet, as he complained repeatedly, he never received just compensation for the dangers and suffering he endured. To the contrary, he was ultimately suspended from his position of NSW superintendent of alpacas and accused of negligence and misconduct, resulting in part from negotiations he initiated with the rival colony of Victoria to bring alpacas there. He fought these accusations and even sued the NSW government

210 | *Llamas beyond the Andes*

for wrongful dismissal and back salary. In the end, the attorney general disallowed his lawsuit, although Ledger did eventually receive the wages owed him by the government.

To understand this change in circumstances, it could be argued that Ledger, himself an imperialist, became a character in a dramatic narrative much larger than his own: a story of imperialism and colonial conflicts, which showed no hesitation in embracing people like Ledger and later casting them aside. Ledger became a victim of the overreach of empire, having believed in its myths and dedicated himself to them, only to discover that in the end he was expendable. Ledger's indignation and frustration continued to grow, especially in the face of increasingly negative press regarding himself and the alpaca venture. He complained bitterly that he had lost all hope of obtaining justice.[3] Convinced that he had no future in Australia, Ledger finally decided to return to South America. He and his second wife, Charlotte Olliver, scraped together money for their passage and set sail on August 20, 1864.[4] They would remain in South America for the next nineteen years before returning to Australia, where they both had family members still living.

In their discussion of travel writing and how the genre foregrounds singular notions of subjectivity alongside themes of movement and transformation, Gilbert and Johnston (2002, 16) note that "travel is, of course, much more than just movement across space; it inevitably involves self-fashioning exercises that deconstruct and reconstruct the traveler in new environments, exercises that are particularly freighted with significance in colonial and postcolonial contexts." These exercises in self-fashioning were continually rehearsed in Ledger's writings when he presented himself to the international public alternately as stouthearted hero, scientific pioneer, and ruined victim of empire. The coherence of his narrative self-representation was further complicated by the presence of the Bolivian shepherds who accompanied him to Australia to work alongside him on the acclimatization project.

The nature of the knowledge-making process in the nineteenth-century New South Wales camelid contact zone was multifaceted and moves us beyond Ledger's personal story, shifting our attention instead to the collaborative relationships in this enterprise. As noted in chapter 5, this move was facilitated by Santiago Savage's drawings, which provided glimpses into the co-construction of knowledge begun in Chulluncayani (Bolivia) and Laguna Blanca (Argentina), and was designed to aid in the alpacas' adaptation to their new environment in the British colony. It is impossible to achieve a full sense of the shepherds' contributions in Australia because their activities were filtered solely through Ledger's self-fashioning narratives and in general their role there was to serve his interests and his own heroic account. Nevertheless, by reading his story against the grain, it becomes possible to uncover bits and pieces of the important role played by the shepherds as key participants in the alpaca acclimatization venture.

The alpacas, like Ledger, also started out as celebrities. Their arrival to Australia was heralded in the newspapers and followed by the public, which expressed great hopes for their successful adaptation to New South Wales. However, the animals did not appear to flourish, and the possibilities for acquiring fresh stock from Peru diminished as time went on. The alpacas also began to decline in public opinion. The NSW government became increasingly impatient with Ledger and the project's rising economic costs, until it finally resolved to rid itself of the animals by dividing the flock into small lots for auction. This action put an end to Ledger's program of crossbreeding llamas and alpacas, which required that all the animals remain together. Neither the first auction in 1864 nor the second in 1866 drew much attention, however. The government eventually decided its interests were best served by disposing of the animals at whatever price the buyer proposed. Most of the surviving animals consequently ended up in small lots on sheep farms or as curiosities or pets, while others were placed at lunatic asylums for the amusement of the patients there. In the end, Ledger's rise and fall did not only mark the course of his personal story. The general lack of interest and poor sales resulting from the two auctions of the alpacas also portended the rise and fall of the global acclimatization movement more generally and the end of major nineteenth-century experiments in the exportation of large numbers of alpacas, the animal that best symbolized the international acclimatization movement's hopes for success.[5]

Pursuing the Camelid Dream in Australia

Ledger's singularity as a transoceanic importer of alpacas can be measured against previous unsuccessful efforts to bring the animal to Australia. The nineteenth-century examples of experiments to acclimatize alpacas in Australia touched on in this chapter all illustrate how camelid importation projects were always already entangled in the desire for imperial expansion, interstate rivalries of various kinds, and even anxieties about

212 | Llamas beyond the Andes

espionage.[6] British interest in acquiring Andean camelids for Australia predated Ledger's project by approximately fifty-five years. Naval surgeon and explorer George Bass prepared his brig, the *Venus*, for an upcoming voyage to South America in 1803. At the behest of NSW governor Philip Gidley King, he hoped to obtain guanacos and alpacas there to introduce into Australia.[7] Bass set sail in early February 1803, never to be heard of again. His ship and crew were presumably lost somewhere in the Pacific.

Several decades passed before serious attention turned again to the topic of introducing camelids into Australia. Thanks to advances in sailing technology, the discovery of gold, and increased grain exports from countries like Chile, the 1850s marked a transition for Australia from economic depression into the "roaring days" of growing trade and commerce opportunities (Bader 1988, 29–32).[8] This upturn in the economy opened the door for many new ventures, including alpaca importation. It was first introduced in the colony of Victoria in 1850 by businessman and wool auctioneer Thomas Sutcliffe Mort and a few years later by Thomas Embling, a medical doctor and member of the Legislative Council. A staunch proponent of bringing the animals to Australia to improve its wool industry (Barnard 1961, 46–47), Mort referred to the animals as "Peruvian sheep." Like those of many of his contemporaries, including Ledger, his descriptions drew from sheep-related terminology, a tradition dating back to the colonial period, as observed in previous chapters. Consequently, the ideal animals for introduction would be females "in lamb" and "rams only brought in proportion of one to twenty ewes" (Mort 1850, 3). This vocabulary might have helped to create suspicion among pastoralists and squatters that the alpaca was a new sort of sheep and would compete with their business, which was recovering from recession at the time.[9]

Mort and his allies were responsible for raising funds to charter the *Julia*, the vessel that was to sail to Peru and return with the valuable livestock (Fletcher 2002, 54). As described in the previous chapter, however, the *Julia's* mission ended in failure due to Peru's prohibition on exporting alpacas. The undertaking nonetheless brought Charles Ledger's name to the attention of Mort and his colleagues, because he served as their main contact in Peru. When Ledger and Ortiz came to explore areas near Sydney in 1853 to determine their suitability for pasturing alpacas, Mort was one of Ledger's influential connections and advocates, even though he was ill at the time and convalescing in England.

Despite this failed attempt, interest in acquiring alpacas did not fade in Victoria. During the late 1850s, Thomas Embling was made chair of the

Legislative Council's Select Committee formed to examine the appropriateness of the alpaca for the colony. Embling's committee found Victoria to be well-suited to the alpaca venture, reinscribing the colonial idea that it was a land with millions of empty acres, "lying utterly waste and unproductive" and perfect for pastoral interests, thus determining that the alpaca would be a significant addition to the economy.[10] The prevailing colonial doctrine of *terra nullius* shaped the acclimatization movement and helped to empty the Australian countryside of native species by introducing exotic plant and animal species: "Moreover, the constant rhetorical portrayals of Australia as blank, inadequate and waiting to be reshaped, indicate that the continent's supposed emptiness was not just a one-off initial assumption. Rather, the alleged vacancy of the landscape was being reinscribed, actively and repeatedly" (Mitchell 2010, 63). In the context of the alpaca importation project, men like Embling favored ending the squatting system and saw the alpaca as playing an important role in this transformation, "leaving the land to be used in a more concentrated fashion" (65). In the committee's opinion, the alpaca undertaking would help populate the land, add jobs and technologies, create more capital, and generate a new and valuable product.[11] Unfortunately, however, the committee was unable to obtain any of the animals. The obstacles the colony of Victoria encountered in attempting to acquire alpacas illustrated more generally how difficult and labor-intensive it could be to introduce new species.

Undaunted by these setbacks, efforts in Victoria to pursue the camelid dream continued, always marked by grandiose claims about empire-building. The rhetoric of Edward Wilson, a newspaper editor and influential promoter of Australian acclimatization endeavors, is a case in point. His 1858 letter to the editor of the *Times* of London concerning a small flock of llamas and alpacas for sale in England is particularly illuminating. "For years past, Sir, the introduction of the alpaca into Australia has been incessantly discussed in all the several colonies as a subject of the most vital interest; and I really do not think that I shall be chargeable with exaggeration in alleging that the whole world could scarcely furnish an instance of a much more interesting experiment than this."[12] The opportunity to make this dream a reality finally arrived when Wilson and merchant, financier, and politician William Westgarth contacted the Victoria government to announce that they had purchased twenty-four animals in total—eight males and sixteen females—and would make a present of them to the colony.[13] As always, the animals came with an exciting story, which helped to "sell" them to the general public and colonial authorities.

214 | *Llamas beyond the Andes*

An anonymous letter published in the *Illustrated London News* told how the Wilson-Westgarth llama-alpacas had "been driven overland from Peru to the Isthmus of Panama, and thence shipped to New York, where they were offered for sale at a very low price, considering the risk and danger incurred in transit through and from their native country."[14]

This story may sound familiar, because the animals originally formed part of a flock brought out of the Andes by Eugène Roehn on one of his early ventures and later sold to British entrepreneur Benjamin Gee. These transglobal animals had survived the journey on foot, by train, and by ship from Bolivia to Ecuador and on to New York City and eventually to Scotland and England. Now some were being readied to sail to Australia. The newspaper story noted that Gee sold five animals to different parties in London, and ten to merchant and businessman George A. Lloyd, who paid £25 for each (see also Ledger 1860–1861, 223). Wilson purchased the remainder of the flock for £700. Both the Wilson-Westgarth and Lloyd animals were shipped to Australia, the former to Victoria and the latter to New South Wales. As Wilson explained in a letter to the *Times*, he hoped that this would mark the beginning of more such experiments in introducing suitable animals, because he believed that Australia's native fauna served no beneficial purpose: "We have the kangaroo, the wild dog, emu, opossum, bandicoot, and many others, furnishing a little sport, an occasional meal, and an interesting study to the physiologist, but of little value for the practical purposes of every-day life."[15] For Wilson and others, the arrival of the Andean camelids would surely lead to the creation of a new and useful stock of animals.

The long-awaited Wilson-Westgarth llamas and alpacas reached the shores of Victoria in early February 1859. Many felt encouraged by the relatively few numbers of casualties even though living conditions on board ship had been less than ideal.[16] Wilson speculated that perhaps the animals fared as well as they did because of their care before sailing. After he had the flock in his possession in London, the animals grazed at Acton and "got quite fat. They started for Australia in high mettle, and, like most other emigrants, they did even better there."[17]

While many heralded the successful arrival of the "interesting immigrants" in Victoria,[18] the event was eclipsed by a much larger shipment of alpacas and llamas landed beforehand in New South Wales by Charles Ledger in November 1858. Back in London, Benjamin Gee was disappointed: even though he was pleased with how well his animals had fared, there was one issue "he felt some delicacy in touching upon." While his alpacas and Ledger's alpacas had reached Australia at very nearly the same moment, the attention all went to Ledger and the successful disembarking of his sizable flock. Gee noted archly that "he was glad to hear from Mr. Macarthur that Mr. Ledger was likely to reap some reward for his exertions; but with regard to himself, he was somewhat in the position of the Irish ostler who, when a gentleman was about to drive off without having handed him the customary gratuity, called after him, 'Please yer honour, if my master asks me what you gave the ostler, what am I to tell him?' and if any one [*sic*] asked him what he got, his reply would be — nothing."[19] Wilson also described his feelings of regret about Ledger's flock overshadowing the Victoria llamas: "The wind had meanwhile been completely taken out of our sails as to the honour of the first introduction of this valuable animal, by the landing in Sydney of the large herd of about 270, collected and brought over direct from Peru with such wonderful perseverance by Mr. Ledger. But as a secondary experiment, in a different neighbourhood, and under different management, our own little venture is not without its interest."[20] Despite Wilson and Gee's disappointment, the arrival of the Ledger, Lloyd, and Wilson-Westgarth animals in New South Wales and Victoria, respectively, signaled the beginning of a new experiment acclimatizing large numbers of alpacas and llamas outside the Andean region, which would be followed with interest by international scientific and business communities.

Australia's Camelid Dreams Finally Come to Life

On November 28, 1858, Charles Ledger, his men, and 256 Andean camelids pulled into the Sydney harbor after a voyage lasting 87 days (Gramiccia 1988, 74).[21] The ocean crossing had been difficult, resulting in numerous casualties along the way. At the beginning of the voyage, seasickness took a toll on many of the animals and required extreme forms of intervention on the part of Ledger and the shepherds and even crew members when necessary: "Three refused to eat although I crammed food into their mouths; two died on the 17th and one on the 21st day of voyage, without tasting food or water all that time. Although the animals were most assiduously attended to by the thirteen natives of South America I brought with me for that purpose, the crew also aiding in every way possible, tempted by the promise of a large reward on successfully carrying through the voyage, and after all I lost 80 animals out of the number shipped" (Ledger 1864a, 98).[22]

216 | *Llamas beyond the Andes*

Soon after landing, the animals were transferred to the cricket enclosure of an area of Sydney called the Domain to recuperate from the voyage. During their stay there, many hundreds of people took advantage of the accessibility of the location to visit the exotic creatures.[23] Within days of their arrival, news began to spread that Ledger would be putting the entire flock on the market. He had 285 animals at the time and was expecting 100 births over the next three months.[24] Given this potential for increase in the animal stock, he set the asking price at £45,000 for the entire flock.[25] Having received word in Melbourne of the impending sale, Embling moved that the Legislative Assembly of Victoria try to obtain some of the NSW alpacas and llamas, emphasizing their superiority over the Wilson-Westgarth llamas that would be arriving from England and highlighting "the danger undergone by the gentleman who had brought the animals to New South Wales." Although Embling's motion was seconded, chief secretary John O'Shanassy seemed less swayed by the proposal and its exciting narrative: he observed dryly that the animals would in all probability already have been sold if they were as valuable as suggested.[26] Despite his reluctance, O'Shanassy approached the NSW government to confirm that the owner would indeed be selling the animals and to inquire about their price, quality, age, and suitability for the new climate.[27] Ledger, however, refused to consider offers for smaller lots for fear that the best animals would be purchased in advance of the sale.

In the information circulated by Ledger's agent J. Herring to parties potentially interested in purchasing the flock of "Peruvian sheep," he emphasized that the animals could be cared for only by those with whom they were familiar. This argument also served as one strategy to justify retaining the presence of the Andean shepherds, because they would be necessary as the flock increased in size, especially when it came time to shear the animals.[28] Projecting a strong future growth rate for the flock, he maintained that it could increase to 1,500 animals by 1864. The wool clip alone would more than compensate the buyer for the initial expenditures, and as a bonus, the flock included five vicuñas to be used for fiber improvement.[29] The author of one newspaper article observed that the number of people willing to take on such risk was probably limited but encouraged those with means to consider the offer not only for their own benefit but for all of Australia: "It is, however, of the utmost importance to these colonies that spirited efforts be made to secure, not only the introduction, but the rapid increase of a tribe of animals which there is every reason to believe would thrive amazingly in our climate, whilst the illimitable demand for their fleeces, and the high prices realized, ensure to the breeder ready and most profitable markets."[30]

As he waited for a buyer, Ledger made himself at home in the public limelight, enjoying a hero's status. Capitalizing on the excitement surrounding him and the animals, he accepted invitations from prestigious venues to speak about his South American travels, such as the meeting of the Australian Horticultural and Agricultural Society.[31] The various events were generally publicized in the newspapers. Many articles related details of the exciting narratives of scientific discovery and adventure that coalesced in the alpaca venture. These reports, in turn, not only helped to boost Ledger's prominence but also enticed the public to take a more active interest in the animal-celebrities and their fate. As a further gesture to the New South Wales scientific community, Ledger presented a stuffed alpaca (one of the first born in the colony) and an alpaca skeleton to the Australian Museum in Sydney.[32] In the accompanying letter to the trustees, Ledger voiced his optimism that the alpaca would one day become a profitable fixture of Australia's landscape: "It is my fond hope that at some future period when this country be teeming with alpacas + exporting abundance of its wool, that this little animal will be looked upon with great interest accompanied with wonderment, that such great ends could ever be attained from such small beginnings as the flock imported afforded."[33] As his remarks suggested, Ledger may well have imagined that these singular gifts would visibly and permanently link his name and heroic effort to the growth of the alpaca industry in Australia.[34]

Ledger's optimism began to fade, however, when the sale of the flock did not go according to plan, due in part to a slump in the wool industry: no buyer offered his asking price (see Fletcher 2002, 57). He found himself in severe financial straits because he owed his investors £15,000, in addition to having lost £7,000 of his own money on the project. These economic troubles compelled Ledger in March to offer the Zoological Society of Victoria a pair of alpacas and three llamas for £350 and his collection of Chilean silver ore to the Australian Museum for £300. Both the NSW Museum Trustees and the Victoria Legislative Council decided that Ledger's asking prices were too high. In each instance, the matter was finally dropped.[35]

No buyer had been found for the animals by April 1859. The NSW Legislative Assembly became concerned that they might be repatriated to South America or, worse, acquired by its rival colony, Victoria. After lengthy discussion, the assembly agreed to purchase the flock from Ledger

218 | Llamas beyond the Andes

for £15,000, under the condition that he would agree to superintend the animals for a certain period.[36] Although this agreement still left Ledger facing a loss of £7,000, he had no choice but to accept the offer. He was heavily in debt to his largest investor, British merchant Joshua Waddington, who had generously lent him money after he had exhausted his own means. As discussed in chapter 5, Ledger refused a French offer of $100,000 (or £20,000 plus £5,000 for shipping) to purchase the animals when he was in Chile (which Waddington at the time had urged him to accept), by claiming a prior obligation to the British. Although the commitment had never been verified in writing, Ledger described it as "public & notorious at the time." Yet his loyalty and patriotic spirit ultimately produced no reward: "Not one of the promises made to me have been fulfilled by the Government of New South Wales; indeed, my loss of 11 years, of every penny I possessed, & the dangers, toil, hardships & the total separation during all that time from my children, not having seen them even, appear but to cause merriment to the Hon. Sec'y for Lands."[37]

As for why Ledger never received further compensation, Gramiccia (1988, 75) surmises that the NSW government had little interest in the hybridization project that Ledger planned to continue with the llamas and alpacas: "On the contrary, [the government] firmly believed that their management would be a routine natural matter that, at most, required only standard bureaucratic procedures as for any other type of government property. They were stunned by the sums claimed by Ledger as compensation for his successful enterprise and still needed for its practical completion in the colony." Bitterly disappointed because the current NSW government had disregarded all promises made by its predecessor, Ledger announced that he would return to South America with the Andean shepherds who had accompanied him from Bolivia, noting in a letter to Sir John Young (governor in chief of New South Wales) that "I accepted my ruin as a punishment for my credulity & implicit reliance in the good faith (with which I fulfilled my part of the compact) of her M's representatives."[38]

However, John Robertson informed Ledger that the government would rescind the offer to purchase the animals unless he and his men agreed to remain in charge of the flock for one year. Ledger thus was obliged to accept the deal, paying his own salary and the salaries of some of his men out of the £300 annual budget he received to manage the animals, with the government agreeing to pay the salaries of the remaining shepherds. Although this contract enabled Ledger to pay off his creditors, it did not save him from economic ruin. As he noted in his letter to Young, he retained some hope that his fortune could change, however, because Robertson implied that the government might eventually agree to resell the animals to him, allow ample time for payment, and even furnish a large run for the alpacas. If this opportunity materialized, he would have the means to recoup some of his losses.[39]

Ledger's first assignment as superintendent of alpacas was to investigate the interior of the colony for a suitable permanent location for the flock. In his communication with the office of John Robertson, the secretary for lands and public works, he referred to this as an "exploring expedition."[40] Ledger likely attempted to elevate the status of his assignment with this strategic choice of phrase by equating it with the highly publicized expeditions taking place in Victoria and NSW during the 1850s. More than half of Australia had yet to be traversed by Europeans in 1860. The large exploration parties, such as the Victoria government-sponsored Burke and Wills expedition (1860–1861), were indispensable to the surveying and mapping of the country's interior (Wilson 1862, 14).[41] Men like Edward Wilson hoped that the alpacas would help to settle and populate these newly charted expanses. Medical doctor David E. Wilkie argued before the Philosophical Institute of Victoria in 1857 that these expeditions were of great national significance from the perspective of science and discovering more about a country that had space enough to settle Europe's excess population. Wilkie emphasized the "indomitable courage displayed by Dr. Livingstone in Africa" and "his extraordinary success as an explorer" as well as the important role of the Australian expeditions organized by leaders such as "[Charles] Sturt, [Ludwig] Leichhardt, [Thomas] Mitchell, and [Augustus] Gregory."[42]

Kociumbas (1992, 267) contends that this discourse of the self-sacrificing explorer formed part of Australia's new national myth-making process, representing "the bastion of white 'civilization' in the Pacific" and embodying the unifying ideal of the new Australian man "who would automatically adopt the militaristic physical and mental discipline which industry and empire increasingly required." Ledger undoubtedly hoped to draw public attention to the comparison between his own celebrated account, the story of Livingstone before him, and now, once again, other prototypical expeditionary leaders and scientists. Moreover, in keeping with the theme of the llamas and alpacas as "new immigrants," Ledger's exploration expedition in search of good pasture for the animals played a key role in their naturalization: he referred to them with the same

220 | *Llamas beyond the Andes*

imperial scientific tropes used to create a foundational identity for the new Australia (see Kociumbas 1992, 263–264). More importantly, these colonial expeditions received full government support, something that Ledger also desired.

Just a few weeks after Wilkie's presentation, Ferdinand Mueller also read a paper before the Philosophical Institute. Although Ledger had not yet reached New South Wales at that time, Mueller's description of the explorer-traveler resonated with the accounts of Ledger's own journeys among hostile Andean peoples and followed a similar logic of imperialism: "If a traveller's progress through a country, densely occupied by native races, domiciled and more or less advanced in industry, is still watched with pleasure or anxiety, even should he gain no space for widening the dominions of the Anglo-Saxon race, of how much more importance is any new information then on that country which we adopt as our home, and which supports, notwithstanding its almost equal size to that of Europe, less inhabitants than many of the capitals of European states?" Like others, Mueller emphasized how these explorations were rooted in a shared patriotic and resolute nationalist spirit: "Our desire to unveil the remaining unknown portions of Australia is not limited at this moment by demands on our patriotism or our progress alone; its future exploration is likewise claimed by our humanity, and by our honour as a nation."[43] As he reiterated time after time, Ledger too had remained steadfast in an honorable spirit of patriotism and loyalty to Britain throughout the course of his alpaca venture. Given this context of heightened interest in the exploration expeditions, Ledger felt even more keenly the possibility that his equally worthy expedition to discover an appropriate permanent location for the animals should be rewarded with public and governmental support.

In his official and private correspondence, Ledger capitalized on this unifying nationalist discourse while also evoking the excitement and exoticism of the South American origins of his venture, which had served him so well rhetorically before reaching Australia. For example, during his exploration in search of a permanent placement for the alpacas in the company of his brother-in-law Major Ortiz, Ledger observed how the Maneroo (or Monaro) landscape visually reminded both men of the Andes. As he explained on his return in a letter to John Robertson, secretary of the Department of Lands and Public Works, "I could easily have believed myself back again in those countries."[44] Ledger also described the trip in a letter to his brother George, similarly highlighting the comparison between the Australian and Andean landscapes and the memories that the Australian mountains evoked: "The chain of snow-covered mountains that suddenly presented themselves to my view, on ascending a hill from Cooma, brought most vividly before me remembrances of past privation and hardships endured among the grand and stupendous Cordilleras; and I gazed with delight and enthusiasm on a landscape similar to those my eye had so continually scanned while on my hazardous journeyings through Peru, Bolivia, and Chili" (quoted in Ledger 1860–1861, 217–218).

In these accounts, the Australian landscape that Ledger and Ortiz traversed evoked powerful memories of the danger and adversities that Ledger and his shepherds had endured in the Andes. Now that the danger was past, however, the associations aroused sensations of pleasure and delight, presumably because he was "safe" within the borders of the British Empire, even though, ironically, this secure space had led to broken promises and economic ruin.[45] Ledger's descriptions that linked the Andean and Australian landscapes made visible the intersections of his own heroic projection and scientific discovery. On the one hand, these connections brought out the relationship between perilous landscape and imperial heroism that was a trademark of Ledger's self-fashioning. On the other, they called to mind British theories of acclimatization, positing that animal and plant species should be moved between places sharing a similar climate.

It was not just the iconic topography that reminded the men of the Andes. Ledger and Ortiz had examined the natural pastures of the Maneroo area, discovering what they believed to be other significant similarities between the two geographies: "Not only are the pasturage and herbage, rocks and stones, identical with those of Peru, but I found throughout the districts I have indicated abundance of a description of wiry grass known as the 'ichu' of South America. It is upon this grass that the llama tribe mostly feed, being extremely palatable and nourishing, and of which they are immoderately fond. The great importance of furnishing the alpacas with fodder as closely as possible resembling that on which they have been accustomed to feed in their native country, need scarcely be pointed out" (quoted in Ledger 1860–1861, 217).[46] Ledger virtually superimposed the Andean landscape and native pasturage on the Australian landscape to such a degree that the Snowy Mountains became the "Australian cordilleras" and thus advanced the logic that the alpacas would flourish in this new location, finding themselves "at home" once again.[47]

222 | Llamas beyond the Andes

Ledger's Struggle to Retain the Status of Hero

Most accounts published about Ledger's life in the decades following his death in 1905 paint a portrait of him as a bold and enterprising man of action. The *Sydney Morning Herald* recounted the history of Ledger's alpaca experiment in 1935, emphasizing the epic nature of his accomplishment in successfully landing such a large number of the animals: "Many romantic and adventurous incidents have occurred in the history of the wool industry in Australia since the day that John McArthur [*sic*] first imported his merinos, but for sheer audacity and daring the methods adopted by Charles Ledger to introduce the Alpaca sheep to New South Wales must surely stand alone."[48] During the months following his arrival, however, Ledger's reputation began to be negatively impacted by the poor sale of the alpacas, even though for the most part the newspapers continued to portray him as a larger-than-life figure with repeated references to the trials and tribulations he and his men had endured. One author argued that Ledger's deeds were the stuff of song and legend, describing him as an "indefatigable merchant," capable of "overcoming a thousand obstacles," the "ravages of beasts," and "the jealousy and vindictiveness of men."[49]

An article published in the *Era* reflected more generally on heroism and the sort of men who become "crusaders of a higher and a purer order of civilization," working to advance the well-being of many. For the author, Ledger personified these very qualities. He had worked tirelessly to promote a new industry for the colony and demonstrated his unwavering support for the British government, no matter what hardships he faced. The author justified the reprise of Ledger's adventures, observing the important role played by narrative in communicating to the reading public the importance of sacrifice and service on behalf of the nation:

> To give anything like a true picture of the wanderings, privations, and perils that beset Mr. CHARLES LEDGER'S career throughout the accomplishment of his purpose would compile a romance of the most extraordinary adventure, and show an heroic devotion to his purpose and flock that is probably without precedent; yet the record of a certain amount of this pilgrimage is absolutely necessary to make the reader cognizant of the service rendered both to the colony and mother country by his exertions.[50]

The article detailed the major events of Ledger's trajectory up to and including the insufficient recompense he received in Australia. Suggesting that the government had not fulfilled its part in the heroic contract, the author concluded by urging the colony to make amends for its neglect.

Ledger himself actively promoted his heroic persona, writing letters to the newspapers and recounting his Andean exploits.[51] A poem penned by "IDUMEA" appeared in the *Sydney Morning Herald*. While the poem lauded the feats of Ledger, Lloyd, and Macarthur, the adventures described seem to come straight from Ledger's accounts of his time in South America. The alpacas speak directly to Australians with one grandiose voice in the poem, echoing imperial themes about the savage Andean landscape and the rewards owed to a selfless patriot and remonstrating with Australia for brushing Ledger aside and leaving him to be forgotten. Despite the poor treatment, the alpacas conclude by announcing that Australia's true heroes will receive due recognition with time:

THE ALPACAS' REMONSTRANCE

Thro' the Andes' savage valleys, o'er each lofty mountain peak,
Where the clouds from far Pacific, in their stormy showers break—
Struggling thro' each rocky ravine, toiling o'er each bleak plateau,
Where the night wind sweeps lee-breathing o'er primeval bedded
 snow—
Days of care and travel ended by a night of anxious ward,
'Till the morning star waned palely o'er the wearied herdsman
 guard—
Thirst and hunger, storm and sickness, met with a determined
 will,
Which defiant of misfortune, braved it boldly, hoping still—
Years and years of stern endeavor, oft frustrated, ne'er subdued;
Force and fraud in time outwitted, soldiers conquered
 when pursued—
Ocean's perils, safely traversed, tho' oft sorely tempest driven,
Half life's best time—all a fortune—to the venture grudgeless
 given.
This, and those, we met unflinching, for we deemed a grateful
 land
Would at least repay the lucre which we spent with thrifty
 hand.

224 | *Llamas beyond the Andes*

But the recompense most sought for was the patriot's
  best reward,
In his country's added welfare, and its grateful shown regard.
How our toils have been rewarded History's page will sadly
  name
In one sentence—"Unrequited to the age's sin and shame,"
In the time of Rome's true greatness, he who suffered in her
  cause.
Or advanced her pride or welfare, was rewarded by her laws;
And his name to after ages, gratefully was handed down—
Honoring both himself and country, who, by giving, shared
  renown.
We, alas! such pagan customs scorn to follow, and our way
Seems to be— "who works unbargained," let him! why should we
  repay?
But the Nemesis, Time, avenges present scorn by future fame,
And brave Ledger, Lloyd, Macarthur, each shall be a [*sic*] honored
  name.
When the pedlars, whose own interest even could not make them
  just,
Are themselves unknown, forgotten—moulder'd to congenial
  dust.[52]

Intercultural Encounters in the Shearing Shed

Ledger did not rely solely on newspaper accounts to throw the spotlight on his achievements. During the first months after arrival, he energetically pursued the public exhibition of the alpacas and the expertise of his men and himself in showman-like events. In October 1859 Ledger informed John Robertson that he and his men would commence shearing all the animals except for the pregnant females in early November. The event was also announced in the newspapers. With regard to shearing more generally, Ledger called the public's attention to the reason for not including the pregnant llamas and alpacas, declaring that Andeans refused to shear them for fear that they would miscarry. Although he dismissed much Indigenous knowledge as superstition, he continued this tradition in Australia.[53] The event took place at Sophienburg, the estate of politician James Henry Atkinson. Invitations to attend the festivities were sent to men and women of Sydney's prominent political and economic circles. Ledger expected that the social occasion would generate enthusiasm among the crowd for the promising addition of the alpaca to Australia's wool industry.

The day of the event, Ledger selected two alpacas, one black and one white, to be the first sheared by his men in front of everyone. The audience reacted with disappointment, however, when it became evident that the South Americans lacked the accomplishment of the famous Australian sheep shearers. As described by the press, "The process was not performed with that dexterity and speed which Australian shearers display, who can shear a hundred sheep a day" ("Shearing the Alpacas" 1859, 5). The dissatisfaction expressed in response to the Andean men's performance reflected local understandings of sheep-shearing as a national theme of significance and a quintessentially masculine activity.

Tom Roberts, the celebrated Australian painter of *Shearing the Rams* (1890), an oil depicting the hard work of the shearing shed, elaborated in a letter to the *Argus* that shearing was a subject "noble enough and worthy enough if I could express the meaning and spirit—of strong masculine labour, the patience of the animals whose year's growth is being stripped from them for man's use, and the great human interest of the whole scene."[54] Together with his famous painting, Roberts's observations represented shearing culture as wholly Australian and a manifestation of a civilizing mission (with imperial overtones): sheep were also an imported animal that, like many new immigrants, had become naturalized. Moreover, the work tested the limits of a shearer's strength when he subdued more than a hundred sheep in a day, "stripping" them of their fleece for "man's use." This was a man who could make a lasting imprint on the colonial landscape and national economy. In contrast, the Andeans' slow speed and seeming lack of adroitness reminded onlookers of the men's outsider status.

In defense of the Andean shearers, Ledger explained that their apparent inexpert performance was due to the larger size of the alpaca, the fleece being closer to the animal's body, the tools used, and, most importantly, a lack of experience, because "in South America the shearing, or rather the cutting off of the wool (as a knife is used in the place of shears) is done entirely by women" ("Shearing the Alpacas" 1859, 5). Although it was not stated, those present may have anticipated that Australian shearers would claim the alpacas once they became acclimatized and incorporate them into the national pastoral myth of "strong masculine labour." At the time of Ledger's event, however, it was preferable for the Bolivians to

226 | *Llamas beyond the Andes*

do the work rather than Australian sheep shearers, who were unfamiliar with the animals. The newspaper recounted that despite the men's awkwardness they nonetheless displayed important skills while handling the alpacas and demonstrated how "their long familiarity with the animals has imparted to [the alpacas] a degree of docility and quietness while in the hands of their own keepers which they would not preserve in the presence of strangers" (5).

During the shearing, onlookers were invited to guess the final weight of the fleeces. All expressed amazement when the black fleece weighed in at over seventeen pounds. Such a remarkable weight would never be found in the Andes, Ledger claimed, impressing upon the crowd that these valuable animals already demonstrated signs of improvement after a short period in their new environment.[55] The consummate host, he answered questions and entertained the crowd with "animated narratives and descriptions" of the animal celebrities, their natural history, and their native land. Afterward, everyone assembled for the luncheon and drank the health of many who had assisted the enterprise. The attendees spent the rest of the day strolling the grounds. All described themselves as pleased with the outing and "much interested in the prospects for colonial enterprise and industry, which the importation and successful rearing of the alpacas in this country have opened out" ("Shearing the Alpacas" 1859, 5).

At the luncheon Ledger had pointed out differences between shearing sheep and alpacas. An unsuspecting sheep shearer had to contend with other contrasts, however, when first working with a camelid. One famous anecdote involved the Lloyd llamas that shipped to Sydney at the same time that the Wilson-Westgarth llamas sailed for Melbourne. Upon arrival, nine of the animals were sold to Gilbert Davidson, of Canning Downs station, Queensland.[56]

When it came time to shear the llamas, Davidson hired Jack Howe, the father of the future champion sheep shearer Jackie Howe. Jack Howe was also an excellent shearer and athlete, having worked as an acrobat at James Aston's circus and Le Rosia's circus.[57] As described later in the *Warwick Examiner and Times*, the people watching the shearing event were "young Australian natives" who helped to capture the llamas and prepare them for shearing. Like most Australians, they knew little of the llama's habits. Davidson apparently did not warn Howe, hoping to enjoy "some fun at the first attempt to shear them." According to the article, "the native of those days wore his hair 'hang-tailed,' or cut straight across the neck, and always had a thick mat of it all over his head. The favourite pomade used, when procurable, was Macassar oil, and the hair always absorbed a fair quantity before the proper glow appeared. A closely plaited, heavy cabbage tree hat, having as a chin strap part of an old-fashioned lady's chain, completed the top male adornment, of what some sarcastic people used to call the 'flash native.'"[58]

Howe had just begun to shear the first llama when it unceremoniously spat all over his hair. Horrified, Howe allegedly exclaimed, "The bastard spat on me!" (Muir 1989, 8). Marsh (2007, 92) also recounts this anecdote: "[Howe] also made the new's, when he shore [*sic*] a batch of Peruvian llamas out on the Darling Downs. Yes, you heard me, Jackie's dad once shore llamas. But they reckoned that he only managed to shear nine in one go because the buggers wouldn't stop spitting on him. Spat all over him, they did." Howe reportedly stopped shearing immediately to shampoo his hair, soaping it up several times, "amidst the chaff of the audience." Before he continued his work, the animal was nosebagged, as was each subsequent llama. "Jack always asserted that the pungent aroma clug [*sic*] to him for weeks and made his presence objectionable" (92). In contrast to this legendary incident, Ledger and his men had the advantage of familiarity and knowledge of the animals so that no such occurrence spoiled the public performance at Atkinson's estate.

Ledger Collides with the NSW Governmental Bureaucracy

Ledger, his men, and the alpacas finally began the 300-mile relocation to Maneroo in late 1859, a journey he estimated would take a minimum of two months to complete (Ledger 1860–1861, 218). Ostensibly, Maneroo was the end of his journeys, because the alpacas would at last be settled permanently and his experiments in crossbreeding and animal improvement could begin in earnest. Ledger put all of his hopes on this final stage of the scientific undertaking, convinced that, given enough time, he could produce the new alpaca and become the vindicated hero. It was not to be, however. The group never reached its destination. The men and alpacas instead seemed condemned to life on the move. Their continued displacement was matched only by Ledger's endless correspondence with John Robertson, in which he expressed outrage and frustration over his poor treatment and financial ruin.[59] Without expecting the government to compensate him for all of the losses accrued during his journeys, Ledger did

228 | *Llamas beyond the Andes*

want to be reimbursed for the £7,000 he had spent on the project out of his own pocket. This sum would allow him to purchase a station, especially if he received an annual salary of £1,000 as superintendent of alpacas. Under these conditions, once he had placed the animals in their permanent location, he could request a nine-month leave of absence, travel to Peru, settle his affairs, and bring his daughters back to Australia.

Ledger also pressed for the retention of the Bolivian shepherds, emphasizing that they would be unlikely to remain in Australia if he left permanently for South America and no one else had their expertise. If these conditions of cash or grants of land could not be met, he stated that he would resign his position once the animals reached Maneroo. He was willing to give instructions to anyone who took over from him, but after that he would not remain in the colony, with no inducement to do so.[60]

Undersecretary for lands Michael Fitzpatrick explained in no uncertain terms in his reply that the business between Ledger and the government had been concluded when he was paid £15,000 for the flock. If Ledger agreed to stay on with the animals for at least another six months, the secretary for lands would raise his annual salary from £300 to £500. Fitzpatrick advised Ledger to make the necessary arrangements for his family and remain in the position of superintendent of alpacas for a while longer. If not, the secretary for lands would select another overseer who would have to learn the job in the time remaining before Ledger left for South America.[61]

This was not the response that Ledger had hoped to receive. He informed the government that he would depart for South America as soon as the alpacas were permanently settled and would take the shepherds with him. However, despite the unsatisfactory outcome of his negotiations with the government, Ledger had difficulty letting go of the venture and appeared genuinely to want to ensure its success. He requested that he be the one to select his replacement, as he alone knew which qualifications were most important. Only someone who was patient and kind toward animals and willing to receive his instructions would do. Ledger also urged that the animals be settled on a permanent run so that they would not have to be moved continually from place to place, which would potentially impact negatively on their ability to reproduce: "it is well known that this peculiar animal is extremely sensitive, attached to its location, and pines when removed from it."[62]

Although he did not want to be further delayed regarding his own affairs, he would remain with the flock until the animals had been properly accommodated. But he added:

It would be assuming a false modesty, were I to refrain from expressing the great chagrin and disappointment which I feel at finding myself ruined and homeless, after years of toil, privation, and expense, at the conclusion of an enterprise that I was distinctly (as fully certified by the written testimony of most respectable parties in this Colony) instigated to carry out by the highest authority in the land, whose assurance of ample remuneration, leaving altogether on one side the reimbursement (which is all that I at present claim), it would have been the height of presumption to question.[63]

In mid-January the group reached Arthursleigh, the 19,700-acre estate of friend and ally Thomas Holt, a wealthy wool merchant. Ledger decided to remain there for the next months because the climate was milder than in Maneroo and he feared the animals might have difficulty adjusting to the change. Once settled on his friend's estate, Ledger had to face the task of replacing most of the Bolivian shepherds, who wanted to return home. Two shepherds and his overseer Pedro Cabrera would remain with him and assist with the training of the newly hired men.[64]

Ledger prepared an accounting of the flock for the previous ten months at Arthursleigh for the NSW government in February 1860. The information he recorded provides further insight into the kinds of frustrating encounters that he and his men experienced when dealing with the NSW bureaucracy. During the period in question, they had lost a total of forty-five animals for reasons that included starvation due to insufficient pasture, problems related to pregnancy and birth, and accidents involving attacks by dogs, falling trees, and poisonous plants, among others. The surviving animals were healthy despite these casualties, and some of the deaths had been offset by births. Ledger was relieved that they would winter over in Arthursleigh, where the animals would be better protected from the late, heavy rains. Had they remained on the road, he feared that many of them might have drowned.[65]

Ledger made his feelings plain as to who bore the responsibility for the high number of deaths. The flock had done well when it spent the previous summer in the County of Cumberland, having been taken there soon after landing. Enjoying ample pasture, the flock increased in number from 256 to 291. However, the government had wanted the animals moved to another spot, despite Ledger's objections. He explained that his resistance to moving the animals had been based on the losses experienced in South America when he had to move the animals in late fall. Furthermore, his familiarity with the animals convinced him that "worse results were to be

230 | *Llamas beyond the Andes*

anticipated from the pining and restlessness of all animals of this species on being moved from a spot to which they had become accustomed, than from a partial scarcity of fodder."[66] In this case, however, it seemed that many of the deaths resulted from starvation. But this problem too had been exacerbated by government inaction. While he was away, looking for a permanent location for the animals, the animals ran out of fodder. The overseer had had to endure a substantial waiting period before receiving authorization from the government to buy more.

Although the losses were regrettable, Ledger assured the government that most of them were among the less valuable animals. He emphasized that alpacas were remarkably strong, capable of resisting a long time with little to no food, and could withstand cold, rain, and drought.[67] Ledger had to exercise restraint in his remarks: while he was obliged to explain the loss of life, he did not want to do so in a way that would downplay the animals' hardiness and thus cause the government to perceive them as too fragile to withstand acclimatization and lose interest in the project. Nor could he appear overly aggressive about blaming the government for the deaths. Moreover, he had to justify new expenses to a government increasingly resistant to approving further resources for the venture. But the shepherds would need a hut if they were not to spend the winter in tents; their three horses needed corn and hay for the winter because each day they averaged ten miles riding around the pastures where the animals were kept. And the alpacas and llamas needed regular tobacco-water baths to stave off skin disease.[68] I concur with Gramiccia (1988) that it must have been very difficult for Ledger, a man used to making his own decisions and changing course spontaneously when necessary to protect the flock, to be forced to seek the government's permission at each turn of events. "Now Ledger found himself in the spider's web of a bureaucratic establishment in which every minor detail had to be accounted for, in which all expenditure had to be sanctioned in advance and, one in which, in particular, all unforeseen and unforeseeable expenditures and actions had nevertheless to be foreseen and laid down in detail for approval months in advance" (Gramiccia 1988, 75).

Ledger and the Bolivian Shepherds: Congruencies and Contradictions

As noted earlier, the continuing presence of the twelve Bolivian shepherds in Ledger's correspondence and in the Australian public press is a critical feature that distinguishes his alpaca story from other accounts of nineteenth-century camelid extraction and acclimatization. They served as an integral part of Ledger's own heroic and scientific accounts, yet he assumed a surprisingly contradictory stance against them when he came under increasing pressure from the NSW government (as discussed later). It is even possible to argue that the Andeans' indispensable participation in the venture ultimately undercut the foundations of Ledger's singular heroic narrative, revealing its fictional constructs. Rather than reinforce the heroic myth, their agency played a crucial part in the construction of what Safier (2010a, 138), drawing from the work of Sanjay Subrahmanyam (1997), identifies as the "connected histories" and stories that link "empires and geographical regions"—in this case, the Andes and Australia. They provided an unmatched example of intercultural collaboration and knowledge-making in a camelid contact zone.

Although relatively little is known about the twelve Bolivian shepherds during their stay in Australia, it is apparent that they carried out much of the actual work and experimentation in the pastures and sheds alongside the animals. Ledger described them as "hardy, frugal, and possessed of great endurance, very sober and quiet people." As he strategically asserted in his correspondence with the NSW government, they were a bargain economically because "the expenses for each would not pass £40 per annum, rations and all."[69] They likely remained comparatively isolated as a group, given that interaction with Australians would have been difficult because only one of the men could communicate in English: James Alexander Ávila (Alexander, as Ledger referred to him). A Portuguese man from the Azores who joined the group at some point in South America, Alexander often served as translator-interpreter for the Bolivians when Ledger traveled.[70] He is the only one of the shepherds who permanently settled in Australia, marrying Margaret Skelly, a woman from Goulburn, in 1862. Two years later, he became a naturalized British citizen (Fletcher 2002, 60).

Because the information available on the shepherds in Australia comes to us almost exclusively through Ledger, it is difficult to disentangle their role in the narrative of alpaca acclimatization from his personal narrative trajectory. From the start, the number of shepherds represented a point of contention between Ledger and the government, which did not want to pay so many salaries. Ledger argued that the shepherds were indispensable to the success of the alpaca acclimatization effort and tried to leverage their expertise in his negotiations with the government for a higher salary by threatening to leave Australia and take the shepherds with him. He also made sure not to limit this ultimatum to his correspondence with

232 | *Llamas beyond the Andes*

the secretary for lands, also announcing it in the newspapers. In response to this potential departure, a letter to the editor of the *Sydney Morning Herald* expressed dismay at the possibility: "The consequence of such a step would be a great loss to the colony, as there was no one here competent to manage the animals, which required special training and accurate knowledge of their habits and instincts, to render one able to take charge of them."[71]

Even though Ledger claimed his own knowledge of the alpacas, gained from many years' involvement with them, he made a point of emphasizing how uniquely specialized his shepherds were due to having grown up in pastoral communities. The NSW government, however, refused to be swayed by this argument and remained unwilling to pay for so many men. In their defense, Ledger reminded Robertson that the twelve men in Australia formed part of his experienced team of thirty men who worked for him in the Andes. All were necessary to care for the 340 animals during the ocean voyage. The shepherds managed the daily responsibilities in Australia and specialized projects focused on the alpacas' maintenance and improvement: "The care required in the systematic cross-breeding so as to produce a race of pure Alpacas, renders it very necessary and advisable that they should be attended to by those who have been from childhood accustomed to their management."[72]

Whenever Ledger traveled, he was required to notify the secretary for lands as to who would superintend the alpacas during his absence. This protocol provided another opportunity for Ledger to communicate the importance of the shepherds and convey his confidence in them. For example, before he and Ortiz traveled in search of a permanent location for the alpacas, he informed the government that he had entrusted the animals' care to his competent overseer, Pedro Cabrera, with Alexander serving as interpreter. Ledger's letter included a copy of his instructions, which stated merely that he had full confidence in Cabrera's ability to look after the alpacas properly. He further advised Cabrera to "not allow the shepherds to leave the flocks for a single moment, except of a Sunday, when I trust that you will send them by turns to Mass."[73] Ledger's simple directives communicated Cabrera's competence because they required no further details or clarification. With the remark about the importance of the shepherds attending Mass, Ledger drew attention to the industrious nature of the Indigenous Andeans and their adherence to Western European values and customs. This might have been an attempt to distinguish them from Indigenous Australians, who at the time were considered by many white European settlers to be "irrelevant to wealth and progress" (Kingston 1988, 109).

By 1860 it was apparent that the anticipated economic rewards from the alpaca enterprise would not be forthcoming any time soon. Ledger's shepherds had become restless with their situation, and pressure continued to mount from the government to reduce the number of his salaried employees. In April, "at the urgent request of the South American shepherds," Ledger sent seven men home and paid for their passage, fulfilling the agreement he had made with them before they accompanied him to Australia. He retained Pedro Cabrera as overseer and two others but raised their salaries,[74] unilaterally overstepping his position by making these decisions without government approval. Displeased when he heard about Ledger's actions concerning the raises, the secretary for lands demanded details of the payment and insisted that government approval be sought for such expenses.[75] Ledger clarified that the men would not have stayed without the raise and that he trusted the government would approve, given that he had not overspent his budget.[76]

Ledger defended his decisions to Robertson by framing them in a larger narrative of science, sacrifice, and British imperial expansion. From the start, he had enticed the shepherds to accompany him with several incentives that included their salary, a certain number of sheep that could be kept free of charge with the alpacas, and passage back to South America.[77] He contended that these men had sacrificed a great deal to participate in this British experiment on Australia's behalf and could all have earned more money had they remained in South America.[78] Given the shepherd-specialists' commitment to the enterprise, Ledger supported a salary increase for them, arguing that it was the least the NSW government could do, especially because the men's hopes for economic gain had been dashed. He could not resist a subtle criticism of the government with his insistence on honoring promises made and rewarding faithful dedication and sacrifice. Moreover, he argued, his actions served the British government's long-term interests, because in the future "natives" would be more willing to "assist them in their enterprises, and its moral effects would be to raise the English name still higher in their estimation."[79]

Later, in an article published in the *Empire*, Ledger publicly justified his decision to give the remaining shepherds a raise, praised their loyalty, and denounced the government's senseless and cumbersome bureaucracy:

234 | Llamas beyond the Andes

My position towards these men was somewhat peculiar and needs some explanation — they had accompanied me for many years, and during their absence from their homes my relatives in South America supplied their families with monthly succor. I explained this to the Colonial Treasurer, and declined going through the *farce* of making out a monthly "acquittance," for the presentation as a legitimate document, when of all the men, those that could write were taught by myself during our peregrinations, and not one of them understood English, two of them but very imperfectly understanding Spanish even.[80]

Thus, in Ledger's correspondence and publications, where he played out his struggle with the NSW government, the shepherds also maintained a vital agency. As specialists, they had the final word on the alpacas and their care and helped ensure the animals' transition from the status of "new immigrants" to naturalized Australians. Furthermore, because the shepherds' fate was so closely intertwined with Ledger's, the argument that they were indispensable to the project's success helped bolster the same claims that Ledger made about himself. After all, if the NSW government determined that the Andeans were superfluous to the management of the alpacas, Ledger and his high salary might also have been deemed unnecessary. Ledger also tried to make the case for how these men would facilitate British imperial projects on their return to South America through their continued loyalty and dedication to those who had treated them with respect and generosity. Finally, the popularity of the exotic shepherds was useful to Ledger in the continual negotiations of his own increasingly precarious relationship with the NSW government and the wider public. They personified the congruence of loyalty, heroism, economic benefit, and scientific advancement in his achievements.

Collaborations and Conflicts: The Camelid Dream Begins to Unravel

Victoria's chief secretary William Nicholson contacted the NSW colonial secretary in July 1860 to inquire whether that government would be willing to loan two male alpacas from Ledger's flock to the Melbourne Zoological Gardens in a plan to improve the fleece of the Wilson-Westgarth llamas.[81] The opportunity to collaborate with the Victoria government provided Ledger with the possibility of making some money and rehabilitating his image as a hero-scientist, which had been damaged by increasingly poor relations with the NSW government. He was keen to have the request approved, pointing to the benefits of having a monopoly of pure alpacas. "They must be got from this at any price, if in any way they wish (which they do in earnest) to carry on this breed to perfection."[82] The requisite permission was granted. After receiving a personal invitation from Ferdinand Mueller, the director of the Botanical and Zoological Gardens, Ledger accompanied the two alpacas to Melbourne on the *Wonga Wonga* steamer on October 20, 1860.[83]

Ledger inspected the Wilson-Westgarth llamas in Melbourne and provided Mueller with a report subsequently published as "Our Llamas" along with a short introduction in the *Argus*. Ledger found the animals to be in overall good condition but of inferior stock; therefore, he recommended that his colleagues put in place the same program of crossbreeding that he was implementing in New South Wales. Keen to encourage Victoria's alpaca enterprise, he characterized the animals as robust and gregarious, even though by doing so he contradicted his statements concerning their adaptability: "No animal in the creation, it is my firm conviction, is less affected by the changes of climate or food, nor is there any one to be found more easily domesticated."[84] As already seen, he had claimed on multiple occasions that the animals in New South Wales could be adversely affected by homesickness if moved. However, it was in his economic interest here to present the alpaca in the most favorable light possible to encourage its promotion in Victoria. He expressed willingness to continue future collaborations with the colony.

During his stay in Melbourne, members of the Royal Society of Victoria invited Ledger to attend one of their meetings, presenting him as "the introducer of the Alpaca to Australia."[85] Ledger had previously contacted the Royal Society to offer his services in obtaining pure llamas and alpacas from South America. The council could not accept the offer at the time because it did not have the funds; however, during his stay in Melbourne, Ledger accompanied a small group from the council to meet with chief secretary William Nicholson to ask for his aid in the effort to increase the colony's number of camelids. After hearing their presentation, Nicholson agreed to bring the proposal to the cabinet and "place the requisite sum on the estimate."[86]

Several months after Ledger returned to Sydney, the chief secretary and the Legislative Assembly of Victoria approved the sum of £2,000 for

236 | *Llamas beyond the Andes*

the introduction of alpacas into the colony, contending that more stock was needed to improve their numbers and quality now it had been demonstrated that the animals could flourish in Victoria.[87] Ledger traveled back to Melbourne in May 1861 to assist the newly formed Acclimatisation Society of Victoria with the arrangements, "for which his local knowledge and great experience ably qualify him."[88] At the society's meeting on May 28, 1861, attended by Ledger, the group specified which animals they wanted for the £2,000 and presented him with the full conditions of their agreement. They requested twelve pure female alpacas and eight male and female vicuñas or as many as possible of each kind for the money. The animals were to be delivered to Melbourne in good condition and within eighteen months from their agreement. They approved advancing Ledger a percentage of the £2,000, with the rest to be paid on his successful return, provided that he first take out a life insurance policy for £2,000 in the name of the trustees for the society to cover its losses in the event of his death during the venture. Ledger agreed to all of the terms but requested the full £2,000 up front because he had already contacted his agents in South America who were in the process of acquiring animals for him. Receiving the whole sum in advance, he argued, would improve the chances of success and enable him to act freely and independently in all related matters.[89] And, one could add, the money would allow him to take control of his own narrative once again.

Ledger's reasoning did not persuade the Acclimatisation Society, which continued to wait for him to send the insurance policy and confirm his dates of departure. The society had understood that Ledger would be leaving immediately for South America, but he continually postponed his departure due to events unfolding in New South Wales. Despite growing misgivings, the society moved forward with the project anyway, even if the sole guarantee was the policy on Ledger's life, deciding "to place implicit reliance on his personal character and reputation, and his acknowledged zeal in promoting the importation and acclimatisation of the animals in question, which are so much in request in these Colonies, where he has already so successfully and creditably proved their adaptability to this climate."[90] The Victoria Treasury advanced £600 to Ledger in Sydney in mid-July 1861 to cover his initial outlay.[91] Two months later, Ledger forwarded to the society one policy for £1,000 from the Australian Mutual Provident Society of Sydney, explaining that he would send a second policy for the same amount before leaving for South America, at which time he would also apply for the remaining £1,400. He had paid the premiums through January 23, 1862, but made no mention as to when he would be traveling.[92] These unsatisfactory exchanges concerning the policies and Ledger's travel dates led to increasing tension between the two parties. There was also disagreement regarding who would be paying the policy premiums, especially in light of Ledger not providing a precise date of departure.

One reason behind Ledger's delayed leave-taking concerned previously initiated negotiations with the NSW government to repurchase the original flock of alpacas. Mort and another financier acted on Ledger's behalf in the discussions with the government, which agreed to introduce a bill to the Legislative Assembly on the matter. Believing that this agreement would be accepted and the matter settled in his favor, Ledger had traveled to Melbourne and commenced arrangements to obtain camelids. A few months later, Ledger learned to his utter dismay that the NSW Legislative Assembly had rejected the proposal, giving as the reason "not obtaining the support of the Government." Deeply disappointed by the decision, Ledger resigned from the position of superintendent of alpacas on October 7, 1861.[93]

Ledger's Triumph at the 1862 London Exhibition

Despite his resignation and mounting pressure to move forward on the Victoria alpaca initiative, Ledger continued to delay his departure for South America. He participated in several events in New South Wales, where his accomplishments with the alpaca project garnered national and international attention, enabling him to achieve some feeling of vindication. Ledger exhibited four alpacas at the Argyle Agricultural Society in March 1862, for which he earned the society's gold medal (Wood 2005).[94] On his return from the show, he received word that the NSW government still required his services, so his resignation appeared to be shelved for the time being.

Ledger received the greatest recognition for his contributions to the 1862 London Exhibition. Queen Victoria had announced that a "Universal Exhibition of the Natural and Industrial Products of all Nations should take place in London in the month of May, 1862" (International Exhibition 1861, 3).[95] William Macarthur, Thomas Mort, and others were appointed commissioners for New South Wales and charged with receiving all submissions and arranging for their safe transport to London (3–4).

238 | *Llamas beyond the Andes*

They designated Ledger's experiments in acclimatizing and crossing the alpaca in New South Wales as praiseworthy entries:

> For the importation of this most valuable animal the Colony is indebted to the enterprise and intelligence of Mr. Ledger. The wool of several animals, a cross between the Alpaca and Llama, has been already exported to England, and entire skins of others, bred in the Colony, and exhibiting, it is believed, special and valuable peculiarities in their fleece, will form part of our contribution to the Great Exhibition. (12)

For Ledger and his supporters, the International Exhibition would be the perfect venue for showcasing his contributions to the science of acclimatization.

Ledger requested permission from John Robertson, the secretary for lands, to have a few animals from his flock killed and stuffed for the event. He planned to display his work crossing the animals and introduce the meat to the public, by having it distributed in Sydney at clubs, private functions, and restaurants, for all to comment freely on whether they found it flavorsome or not.[96] The tallow from the animals killed would be placed in glass containers to accompany the stuffed specimens, along with the public's review of the meat.[97]

After his request was approved, Ledger organized a day-long series of events outside Sydney, centered around the seven animals that would be killed for the exhibition. He selected a pure llama, a pure alpaca, and five others representing the stages of crossbreeding and had them transported to Atkinson's property at Sophienburg, the same place where the shepherds had publicly sheared the alpacas. The *Illustrated London News* carried an engraving (figure 6.1) taken from a photograph of the animals while they grazed on the lawn of Atkinson's estate. According to the article accompanying the engraving, all the animals except for the llama had been born in the colony.[98] A brown and white female, the llama stood opposite a gray male alpaca with the crossed offspring in between (International Exhibition 1861, 76). Public response to the announced demise of the seven animals was mixed. In an article on the affair ("Alpacas for the Great Exhibition" 1861, 12) published in the *Times* (London), a defender of the process scoffed at those who had expressed distress over the killing of the animals, arguing that national benefit and scientific progress required sacrifice:

Camelids in Australia | 239

No small amount of spurious pity has been indulged in at the destruction of these animals, which it was affirmed were too valuable to be consigned to such a fate; but Mr. Ledger, who, more than any other person, is interested in maintaining the completeness of the flock, has distinctly stated that the removal of these animals will not palpably deteriorate the flock, as they were of no use to breed from; but that, even if any loss were incurred, it would still be desirable to exhibit a result of which the most eminent naturalists have denied the possibility—the production of the pure alpaca from the crossing of the alpaca and the llama; and also to show to English manufacturers a sample of wool which in a few years will doubtless constitute one of the principal sources of our national wealth.[99]

The killing of the alpacas did not appear to deter the many visitors who arrived for Ledger's September 7, 1861, event. To the contrary, as Mitchell (2010, 58) has observed, the day's events provided those attending with the opportunity to celebrate and participate in this important British enterprise that combined science, imperialism, and entertainment.[100] The guest list included more than 300 invitees from the colony's elite circles and featured NSW governor John Young and his wife, premier Charles Cowper, members of the Legislative Assembly, prominent members of Sydney's leading commercial businesses, and many families. Everyone came to Sophienburg to stroll through the grounds and view "the colonial alpacas prior to their being handed over to the butcher" ("Alpacas for the Great Exhibition" 1861, 12).[101] In Mitchell's words, "If great exhibitions were about presenting the empire in miniature, it was perhaps appropriate that their displays could also hint at a preparedness for violence" (59–60).

Of the activities planned for the guests, the highlight was the elaborate alpaca luncheon. Ledger compared the menu and the guests' enthusiasm to the much-celebrated eland dinner that had taken place in London the previous January. By making this association, Ledger elevated his event to match the famous dinner, which was considered a landmark event for British acclimatization: "All were delighted with the alpaca soup, cutlets, and roast. I often thought of Dr. Buckland's famous Eland dinner, and wished for his and Professor Owen's presence." In contrast to the more outlandish fare served at a second acclimatization dinner, hosted by the Acclimatisation Society of Victoria, which required elaborate disguise and fanciful aliases to entice the guests to try the food, Ledger highlighted the alpaca meat with unadorned terms like "soup," "cutlets," and "roasts,"

240 | Llamas beyond the Andes

FIGURE 6.1. "*Mr. Ledger's Alpacas and Llamas at Sophienburg, the Seat of Mr. Atkinson, New South Wales. Llama. Cross. Alpaca.*" Illustrated London News 39 (December 14, 1861).

thus rendering this otherwise "exotic" food familiar and tempting.[102] He informed those present that the alpaca meat had already reached Sydney and was attracting attention and, more importantly, profits. "I had more than 100 applications for meat, each accompanied by an order to deliver from the Colonial Secretary. The *cafés* that got some advertised their good luck and were crowded. They charged 5s. for a slice, and must have made a good harvest of the celebrated alpaca feed." The public unanimously concurred with Ledger on the quality of the meat, finding it to be "very tender and savoury" ("Alpacas for the Great Exhibition" 1861, 12).

Those who sampled it were apparently unbothered by what Ledger described as its less than ideal presentation due to the damage caused by the preparation of the carcasses for the exhibition: "I should remark, the finest joints—viz., haunches and shoulders—were entirely disfigured, and the meat much 'mauled,' owing to the necessity of cutting out the bones and sinews to enable the 'setters-up' of the specimens to properly perform their work."[103] He nonetheless felt certain that once people became more familiar with alpaca meat, "its wholesome, nutritious, and palatable qualities" would be appreciated (International Exhibition 1861, 75).

During the luncheon, several of the guests gave toasts, including Ledger, who praised the improvements he had seen in the animals and made the surprising announcement that the Peruvian government had finally granted a concession allowing a large commercial firm the opportunity to export as many alpacas as it wanted, "a consummation which, if nothing else had been attained by his exertions, would be the means of importing the animals into these colonies" ("Alpacas for the Great Exhibition" 1861, 12). This concession would have significant consequences for Ledger's dealings with Victoria, as discussed later in the chapter.

Even before the exhibition took place, Ledger received international recognition for his work. The Paris Acclimatization Society followed his Australia venture with great interest and translated his reports and letters to the newspapers into French for publication in its *Bulletin*.[104] The Paris Society discussed in detail his experiments and findings concerning forage, crossbreeding, and fiber improvement and awarded Ledger its Médaille de Première Class in 1860 for the introduction of llamas and vicuñas in Australia (see figure 4.1).[105] At the first weekly meeting of the Society of Arts in London for the session 1861–1862, the members presented their silver medal "To Mr. Charles Ledger, for the introduction of the alpaca into the Australian Colonies."[106]

Ledger's stuffed specimens and other contributions to the exhibition drew attention because visitors could see for themselves the differences in animal size and fiber quality at each stage of crossing. "I contend, with these *proofs* to support my statement, that the dash of Llama blood infused into the Alpaca produces a larger framed, hardier constitutioned, heavier, finer, and more glossily-fleeced animal than ever could be obtained by the close '*in and in*' breeding so zealously carried out by the Indians of Peru" (International Exhibition 1861, 76; emphasis in the original).[107] According to one newspaper article, "The changes produced by cross breeding are very curiously shown" in the specimens other than the purebred llama and alpaca.[108]

The stuffed animals communicated other discoveries as well, most notably correcting the long-held belief that crossbred offspring were always sterile.[109] For these reasons, Ledger's exhibit promised to have an impact on the scientific world in multiple ways: "Hybridisation assumes through them a complete change. The 'savans' [*sic*] will see that they have been in

242 | *Llamas beyond the Andes*

error for a very long period; and, moreover, the collection will be the first ever exhibited of the 'Auchenia' in its varied crosses, and will be worthy [of] a place in the National Museum."[110] Other commentaries related Ledger's discovery to imperialist claims of progress and advancement, arguing that Peruvians had had the science all wrong and that their breeding traditions were clearly inferior to those now being practiced in Australia: "By process of experiment, and a vigilant attention, it has been found that we can actually improve animals indigenous to other countries, and make them superior to those of the country from whence they came."[111] Edward Wilson went even further, linking the success of the acclimatization of the alpaca to the triumphant advance of the British Empire, as expressed in the chapter's first epigraph (Wilson 1862, 14). For these authors, Ledger's concrete evidence of the successful acclimatization of the alpaca signaled that Australia was poised to play a new and dominant role in imperial trade.

Ledger not only displayed the stuffed specimens but also provided captivating narratives that accompanied the animals. Ever the storyteller, he included colorful incidents of camelid hardiness and survival such as the "'tween-deck tropical voyage of 87 days" (International Exhibition 1861, 77). Through these stories, the alpacas acquired many of the same heroic characteristics that he had employed to describe his own adventures: like Ledger himself, the animals had overcome suffering and adversity and remained relatively unscathed. Wilson (1862, 14) also helped to sell the story of the alpaca exhibition by dramatically playing up the convergence of heroism and scientific discovery in Ledger's persona through pathos: "The animals exhibited are the produce of the flock introduced into New South Wales, after incredible toils and dangers, by Mr. Ledger in the beginning of 1859. They were culled from his present flock, and, at the cost of actual tears from their enthusiastic protector, who has nursed them like his children, slaughtered for the Exhibition, by way of showing to the world the progress of the experiments to which he has devoted his life and sacrificed his fortune."

Ledger's account for the International Exhibition did not focus solely on the stuffed specimens. He chronicled the experiments that he and the shepherds had conducted with the alpaca flock, often portraying the camelids as agential participants. For example, he attempted to determine the healthiest pasture for the animals and compared their overall maintenance with sheep raising. Ledger pitched several of the alpacas' benefits: their fleece did not have to be washed prior to shearing, they were less prone to disease, and the young fared better, as the mothers were "provident and careful nurses" (International Exhibition 1861, 78). The only time that they required assistance was during the breeding season.

The animals' heroic, vigilant nature was perhaps most evident in their success at keeping native dogs away from the flocks. Ledger recommended the alpacas for guarding any sheep station because of their courage and aggressive behavior toward unfamiliar dogs, especially how capable they were "using the fore feet [sic] as offensive weapons with powerful effect" (International Exhibition 1861, 78).[112] As Parker (2007, 70–71) has shown, colonial representations of native dogs (dingos) utilized adjectives such as cunning, treacherous, crafty, and sneaking to depict their hunting techniques and the ways they outwit sheep dogs and farmers when raiding the sheep flocks. In contrast, Ledger's anecdotes personifying the alpacas as intelligent, organized strategists adept at working together to thwart danger made them sound like the perfect remedy for such a perceived pest: "the 'punteras' or leaders are ever on the alert, and on the appearance of danger alarm the flock by uttering a shrill screaming whistle; the young may then be seen running to the centre of a ring formed by the old ones; a steady front is shown to the menaced danger, and the 'punteras' rush forward in concert to meet it. I have repeatedly seen large dogs thus beaten off and now and then killed" (International Exhibition 1861, 78–79). In view of the alpacas' stuffed bodies and compelling story, it was assumed that Ledger would be able to sell the prepared specimens in London at a high price after the exhibition closed.

Given its organization and presentation, Ledger's unusual alpaca exhibit entered international debates on advancements in acclimatization and the human impact on the processes of adaptation. Many prominent Australian scientists of the time opposed Darwinism, including Mueller and others, seeing "evolutionary theory as a threat to Christianity" and maintaining that "the species were clearly defined and immutable" (Mitchell 2010, 72). Although Ledger did not refer to Charles Darwin in the description of his accomplishments with alpaca improvement through crossbreeding, the "aims of transformation and perfection were nonetheless strong in his work" (73).

The camelids chosen for the exhibition thus gained a celebrity identity first when they were captured in the engraving as living creatures displayed on the lawn and featured on the page of the popular *Illustrated London News* and later in the day as exotic menu items for the luncheon. But they gained in status and value due to more than their foreign nature after being killed, materially reconstructed, stuffed, and exhibited. In this

244 | *Llamas beyond the Andes*

reincarnation they served as trophies of empire, demonstrating the promises of acclimatization, the improvements produced through crossbreeding, and the fertility of crossed offspring. It could therefore be argued that their staged physicality was designed to foster desire in the onlooker to encourage the alpaca industry in Australia and beyond. As such, these seven animals were not inert "finished objects" (Patchett and Foster 2008, 102). Rather, they embodied in their lives and afterlives the complexities of their past and present histories and the multiple scientific, geographic, economic, and cultural transformations they traversed.[113]

New South Wales had high expectations regarding the medals it hoped to win at the International Exhibition, thereby showing the world that the colony was not simply "one of [Great Britain's] children which had gone to the bad." Some expressed regret that Ledger's stuffed alpacas had not been better situated at the International Exhibition, their large case having been placed "at the back of the court under the staircase, and rather too far away from the light for advantageous exhibition."[114] Others nonetheless expressed optimism that the attention of the public, "especially those interested in textile manufactures," would be drawn to the stuffed samples as a "new source of our productive wealth."[115] The jurors for the exhibition apparently had no difficulty finding the alpacas. They praised Ledger's specimens but were less kind toward the Victoria llamas. Juror Thomas Clayton reported that Ledger's samples, on display in the Peru Court, "were good and of pure breed. But with respect to those grown in Victoria, he regrets that the same cannot be said. The animals, he observes, 'require further crossing, perhaps three or four times more, before the pure wool will be obtainable'" (International Exhibition 1863, 13). Ledger must have felt vindicated in the eyes of the NSW secretary for lands, John Robertson, when the exhibition jurors awarded him a silver medal "for the introduction of alpacas and specimens of their produce" (14) into Australia.[116]

Much of the excitement over Ledger's exhibit came from his optimistic projections that within fifty years a flourishing alpaca industry would produce an annual income through wool exports to the amount of £9,000,000 (Wilson 1862, 14). An unnamed correspondent had reacted earlier to Ledger's numbers, noting that "at first sight this may look a little like the brilliant day-dream of the barber's fifth brother in the *Arabian Nights*, but let it be observed that the spread of the merino sheep throughout Australia and the consequent increase of wool have gone on outstripping calculation."[117] The comparison of the alpaca with the merino led some sheep advocates to reject the alpacas for fear that they would be competitors. These fears were answered by Wilson (1862, 14), who urged "merino worshippers" to view the alpaca as an addition and "not a supersession" and be assured that "the most enthusiastic sheep-owner may have his alpaca stations, too, with perfect mental quietude."

The linkage of science, ethnicity, and empire came into sharp relief when Wilson echoed many of Ledger's claims about Andean Indigenous peoples and encouraged Australian colonists to transform the alpaca into a profitable commodity. "Once more, we have now got the alpaca; but it will perhaps be found that we have still to create the alpaca. It has been locked up for centuries in the hands of the South American Indian, one of the most superstitious, ignorant, and unimproving of mankind. It rests with us to try what we can make of it, and it seems probable that the care which has made the short-horn ox what we see will scarcely be contented to leave the alpaca as it is" (Wilson 1862, 14). Wilson dismissed the contributions of Indigenous expertise to the success of the acclimatization venture, championing instead a British spirit of liberalism well prepared to improve the state of agriculture in the nation and its colonies.

Given the success of alpaca acclimatization and other similar projects, like the importation of camels, Wilson urged Great Britain to pick up the pace of introducing additional useful animals into its empire. After all, he argued, Great Britain was

> a nation of travelers to see; a nation of merchants to convey; a nation of agriculturists to depasture and improve; a nation of manufacturers to test and to elaborate—what more is wanted to constitute England's special fitness for this particular branch of national progress? . . . It surely is not creditable to find her lag where she ought to lead. And, in relation to her swarm of 50 colonies, especially, it is scarcely edifying to find her standing impassive and unimpressionable, like a stone hen amid a brood of very sprightly, eager, and quick-witted little chicks. (Wilson 1862, 14)

Ledger's alpaca exhibit at the 1862 exhibition accordingly symbolized the hopes that many held for Britain and its colonies and how successful efforts at acclimatization, such as the alpaca venture, enabled all to see how this empire was poised to lead the world in progress and prosperity.

Charles Ledger, a Ruined Victim of Empire

Ledger's success with his contributions to the International Exhibition marked a high point in his Australia venture. He hoped it would continue on the same upward trajectory through his collaboration with the Acclimatisation Society of Victoria. Unfortunately, it was not to be so. As Ledger continued to postpone his departure for South America due to his ongoing negotiations to buy back the alpacas from the NSW government, the society became increasingly impatient over their stalled agreement. Moreover, the dispute between Ledger and the society regarding who would pay the insurance premiums remained unresolved. The relationship became strained even further due to a shipment of two pairs of cashmere goats that Ledger had proposed to send to the society in March 1861 at a price of £20 plus shipping costs.[118] The goats did not arrive until almost a year later. To make matters worse, Ledger admitted only at this late date that he could not guarantee that they were indeed cashmere goats. An outside consultant informed the Acclimatisation Society that the animals were a "common Indian Goat bearing a coarse wool and in comparison with the Cashmere [they] are almost worthless." Following the receipt of this assessment, the society requested that Ledger explain the discrepancy between the animals he had promised and those he had sent.[119] Ledger apologized for the inferior goats, explaining that they had been sold to him as cashmere goats but that he had begun to suspect the truth a few days before dispatching them. His observation that it was the business of acclimatization societies to correct these kinds of errors so that the public could better discern differences between breeds did not endear him to them.[120]

Increasingly concerned about Ledger's reliability, given the botched goat agreement, the lack of an acceptable response regarding the insurance premiums, and the continued postponement of his trip to South America, the Acclimatisation Society requested that he provide a detailed accounting of how he had spent the £600 advance. During the back and forth with Ledger, an unexpected voice emerged, bearing what appeared to be good news for Victoria's effort to obtain alpacas. Businessman Alexander James Duffield approached the society with a proposal to bring a large shipment of alpacas to the colony from Bolivia, having received a concession from the Andean government to do so legally. This was the same concession that Ledger had announced on the day of the exhibition alpaca banquet. Duffield proposed to obtain 1,500 pure alpacas for the colony at a cost of £100 per animal, to be paid either in cash or in cash combined with land and delivered in three separate shipments of 500 animals. The society had already budgeted money for Ledger and therefore could not provide any financial backing at the start of the new venture but otherwise enthusiastically agreed to lend support to Duffield in any way possible.[121]

With Duffield's undertaking potentially on the horizon, Ledger no longer held a monopoly as alpaca supplier. Moreover, the concession meant that the animals could be taken directly to the nearest port with no need for surreptitiousness or long, out-of-the-way driving, in contrast to Ledger's initiative, which would still be illegal.[122] The acting president of the Acclimatisation Society of Victoria reported in April 1862 that he had received confidential information regarding Ledger that "might make it desirable that some extra measures of precaution should be adopted before paying over to him the rest of the money."[123] It is not known what information was given to the society, but presumably it came from the NSW government. The society requested that the chief secretary for Victoria work in cooperation with his NSW counterpart to make further inquiries and that a communication be sent to Ledger ordering him not to proceed with the alpaca project until further notice.[124]

Just as the Australian newspapers were an important vehicle for the dissemination of discoveries and advancements in acclimatization projects, they also participated in public debates on the actions of individuals and institutions and their consequences. In the midst of Ledger's conflicts with the Acclimatisation Society of Victoria and the NSW government, the press began to weigh in on his management of the alpacas. Some articles were signed letters to the editor, others were anonymous, and still others included excerpts from the debates by the NSW Legislative Assembly on Ledger and the ensuing public commentary. Many voiced support for Ledger, rehashing now-familiar discussions concerning his poor treatment and inadequate compensation, while the same number argued that the government should never have become involved in the management of livestock. One common concern involved the costs the government had incurred from the alpaca project. The line of reasoning went that the alpacas were draining the treasury and should be turned over to private ownership. As one observer noted, "While still cordially approving of the purchase of these animals on their arrival in this colony, we cannot fail to recognize in the present embarrassment with regard to their management, a strong similarity to the case of the unfortunate man who suddenly became the owner of an elephant." From his perspective, the animals were

248 | Llamas beyond the Andes

now fully acclimatized to their new environment, the plan of crossbreeding had succeeded, and the improved wool was doing well in the London markets, so it was time to sell the "elephant." Given how much it cost to maintain the flock, he made the case that it would be more profitable to simply give the animals away, if no buyers came forward.[125]

One letter to the editor of the *Empire*, penned by "Citizen," railed against Ledger and the ostensibly deceitful way he foisted the alpacas onto the government. For the author, Ledger was clearly neither a Livingstone nor a Macarthur:

> The artifices by which the animals and their importer were puffed into notice, were rather new in this part of the world, though old elsewhere, and pretty well known to those who have read the most instructive book, the Autobiography of Mr. Phineas Barnum. . . . We were told [by the press] the most wonderful stories about Mr. Ledger. The dangers he had encountered, the deeds he had performed, the sufferings he had endured, and the sacrifices he had made, during his long and laborious efforts to obtain a flock of alpacas, were recorded and reiterated till sensible men became incredulous and suspicious.[126]

In Citizen's opinion, Ledger was nothing short of a humbug and, like Barnum, had hoodwinked the public with his grandiose assertions. The letter mocked Ledger's so-called selfless motives and condemned the deceit he had resorted to in smuggling the alpacas out of South America:

> After violating the laws of a country in which he had been a denizen, if not a citizen, his affectation of higher motives than profit must be peculiarly touching. Was there ever so good a man? After smuggling 300 sheep out of Peru, he is willing to bestow them upon New South Wales, but hopes we will consider his "high motives" before we offer him a price. At what price Mr. Ledger estimated his high motives does not appear; and it is not unlikely that he will yet be so considerate as to tender a bill for the amount. What a great heart the man must have and so kind to the poor people of this colony![127]

The article denounced the NSW government for purchasing these unlawfully obtained animals, arguing that only a despotic government would make such an arrangement. For all of his so-called expertise and knowledgeable shepherds—"as extraordinary nearly as himself"—the affair was a con job from start to finish. Duped or not, the government had lost a great deal of money, the flock was not increasing at a reasonable pace, and the wool showed no signs of turning a profit. Most agreed that it was time for an honest accounting of how much money had been spent on the animals and what they were really worth.

Ledger responded publicly to these denunciations, justifying his management of the animals by arguing that alpacas were relatively unknown, in contrast to well-established information about sheep and their care. He laid special blame on Andeans, decrying their general selfishness and hatred of the "white face." Because of their animosity toward outsiders, he had needed to learn about the animals' care on his own, thereby erasing from his narrative of self-defense the significant role of the shepherds who had accompanied him throughout his alpaca venture and whom he had credited on many other occasions with specialized knowledge and expertise.[128] In a later letter to the press, he made the unanticipated claim that all credit regarding the successes achieved with the alpacas was due to him alone. "With the exception of one lad (who was given to me in Bolivia by his parents in 1854, when about eight years of age) named Ylaco, not one of the men who accompanied me so many years, and came to this colony with me,—I say, that not one of them, the present efficient overseer included, ever saw an alpaca even, before entering my service. It is no vain assumption of great knowledge to ask, who taught them what they do know respecting this animal?"[129] In a complete reversal, Ledger now asserted that his alpaca expertise did not result even partially from interactions with the Andean shepherds but instead had been acquired solely on his own and that he taught those accompanying him.

Despite numerous deaths among the animals, Ledger pointed to evidence of positive trends. He had received word from Titus Salt in London praising the quality of the second clip of the alpacas, which was classed the same as Peruvian alpaca wool. This news substantiated his assertion that the alpacas were becoming more improved with each generation. What the project needed next were a few more male alpacas, which he had planned to obtain while procuring the animals for Victoria: "This Government [NSW], by interfering in a matter with which they had no possible right to interfere, foiled me in my endeavours; and although I am a serious loser, yet the loss to the colony is much greater, and will be evident as the return of each clip comes to hand."[130]

250 | *Llamas beyond the Andes*

Ledger notified the Acclimatisation Society of Victoria in March 1863 that he was leaving definitively for South America and that they should send a representative with him to collect the alpacas and vicuñas that his agents had gathered per their agreement. The council for the society instructed Mueller to reply, stating that there would be no further communication between them until they received a letter of explanation from Ledger regarding his use of the £600 advance.[131] Several months earlier, the society had received word from the colonial secretary of New South Wales that Ledger had been definitively suspended from the office of superintendent of alpacas until his name was cleared with the society. The NSW government also advised Victoria that it should not count on the £600 being returned.[132] Ledger was removed from the position of superintendent for alpacas for two main reasons. The first was his slow response in accounting for the £600. Perhaps even more importantly, Ledger's collaboration with Victoria was seen as a serious conflict of interest precisely because he was an NSW government employee.[133] In reaction to this charge, Ledger observed ironically that perhaps he had made a mistake resulting from ignorance, in his belief that serving one colony was the same as serving another because all formed part of the British Empire.[134]

When the NSW government announced in early 1864 that it planned to divide the animals into small lots and put them up for auction, Ledger tried to appeal the decision, arguing that a move "fraught with so much evil as that contemplated" would put an end to the improvements already accomplished and lead Australia to throw away a significant commercial opportunity.[135] In contrast to Ledger's optimism over how the flock had improved, the Legislative Assembly countered that the entire venture constituted a failed experiment, especially from an economic standpoint.[136] Its statements on the matter reiterated the idea that Ledger had indeed bamboozled the government from the start: "that gentleman was supposed to be the only person in the colony who knew anything about [the alpacas'] management; but it was now strongly suspected that that idea had been a delusion, and that any person of ordinary intelligence, accustomed to the breeding of sheep, could have managed them quite as well."[137] Despite these criticisms, Ledger still had supporters who publicly denounced the NSW government's stance, to argue instead: "We firmly believe that no other deliberative assembly in the world but that which meets at Sydney, would have discussed a question of such importance to the future of the colony in so sordid and pettifogging a spirit."[138] Notwithstanding the protest, the government determined not to delay the planned auction any further.

The auction of the alpacas took place on June 21, 1864, at Wingello Park, where the flock was at pasture. In preparation for the event, the 307 animals were divided into 51 lots of varying classes. A luncheon held in the barn before the auction was attended by the governor and members of the Legislative Assembly along with business leaders and agriculturalists. The auctioneer tried to create interest in the sale by recounting Ledger's heroic story and reminding the public of other attempts to obtain alpacas for NSW and Victoria and how each had ended in failure. The event's officials also pointed out to the potential bidders improvements that had taken place in the animals due to the successful acclimatization and crossbreeding programs. Despite the fact that the animals came with a compelling story, bids came in so low that the auctioneer closed the sale, announcing that private inquiries could be directed to the government but a bid for less than £30 for a pure alpaca would not be considered.[139]

Two years later, in June 1866, the government determined once and for all to rid itself of the alpacas by auction. This time the auctioneer did not put a minimum price on the animals. By the end of the day, every last one had been purchased. Thomas Holt bought a few of the alpacas at the auction for his Arthursleigh estate, where the original flock had pastured. His correspondence indicates that after the auction it became a fairly common practice for those who purchased the alpacas to exchange or lend male and female alpacas to fellow enthusiasts because the animals were difficult to acquire otherwise. In several cases, the animals were placed at lunatic asylums for the pleasure of the patients. As Holt explained to his friend Henry Parkes, "With respect to the Alpacas, Dr. Manning asked me for one to amuse the patients in the Asylum, & I promised he should have the first I could spare. (I have already given one to each of the Lunatic Asylums at Parramatta, and the Cooks' River.)"[140] Ledger's worst fears had come true. It would be difficult or impossible for the alpacas, scattered throughout the colony in small flocks or kept as pets and amusements, to survive in the long run, even if colleagues exchanged animals from time to time. The alpaca endeavor had come to an end. As one commentator publicly observed, the history of Ledger and the alpaca acclimatization project in Australia could be summarized in two succinct words: "expense—disaster."[141]

252 | *Llamas beyond the Andes*

Concluding Thoughts

The case history of Charles Ledger, the Bolivian shepherds, and the flocks of llamas and alpacas remains intriguing today because of its complex narrative frame and layered historical, cultural, and political contexts. When considering his Andean-Australian narrative as a whole, Ledger's alpaca enterprise stands out in the nineteenth-century acclimatization movement because it elucidates the large investments in money, time, and labor required to obtain highly sought-after animals like the camelids and documents the high casualty rates for fragile creatures when extracted from their natural habitat and moved into global markets. Ledger's project provides a glimpse into how Andean Indigenous communities opposed or collaborated with extraction projects. It also highlights problems of cost and competition that arose when a new species was introduced and accounts for why many acclimatization projects failed, especially when economic expenses outweighed potential scientific benefits.

Other stories emerge when Ledger's project is examined in its discrete Andean and Australian sections and in their juxtaposition, because this approach emphasizes further the venture's details and shows how it brought into conflict contradictory narrative scripts that could not be resolved. In one version of his Andean story, Ledger plied tales of danger, adventure, and science into a grand heroic narrative about empire, patriotism, loyalty, and sacrifice. As a story about the circulation and construction of knowledge in intercultural contact zones, however, the venture butts heads against the paradigm of singularity and heroism that Ledger repeatedly rehearsed in his accounts, because it identifies other involved communities that formed around his enterprise and reveals their centrality in its successful completion. Most notable, of course, are the Andean shepherds and their active role alongside Ledger, when they worked together to implement traditional and new camelid technologies. The visual and textual archive of their participation in the Andean leg of the journey depicts the shepherds in a diversity of roles and situations. From working while under duress to enjoying moments of playfulness, the shepherds demonstrate a three-dimensionality scarcely seen in nineteenth-century Western accounts of Andean Indigenous peoples.

Like many heroic narratives, Ledger's Andean story included a plotline recounting a formative phase whereby he learned a number of skills that would later be of use when he found himself in difficulty with authorities and hostile Indigenous communities. This lengthy period of apprenticeship on the ground is one aspect that distinguishes Ledger from other European travelers of the time, including Eugène Roehn. As already seen, Ledger became fluent in Spanish and learned enough Quechua and/or Aymara to be able to interact with the shepherds. From his own account, we know that he learned rudiments of local herbal knowledge and had experience handling popular Western drugs such as laudanum, all of which proved useful at different times. Ledger's daily interactions provide evidence of his savoir faire when it came to navigating the economic, cultural, and ethnic strictures of Andean social relations. By cultivating Andean traditions of civility, respect, and reciprocity through institutions like compadrazgo, he gradually earned the trust of the Andean shepherds.[142] These and other relationships forged across the socioeconomic spectrum sustained Ledger's enterprise throughout his Andean travels.

In contrast, when Ledger and the shepherds reached Australia, he discovered that the practical knowledge gained over the years that had fostered his success was of little benefit when it came to negotiating with the New South Wales government. Furthermore, the government's refusal to honor what Ledger perceived to have been a gentlemen's agreement promising reward and recompense following years of suffering and tribulation transformed his stories of heroic action into bitter complaint. Even as his agency and autonomy of action were increasingly restricted in this new environment, Ledger had to contend with governmental concerns about the growing cost of keeping the flock together, complaints registered against his character, and questions concerning the need for the Andean shepherds. The herders became foils in Ledger's new narrative of self-defense, constructed in the face of these accusations, when he alternately praised or dismissed them, according to how their portrayal best affected his own public positioning.

The shepherds' story is unique, however, in the history of camelid acclimatization, and their presence and importance justify critical attention. Once the shepherds returned home, their story faded from the Australian press of the time. Ledger, however, stayed in communication with some of them, as we discover from letters written years later between Ledger and British chemist John Eliot Howard and from secondary sources. While the primary subject of the future exchanges with Howard was quinine, Ledger nevertheless inserted occasional reflections on the alpaca expedition, including information on the shepherds, suggesting that their fate continued to weigh on his mind. As the men prepared to return home from New South Wales, Ledger ensured that each left Australia with seeds, tools,

254 | Llamas beyond the Andes

clothes, and money—most of which he paid out of his own salary.[143] He expressed concern that when so equipped they might be treated adversely by local South American authorities upon arrival: "In fact, of those that went home last year, some had been impressed as soldiers on arriving, and the others had to purchase their freedom by bribing the authorities not to molest them" (Ledger 1861, 548).

Pedro Cabrera, Manuel's son Santiago, Ledger's servant Pablo Sosa, and one other man (not named) were the last to depart from Australia. Once back in South America, they remained in contact with Ledger, who paid them to go clandestinely into Bolivia to obtain alpacas for his commitment to the Victoria Acclimatization Society.[144] Sosa died due to complications resulting from gangrene that set into one of his legs and one foot, which had been badly damaged by frostbite.[145] Santiago and his father would continue their collaborations with Ledger over subsequent years by helping him to smuggle quinine seeds out of Bolivia. In 1865, after Ledger also had returned to Peru, he sent for Cabrera to join him in Tacna. Unfortunately, the two men just missed each other: Ledger departed for Puno the morning of the same day that Cabrera reached Tacna in the evening. Cabrera rested in Tacna a few days and then set out to find Ledger. On March 4, 1866, Ledger received the devastating news that Cabrera had drowned while crossing a river en route to Puno. He refused to believe that his experienced guide and overseer could have met his death this way and set out to make inquiries, only to discover that Cabrera had been murdered "by two Indians. They confessed having committed the horrid deed so as to rob him. I arrested the villains, taking them more than 50 miles ere I could deliver them up to the authorities. I felt very much inclined to take the law into my own hands, shooting the wretches there & then. One of the murderers died in the gaol of Puno about 4 mths. after, the other one escaped from prison on breaking out of a revolution in 1867."[146] Cabrera's death was a terrible blow to Ledger and undoubtedly personified for him the essential failure of the alpaca venture.

Thus, within a few short years of their introduction into New South Wales, the alpacas were no longer viewed as "the most interesting animals in the world," as Wilson had claimed early on. To the contrary, one government document identified the alpacas as the "first major introduced pest" along with "rabbits, ticks, and wild dogs,"[147] presumably because of the economic toll of their cost and maintenance rather than because they created environmental devastation. Ledger's venture was no longer a narrative of heroism, doggedness, and adherence to patriotic duty. He had been cast aside and objectified as a con man by the very institutions that he had believed would reward him handsomely. Still defending his actions many years later in a letter to the editor of the *Sydney Morning Herald*, Ledger explained that he wanted the greater public to know the details of his story and the unkept promises made to him by British authorities so "that the truth may be known, and that my case may serve as a caution to other enthusiastic Englishmen."[148]

Ledger's return to South America in 1864 marked the end of large-scale acclimatization projects involving the camelids. The same period evidenced the beginning of disenchantment with acclimatization projects in general, primarily due to their expense. Moreover, scientists were discovering that while many imported plants and animals fared poorly, others spread quickly, wreaking havoc on the environment and native flora and fauna. With few exceptions, it would not be until the first decades of the twentieth century that the Andean camelids regained international celebrity status. Improved technology in the latter half of the twentieth century made safe transportation of camelids more feasible. Australia, like the United States and elsewhere, has since become an important center for the alpaca industry outside of the Andes. And this success has imbued Ledger's biography with a new dynamism. The cultural memory of his labor on behalf of the introduction of the alpaca into Australia lives on today. Ledger himself has regained heroic status on the social media pages of the many hundreds of members of the Australian Alpaca Association. Perhaps he would appreciate the irony that one of the association's most important events since 1989 is the annual Charles Ledger Alpaca Show.

CHAPTER 7

US Camelid Contact Zones in the Twentieth Century

Authenticity, Exoticism, and Celebrity

Miss Llinda Llee Llama shines as an ambassador of hospitality, culture, and charity. In 1959, the real Llinda Llee was a guest of The Statler [Dallas] and a feature of the Neiman Marcus Fortnight which showcased textiles and designs from South America. She also visited sick children at Parkland Hospital during her stay. Surrounded by sweeping views of our great city, reflect upon your inner llama and how you can be a part of something greater.

Sculpture plaque: "Miss Llinda Llee Llama" (at the Statler Hotel, created in 2017 by Brad Oldham and Christy Coltrin)

While interest in the camelids in the United States during the nineteenth century was primarily limited to their role as exotica in zoos and traveling menageries, the animals became increasingly visible in the fashion world in the early twentieth century as symbols of a luxuriant modernity, on the one hand, and of a primitive, timeless land, on the other. This contradictory role was especially salient in the marketing strategies developed by S. Stroock & Co., a textile mill in Newburgh, New York. The company was unique because of its specialization in the use of these little-known camelid fibers for the manufacture of fine wool fabrics throughout the first half of the century. Stroock advertised its products by drawing from visual and textual formats already familiar to the public, including circus performance; forms of museum display, such as natural history habitats and dioramas; and even children's literature, most notably the Doctor Dolittle books. Stroock's primary objective, of course, was to sell its products. The company's publications and advertising therefore were designed to accomplish several goals: they sought to educate the retail industry and consumers about these relatively unknown animals and the fine quality of their fiber and demonstrate the excellence of the

258 | Llamas beyond the Andes

finished manufactured product as well as its authenticity and uniqueness. Natural history, the circus world, museum display, and other forms of popular culture provided a signifying system that the company utilized to market its products and accomplish these objectives.

"Edutaining" forms of advertising emphasized the push and pull between the primitive otherness of the animals' original homeland and the fashionable modernity of the lands where their products were manufactured and sold.[1] These discourses and practices, however, as shown throughout this book, were always already embedded in transoceanic networks of extractive colonialism because they referred explicitly to the collection and exhibition of rare animal trophies and the capitalization of exotica. Thus, for example, in the style of the natural-history diorama, Stroock's original storefront included large glass windows showcasing taxidermy animals like those from which the exclusive fiber had been taken. As one article on the company explained, "Camels, llamas and other exotic animals intrigued passersby who inquired where they might find coats made of these fine furs" (Wells 1996, no pagination).

Samuel Stroock founded S. Stroock & Co. in New York City in 1866, when he began to manufacture robes for use in the carriage trade. With the advent of the car, the company produced auto robes to keep people warm while motoring about the countryside.[2] Following World War I, the company turned to luxury fabrics, creating a name for itself in the world of high-end fashion by developing cloth made from 100 percent camel hair.[3] One newspaper article noted that "it was then that the Stroock label began to appear in clothing—a label that signified the real thing and lifted the ego of the wearer."[4] During the 1920s, the company expanded its use of luxury woolens to include camelid blends and eventually produced fabrics made from 100 percent cashmere, alpaca, and vicuña.[5] S. Stroock & Co. had earned a reputation by the 1930s and 1940s as one of the foremost companies of luxury fabrics in the world. Their vicuña coats and jackets symbolized the essence of quality.[6]

S. Stroock & Co. published a series of booklets designed to familiarize wholesalers and consumers with the company's luxurious fabrics and the unusual animals that produced the quality fiber. Modeled on the format of natural-history books, *Llamas and Llamaland* (Stroock 1937a) and *The Story of Vicuna* (Stroock 1937b) included photographs of all four species of the Andean camelids in their native habitat, described their role in the culture and religion of the Incas, detailed the impact of the arrival of the Spanish, and recounted traditional methods of hunting and conservation.

The main purpose of the publications, however, was to capitalize on these colorful lands, peoples, and animals and capture the interest of the moneyed public in the company's quality products. The booklets undoubtedly played another role too. With the development of early Pan-Americanism during the first decades of the twentieth century and the concomitant growth of US international commercial interests, these booklets clearly also helped to educate the business community desirous of opening new markets south of the border and to foment the budding tourism industry. They thus played a role as part of a larger political and economic mission whose goal was the "re-discovery" of South America (Salvatore 2002, 50).[7]

In the autobiographical account of his life as a fashion designer, Christian Dior called attention to the singular role that fabric plays for the designer: "Fabric not only expresses a designer's dreams but also stimulates his ideas. It can be the beginning of an inspiration. Many a dress of mine is born of the fabric alone" (Dior 1954, 34). In the sample booklet *Fine Men's Wear Fabrics* (S. Stroock & Co. 1939, 10) Sylvan Stroock similarly observed that "a good fabric is the 'soul' of the garment. The 'creation' is fashioned not alone by the tailor's hand—but by the quality, softness, sheen, and drapiness of the cloth, as well. These virtues are inherent in the animal fibre. They cannot be 'manufactured.'" The company's fabric sample books displayed beautiful swatches to inspire those dreams and ideas of designers such as Dior. By keeping text to a minimum, the booklets could draw readers' eyes to the colors and patterns with little distraction. The customers were invited to linger over the samples, to inspect their texture and luster, and to feel their softness: "examine these fabrics—and touch them. The eye and hand will tell you why the Stroock 'touch' is a tradition" (S. Stroock & Co. 1948, i).[8] Extolling the intrinsic qualities of the fiber and hence the natural virtues of the fabric, the sample booklets foregrounded the company's unique ability to create the finest product from precious natural resources (figure 7.1). Customers could be assured of the product's quality and authenticity by the Stroock label carefully placed inside the garment, each of which had its own registered number, "like a United States government bond."[9]

The label for the Stroock vicuña cloth coat not only guaranteed the genuineness of the fabric; by including an image of the animal and its native habitat, it also created a narrative of the coat's seemingly unambiguous trajectory from the Andes to the United States, from nature to culture.[10] The picture on the label depicts the slender vicuña in its natural landscape, the serial number attesting to the authenticity of the animal

FIGURE 7.1. *Stroock vicuña cloth coat with numbered label. Used with permission, Hemlock Vintage Clothing (https://hemlockvintage.com).*

(and fabric) as well as its "capture," and ultimately its transformation into a coat. Elsie Murphy, the company's first woman president, described the Stroock label as "the prize of those who place quality above price, who desire the ultimate in luxury, who know and value the vast difference between wool and super-wool, between woolens and *Stroock woolens*" (Murphy 1952, no pagination; emphasis in the original). The label thus became a kind of sartorial trophy for discerning customers on the hunt for quality, exclusivity, and status. At the same time, however, the label concealed that the picturesque place depicted was presumably the site of the vicuña's death. As discussed throughout this book, live captures to harvest the fiber continued to be rare well into the twentieth century.

S. Stroock & Co. enhanced its advertising by constructing a larger narrative around the manufactured products to further entice customers. Like the label, for example, the 1948 fabric book artfully combined a subtle blend of images evoking the lands and peoples where the animals originated and the modern first-world technologies that produced the lovely swatches. In a style reminiscent of circus showman P. T. Barnum, who popularized natural history in the nineteenth century and exploited its commercial possibilities through a variety of enterprises, all of Stroock's publications draw us to the exotic origins of the fabrics by highlighting "elaborate tales of search and seizure" (Adams 1997, 86; see also Betts 1959). Barnum bucked the conventions of nineteenth-century natural-history displays, which were generally void of the presence of animal captors, to foreground stories of the hunt and killing of the animals (Adams 1997, 86).

US Camelid Contact Zones in the Twentieth Century | 261

In its publications, the company directed readers' attention to the efforts made to locate the singular creatures whose fiber served as the raw material for the company's products: "Now, as then, we continue to search the far ends of the earth for rare fibers from animals which are survivors of another age, shunted into remote areas by time and its changes" (S. Stroock & Co. 1948, i). Highlighting the long distances through space and time that the natural fiber had to travel to reach its customers, it depicted the animals as though they were trapped in a barren land of unappreciative Indians, eagerly anticipating their liberation by Stroock, the intrepid explorer-entrepreneur. In a manner reminiscent of some of Charles Ledger's imperialist descriptions of Andean Indigenous peoples, Sylvan Stroock portrayed Indigenous shepherds as knowing "nothing at all of the outside world, caring less. Doomed to spend their lives at altitudes higher than any other inhabited areas of the earth, in the bleak inhospitable territory that typifies the upper Andes, they know nothing of the creature comforts of life, and enjoy few even of its necessities" (Stroock 1937a, 32).

The reference to Barnum is even more explicit in *Stroock's Animal Kingdom* (Raftery 1939), a booklet of poems designed to introduce customers to the unfamiliar fiber-producing animals used in the manufacture of the mill's high-end cloth. On the first page, through images and verse, Sylvan Stroock is presented as someone able to command the animals like a circus ringmaster, while a sketch of a camelid at the bottom of the page depicts the trained animal standing quietly on a small platform, poised to obey. The accompanying poem underscores that Stroock is as exceptional as his product. Readers understand that, like Charles Ledger and Eugène Roehn, he heroically braves the fiercest of enemies in his hunt for success.

The booklet includes descriptive verses for all of the animals whose fiber is used by the company, foregrounding the unique qualities of each. For instance, a poem describes the Suri alpaca as so rare that not even Barnum was able to track it down. Where Barnum failed, Sylvan Stroock prevailed. From its fiber he created a soft, rich, and exclusive fabric. Men, beware! The woman wearing it will "captivate you with one look" (Raftery 1939, no pagination). The comparison to Barnum highlighted the uniqueness of the Stroock name in the fashion world. Just as the exotic animals Barnum collected symbolized the showman's exceptional abilities and influence, S. Stroock & Co.'s "capture" of the valuable camelids conferred prestige on the company as a leading producer of luxury fabrics.

Stroock's 1948 fabric sample book included a series of whimsical drawings running across the top of each page by the French artist and illustrator Charles Cobelle (1902–1994). His simple line drawings, repeated

262 | *Llamas beyond the Andes*

throughout the catalogue, bring an additional visual narrative to the fabric swatches. For example, one sketch depicts two vicuñas witnessing the imminent encounter between Spanish conquistadors and Peruvian Indians. From their lofty vantage point, one vicuña looks out toward the ship while the other turns back toward a scantily clad Indian man and woman. The couple's primitive state is apparent from the woman's bare breasts and the man's spear and feather headdress. The animals' stance, with one looking forward toward the ship and the other back toward the Indians, suggests that they are being asked to choose between one of two possible futures: they can remain in their native land, where fine fabrics go unacknowledged, or depart for more enlightened destinations. In other words, the arrival of the Spanish is represented as a liberation rather than a conquest: the animals' future will result from choice not imposition. The image captures the moment of decision.

Cobelle's sketches throughout the swatch book show that the vicuñas opt to move from nature to culture, lured from home, not by Stroock the hunter but by Stroock the manufacturer of quality fabrics. For example, the male vicuña in one drawing smokes his pipe while perusing a Stroock publication. In another, the camelids don their best Western-style wear and load up suitcases, ready for travel and tourism. Eventually, the vicuñas land in Paris, the center of the fashion world, where they meet up with their distant cousin, the two-humped Bactrian camel. A carriage ride takes them to see the sites, after which they pause for a cocktail at the chic Café de la Paix, located in a swank neighborhood close to Paris's Garnier Opera. In contrast to the Indigenous couple of their native land, the camelids appreciate their new finery and show it off to advantage in the streets of Paris.

Unlike other histories examined in this book, Cobelle's animals are not depicted as having been hunted, captured, killed, or forcibly transported to distant lands. Instead, they seem already acclimatized to their new circumstances, inspired by S. Stroock & Co. to seek a fresh start that promises adventure and profit. These same themes are echoed in *Stroock's Animal Kingdom*, when the vicuña reads about himself in the pages of a fashion magazine and discovers the market value of his fleece. As described in the accompanying poem, he becomes

> wilder and gayer and wisely aware
> That the down off his back is fine fashion fare.
> And legend has had it that years back, egad!
> He happened across a Fifth Avenue ad . . .

Saw the price of a coat that was made from his combings,
Left his habitat flat for loftier roamings . . .
From parts of Peru to Central Bolivia
He feeds on herbs rare and similar trivia.
In fact he's so scarce that by hook or by crook
There are few men can snare him as neatly as Stroock.
Yet Stroock's limited too, by some government stuff
That calls for a permit for each ounce of fluff.
With no ifs, ands, or buts, it's the world's finest fabric
And it costs ninety bucks for a yard—that's the traffic
So beautiful, really, you cannot begrudge it . . .
Though it does cost a mint and will smash up your budget.
Vicuna's the name and no fabric is finer . . .
What joy to exclaim "It's exclusively mine-a."
(Raftery 1939, no pagination)

The poem's narrative moves in a circular direction, beginning and ending with the power of the economy of fashion to charm and captivate. Lured from his remote native land by the discovery of what vicuña "combings" are worth, the animal is easily snared by Stroock. The poem suggests that modern US technologies and the desire for profits were all that was needed to successfully domesticate and acclimatize the camelids to a new home, an accomplishment that none of the adventurers followed throughout this book managed to achieve.

This promotional narrative of acquisition and acclimatization evokes another story: Hugh Lofting's popular children's book *The Story of Doctor Dolittle* (1948). Doctor Dolittle was an animal collector, zookeeper, avid naturalist, and reader of Buffon. He was likely fashioned after nineteenth-century British explorers who traveled about the world in search of exotic natural history specimens (Collett 1997, 83). Lofting's protagonist stands out, however, because he is a skilled polyglot, able to talk to and understand animals. Given this unusual ability, Dolittle did not have to hunt and kill the rare beasts he collected because they willingly agreed to accompany him after conversing together. One of the most famous and unusual members of his menagerie was the pushmi-pullyu, a rare two-headed creature that Dolittle and his monkey companions captured in Africa. The pushmi-pullyu did not want to leave his home at first but was eventually convinced through conversation with the monkeys to accompany the group to England so that the kind but penniless doctor could

264 | *Llamas beyond the Andes*

display the animal, charge admission, and settle his many debts with the profits. Once the pushmi-pullyu understood what a good man the doctor was, he immediately agreed to go with him to England.

Like Cobelle's vicuñas, Dolittle's wild and elusive pushmi-pullyu is transformed through talk into a docile money-making showpiece and fed from the fantasy of acclimatization, utility, and profit.[11] But even in this romanticized story docility does not pay off for the shy creature in the long run. Once the receipts from the exhibition of the pushmi-pullyu have resolved the doctor's outstanding debts and created a cache of funds for future travels, the exotic beast recedes from the story and eventually goes extinct. As the narrator explains in a matter-of-fact way, "That means, there aren't any more" (Lofting 1948, 77).[12]

The rarity of animals like the pushmi-pullyu and vicuña is a major element of their economic value. In a book tracking the recent making of a $50,000 vicuña coat, journalist Meg Lukens Noonan explores the meaning of luxury in her interviews with experts in high-end fashion. The consensus seems to be that luxury is "something no one else has" (Douha Ahdab, quoted in Noonan 2013, 92). Rarity, however, can also signal the danger of extinction, as seen with the death of the pushmi-pullyu. S. Stroock & Co.'s ads did not clarify that vicuña coats are not made from combings, that live catches of the vicuña were uncommon in the 1930s and 1940s, and that the animal was on the verge of extinction. However, *The Story of the Vicuna* addresses the theme of animal conservation and defends the legitimacy of the company's economic enterprise in several ways. First, the publication opens with a letter from F. Pardo de Zela, then consul general of Peru in New York. The letter confers his stamp of approval on the publication and confirms that the information it contains is correct in every way. Second, Stroock incorporates into the text a transcription of the provisions of Peru's 1921 law regulating the sale of vicuña fiber and the measures adopted by the Peruvian government to protect the animal. "The available supply of vicuna fleece at present is very small indeed, and is sold exclusively under license from the Peruvian Government" (Stroock 1937b, 16). S. Stroock & Co. presents itself as keeping to the letter of the law and transforms itself from Stroock the wild animal collector capturing the animal to Stroock the company capturing the market, aggressively going after "the largest possible portion of the annual yield" (16). As further evidence of the company's adherence to the law, each vicuña coat manufactured with Stroock fabric came with a copy of the Peruvian government's license.[13]

US Camelid Contact Zones in the Twentieth Century | 265

With the problem of conservation supposedly resolved, *The Story of Vicuna* turns rarity back into a positive quality, explaining how a vicuña coat bestows upon the wearer a uniquely elite status:

> If you are one of the fortunate few who owns a garment fashioned from the world's most exquisite fabric, vicuna, proud indeed should you be in its possession, for so rare is this costly fabric that only *one out of every 4,000,000 persons living* can enjoy this unique distinction. Emeralds, pearls, and fine jewels; sables, ermines and minks; yachts and horses—costly as they may be—are the prerogative of those with the means to purchase them, but not the garment of the vicuna, which in a given year can be acquired only by approximately five hundred men and women, so rare is the animal which furnishes the fleece used in the weaving of this, the finest of all the world's textiles. (Stroock 1937b, 7; emphasis in the original)

One Stroock coat of pure vicuña cloth required the fiber of forty animals (Stroock 1937b, 19; Potter and Corbman 1959, 191) and the cost of the fabric alone ran anywhere from $90 a yard to $200 a yard (Hess 1958, 219).

Given the expense and exclusivity of Stroock vicuña cloth, it is not surprising to find that ads for the vicuña coats appealed to customers by evoking images of royalty (figure 7.2). This 1944 ad, from the select women's department store Seidenbach's of Tulsa, Oklahoma, marketed the elite nature of vicuña fiber by reminding the public that in Pre-Columbian Peru only the Royal Incas had access to it. The prize of royalty was conferred on the contemporary wearer because the Stroock vicuña coat was a "Queen's Treasure." The image presents a modern, upwardly mobile, white female identity. Dressed for travel and adventure, wearing white gloves and carrying a leather purse, she needs no other companion than her beautiful and exotic Afghan hound with long, free-flowing fur.[14] A light breeze gently blows the woman's hair and coat, suggesting the promise of movement. She is smiling and expectant as she looks up and out toward a bright future. Elegant and fresh-faced, she comes across as confident, poised, and comfortable with her wealth. The caption at the bottom of the page echoes these same themes through its emphasis on the vicuña's proud independence and unwillingness to be subdued and shorn. "If you prize unique possessions . . . or wish to give a queen's gift . . . choose a Stroock vicuna coat. This one is $325."

This and other S. Stroock & Co. ads depict images of contemporary

266 | Llamas beyond the Andes

FIGURE 7.2. *Ad for a vicuña coat at Seidenbach's (1944).*

aristocratic elegance, while evoking the ancient splendor and royalty of the Inca Empire. Yet, like other examples seen throughout the book, Stroock calls attention to the achievements of the Incas but then subsequently relegates them to the realm of the obsolete, dismissing present-day Indigenous peoples and local knowledge and technologies. In this scenario, Stroock becomes the modern incarnation of the Inca, surpassing the quality and stature of the earlier dynasty. "Deep is the debt of gratitude the world owes to Llamaland . . . Land of the Incas . . . of glorious antiquity: For its ageless grandeur . . . for its charm and call to adventure . . . for the secrets of its artistry . . . and for the lovely fleeces of the llamas which through modern, scientific manufacturing skill, as exemplified by the Stroock mills, are expressed in all their magnificence, in the finished fabric. Here, indeed, is 'a lost art, retrieved'" (Stroock 1937a, 52). After the influence and skill of the Inca royalty have been acknowledged and rendered outmoded, a modern royalty emerges in the company's advertising: an elite Anglo-European consumer who follows the sartorial influence of the likes of the Prince of Wales.[15] No wonder Cobelle's vicuñas, like Doctor Dolittle's pushmi-pullyu, never return home to the Andes from their voyage abroad, opting instead to remain in their new environment.

The Incas, authenticity, and adventure also became key signifiers used by the well-known Hickey-Freeman Company in Rochester, New York, when the clothiers produced an exclusive line of menswear developed from Stroock llama fabric and marketed under the registered label "Llamando": "'Llamando' Worn by well dressed men in all quarters of the globe" (S. Stroock & Co. 1939, 5). An ad for "Llamando" (figure 7.3) depicts a lone male protagonist with Anglo-European features exploring the Andean landscape. The man treks alone, autonomous, with no Indian guides, needing only a light-footed llama caravan. Although his physical toughness and his ability to master the treacherous mountainside are reminiscent of similar efforts undertaken by Charles Ledger or Eugène Roehn, his feats now promote a men's clothing line rather than a contraband enterprise.

The background design features ruins suggestive of Machu Picchu, "the lost city of the Incas," and consequently could have evoked in the viewers' imagination the image of Hiram Bingham and the Yale Peruvian Archaeological Expedition (1911–1915), which had resulted in the revelation of the famous Inca site only a few years before the ad's release.[16] In the decades following the excavation of Machu Picchu, the ruins became an increasingly prominent tourist destination. Bingham's life could well have served as a source for fashion advertising, an industry continually in search of the colorful and unique. The reference to Bingham would have been especially apt for Hickey-Freeman's Llamando line, where the advertising linked the Andes and adventure, literally beckoning (*llamando*) the viewer and selling the idea that anyone who wore this clothing was guaranteed to become a hero with an exciting and distinctive life.[17]

FIGURE 7.3. Ad for Llamando from Hickey-Freeman Company ad book (fall/winter 1932–1933 season). Courtesy of the Hickey-Freeman Company.

Although a department store display window advertising the Llamando line (figure 7.4) does not evoke the same spirit of adventure of the previous ad, it does draw attention to the qualities of exoticism, authenticity, and status associated with Stroock and Hickey-Freeman products by displaying images and echoing visual themes common to natural-history dioramas or habitat scenes. Through the use of the taxidermy llama and other realia, such as bundles of fleece, wooden shuttles, photographs of modern looms, and pots of grasses, the storefront display constructs a tableau designed to look "natural," like "the real thing." The Llamando habitat creates a narrative and opportunity for encounters, calling to shoppers and welcoming them to step into the diorama and slip on a coat.[18]

The invitation is hardly open to all, however. Museums and department stores utilize similar methods of display and "claim to welcome a 'general' public, [even though] both actually have codes in place which signal to society what type of audience or customer ultimately they wish to attract" (Sonter 1997, 14). In the case of this display, the use of the gerund ("Llamando") implies action in progress, movement forward and up, not toward the Andean peaks this time but up the socioeconomic ladder.

US Camelid Contact Zones in the Twentieth Century | 269

Hugo Gemignani, vice-president of the Hickey-Freeman Company in the 1940s, emphasized how clothing plays a prominent role in displaying economic status and standing: "So I say to you, wear the garb of your rank and if you aspire to a higher rank, let it be known by the clothes you wear."[19] Quality clothing, in other words, is an essential element for consumers eager to assume a protagonist role in select natural habitats. Hochswender (1993, 9) observes that in the pages of magazines like *Esquire* "fashionable men were portrayed in their natural habitats, almost like nature drawings: in the board room, the fishing dock, the tennis court, the golf course— all the places where glamour and function could be intertwined." The Hickey-Freeman Company's Boardroom Collection struck a similar note as "clothing to suit the Fortune 500 in a man," whereas the Canterbury Collection was designed "for the man who is revered wherever he may reside, be it penthouse or estate."[20]

By combining the trope of the natural-history habitat with the taxidermy llama standing quietly in the center of the window, the storefront display emphasizes the authenticity of the coat and the transformations it promises to the consumer who can afford to answer the call. Haraway (1989, 38) points out that taxidermy is "the art most suited to the epistemological and aesthetic stance of realism. The power of this stance is in its magical effects: what is so painfully constructed appears effortlessly, spontaneously found, discovered, simply there if one will only look." The Llamando display similarly appears to re-create the realism of the seamless narrative from nature to culture, from consumer to elite member of the board. As Haraway (1989) and Patchett and Foster (2008) have argued, however, habitat and taxidermy creations are neither simply "there" nor compliant "finished objects." Instead, their hidden seams, dressed skin, and reinforced construction indicate that they are "active assemblages" or processes, continually accumulating new histories and meanings (Patchett and Foster 2008, 101–102; see also Alberti 2008, 83; and Gosden and Knowles 2001, 4–5).

One company pamphlet suggestively pointed out that understanding the complete story of Hickey-Freeman quality necessitates examining the work behind the visible surface, demonstrating how the finished garment is also an assemblage. "The Hickey-Freeman quality story is not only extremely visible, but the story unfolds behind the seams. The garment does not speak only by its reputation, but it tells another story . . . How it fits . . . How it feels to the customer and the means that the Hickey-Freeman

1937 – Llamando Store Front
Ben Simon & Son in Lincoln, Nebraska

FIGURE 7.4. *Display window for Llamando in 1937. Brayer (1999).*

Company uses to put hundreds of pieces together to accomplish this comfortable soft and easy fitting coat." According to the company's public relations rhetoric, these other elements "also do the speaking." If the finished coat is to fit properly, once all of the pieces and interlinings have been layered and assembled, the fronts must be shaped and molded according to the wearer's body, in much the same way as taxidermy specimens are prepared: "The coat fronts are shaped and custom molded on chest presses so the garments conform to the body. This is one reason a Hickey-Freeman coat feels like a second skin and not a cardboard box."[21] Ultimately, the Llamando showroom display suggests that, just as the taxidermy object is dressed for display, the man who dons the Hickey-Freeman coat is ready to assume his rightful habitat. If he will only answer the call and step into the tableau, he can seamlessly bring the display to life.

The Making of Two Llama Celebrities in the Twentieth Century

Austrian-born photojournalist Inge Morath's now iconic photograph "A Llama in Times Square" first appeared in *Life* magazine on December 2, 1957 (figure 7.5). With its surprising pose, tipped ears, and interested expression, Morath's llama caught viewers' imaginations, and the image has since been regularly reproduced. Reminiscent of Cobelle's vicuñas straining out of their carriage window to take in the sights of Paris, this llama appears to claim a similarly exotic and touristic perspective of downtown Manhattan. Who or what was this llama and why was it riding about in New York City?

Morath herself described the portrait as the result of happenstance. While out driving in Manhattan one day, she spotted the llama after stopping for a traffic light. Grabbing her camera, she jumped out of her car and captured this now-famous image. Untroubled by Morath's actions, the woman sitting next to the llama handed the photographer her business card, which read "Lorraine [*sic*] d'Essen. TV animals." Morath later went to meet the llama and its owner and recounted how the animal, named Llinda, was a sweet and lovely creature. Nonetheless, that first chance meeting with the llama left a definitive impression on her. "I'll never forget that classy look she gave me from under those long eyelashes: a diva on her way to a performance, about to show her stuff as only she can." Morath labeled the image "Encounter on Times Square. 1957."[22]

Morath's photograph is dated "57-1," meaning that it was part of her first series for the year. Her full caption for the photograph reads "Linda, the Lama [*sic*] rides home via Broadway. She is just coming home from a television show in New York's ABC Studios and now takes a relaxed and long-necked look at the lights of one of the world's most famous streets." Founding director of the Inge Morath Foundation, John P. Jacob observes how the shot comes across as "a perfect example of being in the right place at just the right moment." However, Morath's 1956–1957 contact sheet reveals earlier images from 1956 of the photographer standing next to the llama and the llama's owner. For Jacob, the contact sheet belies the impression of serendipity, showing instead that the image "was the result of considerable work and forethought. An appearance of spontaneity, masking the reality of careful planning, is one of the prime characteristics of Morath's work as photojournalist, and shows the degree of comfort that she was able to establish with her subjects while working on their stories."[23]

FIGURE 7.5. *"A Llama in Times Square" (1957). Photograph by Inge Morath, courtesy of Magnum Photos.*

Morath's husband, playwright Arthur Miller (1986, 6), also called attention to the seemingly spontaneous quality of her images: "There is the definite sense of composition in her pictures which appears nevertheless entirely impromptu and unarranged. She seems to have discovered rather than intervened in the formal presence. Many of these pictures could have been the basis of a painter's portrait, but at the same time their atmosphere is devoid of artificiality." Like Hickey-Freeman's department store display, Morath's popular photograph invites us to reflect on the image to discover the narratives hidden behind this seemingly fortuitous moment of encounter.

If, during the first decades of the twentieth century, companies like S. Stroock & Co. and Hickey Freeman utilized taxidermy llamas to create the impression of authenticity for advertising their products, in the 1950s many in the world of fashion photography turned to the use of live animal models. Commenting on the rise of this new practice, one top photographer argued that "animals are not artifice, but a piece of life. . . . I like the disorder, the unexpectedness, the warmth an animal can give."[24] Although the use of animal models often meant that it might take more time to achieve a good set of photographs, they clearly added an element of amusement and exoticism. When asked if animals sold clothes, "[distinguished photographer Irving] Penn, who has shot a menagerie over the years, said: 'I think so. People are always stopped by a photograph that includes an animal.' Then he added wryly: 'But I'll tell you this. I'd rather return to the stuffed variety. They don't bite back.'" The interest in animal models led to the creation of two llama celebrities, Llucky (Lucky) and Llinda (Linda Lee, Llinda Llee Llama). The photogenic Llinda reportedly made a splash in the fashion world when she modeled $1,000,000 in diamonds on her long neck.[25]

Llucky and Llinda belonged to Lorrain and Bernard D'Essen, the founders of Animal Talent Scouts Enterprises in 1952 in New York City. Lorrain D'Essen owned a number of animals that she taught to perform on command for spots in advertising, television, movies, and the stage. As she explained in her memoir on the business, many of the animals, including the llamas, lived in the family's five-story brownstone home on West 18th Street in Manhattan, while the larger ones were kept at a New Jersey farm belonging to Volney Phifer, the owner and trainer of Leo, the Metro-Goldwyn-Mayer lion. D'Essen (1959, 141) purchased Llucky, her first llama, from Roland Lindemann of the famed Catskill Game Farm for $900. She and Llucky could frequently be seen on walks around the neighborhood,

274 | Llamas beyond the Andes

where D'Essen took him for exercise and to accustom him to being around people: "I wanted to share his loveliness with everyone, and when I walked him there were few who could resist stopping to talk" (145).[26]

Llucky became a local personality, working on TV shows and in fashion photography shoots. Using his exotic origins as a reference, D'Essen envisioned the different roles he could play in the world of high-end fashion. "After he'd become established in that area he could tie in with products, promoting silverware (his native land of Peru has fabulous silver mines),[27] cut glass, or diamonds. He could be used to call attention to the luxurious roof garden of a hotel because he is a mountaintop animal. There were many advertising and promotional niches for such a handsome creature" (D'Essen 1959, 169). Llucky also made numerous appearances on *The Garry Moore Show*. According to Herb Sanford, the show's producer, Llucky frequently formed part of a skit or backdrop. "His finest hour occurred when his marriage to Llinda, Lorrain's new llama, was staged on the show. Llinda wore a garland of roses. Llucky was dressed in a high collar and black tie" (Sanford 1976, 137). D'Essen also observed that the llama marriage had been a big hit and brought fresh attention to the animals, especially on the part of educators. As a result, "*Scholastic Magazine*, which circulates to most of the nation's high schools, published a searching zoological story on llamas. Hundreds of letters were received by Animal Talent Scouts, seriously asking for information about the animal" (D'Essen 1959, 200).

D'Essen's second llama, Llinda (also from the Catskill Game Farm), became an instant hit as an exotic animal model after D'Essen convinced skeptical executives that the young creature was the perfect representative for their products. "When I first offered her services to advertising agencies they couldn't understand why I considered a llama luxurious. I'd say, 'But a baby llama is the gift for someone who has *everything*.' The agency executives thought of a llama as a dirty, scraggy-wooled beast of burden. But once they saw Llinda—bathed, combed, and delightfully perfumed—these people did an about-face. She is delectable" (D'Essen 1959, 232; emphasis in the original). D'Essen understood that her llamas carried meaning resonating beyond their embodiment of quality and luxury. Under her care, Llucky and Llinda had shed the ostensibly scraggy character of Andean beasts of burden to become thoroughly modernized and acculturated, as indicated by their well-groomed and perfumed bodies. Each was seemingly individuated with a distinct name.

Llinda could earn up to $100 a sitting.[28] She became a favorite Revlon

FIGURE 7.6. Revlon's "Love That Pink" advertisement. *Seventeen* (June 1955), 6.

model, photographed by the prominent advertising designer Virginia Thoren. D'Essen described the llama's rise to fame: "After the first llama photo was submitted to the client the entire nature of the advertising and marketing campaign was altered so that the llama would be featured. A slogan, as well as a nail-polish shade, was devised, 'Love that Pink'; and Llinda received bushels of fan mail from admirers. [D'Essen's assistant] Maria was kept busy many evenings replying to these letters, each one signed with a miniature llama footprint in pink, made by a rubber stamp devised by Bern" (D'Essen 1959, 233).

A Revlon ad, published in *Seventeen* magazine, capitalizes on the between-stage status of teen girls: not quite women, no longer young girls (figure 7.6). The suggestive image implies that Revlon cosmetics will enable any teenager, of any coloring, to develop a sensuous and attractive appearance like the bejeweled woman in the image, while maintaining a childlike innocence. The model's deliberately posed hands on the llama's neck show off the pink nails of the adult woman, while her pose alongside the animal's swanlike body gives the appearance that she still holds onto her childhood: the white llama looks almost like a fluffy stuffed toy that a teen might have in her bedroom.[29]

276 | Llamas beyond the Andes

According to D'Essen, everyone who saw Llinda became instantly charmed. One family friend wryly commented on the way the animal claimed a conspicuous presence in the D'Essen home: "We all know she's beautiful, but does she have to walk around as though she holds the mortgage on the house?" (quoted in D'Essen 1959, 273). No longer did llamas like Llinda require the specialized knowledge of Bolivia's Indigenous shepherds or even the assistance of an intermediary like Charles Ledger. Communication between the llama and D'Essen had been successfully established. In the Revlon ad, the beautifully manicured hands of white femininity were all that was required to keep Llinda compliant and well behaved.

Llinda Llee Llama's Starring Role at Neiman Marcus's South America Fortnight

Having gained popularity in New York City as a fashion model and television star, Llinda Llama's celebrity status reached new heights in 1959 when she was flown to Texas to participate as a model and goodwill ambassador in the glamorous South America Fortnight, an extravagant event hosted by Dallas's famous department store Neiman Marcus. She played a prominent role there for two weeks in the US business community's efforts to strengthen economic, diplomatic, and tourist ties with South America. As indicated by the textual and photographic archive of the event, Llinda Llama became one of the Fortnight's most featured guests, embodying complex, intersecting narratives of exoticism, authenticity, indigeneity, consumerism, charity, and Pan American unity.

The South America Fortnight was the third such event hosted annually by Neiman Marcus. Stanley Marcus, the chief executive of the company, created the tradition to generate more traffic in the store during the month of October, an otherwise slow time of year in the pre-Christmas season. The Fortnight tradition featured a specific country or region of the world to showcase its clothing, customs, and crafts. With each successive year, more and more people came to the store to see the elaborate decorations and feel "the lure of many foreign lands" (Alexander 2009, 59). In preparation for the event, Neiman Marcus merchandisers spent weeks touring the designated country, searching out ideas for new fashions, handicrafts, and fine artwork that could be incorporated into displays and placed on sale.

Given the wider context of US foreign policy toward Latin America in the Cold War years, the South America Fortnight carried political as well as economic and cultural overtones. Roy Richard Rubottom, assistant secretary of state for Western Hemisphere affairs, gave his blessing to the preparations, confident that Neiman Marcus's "salute to our South American neighbors which you are undertaking in Dallas will make a valued contribution to Inter-American friendship."[30] Citywide institutions such as the Dallas Council on World Affairs were invited to cosponsor the event with the department store,[31] while invited panelists from North and South America participated in discussions on the politics, economics, and artistic movements of the two hemispheres.[32] The Dallas Symphony, the State Fair of Texas, and the Dallas Museum of Fine Art organized concerts, lectures, expositions, and roundtables, and Pan American–Grace Airways and the Grace Line with Braniff International Airways assisted with advertising for the Fortnight and promoting a South America Fortnight Tour to take place in the months following the gala events.[33] Local schools joined in on the excitement, bringing their students to see the store's exhibits and assigning essays on the featured region (Alexander 2009, 60). Playing up the Fortnight's overarching theme of friendship, American industrialist J. Peter Grace expressed the hope that the event would create "'a family spirit' between the Americas."[34]

Despite the importance of the diplomatic and cultural relations surrounding the South America Fortnight, there was no mistaking the underlying moneymaking impetus. According to Thomas E. Alexander (2009, 59), executive vice-president of marketing for Neiman Marcus (1970–1986),

> The Fortnights were never, in truth, intended to present anything resembling an actual picture of any particular country. . . . If school children learned something about a particular land, so much the better, and if the many cultural entities located in the city were pleased to unite under one international theme for a few weeks each autumn that, too, was wonderful. The fundamental idea behind it all, however . . . was to provide customers an intriguing and compelling reason to come into the store at a time when they did not traditionally do so.

What better way to persuade customers to visit Neiman Marcus than the promise of seeing South America embodied in a living llama? As an official greeter at the South America Fortnight, Llinda Llee Llama's

278 | *Llamas beyond the Andes*

appealing image adorned advertisements for the event. Sporting a derby displaying the flags of the ten featured South American countries,[35] she posed like an ambassadorial tour guide (figure 7.7). Her welcoming salutation invited customers to join her at the Fortnight on an exciting exploration of South America. A full-page ad published in high-society's *Town & Country Magazine* served as a guarantee that the festivities would be authentic and enjoyable. As illustrated by the image of Llinda Llee Llama, one key to the success of the Fortnights was what Stanley Marcus identified as a "new theatrical form of retailing" that would strike a note of authenticity. To entice crowds into Neiman Marcus, careful attention was paid to designing the layout and décor of the exhibits on all six floors of the store and to planning the extensive advertising campaign. The theatricality of the store's ornamentation and design was directed specifically at entertaining the customers and creating a stylized illusion of realism (Alexander 2009, 60, 75).

Veteran set designer Alvin Colt recognized the importance of the Fortnights to influence patrons: "There must be an impact on the audience so that when people come into the store, they are completely engrossed in what is happening. It's not display, interior design or anything like that. . . . It's an experience, and it's just the same as when the curtain goes up on a show."[36] Taking inspiration from theaters and museums, Neiman Marcus staged the experience of authenticity by constructing what might be called living dioramas throughout the store's showrooms and galleries.[37] As in the Hickey-Freeman window display examined earlier, store designers cultivated the model of the museum diorama as a way of drawing the customer into a "real life" scene. These settings were then animated on all six floors with the theatrical addition of costumes, lighting, and set decoration.

In the case of the South America Fortnight, visitors found themselves entering the spirit of the event as they approached the store on the street. Like Llinda Llee Llama's hat, the building's façade was decorated with the featured countries' colorful flags and attractive metallic discs representing Argentine carnival celebrations.[38] Inside, "South America" was brought to life on every floor with the dramatic use of authentic realia and decked out salespeople. A "typical South American Coffee Bar" featured a special South American blend sponsored by Chase and Sanborn served to shoppers by "a costumed senorita [*sic*]."[39] Decorators transformed the first floor into a "typical small village," using painted façades to demarcate departments and counter areas as village shops, markets, and homes. Baskets of "South American-inspired objects," including ceramics and

FIGURE 7.7. Advertising insert: "Town & Country. Sunrise in South America. October 1959." Dallas Public Library Archives, Neiman Marcus Box 10-5.

fabrics, vicuña rugs, and Peruvian retablos or household shrines, were on sale throughout the store.[40] Maps and photomurals of Braniff International Airway's model of Brazil's future capital city Brasília lined the walls of the men's department.[41]

Stanley Marcus selected the fifth floor's Oak Room for a popular exhibit of priceless South American gold, with pieces not from South America but from private collections across the United States.[42] Customers could dine on traditional South American fare in the famous Zodiac Room, which was transformed into a replica of two renowned Peruvian restaurants, Granja Azul and Trece Monedas. The Amazon, Machu Picchu, and Inca art inspired designs for other areas of the store, like the escalators, which were trimmed in lush greenery and hanging baskets "studded with feather headdresses, bands of bone, noise-makers and other objects gathered from the native villages."[43] Other items brought from the Andean republics were repurposed for sale, such as "Bolivian silver pisco cups you'll use as candleholders."[44] These hammered-silver cups, claimed to be of great interest to collectors, caught customers' attention with their unique "collection of Indian faces and expressions."[45]

Indigenous designs inspired pretty fabrics and other unusual gift items.

280 | *Llamas beyond the Andes*

Ecuador's woven faja belts were especially popular due to their attractive colors and folkloric resonance. Store designers made use of these as trimming on clothing, shoes, placemats, and gift wrapping.[46] Throughout the store, these and other eye-catching items paid homage to the way the "history, romance and color of South America have been translated into contemporary fashion by Neiman-Marcus for the South American Fortnight."[47] Moreover, the material and sensorial delights of the Fortnight experience encouraged interested visitors to contemplate "the rewards of an eventual journey to South America," where they too might discover beautiful treasures for themselves.[48]

This elaborately prepared stage came to life with the arrival of a glittering cast of invitees brought to Dallas for the featured events. Ambassadors from the ten participating South American countries traveled from Washington, DC, to take part in the opening ribbon-cutting ceremony and the ambassador's evening dinner and ball. They were accompanied by ten "junior ambassadresses" brought along for an Elizabeth Arden–sponsored beauty pageant. Entertainment was provided by the 35-member Carmen Cuevas Conjunto from the Chile Musical Conservatory of Guitar and Folklore. Other renowned musicians included 18-year-old Bolivian violinist Jaime Laredo, who had recently won the Queen Elizabeth of Belgium International Competition, and famed Brazilian pianist Guiomar Novaes, both of whom performed with the Dallas Symphony.[49] Guests providing "Special South American flavor" included a "Peruvian town mayor and Argentinean gauchos," while representatives from Pan American–Grace Airways and from Grace Line promoted the comforts and pleasures of modern travel and tourism.

The unquestionable star of the show, however, was Llinda Llee Llama.[50] "Despite our impressive guest list, which included the entire South American diplomatic corps from Washington, [American socialite and diplomat] Perle Mesta, and other notables from the various countries, the guest who made the headlines was a live llama from Peru. Her name was Llinda Lee [*sic*] and she had perfect house manners. She appeared on every floor of the store and on television, attracting great crowds of delighted children and adults, who had never before seen a real, live llama" (Marcus 2001, no pagination). Although Llinda Llee was not actually from Peru, her presence provided an authentic flourish to the festivities.

Accompanied by Lorrain D'Essen, Llinda Llee Llama arrived in Dallas on a Braniff International Airways flight and, like a star, was photographed while disembarking. Once on the ground, she was met by Neiman Marcus officials and the Air Force Band from Sheppard Air Force Base, before being whisked away to her hotel in a liveried Cadillac convertible. Llinda Llee and D'Essen were taken to the Statler Hilton, where they would stay for the duration of the events. At the registration desk, the llama was greeted with an epicure basket from Neiman Marcus.[51] It was not usual for the hotel to house large animals, but an exception was made on this occasion for Llinda Llee. According to Marcus (2001, no pagination), "In order to get hotel accommodations for her at the Statler-Hilton, we had to persuade the hotel's board of directors to convene an emergency meeting to lift its ban on the housing of livestock in its hotel." Several celebrity-style photographs capture the anthropomorphized llama checking in to the hotel, picking up her mail, and demonstrating beyond doubt that she was not common livestock.[52]

Over the course of the next two weeks, Llinda Llee made appearances dressed in pretty pompoms and colorful folkloric blankets, reminiscent of the ways in which Indigenous pastoral communities adorn camelids in the Andes (see figure 0.3). She was featured at the ambassadors dinner and ball and at all the major events, including an opening parade, where she walked along between D'Essen and Stanley Marcus.[53]

No matter where she was (standing elegantly, snuggled up to a guest, or seated on the floor amid an event), Llinda Llee Llama was the center of attention. Children and adults flocked to have their photos taken alongside her. When not participating in a Fortnight-related event, Llinda Llee appeared in photo shoots with models and visited patients in the Children's Medical Center.

Llinda Llee's presence at a traditional South American barbecue charmed newspaper reporter Ethel Woodby, who described how she lost her heart to the llama and to the Carmen Cuevas Troupe at the event. Although she expressed surprise to learn that the llama was actually a native New Yorker, Woodby nonetheless sensed that the animal seemed captivated by the musical performers, reacting to "South American music like a far-removed Irishman to St. Patrick's Day. Right in the middle of the singers she would go, taking advantage of her nationality to nuzzle the performers." Apparently, the llama was partial to some of the men around her: "The singers weren't the only ones the animal kissed. She was captivated by her host, [brother of Stanley and executive vice-president] Edward Marcus—or maybe it was the other way around. Marcus, when he introduced me to Linda Lee, said she was the only girl his wife will permit him to pet." The reporter described the llama as the consummate

282 | Llamas beyond the Andes

performer: "Linda Lee isn't the least bit shy. In fact she can spot a camera a block away, then begins to pose. She prefers a profile shot with her long swanlike neck arched high."[54]

As the archival record demonstrates, Llinda Llee was the perfect choice to serve as a goodwill ambassador for the Neiman Marcus South America Fortnight. A thoroughly acculturated model and appealing performer, she mingled easily with ambassadors, customers, and children. Although not a genuine Peruvian llama, she nonetheless performed an exotic, nonthreatening authenticity throughout her two-week stay in Dallas. Against the backdrop of the department store's folkloric decorations and costumed personnel, the charming llama led the way to a touristic "rediscovery" of South America, embodying the North's romanticized understanding of the southern continent as "the site of projected utopias, dreams of gold, and exotic reveries" (Majluf 1997, 874).[55] For Stanley Marcus, the process of rediscovery formed part of a historical continuum, beginning with the initial arrival of Spanish "tourist" Francisco Pizarro to South America and culminating in Neiman Marcus's commercial exploration of the region in preparation for the two-week-long event.[56]

Although the expressed objectives of the Fortnight included strengthening the bonds of friendship and encouraging a family spirit within the Americas, the event presented South America as the site of exotic difference and reinforced a vertical understanding of the relationship between North and South America rather than one of equal participation.[57] The llama's seemingly foreign identity encapsulated the contradictions and ambiguities of the South America Fortnight, which, in its theatrical excess, functioned in a way similar to what Majluf (1997, 881) has observed regarding picturesque or *costumbrista* illustrations in nineteenth-century travel narratives, which "tend to open up a vista, allowing the viewer the illusion of unmediated access to a particular scene." For this reason, they were an important vehicle for travel accounts, which "depended on their ability to transport readers to distant and exotic sites as if those places were immediately present. The rhetoric of description, the profuse detail, and the vistas that opened out from the pages of journals and travel books helped to sustain that illusion" (884). In the case of the Neiman Marcus Fortnight, the large colorful displays, the costumed salespeople, and the beautiful white llama were all in place to provide customers who came to the store with a similar illusion of being directly transported to a South America that opened itself out to them.

But this transfer came, literally, at a cost. In this context, the South

US Camelid Contact Zones in the Twentieth Century | 283

America Fortnight and Llinda Llee's starring role can be read as the culmination of the advertising strategies studied in this chapter. In each instance, consumers were invited to step into new, more luxurious, and even more adventurous identities and habitats. In the case of Hickey-Freeman, male buyers were encouraged to imagine themselves as a new Hiram Bingham, climbing into the Andes in search of the next beautiful coat made from Stroock llama cloth. Women, simply by slipping into an exquisite Stroock vicuña coat, became royalty, free to travel the world independently. As a cultural ambassador, television star, and live model, Llinda Llee helped Neiman Marcus customers imagine that they too could enter directly into an authentic South American scene full of exotic and colorful merchandise waiting to be purchased. This body of advertising relied on forms of display, illusion, and theater, which all came together to create a dramatic space where customers with purchasing power could hope to possess whatever they wanted.

CONCLUSION

The Afterlives of Camelid Contact Zones

Bigelow (2016) raises a methodological problem in her study of the colonial silver extraction industry in Latin America with which historians of the field have had to grapple: how to recover Indigenous contributions to the technological transformations taking place in mining and the science of metallurgy at the time. She approaches the question with a "linguistic-discursive method" of analysis and close reading of Quechua and Spanish language forms, sounds, and concepts appearing in colonial mining texts and their translations (117). Her contention is that "extractive industries" can serve as novel sites for investigating "the production and dissemination of hybrid knowledge" (118). The history of efforts to remove Andean camelids from their native habitat for export documents another kind of extractive industry, which created a proliferation of intercultural junctures of knowledge production and encompassed a wide variety of activities and actors, many of whom were Indigenous. As this book shows, camelid contact zones produced as a result of these encounters offer a unique investigative tool that brings to light a largely unexamined, centuries-long trail of documents and artifacts.

The significance of the camelid contact zones can be assessed in at least two fundamental ways. The first perspective takes the long view, focusing on what camelid-human intersections have shown us in more than five hundred years. This broader standpoint gives an account of the ways that imperial, scientific, economic, and ecological interests converged over time in human and nonhuman animal histories. For example, these sites of investigation document how the animals were slowly transformed from exotic creatures into important commodities for large-scale export. In the same vein, these histories consider European countries that wanted to acquire camelids with the expressed goal of improving their own economies or those of their colonies.[1] They draw attention to governmental institutions and scientific societies that initiated or became involved

286 | Llamas beyond the Andes

in these projects and uncover the debates that evolved concerning the scientific, political, and economic challenges such ventures might create and how best to overcome them. Camelid contact zones provide evidence of how changing political relations among countries influenced the outcomes of these imperial ventures.

The comprehensive study of these key sites sheds light on the impact that extraction undertakings had on Indigenous herding communities, especially in areas around Lake Titicaca, where alpacas and llamas are more numerous. The book provides instances of consequence where Indigenous shepherds joined extraction projects, actively participating in the preparations to ready the animals for transoceanic crossings and accompanying the flocks abroad. Despite these important examples, by and large Andean pastoral communities refused to take part in these ventures or sell their animals to outsiders. If compelled to do so under pressure from governmental forces or local intermediaries, they appear to have deliberately selected old or infirm animals, even some that were unable to reproduce. For Indigenous communities already under assault due to the imposition of new labor taxes and territorial losses resulting from liberal land reforms (Larson, 2004, 149–164), the forced sales of camelids led to a further unraveling of traditional ways of life.[2]

The study of these contact zones over the years brings to the foreground a second ecological consequence that marked all efforts to move the animals overseas: the high fatality rates that occurred without exception among the flocks during transit. The large number of camelid deaths makes it impossible to overlook this aspect of extraction ventures and shines a light on the limits of science at the time. Given the enormous cost in terms of money, labor, and animals, most camelid extraction projects came to an end by the 1870s.

During the early decades of the twentieth century, the animals' valuable fiber slowly became more accessible internationally, a transformation that helped to reshape new camelid contact zones. Specialty textile mills in the United States like S. Stroock & Co. began sourcing their camelid wools directly from Peru in the 1930s. Department stores wanting to introduce the luxury products made from the fabric of these exotic creatures and pique the interest of potential customers strove to create an atmosphere of authenticity by using taxidermy animals and other genuine Andean objects to create storefront displays reminiscent of museum dioramas. Toward the middle of the century, as it became popular to employ living animals in advertising campaigns, live llamas were introduced as

Conclusion | 287

attractive props for selling luxury products, as goodwill ambassadors, and as symbols of authenticity for events featuring US–South American commercial and political relations.

While the examination of camelid contact zones from a broad perspective elucidates their common features and moments of transformation, an in-depth analysis of individual case histories brings to light another key vantage point that enables us to discover these intercultural sites in all of their complexity. A close reading of particular examples uncovers the many stories proliferating around each intercultural site and highlights the convergence of diverse actors and interests. This more intimate standpoint enables us to look over the shoulder of the person exploring the camelid body-interior or follow the biogeographies of individual animals overseas and in new environments. These sites of investigation reveal protagonists who reside at the margins of colonial society, like Julián García, the postal worker from Lima who guided Josephine's camelids hundreds of miles across the South American continent and overseas to Spain, despite hardship and myriad difficulties. And they enable us to hear the angry reactions of the Indigenous women (furious that the men had accepted money in exchange for alpacas and llamas), who traveled hundreds of miles behind the flocks, demanding that their animals be returned.

Camelid-human junctures have additionally produced unique visual and material archives that enhance our understanding of their significance. Skeletal remains scattered around the world in museums of natural history affirm the distances that camelids and/or camelid fragments traveled. Visual images (such as the collection created by Santiago Savage, portraying the activities carried out at Laguna Blanca by Charles Ledger and the group of Bolivian shepherds that accompanied him) provide historical evidence of the contingent nature of knowledge-making in this intercultural context. Savage's colorful scenes give prominence to these singular Indigenous protagonists who participated fully in each task at hand, many of whom emerge from the pages as individuals. It is hard not to feel empathy toward the young shepherd boy Pepe, depicted by Savage as someone who would trip and fall headfirst into a scene at the worst possible times. Other images draw viewers into the narrative, where they too experience uneasiness at the approach of condors along the horizon or perceive the distress of the family that walked miles carrying heavy containers of water to aid Ledger's exhausted and dying animals.

Finally, the histories emerging from close readings of camelid contact zones frequently come to a premature ending when archival trails

288 | Llamas beyond the Andes

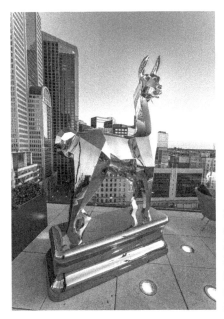

FIGURE 8.1. "'Miss Llinda Llee Llama' at the Statler in downtown Dallas by Brad Oldham & Christy Coltrin of Brad Oldham Sculpture. 8.5' x 6' x 3'. Stainless Steel. 2017." Photograph courtesy of Christy Coltrin of Brad Oldham Sculpture.

disappear before the stories have concluded. Moreover, some protagonists emerge and then recede in significance too soon, like García, while others never come fully into view due to the incomplete record, like the Black men hired to domesticate Josephine's vicuñas in Lima before departure or the Indians who reportedly accompanied the postal worker throughout the journey to Spain but rarely receive mention. The story of Llinda Llee Llama serves as another prominent example of untimely archival silence: the account of her life ends abruptly after her participation in the Neiman Marcus South America Fortnight. Despite the success of her appearance at the event and her acclaimed celebrity status, the white llama vanished from the historical record after October 1959.

Although news about the llama faded, the lasting impression she made on the Dallas community did not. In 2017, after being closed for a sixteen-year period of renovation, the Statler Hilton Dallas reopened its doors, paying tribute to this famous guest on December 8 by unveiling a polished stainless-steel sculpture of the star created by local artists Brad Oldham and Christy Coltrin for the hotel's rooftop Waterproof bar and lounge.[3] Praised for her charitable spirit in the statue's plaque (see the epigraph in chapter 7), Llinda Llee graces the Statler's rooftop setting, where today she lives on in her afterlife as an ambassador of hospitality, culture, and service.

Reminiscent of Morath's iconic photograph of the llama riding through New York City's streets and Cobelle's whimsical vicuñas taking in the sights of Paris, Oldham and Coltrin's Llinda Llee Llama inhabits a modern, urban space. The proud carriage of her neck, head, and tail as well as her flexed front left leg project liveliness and vitality rather than fixity or docility. At the unveiling, Oldham explained how he and Coltrin had taken a "great concept and tried to create an iconic sculpture that wasn't just a literal rendition of a llama."[4] The sculpture represents the historic Llinda Llee Llama but also something more. As shown in figure 8.1, the ever-changing play of light and shadow that moves across the glittering surfaces of her fleeceless body beautifully mirrors, fragments, and distorts the reflections of Dallas's downtown skyline and transforms her into a resplendent and evocative three-dimensional creation. While these fluctuating images emerge and recede across her angular body with the changing light, she becomes both self and other, a polysemic symbol reflecting a proliferation of camelid histories and their biogeographies across space and time.[5] Comparable to the taxidermy llama in figure 0.1, the sculpture of Llinda Llee represents a specific animal and her history. But it also stands in for other camelid stories that carry no physical markers. Although we cannot yet fill the 58-year gap in her life story, we can see new histories and narratives beginning to emerge through this gleaming memorial. It becomes a contact zone, around which all of the case studies examined in the book converge. Llinda Llee Llama reflects and refracts this complex genealogy of roots and routes, all of which are part of her brilliant afterlife.

Acknowledgments

This book took much longer to finish than I ever could have anticipated, and along the way I have incurred many debts of gratitude. I am beholden to the assistance and guidance of many people and institutions, without whom its completion would not have been possible.

First and foremost, I want to express my deep appreciation to Nancy Peterson and Aparajita Sagar, who have accompanied this project from the beginning and directly influenced its shape. They graciously read multiple drafts of each chapter and provided rigorous feedback and immensely helpful suggestions for revision. Their camaraderie, generosity, and encouragement have sustained me over the years.

At various stages of the writing process, a number of friends and colleagues read individual chapters and offered useful comments and helpful suggestions that significantly improved earlier drafts. I gratefully acknowledge Reed Benhamou, Brooke Larson, Joy Logan, Víctor Maqque, Jessie Mitchell, Katherine M. Moore, Kerry Rabenold, Josefa Salmón, and Whitney Walton.

Several colleagues generously invited me to present my work at scholarly venues, especially during early stages of the research. These occasions generated valuable comments, questions, and discussions. I thank Maggie Bolton, University of Manchester (England); Salvador Fernández, Occidental College; Jill Kuhnheim and Danny Anderson, University of Kansas; Joy Logan, University of Hawai'i at Mānoa; Fernando Unzueta and Ileana Rodríguez, Ohio State University; Estelle Tarica, University of California, Berkeley; Guillermo Bustos, Universidad Andina Simón Bolívar; Marta Irurozqui Victoriano and Víctor Peralta Ruiz, Consejo Superior de Investigaciones Científicas; Kathryn Lehman, University of Auckland; Carlos Mamani Condori, Universidad Mayor de San Andrés; Mariselle Meléndez, University of Illinois, Urbana-Champaign; Antonio Tillis, Dartmouth College; and Museo de Arte Indígena ASUR.

I am indebted to the following colleagues and friends who took time from their own work to engage in stimulating conversation, answer queries, share references, chase down etymologies, solve paleography-

292 | *Acknowledgments*

related uncertainties, and assist with translations: Denise Arnold, Paul Benhamou, Chad Black, Vit Bubenik, Heather Burke, Tom Carr, María Eugenia Choque Quispe, Chuck Cutter, Guillermo Delgado-P. , Ariel de la Fuente, Sabine Dedenbach-Salazar, Laura Escobari de Querejazu, Nuur Hamad-Zahonero, Cody Hanson, Peter Henderson, Eric Hoffman, Wei Hong, Alberto Gallo, Ana Gómez Bravo, Shaun Hughes, Ahmed Idrissi Alami, Christian Jouanin, Norma Klahn, Erick D. Langer, A. Darío Lara, Enrique Martín Nogués, Fernando Martín Polo, Esteban Mayorga, Luis Millones, Michael A. Osborne, Niall Peach, Tristan Platt, Francisco Rigalt, Iñigo Sánchez-Llama, Patience Schell, Wendy Stephenson, Dawn Stinchcomb, Cecilia Tenorio, Jane C. Wheeler, Alex Wei, and Juan de Dios Yapita.

Generous funding and institutional support made work on the book possible. During the book's initial stage, I benefited from a Cornell University Summer Library Research Fellowship, where I was able to begin investigating international camelid trajectories. I thank Mary Jo Dudley for her mentorship during the period of the grant. A year-long fellowship with the Purdue University Faculty Program of Study in a Second Discipline provided valuable opportunities and enriched my project in countless ways by enabling me to work with faculty from Purdue's College of Veterinary Medicine, where I studied small ruminant medicine and camelid physiology and anatomy through dissection. The experience I gained under the guidance of my faculty mentor Michel Levy has been fundamental to much of my understanding of the health and medical issues affecting the camelids in their travels. I thank Karin Kooreman and Wael Khamas for their instruction in llama dissection and David Williams for sharing his expertise in the history of medical illustration. Laurent L. Couëtil graciously assisted with the interpretation of several dissection reports. An important part of the fellowship included herd visitations, which provided the unique opportunity to work with the alpaca flock at the White Violet Center for Eco-Justice, a ministry of the Sisters of Providence. I am thankful for the center's directors, Sister Ann Sullivan, who kindly welcomed me at the start of my fellowship, and Sister Maureen Freeman of the Congregation of the Sisters of Saint Joseph (CSJ), who encouraged me to continue my volunteer work after the grant. Several of the Sisters took me under their wing. I want to express my gratitude to Sister Michael Ellen Green and Sister Ruth Johnson. Working alongside Sister Paul Bernadette Bounk, CSJ, and Tracy Wilson in the alpaca fields and barns shoveling poop, assisting with the spring shearing, and skirting fleece was an unforgettable experience. Their guidance in the daily care of alpacas helped me gain a greater understanding of the animals and their remarkable personalities. Candace Minster generously shared her knowledge of fiber processing and organic gardening.

I am extremely grateful for a year-long Research Fellowship from the National Endowment for the Humanities (NEH). For their assistance with the grant writing, I thank Sally Bond with Purdue's Office of the Executive Vice President for Research and Partnerships and David Morrison with Grant Writers' Seminars and Workshops. The NEH and a Purdue University Enhancing Research in the Humanities and Arts grant provided valuable time and support to carry out research in Australia, Chile, Argentina, Bolivia, and Ecuador. Two grants from the Center of Humanistic Study enabled me to dedicate time to writing the book.

I express my heartfelt appreciation for the support that Purdue's School of Languages and Cultures has continually provided. I especially thank Jen William for her wisdom, generous mentoring, and friendship. I am beholden to Joni Hipsher and Soledad Morales-Serrano, who helped me find time for writing, and their kindness and sense of humor make every day brighter. Paul Dixon fortified me with support and chocolate cookies. My students over the years have been an inspiration, I thank particularly Johana Barrero, Débora Borba, Rafael Climent-Espino, Michelle Medeiros, Esther Teixeira, and Sandra Úsuga.

While constructing Charles Ledger's itinerary through Bolivia and northern Argentina, I was contacted by Sabine DuPuy from the Instituto Interdisciplinario Puneño (IPP) of the Universidad Nacional de Catamarca. A highlight of the book project was meeting the archaeologists from the university and the IPP and sharing research on Ledger. I gratefully acknowledge Daniel Delfino Edery, who invited me to visit the Museo Integral de la Reserva de Biosfera de Laguna Blanca. Thanks to Daniel, I had the opportunity to visit the archaeological site where the team of faculty and students have located artifacts and structures associated with Ledger and the Bolivian shepherds.

It gives me great pleasure to thank Dr. Clemency Fisher, emeritus senior curator of vertebrate zoology with the National Museums of Liverpool (NML). Clem generously guided me in the NML's zoology archives, shared her research, and accompanied me to the estate of the Earl of Derby, where I consulted the collection of Edward Smith Stanley, 13th Earl of Derby.

294 | Acknowledgments

I give heartfelt thanks to Dr. Christophe Degueurce, professor of anatomy and curator of the Fragonard Museum at the École Vétérinaire, Maisons-Alfort. Dr. Degueurce prepared a fascinating tour of the unforgettable museum and introduced me to the Fragonard llama.

Linden Gillbank deserves special recognition for her assistance while I was in Melbourne. I benefited greatly from our conversations on the history of the acclimatization movement in Australia and especially on topics concerning native pastures and plants, including "pig's face," that would have been relevant to the arrival of Ledger's alpacas and llamas.

Lucio Aguilar del Río kindly furnished me with photographs of his great-grandmother, Charles Ledger's daughter Isidora, and the extended family.

Lori Czerwionka and Dan Olson ran the statistics on camelid survival rates in overseas journeys, giving precision to the conclusion that I had reached: the animals fared poorly on the long transoceanic voyages.

Special thanks go to Noel Vietmeyer, who generously sent me his archives of notes, correspondence, photographs, and photocopies on Charles Ledger.

In Arequipa I had the pleasure of meeting Frances E. B. Rainsford, owner and operator of Conchotex EIRL and honorary British consul for the regions of Arequipa, Moquegua, and Tacna. I thank Francis for our conversations regarding Charles Ledger and Henry Swinglehurst.

For their generous hospitality during my research travels, I give my heartfelt thanks to Sue and Joe DeGeorge; Ana Gómez Bravo, Felipe Gómez, and Boni Bravo; Monica Macaulay and Joe Salmons; Josefa Salmón; Javier Sanjinés C.; Sally Staley and Keith Keller; and María del Mar Torreblanca López.

I warmly thank the directors and staff who generously assisted me with my research at the following institutions. In England, the Bodleian Library, British Library, Cambridge University Library, Collection of the 13th Earl of Derby, Hunterian Museum and Archives, Liverpool Customs Museum and Archives, National Archives of the United Kingdom, National Museums of Liverpool (Zoology Department), Royal College of Surgeons Library and Archives, and Zoological Society of London Archives. In Spain, the Archives of the Real Jardín Botánico, Archivo del Palacio Real, Archivo General de Indias, Archivo Histórico Nacional, Archivo Municipal de Cádiz, Biblioteca Nacional, Museo Nacional de Ciencias Naturales, and Museo Naval Archives. In France, the Archives Départamentales des Vosges, Archives Départamentales Meurthe et Moselle,

Archives Diplomatiques: Ministère de l'Europe et des Affaires Étrangères, Archives Municipales–Bibliothèque d'Étude et de Conservation de la Ville de Remiremont, Archives Nationales, Bibliothèque Nationale, Château de Malmaison Archives, École Vétérinaire Maisons-Alfort Library and Archives, Musée Fragonard, and Muséum National d'Histoire Naturelle. In Australia, the Australian Museum Archives and Research Library, Goulburn Mulwaree Library, Mitchell Library (State Library of New South Wales), National Library of Australia, New South Wales State Archives, Public Record Office Victoria, and State Library Victoria. In Bolivia, the Archivo y Biblioteca Nacionales de Bolivia, Archivo de La Paz, and Archivo Histórico de la Casa Nacional de Moneda "Mario Chacón Torres." In Peru, the Archivo Central del Ministerio de Relaciones Exteriores del Perú and Archivo Regional de Puno. In Ecuador, the Archivo Histórico of the Banco Central del Ecuador, Archivo Histórico Nacional del Ecuador, and Archivo Histórico y Biblioteca Central del Ministerio de Relaciones Exteriores del Ecuador. In Chile, the Archivo Nacional de Chile. In the United States, the Angelo Bruno Business Library (University of Alabama), Beinecke Rare Book and Manuscript Library (Yale University), Buffalo and Erie County Public Library, City of Newburgh Historian's Office, Dallas Municipal Archives, Dallas Museum of Art Archives, Dallas Public Library, DeGolyer Library (Southern Methodist University), Indiana State University–Cunningham Memorial Library, Inge Morath Estate, National Library of Medicine, Inge Morath Estate, Purdue University Libraries, and University of Rochester Libraries (Department of Rare Books and Manuscripts).

For their research assistance, I recognize Jean-Claude Baumgartner, Paul Brothers, Margie Compton, Tina Craig, Patricia Eagan, Dennis Evers, Javier Fernández Reina, Jane E. Hamby, Béatrice Houot, Mary Huth, Sandy Ingleby, Sana Manzoor, Nancy Martin, Mary McTamaney, Peter Minard, Christophe Pincemaille, Sonia Rosario Sotomayor Vargas, Patricia Summerling, Michel Tranier, M. Carmen Velasco, Stéphanie Ysard, and Grace Zimmermann.

Many friends and associates have offered their support and encouragement. I am pleased to have this opportunity to thank them: Norma Alarcón, Dorothy Bethel, Becky Brown, Tom Brush, Elena Coda, Guillermo Delgado-P, Annabel Drazin, Geraldine Friedman, Patty Hart, Johnny Henry, Emma Hughes, Cara Kinnally, Norma Klahn, Howard Mancing, Françoise Martínez, Colleen Neary-Sundquist, Íñigo Sánchez-Llama, Kyle Schwipps, Sally Staley, Dawn Stinchcomb, John Sundquist, Annie

296 | Acknowledgments

Thomas, Cassandra Torrico, Margie Towery, Nadège Veldwachter, Alex Wei, Mariko Wei, and Jane Yatcilla.

It has been my good fortune to work with two outstanding editors in chief at the University of Texas Press. Theresa May gave strong support to the book at its early stages. I have additionally been privileged to work with Casey Kittrell. I owe Casey a special debt of gratitude for his patience, attention, and care throughout the editorial and evaluation process. Many thanks go to Christina Vargas and Lynne Ferguson for their expert assistance with the manuscript. I am grateful to Kathy Lewis for her meticulous copyediting of the book and to Sue Gaines for preparing a comprehensive and concise index. Special recognition goes to Mariselle Meléndez and Gregory Cushman for their thorough reading of the manuscript, insightful feedback, and strong endorsement of the project.

I owe a special debt of gratitude to Tom Stephenson, who prepared many of the visual images for publication. Ed Lausch, of Lausch Photography, generously assisted with one set of photographs. I thank Molly O'Halloran for the fine map, which clearly communicates to readers the range and scope of the camelids' travels.

My greatest gratitude goes to my family, the Stephensons and the Brodens. My favorite birders, brothers Tom and Mark Stephenson and sisters-in-law Wendy and Kris, have been a constant source of inspiration and love. Graham, Claire, Lucas, Michael, and Dani, you never cease to fill me with joy. I could not imagine a more kindhearted and generous extended family than the one I have in Judy and Dennis, Tim, Jane, and John and Jo: my warm recognition goes to you all. Most of all, I thank my beloved husband, Tom Broden, who has been a part of this project from the beginning. From reading chapter drafts and offering valuable feedback to accompanying me to distant collections in search of camelid skeletons, you have always been there for me. Life with you is the greatest of adventures.

Notes

Introduction. "The Most Interesting Animals in the World"

1. The chapter title "The Most Interesting Animals in the World" comes from the first epigraph in chapter 6 (Wilson [1862]).

2. The camelids are members of the family Camelidae, order Artiodactyla (even-toed ungulates or hoofed mammals), and suborder Tylopoda (pad-footed ungulates).

3. On the North American origins of the camelids and the archaeology of their range and history of domestication, see Dransart (2002, 15–26); Flores Ochoa and MacQuarrie (1994a, 1994b); Wheeler (2005a, 2005b); and Wheeler et al. (1995).

4. In recent years, Indigenous communities, governmental organizations, and non-governmental organizations have reimplemented *chacos* for sustainably harvesting the fiber of the endangered vicuña. See Vilá (2006).

5. Patchett, Foster, and Lorimer (2011, 126) note that a specimen's afterlife as a museum and/or artistic artifact remains "unfinished" and that it can be extended further through new critical and aesthetic engagements.

6. In the wake of his project to reconstruct the afterlives of taxidermy polar bears in the United Kingdom, Marvin (2006, 157) concludes that most wild animals "do not have a recoverable history until their final fatal encounter with humans." This sometimes holds true for the reconstruction of histories of nonwild animals.

7. For example, in 1855, while in exile in Europe, Chilean political figure and writer Benjamin Vicuña Mackenna corresponded with the Paris Zoological Acclimatization Society, noting that he had contacted his father in Valparaíso to request that he approach the Peruvian government to advocate lifting the ban prohibiting the extraction of alpacas and vicuñas. There appears to have been no follow-up on the subject (*Bulletin de la Société* 1855: 231).

8. See Mason (2009) for the chronological history of the image of the four-toed "Chilean sheep." Perhaps one of the best-known examples of jigsaw-puzzle camelids is Swiss naturalist Conrad Gesner's strangely large *Allocamelus scaligeri*, brought to Middelburg (Netherlands) from the "land of the Giants" (Patagonia) and exhibited in June 1558 (Gesner 1560, 42). Described as a male, with a head and ears similar to those of a mule, a white, swan-like neck, feet like an ostrich, and a horse-like tail, this strange, four-year-old creature displayed a mild, sheep-like temperament. Unlike sheep, however, it urinated backward, to the amazement of eyewitnesses.

9. For a discussion of the persistent misidentification of Andean camelids by Europeans, see Gade (2013).

10. On wonder and curiosity as a method of inquiry, see also Bleichmar (2017, 91) and Greenblatt (1991).

11. According to Dutch travelers, translator-interpreters played an indispensable role in their colonial enterprise because the Mapuches' use of Spanish was "so peculiar that none of us could understand anything of what they said" (quoted in Mason 2009, 186).

12. Mason (2009, 186) speculates that the figure standing to the far right of the

298 | Notes to Pages 12–28

image may represent a Moorish servant to the Dutch. On the reliability and authority of the eyewitness, see Bleichmar (2017, 20–21) and Daston and Park (2001, 62–63).

13. Daston and Park (2001, 16) remind us that in early modern Europe the Latin word *admiratio* expressed the contemporary idea of "wonder," while *mirabilia* and *miracula* were employed for the objects that generated the emotional response. The latter two terms are etymologically related to an Indo-European term meaning "smile."

14. My discussion of masculine heroic tropes draws from Freedgood (2000); Logan (2011); Ritvo (1987, 241–288); Ryan (2005); and Terrall (1998).

15. For more on Peru's fiber industry and exports in the twentieth century, see Orlove 1977.

16. According to Hoffman (2001–2002), the Hearst llamas were likely imported from Germany and South America.

17. I draw from Cushman (2013) and Crosby (2004) for my use of the term "neo-ecological imperialism." If "ecological imperialism" (Crosby 2004) describes the impact of initial conquest, "neo-ecological imperialism" refers to postconquest colonizing forces and their repercussions on local and/or national environments (Cushman 2013, 77). On ecological imperialism more generally, see Ross (2017).

18. Three important exceptions are Cowie (2017a, 2022) and Mello Pereira (2013).

Chapter 1. From Marvelous Antidote to the Poison of Idolatry

1. A list of ailments treated with bezoars as well as recommended dosages can be found in Pomet (1694, 10–14).

2. Burton ([1621] 1676, 244) highlighted how the stone "takes away sadness, and makes him merry that useth it; I have seen some that have been much diseased with faintness, swouning [*sic*], and melancholy, that taking the weight of three grains of this stone, in the water of Oxtongue, have been cured."

3. The list of jewels that King James I sent in 1622–1623 to the Prince of Wales and the Duke of Buckingham for their use while they were in Spain included diamonds, unicorn horn, and bezoar stones, one of which was large and set in gold and had belonged to Elizabeth I (Lemon 1828, 150, 153). Archival documents also highlight the link between jewels and medicinals. See Archivo General de Palacio (hereafter cited as AGP), "Memorial del Boticario Mayor: Madrid a 25 de julio de 1650," Sección Administrativa, Casa, Dependencias, Botica, Legajo 429. For more on royal collections and bezoars, see Alfonso Mola and Martínez Shaw (2003); Al Tifaschi ([ca. 1243] 1998); Bauer and Haupt (1976); Julien (1968); Pérez de Tudela and Jordan Gschwend (2001); and Trnek and Vassallo e Silva (2001).

4. To provide one example the Cardinal of Este sent the Duke of Lerma a gilded silver cup from Toledo, Spain, in 1614 that contained a large and costly bezoar stone (Cabrera de Córdoba 1857, 562). For the role that bezoar stones and other exotic objects played in the decorative arts of the period, see Duffin (2013); Esteras Martín (2006); Fučíková et al. (1997); Sameiro Barroso (2014); and Stark (2003–2004).

5. Daston's (2000a, 6) description of how scientific objects become historically salient fits the bezoar stone (see also Daston 2000b). On the effectiveness of bezoar stones against arsenic poisoning, see Malcom (1998) and Sameiro Barroso (2014, 94).

6. Andean huacas were complex material, symbolic, and performative sites, including tombs and shrines as well as agential forces of ancestral beings or gods. Huaca ancestors could become angry and even dangerous when the proper rituals were

Notes to Pages 29–34 | 299

neglected or enacted incorrectly. See Abercrombie (1998); Brosseder (2014); Duviols (1971); Mills (1997); and Salomon, Urioste, and Ávila (1991).

7. Martín's (2001) discussion of the large quantity of Peruvian bezoars circulating between the Colegio Jesuita and Rome and Valdizán and Maldonado's (1922) inventory of the Colegio Jesuita's pharmacy provide additional evidence for my assertion that the search for bezoars impacted camelid populations.

8. Martínez de Leyua (1597, 128) advocated use of the bezoar stone for combating the plague, noting that it was "first and foremost for curing and protecting."

9. All subsequent references to the text are from this edition, unless otherwise noted. Pardo Tomás (2002, 110–111) refers to the 1574 *Historia medicinal* as a "mixed" or hybrid work that brings together European, Asian, and American products and knowledge.

10. For a discussion of the politics and economics of pharmacological publication during the sixteenth century, see Guerra (1966), especially 50–52.

11. Barrera-Osorio (2006, 44–48) examines how the study of nature and the institutionalization of empirical practices in sixteenth-century Spain were linked to the search for commodities and commercial sources of revenue; see also Guerra (1966).

12. Physician Garcia da Orta (ca. 1501–1568, Monardes's contemporary), known for his writings on Asian materia medica, provided the following information on the origin of the word "bezoar": "This stone is called *Pazar*, from *pazam* (the word for goat), and so, here, when you ask for a medicine or antidote for poison, it's called *pazam*, and some also call unicorn [horn] and composite remedies by the same name. The word *pazar* is used by Persians, Arabs, and people from Coraçon; and in Europe it has been modified to *bezar*, while Indians have altered it further to *pedra de bazar*, which means a stone from the plaza or market; because *bazar* is the place where things are sold" (Orta [1563] 1895, 233).

13. Fernández de Oviedo y Valdés (1851–1852, 2:79–80), for example, offers the story of the fatal poisoning of the Spanish captain Martín Íñiguez de Carquiçano by the Portuguese Fernando de Valdaya. Valdaya hid the poison in his fingernail, which he dipped unobserved into Íñiguez de Carquiçano's wine glass while passing it to him.

14. In his book on Chinese, Persian, Arab, and Indian merchants in Asia, Chau Ju-kua (1170–1231), the Chinese inspector of foreign trade during the Song dynasty, referred to the bezoar or "mo-so" (*mu-suo*) stone as a "life preserver." He observed foreigners visiting the province of Canton who wore finger rings set with a bezoar so that they could lick the stone if they were poisoned and be cured immediately (Ju-kua [1783] 1911, 90n7). Avenzoar ([12th c.] 1992, 151) recommended having a bezoar set in a ring, as poisonous serpents would avoid the person who wore one.

15. Georges-Louis Leclerc, Comte de Buffon, in consultation with fellow naturalist Louis-Jean-Marie Daubenton, theorized about the formation of bezoars. Having observed how gastric and plant juices adhered to the teeth of ruminants to form a tartar or plaque, he posited that the same substances might form inside the animal around a small ingested object, such as a seed or kernel, eventually creating a bezoar over time. Subsequent layers could form around the original, while movement along the walls of the stomach or intestines would polish and smooth the stone (Buffon 1764, 278–293).

16. For observations regarding the healing power of bezoar stones and the influence of celestial forces, see Morales (1605, 205v–206r, 207v–208r). Other sources similarly noted that the stones' physical characteristics and medicinal virtue could be impacted

300 | Notes to Pages 34–40

by the astrological sign under which they were formed (see Elgood 1935, 79; Levey 1966; Alfonso X el Sabio [1250] 1981, 62).

17. My discussion of how Monardes empowered his readers draws in part from Kavey (2007, 5). See also Asúa and French (2005, 107).

18. For more on how such a methodology could work, see Kavey (2007, 59–94).

19. In regard to the development of ideas central to this discussion and the final section of this chapter, MacCormack (1991a, 126) theorizes about the epistemological relationship of authority and divine and demonic power as worked out in the 1530 writings of the Spanish priest Pedro Ciruelo:

> In Ciruelo's mind, the distribution of natural and divine power in the universe was mirrored and made effective by designated experts. Ordained priests were authorized to administer words imbued with divine power, while physicians after prolonged study administered the natural power inherent in certain plants and minerals. There existed no such thing as knowledge "infused by God without the need of a teacher's instruction or the study of books." Practices described by Ciruelo as "idolatrous superstition" threatened, not only true religion and scientifically accurate knowledge, but also the proper ordering of society.

See also Pardo Tomás (2002, 118).

20. Pardo Tomás (2002, 108) similarly observes that the publication of the first part of Monardes's work resulted in such fame and notoriety that he did not have to conduct much investigation on his own to discover new materia medica in America, as people returning from the New World began bringing him samples of all kinds (see also López Piñero 1990, 18). For more on Monardes's method of collecting New World medicinals and information about them, see Asúa and French (2005, 106–107). Bleichmar (2005, 89–95) describes Monardes's networks of travelers, patients, and others, from whom he gathered information regarding these heretofore unknown products.

21. Many who wrote about bezoar stones warned against counterfeits, which could be found in abundance in Peru, Asia, and Europe (see Primerose 1651, 354). In England a fake bezoar was at the center of the now famous *Chandelor v. Lopez (Lopus)* case (1625), which led to the principle of "caveat emptor": let the buyer beware (Baker 2006, 552–555). Along with rising concerns over fraudulent bezoars, some physicians raised questions concerning the genuine stone's medical efficacy. Pitt (1702, 33–35) argued that the bezoar was an ineffective remedy that served only to line the pockets of deceitful medical practitioners (see also Guybert 1629). Given its cost, Pitt (1702, 39) suggested that the stone's only noticeable result was on the individual who received the bill: "But the most visible Operation it has, is seen when the Bill is paid. Then it changes the colour, and causes paleness and chilness [*sic*]."

22. On the relationship between nature as a source of both commodities and wonder, see Asúa and French (2005); Barrera-Osorio (2006); and Smith and Findlen (2002b).

23. Neither Monardes nor Osma ever identified the animals by name. Readers learned only in later publications that they were vicuñas, guanacos, and deer.

24. Further research is required to complete our understanding of how Peruvian stones circulated. For example, the extent of the role played by the Jesuits is not yet known. Martín (2001) has shown that the Jesuits were actively involved in shipping sizable quantities of bezoars from the Colegio Jesuita de San Pablo in Lima to Rome. The Colegio de San Pablo's inventory of medicines indicated that large amounts of bezoars

Notes to Pages 40–42 | 301

were kept on hand in the pharmacy and dispensed alone or as key ingredients in compound recipes (see Valdizán and Maldonado 1922, 3–106). Contreras y Valverde ([1640] 1965, 10) noted that pharmacies in Spain were always looking for bezoars. Trade in bezoar stones was still active even in the eighteenth century (see also Juan and Ulloa 1748, 1:140). Europeans likely acquired the stones in three ways: through trade with Indigenous peoples and others; by hunting the animals themselves; and by ransacking huacas and homes. Indigenous peoples from the Atacama province were regularly hunting vicuñas even in the mid-eighteenth century, trading their skins and bezoar stones (Cosme Bueno y Alegre 1764–1778). The *Relaciones* and *Descripciones* of provinces and bishoprics also identified where bezoar-producing animals could be found (for example, Castro y del Castillo [1651] 1906, 205–207, 209–210, 219–220; Contreras y Valverde [1640] 1965, 11).

25. My reading of the symbolism of the hunt draws from Eamon (1994, 269–300). Cañizares-Esguerra (2006b, 120–177) has also shown how the languages of medicine and demonology converge in early colonial writings.

26. As Eamon (1994, 297) points out:

the repeated references to the "secrets of nature" in seventeenth-century scientific literature should not be dismissed as mere rhetoric. Far from being a mere hackneyed metaphor, the continual appearance of that well-worn phrase indicates a fundamental shift in the direction of natural philosophy. The conception of nature's "secrets"—that is, the exterior appearance of things—was the foundation of the new philosophy's skeptical outlook, and of its insistence upon getting to the bottom of things through active experimentation and disciplined observation.

See also Daston and Park (2001, 129). Barrera-Osorio (2006, 2) argues that these discoveries resulted in an early scientific revolution emerging in sixteenth-century Spain and its New World colonies. See also Bleichmar and Mancall (2011) and Smith and Findlen (2002b).

27. The way some medicines and poisons worked to cure or harm an animal or person could not always be perceived directly through the senses, although the symptoms were clear enough. In such cases, the beneficial or harmful qualities were considered to "depend on occult qualities and, therefore, on occult causes; they were the subjects of experience (even in the sense of experiment), not of rational explanation" (Clark 1997, 228; see also 214–232). Monardes (1574, 133v) noted the occult qualities of bezoar stones in his treatise on poisons and their antidotes. The bezoar's occult properties gave it versatility as a remedy. In addition to being mixed in powdered form in a drink or placed directly on a poisoned wound, it could also be worn as an amulet on a cord around the neck and kept near to the wearer's heart, as Martínez de Leyua observed in 1597 (128). See also Porta ([1558, 1559] 1669, 227).

28. For more on the nature and properties of poison and its place in early modern medicine, see Gibbs (2013).

29. Indeed, some of the bezoars in Peru had seemingly miraculous qualities. Cobo ([1653] 1956, 130) told of a bezoar that at one point belonged to Pedro Sórez (Ozores) de Ulloa, the *corregidor* of Potosí. The size of a chicken egg, the stone had been pierced by an arrow; the tip and a portion of the shaft remained embedded in it. The animal did not die from the arrow, as the stone had continued to grow around it. A reliable clergyman told Cobo of a second stone that had at its center an arquebus ball. Calancha ([1638] 1974, 1:129) wrote of yet another that had formed around a

302 | Notes to Pages 44–51

mattress-maker's needle, and Acosta ([1590] 1962, 214) described two stones that he himself had seen, which had at their center pine nuts from a tree found in Spain but not in Peru.

30. As already noted, for Monardes (1574, 133v), the bezoar stone constituted the most sovereign medicine for curing the ills of the flesh. Zurbarán's painting represented divine intervention in the form of the bezoardic antidote because it preserved not only the flesh but also the spirit. In similar fashion, Ramos Gavilán ([1621] 1988, 313) described the Virgin Mary as a "pharmacy of spiritual medicinals," the purest and most noble antidote for the bite of the serpent. See Peyrebonne (2011) for a discussion of wine as a symbol of the triumph of life over death and salvation from corruption or poison.

31. Garcilaso de la Vega ([1609] 1985, 1:34–35; see also 1:130–131) claimed that the use of poison had been widespread among pre-Inca Indigenous peoples, referring to them as "the Indians from the time of gentility." On Indigenous use of poisons, see Elferink (1999, 339) and Murúa ([ca. 1611] 2001, 333).

32. Bouysse-Cassagne with Bouysse (1988, 56) found connections between the Collas and the present-day Callahuayas, who are well known for their knowledge and practice of traditional forms of medicine.

33. Drawing from what he had seen as extirpator of idolatries, Arriaga ([1621] 1968, 204) explained:

> there are also specific *conopas* [small figures], some for corn, called *zarap conopa*; others for potatoes, *parap conopa*; and still others for the increase of their cattle, called *caullama*, which sometimes are small figures of rams [llamas]. All the *conopas*, no matter what kind, are worshipped in the same way as the huacas, except that huaca-adoration is public and common throughout the province, while *conopa*-adoration is secret and specific to each household. This cult and its veneration are carried out either by individuals . . . or a sorcerer is called in, and so in this way the sorcerers know all the *conopas* that everyone in a village has and gives the signs for them.

34. For more on the role that *illas* play in herding communities, see Arnold and Yapita (1998, 224–238).

35. See Platt et al. (2006, especially 167–174) for a discussion on the relationship between the shining radiance of lightning (Chu'qi Illa), fertility, and precious metals.

36. Cuba (ca. 1499–1502, 136r) described a burnished radiance that he had noticed in Eastern bezoars: "This gleaming stone, its color like that of pale yellow wine, shimmers with light."

37. My analysis in this last section takes as its point of departure studies by Harrison (1995) and Delgado-P. (2005) that examine how the early bilingual dictionaries and religious documents became tools used in the attempt to dismantle Andean epistemologies specifically through language. On the concept of *illa* and the problem of translation, see Bouysse-Cassagne and Harris (1987).

38. In Cobo's (1653) description, the bezoar appeared to function as a sort of magic talisman that would bring wealth to its fortunate holder when carried about. Many Europeans similarly believed that the bezoar had talismanic powers, especially if worn and kept close to the heart, as observed earlier in the chapter. The stone's occult properties were also described in early Arabic texts (Qaddumi 1990, 175).

39. Solórzano y Pereira ([1648] 1972, 335) defined treasure as "any money, gold,

Notes to Pages 51–54 | 303

silver, jewels, or other valuable personal property whose owners are no longer known and of whom there is no information, and these items, having been hidden long ago in secret places, are preserved for the future."

40. The Spanish largely referred to Andean camelids as *carneros* (sheep, rams) and *ovejas* (ewes, sheep). See also Gade (2013).

41. Describing the inspection tour of the *visitador* (inspector) Cristóbal de Albornoz, Felipe Guaman Poma de Ayala (1615/1616) noted that he punished the corrupt religious fathers as much as the Indians. He also castigated the "false sorcerers" (Taqui Oncoy) and those who followed or had in their possession any sort of *conopa* or *illa*. For more on *conopas*, see Brosseder (2014); Mills (1997, 75–100); and Uhl (1906).

42. Mills (1997, 42) has traced a shift during the sixteenth century from the depiction of huacas as a sacred place or shrine to a site where treasures were buried or hidden with the bodies of dead ancestors. See also Duviols (1971, 299–333).

43. An extraordinary stockpile of bezoars was found concealed in a huaca in 1580:

This year, in Acoya, near Guancavélica, some men discovered a *guaca*; upon excavating it, they found small gold and silver idols and in the furthest chamber they came upon a pile of bezoar stones, at least 10 *quintales* worth. Among them they found beautiful and large stones. There were also items of clothing that, when touched, turned into dust. When the *guaca*-excavators saw these unfamiliar stones and rotted clothing, they burned everything without realizing what they were doing. Old people told me that these stones, which Indians found in vicuñas, guanacos, and other animals, were given as offerings, serving as a sign of the good fortune and events that they awaited. (Montesinos [1605] 1906, 79–80)

The narrator hid neither his amazement at the immensity of the find nor his sense of regret at the unnecessary loss of treasure that these stones and pieces of clothing represented.

44. Las Casas ([1563] 1958, 11–27) put forward three fundamental propositions spelling out the reasons why the Spanish had no legal jurisdiction over these riches, which he then explicated in all of their legal ramifications. First, these riches had been used to glorify and honor the dead with whom they had been buried. Second, the treasures and the glory and fame associated with them also honored the living, who continued to have connections with the dead. Third, these treasures had not been abandoned; rather they belonged to the families of the dead. His general conclusion argued that it was a mortal sin to disturb a tomb in the search for treasure (33). On the topic of Las Casas and the restitution of treasures, see also MacCormack (1991b, 240–248).

45. Drawing from authors and texts that treated this subject, Solórzano y Pereira ([1648] 1972, 335, in the chapter on treasures, huacas, and burials) defined as treasure "any money, gold, silver, jewels, or other valuable personal property that was hidden long ago in secret places and reserved for the future, and of whose owners we no longer have news." His definition pointed out the occult, hidden quality of a treasure passed down through time and seemingly lying in wait for future use to be made of it. Accordingly, the bezoar stone constituted for the Spanish a treasure par excellence.

46. Álvarez ([1588] 1998, 69) defended the priests' practice of selling items confiscated from Indigenous peoples, claiming that commodities trade was useful and necessary to human existence and had nothing to do with idols and idolatry. Whether or not the priests engaged in this business was no excuse for Indians to be heretics.

47. Boxer (1963, 24) argues that both Garcia da Orta and Monardes were obviously

304 | Notes to Pages 54–59

swayed by the predominant tenets of their times and for this reason included the bezoar stone in their studies. Guerra (1961, 78) is even more critical of Monardes for including the bezoar stone in his *Historia medicinal*:

> In spite of his good training at the Complutense, Monardes included in his work all of the Arab writers' fantasies and repeated the stories written by Ahmad al-Ghafiqi, Avenzoar, Avicenna, Averroes, and especially Serapion. For this reason, the reader will find everything in his writings, from the poisoning of Miramamolín, King of Córdoba, miraculously saved by using the bezoar stone, to the case of King Edward of England, wounded with deadly poison by the Great Soldan and cured with the bezoar stone by the Grand Master of the Knights Templar.

48. Bezoar stones were still being collected during the eighteenth century. Pedro Franco Dávila had more than one hundred in his collection, considered to be the most complete assortment found in Paris (Amorós 1963, 32; Dávila 1767, 501–505). Throughout the eighteenth century, the Spanish Royal Pharmacy continued to send requests to New World governors for materia medica, including vicuña and guanaco bezoar stones, especially from La Paz, Oruro, and Chucuito provinces. See Archivo General de Indias (hereafter cited as AGI), Indiferente, 1552 (1736–1784). "Remisión de especies medicinales para la Real botica," in particular 1746–1747, 13–47v, and 1746, 68.

49. For instance, the Hunterian Museum in London received a bezoar in May 1827 from Henry Miller, who had acquired the stone in Patagonia: "The story or History attempted to be palmed upon Mr. Miller in the Country was, that it was a Stone from the head of a Lama, and possessed wonderful properties as a remedy; (or Antidote) if grated and taken in Cold Water it relieved Fainting etc. etc.!!! (I rather think Mr. Miller had given a good price for it, as he was a long time rather sceptical about its being valuable.)" Archives, Hunterian Museum—Royal College of Surgeons (hereafter cited as HM-RCS), "Donations Book to the Hunterian Museum" (1814).

Chapter 2. Exploring the Body-Interior

1. The Scottish anatomist John Hunter (1861, 189) observed, while writing about the dissection of the male sexual organs, that generative secretions could be tested by taste: "The semen would appear, both from the smell and taste, to be a mawkish kind of substance; but when held some time in the mouth, it produces a warmth similar to spices, which lasts some time." Moore (2005, 79–80) has similarly indicated the attention that Hunter gave to anatomy as a multisensorial art.

2. My reading of knowledge as a form of gain draws from Van den Abbeele (1992). According to Raj (2007, 29), in the field of natural history the resulting specialized knowledge itself constituted a product of value because its possession was a significant move toward the commoditization of newly discovered objects of natural history and the control of their circulation in global economies, which Europeans wanted to shape for their own benefit.

3. See Pomata (2011, 65–66) for an analysis of early usage of the term "autopsia." On autopsia as truthful reporting by authors, see Asúa and French (2005, 178–179).

4. Cook (2007, 21) notes that *historia* in the context of natural history emphasized learning or knowledge acquired from a process of inquiry. In this regard, as explored in the previous chapter, *historia* was linked to "hunting," insofar as "the hunt was no mere

Notes to Pages 60–69 | 305

leisurely academic examination of old books but an urgent investigation of natural things themselves" (22).

5. On building a new body of knowledge through *historia*, see Asúa and French (2005, 88–89).

6. Dransart (2007, 163) writes about how woven textiles can be compared to the tissue of the skin, which, as a living membrane or fabric, envelops or wraps the body. In parallel with these ideas, Roberts and Tomlinson (1992, 128) describe the enduring idea of skin as the "fabric of the body" in European dissection and anatomical studies from the early modern period, which serves as "a metaphor for the intricacies of the tissues and organs of human anatomy."

7. See Lecoq and Fidel M. (2000, 167–174) on the marking of camelids in southern Potosí. Ávila ([1598?] 2009, 53) described the use of the cut pieces from llama ears in the colonial period.

8. Abercrombie (1998) similarly highlights this difficulty for Andean scholars and their research.

9. These included minister (*ministro*), sorcerer (*hechicero*), priest (*sacerdote*), pontiff (*pontífice*), diviner or seer (*sortílego*), and augur (*agorero*). This terminology reinterpreted the role of officiant in the context of Catholic doctrine and provided a sense of the range and variety of functions understood to be a part of the idolatrous ritual of sacrifice (see Dedenbach-Salazar Sáenz 1990, 188). On Andean specialists more generally, see Mills (1997, 101–136).

10. Other colonial chroniclers and extirpators of idolatries described this method of sacrifice: Arriaga ([1621] 1968, 210) and Cieza de León ([1553] 1853, 430, 454). In addition to this form of sacrifice, known as *ch'illa*, some Andean communities sacrificed camelids by means of a ventral throat slit (Miller 1979). Based on ethnoarchaeological evidence and colonial documents, Miller (1979, 25–39) hypothesizes that the *ch'illa* method of slaughter may have been limited to Quechua-speaking communities, as to date there is little evidence of its practice in Aymara territory. See also Dedenbach-Salazar Sáenz (1990, 196).

11. Miller (1979, 30) provides four reasons in support of the *ch'illa* method of slaughter. First, it kills the animal quickly so that it suffers less; second, the blood does not spill out and can be more easily collected; third, Pachamama is not stained because the blood is contained in the thoracic cavity; fourth, in contrast to the belly's soft tissue, which can be easily pierced, the skin of the neck is thicker and tougher and more difficult to cut if a sharp knife is unavailable.

12. According to Sawday (1995, 25), "The [early modern] scientist who searched the cavities and recesses, the interior secrets, of the body was not faced with the 'ne plus ultra' confronting earlier, theologically-bound patterns of knowledge. Instead 'Plus Ultra'—'yet further,' the motto of the Emperor Charles V—became the watchword of the natural philosophers. . . . No limit was to be placed on the possibility of gaining understanding." Asúa and French (2005, 220–228) also explore the idea of "Plus Ultra" in the context of dissection-as-exploration.

13. Including the desire to uncover the precious metals secreted away in the heart of a mountain like Potosí.

14. My discussion here has benefited from Barthes (1975, 64) on the intersections of text, tissue, and textile. Pedro de Osma's reliance on Monardes's *Historia medicinal* can be understood in a slightly different context of knowledge generation that would

306 | Notes to Pages 69–76

have been familiar to many of the Spanish physician's European readers: the university anatomy lesson, where direct observation of a cadaver was guided by an authoritative text and a "demonstrator" (Carlino 1999, 11–12; French 1999, 15). In the field, however, Monardes's book was ultimately unhelpful, which is why the Indian boy had to "demonstrate" to the Spanish soldiers where and how to find the stones.

15. *Buche*, in its figurative sense, also signified "the heart's secret," as in someone loyally guarding a confidence or secret (*Diccionario de autoridades* [1726] 1963, 1:695).

16. On how visual representation bolstered scientific claims, see French (1999, 170) and Long (2002, 63, 76).

17. Pedro de Osma's letter indicates that scores of camelid guts were opened and searched for bezoars and that many people may have acquired a working knowledge of camelid anatomy. Osma and especially Feuillée, however, were the first known Westerners to dissect the camelid body and describe the details of the animal's anatomy. English naval commander John Narborough in the mid-seventeenth century documented his efforts near Port Desire to search the guanaco body for bezoars, but he did not provide information on the body-interior (Narborough et al. 1694, 32–33).

18. On the importance of the bezoar stone in eighteenth-century commerce, see Savary des Bruslons (1741, 1:477–478, 492).

19. Pratt (1992, 136) has similarly observed how "the conventions of travel and exploration writing (production and reception) constitute the European subject as a self-sufficient, monadic source of knowledge": therefore, most interactions that a traveler may have had with Indigenous peoples or other locals disappear, only to emerge here and there in the text as mere traces.

20. National Library of Medicine, History of Medicine Collection (hereafter cited as NLM HMC), W6P3, vol. 7481, Box 354, no. 13: John Hunter, *Directions, for Preserving Animals, and Parts of Animals for Anatomical Investigation; and Concerning Extraneous Fossils* (London: J. Adlard, 1809), 7. On the different tools, equipment, and guidebooks collectors needed in the field, see Larsen (1996).

21. Portús (1994) has identified a similar shift in eighteenth-century pictorial representations of the camelids. He argues that images of the animals prior to that century customarily depicted them in human and ethnographic environments, yet they increasingly appeared in isolation from any specific contexts during the eighteenth century. He suggests that this transformation is due to the camelids' diminishing role in most of Peru and Chile in comparison to the growing importance of imported European animals (1994, 66). Abercrombie (1998, 194) and others have argued that this kind of decontextualization and depersonalization had already commenced during the early colonial period.

22. For critiques of Buffon's ideas, see Cañizares-Esguerra (2001, esp. 44–51); Gerbi (1973, 3–34); and Poole (1997, 58–84).

23. According to Landes (2012, 27), Buffon and many of his contemporaries had the opportunity to examine exotic specimens coming in from the New World and the East, thanks to expanding global exchanges.

24. The two llamas were likely collected in England by Pierre Flandrin, who had worked as the director of the veterinary school at Lyon and later came to Alfort as the new chief director, following the death of former director Claude Bourgelat (Degueurce 2011, 43, 108). Flandrin traveled to England to acquire horses and mentioned seeing two llamas. It is likely that the llamas were brought to Alfort along with a nilgai,

Notes to Pages 76–82 | 307

several stallions, and other unidentified animals, one of which may have been the vicuña.

25. This portion of the chapter draws from Alberti (2011b) and Patchett, Foster, and Lorimer (2011).

26. The Spanish traveler Fray Diego de Ocaña ([1605?] 1969, 188) illustrated the male llama anatomy, possibly the only visual representation prior to the twentieth century.

27. A full history of the classification and nomenclature of the South American camelids can be found in Dransart (2002, 17–23) and Wheeler (2012).

28. Writing in the context of the arrangement of specimens in taxidermy exhibits and museum dioramas, Poliquin (2012, 101) raises the question of what constitutes a "typical" pose for animals and humans on display.

29. As Landes (2012, 24) clarifies, "By the time Buffon undertook his study of nature, embracing animals, plants, and minerals . . . naturalists had already done a great deal of work to clear away the mythical and fantastical presentations of animals, deriving particularly from the custom of combining real and imaginary animals in medieval bestiaries and illuminated manuscripts."

30. Bleichmar (2009, 305) also highlights the importance of visual images in the production of natural history knowledge in the eighteenth century.

31. As Alberti (2008, 83) observes, "Naturalization is what happens when categories or objects cease to be strange, and as such is an integral part of classification."

32. According to Lacépède and Cuvier (1801, 1), the llama lived at Alfort from 1773 to 1778.

33. See Degueurce (2011) and Simon (2002) for a detailed description of Fragonard's technique of preservation.

34. Boitard (1842), writing about the Menagerie of the Muséum d'Histoire Naturelle in Paris, noted how much could be learned from studying living animals but also that dead animals' dissected organs and their afterlives as stuffed specimens provided significant information for the anatomy laboratory. On the use of museum specimens as important resources for communicating an artifact's complex biogeographical narratives and the blurred border between nature and culture, see Alberti (2011a, 2011b) and Patchett, Foster, and Lorimer (2011).

35. Archives Nationales de France (hereafter cited as ANF), F/10/1294, Instruction Publique, Inventaire du Cabinet d'Anatomie de l'École Vétérinaire Nationale d'Alfort, 1783.

36. The Fragonard llama was likely prepared by someone other than Fragonard himself, because the animal did not arrive at the Veterinary School until two years after the anatomist's dismissal. Degueurce (2011, 210) has recently identified its creator as Fragonard's student, collaborator, and successor Jacques-Marie Hénon.

37. In this regard, see Degueurce's (2011, 14) discussion of Fragonard's *écorché* of a horse and rider.

38. For methods of preservation, see also Simon (2002, 66–67).

39. ANF, F/10/1294, Instruction Publique, Inventaire du Cabinet d'Anatomie de l'École Vétérinaire Nationale d'Alfort, 1783. The English translation is from Degueurce (2011, 110), but with two modifications. Degueurce rendered the French *pied* as "hoof" and *pieds* as "hooves"; I changed this to "foot" and "feet," respectively, since the llama does not have hooves and Fragonard did not use the term *sabot*.

308 | Notes to Pages 82–94

40. For instance, Ellenberger (1981, 10) observes how Fragonard masterfully brought dissected flesh to life, like a surgeon or sculptor. Poliquin (2012, 107) has shown how taxidermy creations can achieve "that uncanny spark of animation" and provoke a "tingling sensation" in the viewer, as if the animals had suddenly come back to life.

41. Alberti (2008, 81–84) shows how museum objects and museum nature and their meanings crisscross the nature/culture divide in complex and ever-changing ways.

42. For Degueurce (1999, 91–92), the Fragonard collection is as difficult to categorize as the objects displayed within it. Positioned somewhere between the pedagogical laboratory and the cabinet of curiosities, it reflects changing perceptions in the understanding of veterinary medicine as well as in the cultural reception of disease and anatomical display. Alberti (2005) and Simon (2002, 69) also discuss how museum objects inhabit multiple spaces. For more on the intersections of art and science in the study of picturesque anatomy, see Callen (1997).

43. Sue's work likely influenced Fragonard's own anatomical and preservations projects (Degueurce 2011, 48).

44. Commenting on the importance of color, Philippe Ariès noted how the beautiful hues of a cadaver just beginning to decompose could achieve the subtlety of works by Peter Paul Rubens and Nicolas Poussin (quoted in Blin 1981, 6). Price (1796, 183–184) found autumnal hues to be picturesque, arguing that subtle plays of color, "as well as forms, arise from age and decay."

45. Sournia (1981, 5) also suggests that the overinflation of the vessels was prepared deliberately, while Simon (2008, 153) observes that the process of injecting the veins and vessels with resins tended naturally to overinflate them, although he does not deny that Fragonard may intentionally have sought to create this dramatic effect.

46. As Carter (1988, 231–232) puts it, "Picturesque views might give rise to all kinds of pleasant ideas, but the primary pleasure they gave resided in their picturesqueness itself—in the fact that their structure of casually interlinked and contrasting forms enticed the eye (and the mind) to wander."

47. As Alberti (2008, 83) similarly notes, "Museum nature, so wild in appearance, is domesticated in its familiarity."

48. Drawing from Hetherington's (2004) work on the agential categories of absence and presence, Patchett, Foster, and Lorimer (2011, 126) describe haunting as the "persistence of processes that remain." Gordon (1997, 15) has also explored ghostly haunting, describing it as a sign that "something is missing—that what appears to be invisible or in the shadows is announcing itself, however symptomatically."

Chapter 3. From Curiosity to Commodity

1. For example, in April 1537, Venetian explorer Sebastian Cabot sent three llamas (*ovejas de la tierra*) to King Carlos V of Spain (Toribio Medina 1908, 181–182).

2. Fernández Oviedo y Valdés (1851–1852) told of taking on board a "Peruvian sheep" that had been given to him by Diego de Almagro in the city of Panama. The unfortunate animal died shortly after the vessel set sail and the remains were consumed by the men. He described the meat as "one of the most delicious in the world" (1:418).

3. Juan and Ulloa's complete manuscript was later published in London in 1826 with the title *Noticias secretas de América*.

4. For a description of Indigenous methods of hunting vicuñas, see Tschudi (1847, 313–315).

Notes to Pages 94–101 | 309

5. Archivo Histórico Nacional de España (hereafter cited as AHN), Códices, 751-B, "Vicuñas: Cédula de 30 de Agosto de 1777," Vid. Tom. 29, f. 205, no. 68.

6. *Mercurio Peruano* 1 ([March 27, 1791], 233) described the annual monies coming in from exports of vicuña wool as averaging 10,000 pesos, although this figure certainly did not consider internal or illegal trafficking in the fiber.

7. Other natural histories of that period covered similar themes, although they did not necessarily come to similar conclusions. See Molina (1788, 357, 363).

8. A copy of the entire *Quadro* can be viewed at https://museoecologiahumana.org /en/obras/encyclopaedia-and-mural-museum-of-peru-in-the-18th-century (2023).

9. Soule (2014, 4) describes the same use of local terminology in Martínez Compañón's *Trujillo del Perú*. For more on the history of the *Quadro*, the commissioner, the artist, and the images, see Bleichmar (2011) and Peralta Ruiz (2006).

10. The *Quadro*'s full text is transcribed in Barras de Aragón (1912).

11. Drawing in part from Peralta Ruiz (2006), Bleichmar (2011) has identified interconnections between the images in the *Quadro* and other pictorial collections, such as the *Trujillo del Perú* and the Alejandro Malaspina expedition (1789–1794). As for the *Quadro*'s camelids, the llama and alpaca especially appear to be adaptations from the Malaspina illustrations. Archivo del Museo Naval (hereafter cited as AMN), "Pinturas de la Expedición Malaspina 24 C-II-Llama, 1726-1-Paco, 1726-2-Llama."

12. AGI, Signatura Lima, 652, no. 24, "Duplicados de virreyes: Manuel de Amat y Junyent, Fecha Inicial: 14-03-1770," letter 282 from Manuel de Amat y Junyent, *virrey* of Peru, to Julián de Arriaga, secretary of the Indies, "Acusa recibo de la R.O. de 19 de junio de 1768 sobre las precauciones con que se deben criar y conducir las vicuñas, comunica las providencias tomadas no obstante las dificultades," 104–105. For additional attempts by Viceroy Amat to ship camelids to Spain, see AGI, Signatura Lima, 651, no. 59, "Duplicados de virreyes: Manuel de Amat, Fecha inicial 29-07-1769," letter 189 from Manuel de Amat, *virrey* of Peru, to Julián de Arriaga, secretary of the Indies, "Avisa del envío de tres carneros de la tierra y una vicuña en el navío de registro 'San Miguel' y seis liebres silvestres en el llamado 'El Aguila,'" 1; AGI, Signatura Lima, 652, no. 182, "Duplicados de virreyes: Manuel de Amat y Junyent, Fecha inicial: 15-01-1772," letter 514 from Manuel de Amat y Junyent, *virrey* of Peru, to Julián de Arriaga, secretary of the Indies, "Avisa el envio de tres vicuñas, un guanaco y un papagayo en el navío 'San Lorenzo,' bajo la custodia del capitán de fragata José Bustillos."

13. Archivo General de Palacio (hereafter cited as AGP), Patrimonios Aranjuez, Ganado, Caja 14242, 1787, Aranjuez, October 24, Orders sent to Gobr. de Aranjuez. Palacio, December 24, 1787, Adm. Miguel de Trejo, 1–1v.

14. Wheeler, Russel, and Redden (1995, 834) have shown how both Quechua and Aymara pastoralists developed strategies for breeding for pure colors in llamas and alpacas, primarily for use in sacrifices and textile production. See also Dransart (2002, 138–141) and Flores Ochoa (1988).

15. On the preference for white alpaca fiber, see Gosse (1855, 321); Mort (1850, 59); Orlove (1977, 98); and Walton (1811, 136–137). As noted, herding communities have been obliged to privilege white fleeces over other colors because of the money they bring in (see Bustinza Choque 1989, 117–118; and Flores Ochoa 1988, especially 127n8). Today Andean herders are working to recover the full range of natural colors, although white fleeces still produce the most revenue.

16. See Mello Pereira (2013, 115–116) for more on ventures to ship guanacos from Río de la Plata to Spain.

310 | Notes to Pages 102–111

17. Beliardy, Bexon, and Folie's original memoirs referred to by Buffon are found in Muséum National d'Histoire Naturelle (hereafter cited as MNHN) Archives, MS 864 IIID. The documents include Beliardy, "Mémoire sure les lamas" (Paris, April 21, 1779); Folie, "Observations concernant le mémoire remis à Monsieur de Tolozan au suget des lamas, alpacas et vigognes" (Paris, n.d.); and Bexon, "Observations relatives à l'utilité et à la possibilité de l'education du lama et de la vigogne en France: D'après le mémoire communiqué de M. Béliardi" (Paris, n.d.). Given some differences between the archival documents and Buffon's published report, I refer to both sources.

18. MNHN Archives, MS 864 IIID. During the eighteenth century, the French engaged in substantial commercial activity on South America's west coast and were very familiar with these trade routes (Hanke in Hanke and Mendoza [1700–1736] 1965, lxxi–lxxii).

19. MNHN Archives, MS 864 IIID.

20. MNHN Archives, MS 864 IIID.

21. In addition to these larger projects from the late eighteenth century to extract camelids, smaller efforts in Europe were contemplated as well. See, for example, Nélis 1780.

22. Other sources have the llamas arriving in 1803 (Houdaille 1959, 118n38; Jouanin 1997a, 117).

23. See McClellan (1992) on Saint Domingue as a thriving center for the combined enterprises of scientific and colonial development.

24. Walton (1844, 185) provided a brief account of the animals' travels overland to Cartagena from Peru, stating that they were accompanied by an Indian shepherd.

25. While Rojas de Clemente undoubtedly was correct about Zea sharing information with Josephine, archival and published documents indicate that her interest in vicuñas and alpacas began well before the publication of the second piece. The two articles cited by Rojas Clemente were published in "De las vicuñas" (1801) and Le Goux de Flaix (1804), respectively. The first article described the economic benefits to be derived from vicuñas, llamas, and alpacas. Bringing these animals to Spain, the author argued, would provide recompense for Europe's enrichment of America with its horses, cattle, and agricultural imports ("De las vicuñas" 1801, 263–269).

26. A copy of Camacho's letter is transcribed in Harcourt (1950, 260–261). The president of the Real Audiencia of Quito, Francisco Luis Héctor, Baron de Carondelet, was to confer upon Camacho a "maestría de plata" (authorization entrusting him with the care of the valuable cargo) for the project. AGI, Lima, 727, no. 31, letter 167 from Marqués de Avilés, *virrey* of Peru, to Miguel Cayetano Soler, minister of finance, "Se conferirá una maestría de plata de las del puerto del Callao a José Camacho y le encargará que éste conduzca, si las tiene domesticadas, algunas alpacas, vicuñas, y guanacos."

27. Musée de Malmaison (hereafter cited as AMM) Archives, MM.68.8.6.i. (2 pluviôse an XII, January 23, 1804), "Onze brouillons de lettres intimes de Francastel à l'impératrice Joséphine."

28. AMM, MM.68.6.c. (29 pluviôse an XII, February 19, 1804), "Onze brouillons de lettres intimes de Francastel à l'impératrice Joséphine."

29. Quoted in communication from Viceroy Sobremonte, March 25, 1804: Archivo y Biblioteca Nacionales de Bolivia (hereafter cited as ANB), ECn.69 1804–1805, correspondence regarding Josephine Bonaparte's request for vicuñas and alpacas, 9.

Notes to Pages 111–121 | 311

30. ANB, ECn.69 1804–1805, correspondence regarding Josephine Bonaparte's request for vicuñas and alpacas, March 25, 1804, 1r–2v.

31. ANB, ECn.69 1804–1805, correspondence regarding Josephine Bonaparte's request for vicuñas and alpacas, letter to Ramón García de León y Pizarro, president of the Real Audiencia and governor of Charcas, November 28, 1804, 5r–5v.

32. ANB, ECn.69 1804–1805, correspondence regarding the request of Josephine Bonaparte for vicuñas and alpacas, letter from Manuel M. Garrón, Guayllamarca, November 13, 1804, 6r–6v.

33. ANB, ECn.69 1804–1805, correspondence regarding Josephine Bonaparte's request for vicuñas and alpacas, 5r–8v.

34. ANB, ECn.69 1804–1805, correspondence regarding Josephine Bonaparte's request for vicuñas and alpacas, letter from viceroy Sobremonte, Buenos Aires, January 25, 1805, 9r.

35. The archival record does not explain how García came by the animals. According to Escobari de Querejazu (2014, 146), the animals were collected in Huancavelica.

36. Archivo Nacional de Chile/Archivo de la Capitanía General (hereafter cited as ANC/ACG), vol. 405, no. 6, 5-3-1805, "Sobre conducción a España de llamas y vicuñas," Santiago, letter from Julián García to Royal Treasury, March 20, 1805, 105–105v.

37. ANC/ACG, vol. 405, no. 6, 5-3-1805, "Sobre conducción a España de llamas y vicuñas," Santiago, 114. See also Escobari de Querejazu (2014, 145–150).

38. ANC/ACG, vol. 405, no. 6, 5-3-1805, "Sobre conducción a España de llamas y vicuñas," Santiago, receipts, Julián García to Royal Treasury, March 20, 1805, 107–109.

39. ANC/ACG,, vol. 405, no. 6, 5-3-1805, "Sobre conducción a España de llamas y vicuñas," Santiago, letter from Julián García to Royal Treasury, March 20, 1805, 105v.

40. ANC/ACG, vol. 405, no. 6, 5-3-1805, "Sobre conducción a España de llamas y vicuñas," Santiago, March 21, 1805, letter from Manuel Hernández and José Samaniego y Córdoba, Royal Treasury, Santiago, March 21, 1805, 119–119v.

41. See Ridder de Zemboraín (1998) for more on Correa Morales and his spendthrift ways.

42. According to Ridder de Zemboraín (1998, 46), the flock consisted of three alpacas, two vicuñas, three alpaca-vicuña crosses, two llamas, and three alpaca-llama crosses, for a total of thirteen animals. Terán (Theran 1821, 19) described the shipment as originally consisting of thirty-six animals. Terán's account of the royal camelids was published in Portuguese in Paris, where his name appeared as Francisco de Theran. See also Núñez (1898, 301).

43. This appeared to coincide with King Carlos IV's initial intentions. The original order had had two objectives: to fulfill Josephine's request *and* to bring some of the animals to Spain for acclimatization (Theran 1821, 16).

44. Martín Polo (personal communication, June 20, 2015) calculates that Rojas likely wrote the manuscript in December 1809, before he left for France in January 1810.

45. On Quechua and Aymara nomenclatures for alpaca-llama crosses, see Dransart (2002, 67); Moore (1989, 126); and Yapita, Arnold, and Espejo Ayca (2014, 37). Regarding the coarsening of camelid fiber through the intermixing of the species, see Wheeler, Russel, and Redden (1995, 834, 839).

312 | Notes to Pages 122–135

46. As for the animals' fate, a few survived at the Sanlúcar garden for three years. Their demise was attributed to the climate being too mild and the scarcity of food resulting from political turmoil. Archivo Municipal de Cádiz (hereafter cited as AMC), Sociedad Económica Gaditana (SEGAP), Legajo 3.420, "Carta de Juan Colón a la SEGAP, Sanlúcar el 4 de diciembre de 1843"; see also Bory de Saint-Vincent (1823, 216).

47. *Revue Encyclopédique ou Analyse Raisonnée des Productions les Plus Remarquables dans la Littérature, les Sciences et les Arts* (Paris) 14 (March 4, 1822): 204.

48. *Revue Encyclopédique ou Analyse Raisonnée des Productions les Plus Remarquables dans la Littérature, les Sciences et les Arts* (Paris) 14 (March 4, 1822): 204. For the commission's decision to send its report to the minister of the interior, see *Annales de Chimie et de Physique* (Paris) 19 (1822), 419–420.

Chapter 4. The Science of Acclimatization

1. One such project was the flock of alpaca-vicuña hybrids of a priest from Macusani: see Stephenson (2023).

2. For a history of the term "acclimatization" and the development of acclimatization societies, see Gillbank (1986, 1996a); Lever (1992); and Osborne (1994).

3. Brantz (2007, 87) calls attention to a basic paradox structuring acclimatization projects: "on the one hand, to acclimatize an animal or plant meant to bring it under the civilizational forces of a nation and its socioeconomic landscape; yet, on the other hand, it also underscored that nature continued to be the decisive force in acclimatization since humans might bring animals to new habitats, but natural factors like climate, diet, and specific modes of life still determined whether an animal or plant would be able to adapt."

4. Archivo, Museo Nacional de Ciencias Naturales (Madrid), ACN0328/017, "Expediente sobre la concesión de una medalla de oro al Rey de España y condecoraciones a otros Españoles," Paris/Madrid, 1858-02-10/1858-06-30, doc. 1, letter from Isidore Geoffroy Saint-Hilaire to Mariano de la Paz Graells, February 13, 1858.

5. ANF, F/17/3213, "Mr. ROEHN, Eugène. Voyageur-naturaliste, zoologist. Mission, Indemnité: 1860–1883"; ANF, F/12/5257, "Eugène Roehn naturaliste à Paris. Légion d'honneur 1861."

6. The itemized budget of Barthélemy-Lapommeraye (1847, 214–215), based on total expenditures of 100,000 francs, details the (anticipated) costs such an expedition might incur.

7. ANF, F17/3003/B, 1867, "Demande de mission pour l'Himalaya (exploration au point de vue de la flore médicinale, et la zoologie et de la minéralogie)"; ANF, F/12/5257, "Eugène Roehn naturaliste à Paris. Légion d'honneur 1861"; Roehn (1855).

8. Though the full story of Roehn's first two shipments falls outside the scope of this chapter, let me offer an overview here: the first flock that Roehn sold in Havana eventually landed in Spain and resulted in the king's gold medal, while the second flock was taken to New York City, where it was purchased by Benjamin Gee, a British entrepreneur, and taken initially to Glasgow. Ten of Gee's animals were eventually shipped to Australia.

9. Roehn and the Acclimatization Society reached an agreement on the alpaca expedition in early March 1859. He departed for South America a few weeks later after acquiring financial backing from the French commercial house Lefebre, Roussel et Cie of Panama (Roehn 1860, 498).

Notes to Pages 135–146 | 313

10. On the way in which the popular press helped to create scientific celebrities, see Dawson, Noakes, and Topham (2004, 17).

11. See, for example, "Le Chimborazo: Ascensions diverses" (1851).

12. A copy of the painting can be found at https://www.metmuseum.org/art/collection/search/10481 (2023).

13. The inclusion of the figure of a child near the cauldron suggests that men and their sons, or even families, may have accompanied Roehn, a feature not uncommon in Andean llama caravans (see Browman 1990, 402; Lecoq 1997, 180; Medinaceli G. 2010, 190).

14. On conflicts between Indigenous communities and the state, see Choque Canqui et al. (2003) and Larson (2004, 214–215).

15. The Panama railroad was completed in 1855, shortly before Roehn's expedition, making it possible to cross the isthmus in just a few hours (see Manthorne 1989, 47).

16. The author's comparison of the alpacas and their range of colors to those found in a bed of flowers anticipates similar language used by Fuentes (1866, 75–76, 1867, 78–79) to describe the ethnic and racial diversity of the city of Lima at the time. See Poole (1997, 161) for an analysis of Fuentes's description of Lima as a "field of flowers." So-called weaker physiognomies were perceived to be less likely to survive in the long run, giving rise to the idea among nineteenth-century Andean urban elites that the Indigenous populations were slowly dying out.

17. Although some European scientists believed that vicuña hunts were responsible for diminishing numbers of the animals, others, like Tschudi (1847, 315), argued that these assertions were exaggerated.

18. ANF, F17/3003/B, 1867, "Demande de mission pour l'Himalaya (exploration au point de vue de la flore médicinale, et la zoologie et de la minéralogie)."

19. The archival evidence suggests that this was Roehn's last effort to obtain Andean camelids. For information on his later life, see ANF, F/12/5257, "Eugène Roehn naturaliste à Paris. Légion d'honneur 1861"; *Sydney Morning Herald,* July 9, 1870, and December 30, 1875; *Votes and Proceedings of the Legislative Assembly, with the Various Documents Connected Therewith* (hereafter cited as *VPLA-S*), vol. 4, 1875, 631–635; and *Argus* (Melbourne), February 5, 1880.

20. Archivo Histórico Ministerio de Relaciones Exteriores/Fondo: Comunicaciones Recibidas de la Legación del Ecuador en Francia (hereafter cited as AHMRE/F: CRLEF, 1861–1884. C.19.2. vol. 2, doc. 000084, March 15, 1862; and doc. 000165–166, November 30, 1862. In 1857 García Moreno pushed for an expanded curriculum in the theoretical and applied sciences in the Ecuadorian secondary school system that would better prepare students for industry and manufacturing as well as for further training at the higher level. His goal was realized with the founding of the Polytechnic School in Quito a few years later (Pólit Laso 1923, 60–70).

21. AHMRE/F: CRLEF, C.19.2, vol. 2, doc. 000078, February 28, 1862.

22. Archivo Histórico Banco Central del Ecuador/(Fondo) Jacinto Jijón y Caamaño (hereafter cited as AHBCE/JJC), 01535, Correspondencia Antonio Flores, invitations to scientific institutes, Paris, January 8, 1863.

23. García Moreno cautioned Flores that the arrangement would require great care to keep the animals alive en route (Villalba F. 1976, xxi).

24. AHBCE/JJC, 01529, Correspondencia Antonio Flores, 1862, letter from minister of foreign affairs (Paris) to Antonio Flores, August 11, 1862.

25. AHMRE/F: CRLEF, vol. 2, C.19.2, doc. 000188, December 5, 1862.

26. AHMRE/F: CRLEF, vol. 2, C.19.2, doc. 000173–000174, December 15, 1862.

314 | Notes to Pages 146–157

See also Drouyn de Lhuys's thank-you to Flores: AHBCE/JJC 01535, Correspondencia Antonio Flores, 1863, letter from Drouyn d'Lhuys to Antonio Flores, February 11,
1863; AHBCE/JJC, 01537, Correspondencia Antonio Flores, 1863, letter from Antonio Flores to his father General Juan José Flores, January 15, 1863.

27. AHMRE/F: CRLEF, vol. 2, C.19.2, doc. 000227, January 31, 1863; AHBCE/
JJC 01537, Correspondencia Antonio Flores, 1863, letter from Antonio Flores to his
father General Juan José Flores, January 31, 1863. For similar observations by García
Moreno, see AHBCE/JJC, 00161, vol. 1, letter 127, from García Moreno to General
Juan José Flores, April 16, 1862.

28. AHBCE/JJC, 00167, vol. 4, 1863, letter 75, from Gabriel García Moreno to
General Juan José Flores, August 22, 1863. On the reception and gifts offered to the
French warship commanders and their officers on arrival, see AHBCE/JJC, 00.63,
"Copiador de oficios año de 1862 (y 1863)," July 26, 1863.

29. AHBCE/JJC, 00167, vol. 4, 1863, letter 73, from General Juan José Flores to his
son Antonio Flores, August 19, 1863.

30. AHBCE/JJC, 00167, vol. 4, 1863, letter 67, from García Moreno to General
Juan José Flores, August 19, 1863.

31. AHBCE/JJC, 00167, vol. 4, 1863, letter 91, from Gabriel García Moreno to
General Juan José Flores, August 26, 1863.

32. The territorial extension for alpacas is generally limited to southern Peru and
Bolivia (Flores Ochoa and MacQuarrie 1994b, 133).

33. Fabre included with his letter a memoir on llamas (Wisse 1849) prepared by a
French engineer. Wisse was an old friend of García Moreno's and one of his mentors
in scientific matters (Henderson 2008, 14).

34. See Bourguet (2010, esp. 397) for the multiple roles played by scientific travelogues and notebooks.

35. Upon arrival in France, seven of the Ecuadorian animals were shipped directly
to Algiers (*Bulletin de la Société* [1864], 213). Their safe arrival was later confirmed by
the governor of Algeria, who announced that the llamas would be distributed between
the Algiers acclimatization garden and the sheepfold of Ben-Chicao, near Médéah
(288).

36. In 1859 the society awarded Barbey a "médaille de 2ᵉ classe" (second-class medal)
for having brought llamas into France and generously distributing them throughout
the country (*Bulletin de la Société* [1859], lxxxi). On the llamas placed in the Paris
Museum of Natural History, see ANF, AJ/15/844, Ménagerie, "Muséum d'Histoire
Naturelle. Ménagerie: Liste des lamas existant à la Ménagerie au 21 juillet 1860."

37. He later used the fleece to make a warm vest for himself (*Bulletin de la Société
Régionale* [1858], 345).

38. At the meeting of the Regional Society's General Assembly, the president
applauded the acclimatization project, although some concerns were raised about the
quality of Galmiche's llama-fiber yarn (*Bulletin de la Société Régionale* 2 [1860], 49).

39. On this same point, the Haute-Garonne Agriculture Society opted to use the
Spanish orthography (*llama*) to avoid confusion between the animal and the Buddhist
monk (Joly 1869, 1n1).

40. The 1861 price for Lima was 2,000 francs, while a second female was purchased
the following year for 1,100 francs. Archives Départementales de Meurthe et Moselle
(hereafter cited as ADMM), Folder 7M12: "Diverses Sociétés Agricoles. Renseigne-
ments, Société Régionale d'Acclimatation pour la Zône Nord-Est," December 28,
1861, and December 31, 1862.

Notes to Pages 157–169 | 315

41. Galmiche attributed the cause of death to Lima being overly sensitive to touch, because she refused to feed the baby. He reported that those working with the llama had made the mistake of using violence to constrain her, speculating that death may have been the result of a kick rather than starvation. The meat of the baby llama was shared with nearby residents, who pronounced it delicious (*Bulletin de la Société* [1862], 994–995).

42. The Paris Acclimatization Society indeed awarded Galmiche a first-class medal for his work training the llamas for household chores in the Vosges (*Bulletin de la Société* [1865], lxxiv).

Chapter 5. Andean Itineraries of Nineteenth-Century Camelid Science

1. Vietmeyer (1978) published an account of Ledger's life in *Smithsonian*, followed by Turner (1981). The biography by Gramiccia (1988) to date has served as the primary source of information on Ledger, his Indigenous companions, and his initiatives involving alpacas and quinine. Several articles have been published on or including Ledger since then, situating his alpaca and quinine projects in the context of the history of Australia, the wider acclimatization movement, and/or British colonial expansion (for example, Cowie 2017a; Gillbank 1986, 1996b; Mitchell 2010; Young 1983).

2. On entanglement and how an examination of its etymological and metaphorical nuances can serve as a fruitful avenue of approach for scholarship grappling with the complexities of intertwined European and Indigenous histories and legacies, see Bauer and Norton (2017).

3. The first shipments of alpaca fiber in Great Britain created problems for its processing because of the length of the staple. Ledger was sent to the Peruvian highlands in 1839 to persuade the Indians to shear their animals annually instead of the customary every two or three years. He explained that the Indians refused, claiming that it was "not their tradition and the animals would die" (Ledger 1864a, 96). British manufacturer Titus Salt (1803–1876) eventually developed machinery capable of spinning it. Peruvian exports in alpaca, llama, and vicuña fiber rose significantly as a result (Flores Galindo 1977, 69). The Andean tradition of shearing camelids every other year continues today (Dransart 2002, 107).

4. Charles Ledger's brother George (Ledger 1860–1861, 213–214) described how wool contracts were made between the mercantile company and the governor of an Andean district and the subsequent coercion of Indigenous pastoral communities in the process. See also Flores Galindo (1977, 61–78) and Orlove (1977, 51–62).

5. The *Sir Charles Napier* landed in Liverpool on April 15, 1843. Its cargo, financed by the shipowners and the Liverpool merchant company William & John Lockett, included "3 alpacas, 1 llama, and 250 llama and alpaca skins" and "300 t & 6000 bgs guano." Maritime Archives and Library, Merseyside Maritime Museum (hereafter cited as MALMMM), Customs, Liverpool, Bill of Entry. no. 7501, Saturday, April 15, 1843, "Ships' Reports." German immigrant and businessman Heinrich Witt (1992, 14) in his diary at the time ascribed the animals' deaths to their inability to withstand the heat of the tropics.

6. In some of his writings, Ledger (1859, 155) situated Indigenous unrest historically, describing how it resulted from centuries of oppression. Flores Galindo (1977, 88–89), drawing from the work of Piel (1973), argues that Indigenous unrest took place in a context of transformation of the southern region of Peru and growing power of the oligarchy, with the rise in the wool industry, inauguration of the railroad, transformation of Mollendo into a new port, growing British presence, incitement by military bosses,

316 | Notes to Pages 169–174

and emergence of banks and English-style clubs. On Indigenous unrest and changing social and economic structures in the Peruvian and Bolivian altiplano, see Jacobsen (1993, 107–197); Larson (2004); and Rivera Cusicanqui (2012, 96).

7. On behalf of the Peruvian treasury and prefects and governors, Manuel de Mendiburu published the official notice of legislation prohibiting the exportation of alpacas, arguing that the unique animals should be protected at all costs from extraction and advising customs officials to watch for anyone attempting to take them out of the country (*Suplemento al Peruano* [Lima] 16.11, August 7, 1846). The prefect of Arequipa had suspended the extraction of live vicuñas and alpacas the previous year. Archivo General de la Nación (hereafter cited as AGN), Libros Manuscritos Republicanos, H-4-1982, Ministerio de Hacienda, R-0423 (1843–1851): Expediente 202, Legajo 140, "Vicuñas: El Prefecto de Arequipa sobre haber mandado suspender la extracción de las alpacas y vicuñas vivas."

8. For more on the movements of camelids overseas to Great Britain during the 1830s–1840s, see Cowie (2017b, 106–113) and Fisher (2002a).

9. Ledger's estate may have been the Hacienda Chulluncayani, located in Bolivia near the town of Berenguela and conveniently close to the Peru-Bolivia border, between La Paz and Tacna, not far from Corocoro (Carlos Mamani Condori, personal communication, August 1, 2017). See also Ballivián and Idiáquez (1890, 45) and Weddell (1853, 97–98). Ledger's work smuggling cinchona seed with the aid of his longtime travel companion, Bolivian native Manuel Incra Mamani, falls outside the scope of this project.

10. For example, Weddell (1853, 99) describes his frustrated attempts to purchase alpacas from shepherds.

11. On the key role that camelids played in Andean social relations during the colonial period, see Medinaceli G. (2010).

12. The *Sydney Morning Herald* blamed the failed effort on Duniam for making promises that could not be fulfilled. He apparently was not the most scrupulous of men, having absconded earlier with monies raised for the purchase of some mummies from Peru (Carter, Vilches, and Santoro 2017, 400).

13. On the confidential negotiations, see Gramiccia (1988, 29); and New South Wales State Records Archives, Lands Dept. Miscellaneous Papers Re: Introduction of Alpacas to NSW (hereafter cited as SRNSW, NRS8362 (9/2659), letter from Charles Ledger to Sir John Young, captain general and governor in chief of New South Wales, Sydney, August 31, 1863.

14. On trust and gentlemanly civility in British history, see Shapin (2011).

15. Gramiccia (1988, 35–36) describes Ledger's arrangements before departing for Australia and his frustrated plans to ship the animals from Peru. See Pentland (1974, 226) concerning the poor condition of roads throughout Bolivia and between Bolivia and Salta.

16. Upon departure for New South Wales, Ledger had £15,000–£16,000 in capital. Mitchell Library Archives, MS 630/1: Series 01: "Annotated watercolour sketches by Santiago Savage, 1857–1858, being a record of Charles Ledger's journeys in Peru and Chile; with maps and notes" (hereafter cited as ML MSS 630/1).

17. Years later, Ledger (1864a, 93) described camelid manure as being more precious than gold during such extreme circumstances, especially as a much-needed fuel in areas of few trees: "On one occasion in particular, I believe that several, perhaps all of us, would have perished from the effects of intense cold, hunger, and dreadful

Notes to Pages 175–183 | 317

winds, but for meeting with two of these deposits that supplied us with two large fires for thirty hours, besides allowing our filling some forty sacks for future use."

18. Dalence ([1851] 1975, 180) notes that llamas from Carangas were known for being larger and more robust than those from other provinces, resulting in a lively commerce of the animals. Manrique (1983) highlights the significance of llamas and mules for these commercial routes, especially prior to the construction of the railroad.

19. Works on the history of Indigenous resistance to land reform and the assault on Indigenous territory on the part of hacendados include Choque Canqui et al. (2003); Choque Canqui and Quisbert Quispe (2010); Rivera Cusicanqui (1993); Serulnikov (2013); and Thomson (2002).

20. For more on the complexities of Andean Indigenous economic practices during the nineteenth century, see Langer (2004) and Platt (1995, 261).

21. On the connection between age, memory, and wisdom in the Andes, see Huanca L. (1991).

22. Harris (1995, 304) also observes how the tenets of liberal discourse described women as overall more irrational than men.

23. Ledger (1864a, 97) explained that the Peruvian authorities took immediate diplomatic action when they learned of his plan to export alpacas from their consuls in Bolivia and requested that the government of Bolivia impede his journey through the country.

24. Archivo Histórico de la Casa Nacional de Moneda (hereafter cited as AHCNM), PD 811 1855, Ministerio de Hacienda, Sucre, June 26, 1855, Ministerio de Estado del Despacho de Hacienda, 60–60v; and ANB, Ministerio de Hacienda, MH1855-177-9, Prefectura de Potosí, no. 60, Sucre, June 26, 1855, 12–12v.

25. ANB, Ministerio de Hacienda, vol. 140, no. 34, Tupiza, From the Southern General Command to the minister of state in the Office of Finance, letter, from Rafael Castro (governor of Chorolque [Tupiza]), July 5, 1855; AHCNM, PD 807, governor of Chorolque, Tupiza 1855, letter from Rafael Castro to prefect of Potosí, Tupiza, September 20, 1855, 42; AHCNM, PD 808 1855, Subprefectura Nor Lípez, letter received from José María Benavides, Gobierno de la Provincia de Lípez, Tagua, October 7, 1855, 54.

26. ANB, Ministry of Finance, MH1855-140-34, letter from José V. Rivera, Calama (Province of Atacama), to the state minister in the Office of Finance, September 30, 1855. With regard to the challenging circumstances of this region, Platt (1995, 293n64) observes that Lípez herders and muleteers refused to travel through the desert to the port of Cobija, surmising that this was due to the unavailability of food and water.

27. SRNSW, NRS8362 (9/2659), letter from Charles Ledger to Sir John Young, captain general and governor in chief of New South Wales, August 31, 1863. On the ill-defined borders between Bolivia and Argentina during the nineteenth century, see Abecia 1952.

28. *Unca*, also called *saguaipé*, is the common liver fluke (*Fasciola hepatica*), a parasite that infects the liver and other parts of the mammal's body (Francisco Rigalt, personal communication, January 17, 2017).

29. Rosa Olmos (1970, 32) speculates that Ledger selected Laguna Blanca after having seen reports of the area prepared by English businessman Samuel Fisher Lafone. For Bertrand (1885, 238), Ledger's experience in Laguna Blanca provided a valuable blueprint for introducing alpacas into Chile.

318 | Notes to Pages 183–197

30. ML MSS 630/1. Benjamin Poucel, who visited Ledger at Laguna Blanca, was less generous in his description of the place, observing how the violent force of the gale coming down off the cordillera felt like "a knife flaying the skin" (quoted in Rosa Olmos 1970, 29–30).

31. The Scientific and Literary Society was founded in Valparaíso on December 1, 1856, and was mainly composed of wealthy British and North American merchants, bankers, miners, railroad engineers, and stockbrokers residing there at the time. Swinglehurst became the group's first treasurer (Valenzuela González 1968).

32. The anonymous author went on to report that Ledger was elected unanimously to be an honorary member of the society, noting that "[t]he meeting was the most numerously and respectably attended of any we have ever witnessed" (quoted in Bradshaw 1858). The anonymous author was probably Ledger. Gramiccia (1988, 72) speculates that "Mr. Bradshaw" was also Ledger.

33. As late as 1864 there was still talk of Ledger bringing out his travel narratives (see Ledger 1864a, 90). Ledger published what were likely drafts of his book project in different venues, the most important being Ledger (1859). He presented this manuscript serially before the Australian Horticultural and Agricultural Society at its monthly meetings in 1859, the transactions of which were subsequently published in the *Sydney Magazine of Science and Art* (Ledger 1859). Unfortunately, Ledger's manuscript never appeared in its entirety, the journal having gone out of business before the final sections could be printed.

34. The Mitchell Library has recently digitized the images from Ledger's diary, which can be accessed through its online catalogue (2023: https://collection.sl.nsw.gov.au/record/94Rxr6y1).

35. Although the scouts were not identified, their clothing indicates that they were likely from the inter-Andean valleys north of La Paz. A description of this style of clothing and hair braid can be found in d'Orbigny (2002, 1090–1091). The Indian in the vicuña hunt (figs. 5.4, 5.5, 5.6) sports a similar hairstyle and clothing. See also Mercado (1991, 105, plate 35).

36. ML MSS 630/1; Stephenson (2023).

37. See Wonders (2005) on gender construction, hunting, and landscape.

38. Increased pressure from merchants in Peru required local Indigenous hunters to kill vicuñas at alarming rates to meet the demand for their fiber (Flores Galindo 1977, 76). The situation in Argentina was similar. Moreover, although Ledger proposed an alternate model for obtaining the precious fiber, he was not averse to dealing in vicuña skins: "To obtain the wool, the animal is killed, and some idea of the abundance of them can be formed, when I alone collected in one year 6,500 skins—they were sold in London, in 1850, at 3. 6d. each" (Ledger 1864a, 91).

39. Ledger paid the hunters five pesos for each baby vicuña, while they only received one peso for an adult hide (Poucel 1858, 183).

40. ML MSS 630/1.

41. ML MSS 630/1.

42. The going price for vicuña fiber was exorbitant. Poucel (1858, 184) describes hand spun and dyed garments made from vicuña that sold for six to twelve ounces of gold.

43. ML MSS 630/1.

44. Poucel attempted to export llamas and alpacas to France from Argentina, partnering for the project with Emilio Quevedo (Poucel 1860, 257); Ministère de l'Europe

Notes to Pages 197–212 | 319

et des Affaires Étrangères, Archives Diplomatiques, Affaires Diverses Politiques (hereafter cited as MEAE), vol. 2, Conf. Argentine, 1858, B. Poucel, "Lamas offerts au Jardin des plantes."

45. *Carte, provinces de Salta et Jujuy, partie de la Bolivie* (Paris: Fermin Didot Frères, 1873), David Rumsey Historical Map Collection, http://www.davidrumsey.com /luna/servlet/detail/RUMSEY~8~1~20544~510070:Carte,-provinces-de-Salta-et-Jujuy (2023).

46. ML MSS 630/1.

47. On the names and occupations of the members of this community of admirers and potential backers of Ledger's project, see Swinglehurst (1893, 173).

48. National Archives, United Kingdom (hereafter cited as KEW), JEH/1/41, Correspondence: Letters to John Elliot Howard from Charles Ledger: 1877–1883, Charles Ledger to John Elliot Howard, Salta, December 22, 1874 (emphasis in the original).

Chapter 6. Camelids in Australia

The source of the chapter epigraph is Charles Ledger to Sir Henry Parkes, June 1, 1860. ML. "Autograph Letters of Public Men, Australia." A68 CY Reel 822, 372–373.

1. "Mr. Charles Ledger and His Alpaca Contract with New South Wales," *Era* (Sydney), September 25, 1859.

2. New South Wales, *Votes and Proceedings of the Legislative Assembly, during the Session of 1861–62*, vol. 2, doc. 58-A, "Flock of Alpacas, and Claims of Mr. Ledger (Return in Reference to)" (hereafter cited as NSW, *VPLA*), letter from Charles Ledger to John Robertson, November 18, 1859, 1387; see also SRNSW, NRS8362 (9/2659), letter from Charles Ledger to Sir John Young, captain general and governor in chief of NSW, August 31, 1863.

3. SRNSW, NRS8362 (9/2659), letter from Charles Ledger to John Bowie Wilson, the secretary for lands, August 1, 1864.

4. Ledger's first wife, Candelaria Ortiz, died while he was in Laguna Blanca. For more on Ledger's biography, including his later life in South America and Australia, see Gramiccia 1988.

5. The New South Wales Acclimatisation Society was active from 1861 through the 1870s, when the government began adopting measures to control environmental damage caused by newly introduced species (Fletcher 2002, 53). On acclimatization in Australia, see Gillbank (1986, 1996a, 1996b) and Lever (1992).

6. With regard to espionage, see the proposal to bring alpacas to Australia by Bolivian Manuel Antonio Flores (1852–1854) and subsequent concerns that arose regarding his character and his venture: Mitchell Library, State Library of New South Wales (hereafter cited as ML), CY2217 A2364 A 2367, Secretary of State for Colonies— Circulars to the Governors of Victoria, 1851–1855, British Legation, Copy No. 111, letter from Colonel John Augustus Lloyd to rear admiral and commander in chief Fairfax Moseby, November 28, 1853, 242–243. See also ANB, Argentina, Consulado de Bolivia en Salta-Argentina: Correspondencia, 1854–1870, June 14, 1854, and June 27, 1854; "Al público," *La Época* (Cochabamba), April 27, 1852.

7. ML, Bonwick Transcripts Biography, A2000/vols. 1–4, Microfilm: CY 679, vol. 1: A–C, letter from George Bass to Captain Waterhouse, Sydney, January 5, 1803, 211.

8. Bader (1988) borrows the phrase "roaring days" from a poem by Australian poet Henry Lawson.

9. New South Wales and Van Dieman's Land were already exporting 200,000 pounds

320 | Notes to Pages 213–215

of sheep wool to England by 1821, and "the pastoral invasion of the country was underway" (Kociumbas 1992, 125). The average sheep required a minimum of three acres for grazing. Hence large herd holders moved their animals frequently to occupy increasingly distant pasturelands, leading to the practice later referred to as "squatting" (126).

10. *Victoria: Votes and Proceedings of the Legislative Council* (hereafter cited as VVPLC), vol. 15, February 1856, 161; VVPLC, *Victoria: Report from the Select Committee of the Legislative Council on the Alpaca* (hereafter cited as RSCLCA), March 7, 1856, iii–iv.

11. VVPLC, RSCLCA, March 7, 1856, iv. The report was accompanied by Minutes of Evidence, which consisted of queries made to those who had resided in South America. Topics included the alpacas' habits, diseases, acquisition, and care during the ocean voyage, including whether an Indigenous herder should be brought along. VVPLC, RSCLCA, February 13, 1856, and February 20, 1856, 1–5.

12. Edward Wilson, "The Alpaca," letter to the editor of the *Times* (London), July 17, 1858, 10. For more on Wilson, see Gillbank (1986, 1996a).

13. *Victorian Hansard Containing the Votes and Proceedings of the Legislative Council & Assembly of the Colony of Victoria* (hereafter cited as *VH*), vol, 4. 1858–1859, August 16, 1858, 15–16.

14. "Llamas," *Illustrated London News* 926.33, July 10, 1858.

15. Edward Wilson, "The Distribution of Animals," letter to the editor, *Times* (London), October 20, 1858. Wilson continued:

Why should the tables of our colonists not be supplied with an occasional hare or pheasant as well as yours? Why should our alderman be baulked of his salmon cutlet, or slice of venison, more than your alderman? Why should the heart of our ploughman not be gladdened by the song of the skylark? And why should the daughter of Australia, as she lingers with her lover upon a moonlit evening, be deprived of one more felicity, one more topic of conversation, in the nightingale perched in the neighboring thicket? We do not know how many such things are capable of much more extended distribution than at present, and we never shall know unless we try.

16. "Animals on Board the *Goddess*," *Argus* (Melbourne), February 17, 1859.

17. "Mr. Ledger and the Alpacas," *Sydney Morning Herald*, April 30, 1861.

18. "Animals on Board the *Goddess*," *Argus* (Melbourne), February 15, 1859; "The Alpacas," *Argus* (Melbourne), February 19, 1859.

19. "Mr. Ledger and the Alpacas," *Sydney Morning Herald*, April 30, 1861.

20. Wilson, "The Distribution of Animals," *Times* (London), August 29, 1860.

21. For a complete list of the animals landed and their place on the continuum of species purity, see *Journal of the Legislative Council of New South Wales* (Sydney) (1859–1860), vol. 5, part 1: "Alpacas (Correspondence Respecting)," Charles Ledger, letter to John Robertson, April 16, 1859, 372; also *VPLA-S* (1859–1860), vol. 4, 997–1005.

22. In reference to problems that could arise during a sea voyage, the British curator of the South African Museum argued that at least one person on board should have sole responsibility for the care of any animals and birds transported:

It is of little use putting them into the charge of one of the crew; even though the

Notes to Pages 216–217 | 321

captain be ever so obliging, bad weather comes on, every one has his station and *must* attend to it, and at the very time that the animals require most care and attention, and the reassuring presence of a face they know, are left to themselves; cages overthrown and deluged with salt water, food and water spilt, bedding wetted, and the animals themselves in mortal terror. Many are killed and maimed in their frantic efforts to escape, and not a few die of fright. This is no overdrawn picture. I have *seen* it many times in my frequent voyages (Layard 1865, 73; emphasis in the original).

23. "The Alpacas," *Sydney Morning Herald*, December 4, 1858.

24. *Victoria: Votes and Proceedings of the Legislative Council* (hereafter cited as VVPLC) (1858–1859), vol. 1, "Alpacas," letter from Charles Ledger to Joseph Herring, December 18, 1858, 2.

25. VVPLC (1858–1859), vol. 1, "Alpacas," letter from E. Montefiore to John O'Shanassy, January 3, 1859, 1–2.

26. *VH*, vol. 4 (1858–1859), December 14, 1858, 556. One assemblyman "hoped that the Chief Secretary would not enter into the communication in a very lukewarm spirit, but would initiate his correspondence in such a way as to show that he was really anxious to obtain the animals. When Mr. Macarthur introduced the merino sheep into New South Wales he was considered quite as much of an enthusiast as the hon. member of Collingwood [Embling] is at present" (556). Another member argued that this sort of enterprise was better suited to private initiative than to government involvement (556–557). A third asked Embling "why he had transferred his sympathies from the 'regal Koodoo' (a laugh) to the llama, the alpaca, and the vicuna (a laugh)" (557).

27. PROV, VPRS 1187/P0000/000003, "Letters out from Chief Secretary," May 1858–December 1858, letter from John Moore to Montefiore (Montefiore, Graham, and Co. of Melbourne), December 24, 1858, 491.

28. The crew and passenger list of the *Salvadora* registered Ledger as being accompanied by one servant and eleven passengers in steerage, who were described as non-European caretakers of the "llamas." A "J. Alexander" appears as a member of the crew, of British nationality, age twenty-four, listed as "AB" (able-bodied seaman). This was likely James Alexander Ávila, another of Ledger's shepherds (Ledger referred to him as Portuguese). A "Maria Ortez [*sic*]" was also with the group. Presumably this was Ledger's brother-in-law, Major Ortiz. SRNSW: Shipping Master's Office, Passengers Arriving 1855–1922, NRS13278, (X98-100) Reel 406, transcribed by Barbara Farquharson, 2005. A scan of the original is available online: https://marinersandships .com.au/1858/11/057sal.htm (2005).

29. VVPLA (1858–1859), vol. 1, "Alpacas," "Report of J. Herring [Ledger's agent] for information of such parties as may become purchasers of a flock of Peruvian sheep, now depasturing at Collingwood in New South Wales," 2–3.

30. "The Flock of Alpacas," *South Australian Advertiser* (Adelaide), March 9, 1859.

31. "The Llama," *Sydney Morning Herald*, January 4, 1859.

32. The records of the Australian Museum indicate that on June 15, 2009, three "llama-pacos" donated by Ledger, one a juvenile, were ordered to be destroyed by the museum's trustees. The collection's register lists the juvenile, likely the stuffed specimen noted here, as born in New South Wales (Original Registration, Old Collection 1717, 1718, 1719). On the destruction of museum taxidermy specimens, see Poliquin (2008).

322 | *Notes to Pages 217–221*

33. Archives of the Australian Museum (Sydney) (hereafter cited as AAM/AMS), 7 C: 30.59/19.

34. As Alberti (2005, 564) observes: "Collecting was civilizing; subsequently to donate to a worthy museum ensured that such an act remained visible in perpetuity and secured a lasting connection between person and object."

35. Public Record Office, Victoria (Melbourne) (hereafter cited as PROV, VPRS), 02223/P0000/000002/V2 Minute Book, Acclimatisation Society of Victoria (Melbourne), 1858–1861, March 15, 1859; *VH*, vol. 4 (1858–1859), February 22, 1859, 924. Regarding the silver ore collection, see AAM, Australian Museum Minutes Book, 1859, March 3, 1859; June 2, 1859; July 7, 1859.

36. NSW, *VPLA* (1858–1859), vol. 1, April 7, 1859, 277–278.

37. Ledger proudly described his warm reception by the British in Chile, including a dinner hosted in his honor in Valparaíso by "all the principal English Merchants at the Exchange" in August 1858. SRNSW NRS8362 (9/2659), letter from Charles Ledger to Sir John Young, Sydney, August 31, 1863.

38. SRNSW NRS8362 (9/2659), letter from Charles Ledger to Sir John Young, August 31, 1863.

39. In September 1859, in the effort to procure better compensation for Ledger and encourage him to stay in Australia with the alpacas, a group of his supporters raised a subscription "for the purpose of presenting Mr. Ledger with a testimonial." "Testimonial to Mr. Ledger," *Sydney Morning Herald*, November 19, 1859. An unspecified amount of money was presented to Ledger nearly a year later for the danger and financial sacrifice he underwent in introducing the alpacas to New South Wales. "Alpacas: Testimonial to Charles Ledger, Esq." *Sydney Morning Herald*, September 5, 1860.

40. *Journal of the Legislative Council of New South Wales* (Sydney), vol. 5, part 1 (1859–1860), letter from Charles Ledger to John Robertson, secretary for lands, May 13, 1859, 373.

41. Mitchell (2010, 66) notes that these exploration expeditions "could not be separated easily from the cultural power attached to the figure of the explorer in the mid-nineteenth century, associated with the conquest of the colonial landscape." See also Gillbank (1986) and Minard (2021, 19).

42. David E. Wilkie, "Minutes of Meetings" November 11, 1857, *Transactions of the Philosophical Institute of Victoria* (Melbourne) 2 (1857), xlvi.

43. Ferdinand Mueller, "An Historical Review of the Explorations of Australia," *Transactions of the Philosophical Institute of Victoria* (Melbourne) 2 (1857), 148 (delivered on November 25, 1857).

44. Letter from Charles Ledger to John Robertson, August 23, 1859, *Journal of the Legislative Council of New South Wales* (Sydney), vol. 5, part 1 (1859–1860), 377.

45. Writing about how voluntary risk-taking, such as ballooning, produces satisfaction and pleasure in Victorian travel accounts, Freedgood (2000, 76) argues that even though "fear is aroused, it is intentionally aroused, and for this reason it is accompanied by a sense of pleasure and security, as well as a more or less confident hope of a return to safety."

46. George Ledger (1860–1861, 218) also noted the significance of this discovery, observing that the wiry grass was not found in England, which might explain why the alpaca had not prospered there. Its discovery in the colonial antipodes portended the animal's successful adaptation.

47. George Ledger, Charles's staunch supporter, assisted him in many ways,

Notes to Pages 222–229 | 323

including by helping to confirm the importance of his scientific discoveries. He followed up on Charles's speculation that the native grasses of Australia were the same as the Andean *ichu* in correspondence with botanist William Hooker, the director of Kew Gardens. KEW, (George Ledger) Director's Correspondence, vol. 40: English Letters I–Y (1858–1861), 32–34.

48. "Alpaca Sheep: An Experiment Which Failed," *Sydney Morning Herald*, January 26, 1935.

49. "Interesting Narrative Respecting Alpacas in Australia," *Era* (Sydney), February 20, 1859.

50. "Mr. Charles Ledger and His Alpaca Contract with New South Wales," *Era* (Sydney), September 25, 1859.

51. See Charles Ledger, "Exports of Alpaca Wool," letter to the editor, *Sydney Morning Herald*, April 27, 1859.

52. IDUMEA, "The Alpacas' Remonstrance," *Sydney Morning Herald*, March 10, 1859; reprinted in *Argus* (Melbourne), May 4, 1859.

53. NSW, *VPLA*, letter from Charles Ledger to John Black, secretary for lands October 31 1859, 1387; "Shearing the Alpacas in New South Wales," *Star* (Victoria), November 17, 1859; "Probable Increase of the Alpacas," *Sydney Morning Herald*, August 13, 1860.

54. Tom Roberts, "Mr. Tom Robert's Picture, 'Sheep Shearing,'" letter to the editor, *Argus* (Melbourne), July 4, 1890. A digital copy of Roberts's painting (1890) can be found at https://www.ngv.vic.gov.au/explore/collection/work/2920 (accessed August 25, 2021).

55. Ledger collected eleven small bales of the shorn wool and forwarded them to London (NSW, *VPLA*, 1391–1392). Although Ledger expressed optimism over the fiber's improvement, Titus Salt, who purchased the bulk of the shipment, described the fleeces as only of fair quality. He found that they had been clipped too soon and therefore were too short for processing (Ledger 1860–1861, 217).

56. ML MSS 4651, PXB 528 Grambox2BunC2, *Local Government*, Brian Turner, "Llamas on the Darling Downs," March 1968, 25, 27.

57. One circus act for which Howe was famous involved "a flying somersault from a springboard over fourteen horses" (Muir 1989, 7).

58. Thomas Hall, "Llamas at Canning Downs: Amusing Shearing Operations," *Warwick Examiner and Times*, November 20, 1918. See also Clem Lack, "A Llama Farm That Failed at Canning Downs: Sheep Grazed Where Warwick Is Built Today," *Courier-Mail* (Brisbane), April 30, 1938.

59. NSW, *VPLA*, letter from Charles Ledger to John Robertson, October 8, 1859, 1386.

60. NSW, *VPLA*, letter from Charles Ledger to John Robertson, October 8, 1859, 1386; letter from Charles Ledger to John Black, November 18, 1859, 1387–1388.

61. NSW, *VPLA*, letter from Michael Fitzpatrick to Charles Ledger, November 28, 1859, 1389.

62. NSW, *VPLA*, letter from Charles Ledger to John Black, December 6, 1859, 1390.

63. NSW, *VPLA*, letter from Charles Ledger to John Black, December 6, 1859, 1390.

64. NSW, *VPLA*, letter from Charles Ledger to John Black, January 18, 1860, 1393–1394.

324 | Notes to Pages 230–234

65. NSW, *VPLA*, letter from Charles Ledger to the John Black, February 17, 1860, 1396; SRNSW NRS8362 (9/2659), Charles Ledger to John Robertson, "Classification of flock on 1st Instant, also specification of losses from April 28, 1859, to 1st February 1860."

66. NSW, *VPLA*, letter from Charles Ledger to John Black, February 17, 1860, 1396.

67. NSW, *VPLA*, letter from Charles Ledger to John Black, February 17, 1860, 1396–1397. Ledger updated the public in August 1860 on the health of the alpacas, including the successful births of many young, all while enduring nine days of nonstop rain with no shelter. Along with improved wool, he contended that this was a sure sign that the animals were adapting to the Australian climate. *Yass Courier*, reprinted in "The Alpacas," *Empire* (Sydney), August 22, 1860.

68. NSW, *VPLA*, letter from Charles Ledger to John Robertson, May 11, 1860, 1403–1404. Ledger sent the secretary a bill in July for expenses related to the alpacas. His purchases included tobacco for dipping the animals, barrels for soaking the tobacco, lard to smear on the alpacas, "[m]ercurial ointment and sulphur," and strychnine for poisoning the dingos. NSW, *VPLA*, letter from Charles Ledger to John Robertson, July 18, 1860, 1406. These expenditures were allowed. NSW, *VPLA*, letter from Michael Fitzpatrick to Charles Ledger, August 8, 1860, 1406.

69. VVPLA, "Alpacas," doc. A—no. 5 (1858), vol. 1, letter from Charles Ledger to Joseph Herring, December 18, 1858, 2.

70. "Alpaca Correspondence," letter from Charles Ledger to John Robertson, June 15, 1859, and "Enclosure in No. 9. (Translation from Spanish)," June 15, 1859," *Journal of the Legislative Council of New South Wales* (Sydney), vol. 5, part 1 (1859–1860), 375–376. Ledger described Alexander elsewhere as "tolerably useful" and "intelligent and willing," although not overly knowledgeable about the alpacas. NSW, *VPLA*, letter from Charles Ledger to John Black, November 18, 1859, 1388.

71. "Testimonial to Mr. Ledger," *Sydney Morning Herald*, November 29, 1859.

72. NSW, *VPLA*, letter from Charles Ledger to John Black, November 18, 1859, 1388.

73. "Alpaca Correspondence," letter from Charles Ledger to John Robertson, and "Enclosure in No. 9 (Translation from Spanish)," *Journal of the Legislative Council of New South Wales* (Sydney), vol. 5, part 1, June 15, 1859, 376.

74. NSW, *VPLA* (1861–1862), vol. 2, letter from Charles Ledger to John Robertson, April 13, 1860, 1400.

75. NSW, *VPLA* (1861–1862), vol. 2, letter from Michael Fitzpatrick to Charles Ledger, April 19, 1860, 1400.

76. NSW, *VPLA* (1861–1862), vol. 2, letter from Charles Ledger to John Robertson, May 11, 1860, 1400–1401.

77. NSW, *VPLA* (1861–1862), vol. 2, letter from Charles Ledger to John Black, February 22, 1860, 1398.

78. NSW, *VPLA* (1861–1862), vol. 2, letter from Charles Ledger to John Black, February 17, 1860, 1397.

79. NSW, *VPLA* (1861–1862), vol. 2, letter from Charles Ledger to John Robertson, February 28, 1861, 1415. Ledger's request was approved. NSW, *VPLA*, 1861–1862, vol. 2, letter from Michael Fitzpatrick to Charles Ledger, April 12, 1861, 1415.

80. "Mr. Ledger and the Alpacas," *Empire* (Sydney), November 13, 1862 (emphasis in the original).

Notes to Pages 230–234 | 325

81. NSW, *VPLA*, 1861–1862, letter from Charles Ledger to John Robertson, August 7, 1860, 1409. Ferdinand Mueller reported that the wool of the Victorian llama-alpacas was much coarser than the wool of pure alpacas and the overall yield was relatively low. He anticipated that the addition of the NSW male alpacas would hasten the process of improving the wool. *Victoria: Papers Presented to Both Houses of Parliament by Command of His Excellency the Governor* (hereafter cited as *VPPHP*) (1859–1860), Legislative Assembly of Victoria (hereafter cited as LAV), vol. 4, doc. 37, January 12, 1860, 7–8; NSW, *VPLA* (1861–1862), letter from Michael Fitzpatrick to John O'Shanassy, chief secretary of Victoria, October 19, 1860, 1411.

82. NSW, *VPLA* (1861–1862), letter from Charles Ledger to John Robertson, September 1, 1860, 1408.

83. NSW *VPLA* (1861–1862), letter from Ferdinand Mueller to John Robertson, November 5, 1860, 1410; see also NSW *VPLA*, letter from J. Moore, under colonial secretary for Victoria, to Charles Cowper, colonial secretary, New South Wales November 7, 1860, 1411.

84. Letter from Charles Ledger to Ferdinand Mueller, *Argus* (Melbourne), October 30, 1860, included as part of Mueller's report "Our Llamas," *Argus* (Melbourne), November 3, 1860.

85. *Transactions of the Royal Society of Victoria* (Melbourne), vol. 5 (1860), Meeting, October 29, 1860, xx. The Royal Society became the Acclimatisation Society of Victoria in 1861. See Gillbank (1986) for a history of the society.

86. PROV, VPRS 02223/P0000/000002/V2 Minute Book, Acclimatisation Society of Victoria (1858–1861), letter from Charles Ledger, read at the August 20, 1860, meeting, which noted that the consultation with Nicholson was reported at the November 5, 1860, meeting of the society.

87. *VH* (1860–1861), vol. 6. The Legislative Assembly voted on the monies at its April 30, 1861, meeting (780).

88. PROV, VPRS 08850/P00001/000050, Royal Melbourne Zoological Gardens Archives (1861–1981), Box 050, "Report of the Provisional Committee to the Members of the Acclimatisation Society of Victoria," August 7, 1861, 10. The report states that Ledger was nominated to be an honorary member of the society "in testimony of his great services to the cause of acclimatisation by the introduction of a large number of Alpacas to Australia."

89. PROV, VPRS 2223/P/0000/000001/V2, Acclimatisation Society of Victoria, First Minute Book, 1861–1863, Meetings, May 28, 1861, 28; and June 3, 1861, 34–37.

90. PROV, VPRS 2223/P/0000/000001/V2, Acclimatisation Society of Victoria, First Minute Book (1861–1863), June 3, 1861, meeting, 35.

91. PROV, VPRS 2223/P/0000/000001/V2, Acclimatisation Society of Victoria (Melbourne), First Minute Book (1861–1863), Meetings, June 19, 1861, 45; and July 17, 1861, 51–52.

92. In the event of his demise, Ledger requested that any monies owed him be distributed among his children. SRNSW, NRS8362 (9/2659), letter from Charles Ledger to the treasurer, Acclimatisation Society of Victoria, September 4, 1861.

93. SRNSW, NRS8362 (9/2659), letter from Charles Ledger to Sir John Young, August 31, 1862.

94. See also "Goulburn, from Our Correspondent," *Sydney Morning Herald*, March 24, 1862.

326 | Notes to Pages 238–241

95. In the year of the London Exhibition, Charles Ledger and Charlotte Olliver (1818–1892) were married on October 23, 1862, in Liverpool, New South Wales.

96. In a lecture on acclimatization presented in Sydney, Bennett (1862, 18) characterized alpaca meat as "tender, wholesome, and savory. When of a proper age, and well fed, it is described as small-grained and rather mottled, the fat white and firm, and when from three to four years old, of full flavour. It is not a greasy, but rather a juicy meat, and easily digested."

97. NSW, *VPLA* (1861–1862), letter from Charles Ledger to John Robertson, June 25, 1861, 1416. Fitzpatrick's letter authorizing Ledger's request was dated July 10, 1861.

98. "Alpacas and Llamas in Australia," *Illustrated London News* 39, December 14, 1861.

99. See also "The Alpacas," *Sydney Morning Herald*, September 21, 1861; and "The Ministerial Alpaca Lunch," *Maitland Mercury & Hunter General Advertiser*, September 12, 1861. Ledger speculated that in fifty years the number of alpacas in Australia would reach 5,606,720, with wool production reaching some 39,247,040 pounds. "Ledger's Alpacas in Australia," *Illustrated London News* 39, December 14, 1861.

100. Drawing from the work of Darian-Smith (2008) and Edmonds (2006) on the significance of nineteenth-century exhibitions, Mitchell (2010, 58) notes how these displays became "sites of confidence, exuberance and power, which slipped back and forth between capitalism, science and populist entertainment," thereby enabling "empire-builders" to "celebrate their Britishness, flaunt their achievements and play out colonial and racial dynamics," all while encouraging the attending public's participation.

101. See also "The Alpacas," *Sydney Morning Herald*, September 21, 1861; and "The Ministerial Alpaca Lunch," *Maitland Mercury & Hunter General Advertiser*, September 12, 1861.

102. The Acclimatisation Society of Victoria's acclimatization dinner took place at Menzies Hotel in Melbourne. Although no alpaca was served, the fare included a number of exotic dishes created from local and imported animals and fowl. These dishes were given elegant French names to alleviate potential misgivings: "le wombat au lièvre" (wombat with hare) and the Cape Barren goose "à la Soubise." The "fretful porcupine" became "le porc-épic aux truffes" (porcupine with truffles) as an important part of the "second service, a real luxury, divested of the horrors of his quills." Attendees praised the skillful cooks and the contributors of the animals sampled. "What amount of Machiavellian craft was wanted to disguise a 'musk duck,' and to serve it as 'le canard musc roti,' was a problem second only to the amount of courage required to eat it. But the difficulty was met and managed." "The Acclimatisation Dinner," *Argus* (Melbourne), October 16, 1861.

103. Mitchell (2010, 59) similarly called attention to these "visceral" and "even bloodthirsty" aspects of the alpaca meal and the presentation of the damaged meat and carcass.

104. See, for example, Ledger (1860a, 1860b, 1864b).

105. "Introduction des lamas et vigognes en Australie," *Bulletin de la Société* 7 (1860).

106. "Alpacas and Llamas in Australia," *Illustrated London News* 39, December 14, 1861. The meeting took place on November 20, 1861 (*Journal of the Society of Arts and of the Institutions in Union*, November 22, 1861, vol. 10, no. 470, 16). The Mitchell Library holds Ledger's medals today (see ML Yold8qW9).

Notes to Pages 241–244 | 327

107. Although Ledger openly criticized the Peruvian Indians for their breeding practices here, Ritvo (1997, 113–120) has shown that Victorian breeders of dogs, horses, and cattle included strong proponents as well as critics of "in and in breeding" or inbreeding.

108. "New South Wales Products at the Great Exhibition," *Empire* (Sydney), August 18, 1862.

109. See, for example, "Notes on Wool," *Courier* (Brisbane), July 31, 1862.

110. Charles Ledger quoted in "The Industrial Exhibition of 1862," *Sydney Morning Herald*, July 20, 1861. Following the exhibition, Ledger had a legal run-in with natural-history dealer James Samuel Palmer, who had stuffed some of the alpacas. Palmer was a former convict who had been sent to Australia for life and opened a natural-history shop in Sydney in the mid-1850s (Coote 2013, 4). Ledger claimed that Palmer had attempted to extort from him some money for his taxidermy work with the alpacas. Ledger could not recover the money from the secretary for lands because there was no provision for an expense like this in the budget. SRNSW, NRS5239, letter from Charles Ledger to George Benbow, the acting secretary to the exhibition commissioners (copy), May 27, 1862. The matter reached the Supreme Court as *Palmer v. Ledger.* Ledger eventually won the case but never received any settlement because Palmer was deemed "of no means." SRNSW, NRS5239, letter from George F. Benbow to Charles Ledger (copy), July 1, 1862.

111. "Notes on Wool," *Courier* (Brisbane), July 31, 1862. See also Mitchell (2010, 72–75) on Ledger preparing the camelids for imperial trade.

112. As Ledger explained, "Previous to the arrival of the Alpacas at Arthursleigh, the native dogs caused great havoc, both day and night, to a flock of sheep there—since the arrival of the Alpacas, we have not been once troubled by visits of these pests, and every day may be seen a few sheep accompanying one of the flocks to graze, returning with them at sunset to the fold. In South America it is customary to have 8 or 10 wether Alpacas with a flock of 1000 ewe sheep; these Alpacas conduct the flock to pasture, defend it from the foxes, condors, and strange dogs during the day, and bring it back to fold by sunset" (International Exhibition 1861, 78–79). Many of Ledger's budgets presented to the secretary for lands included money for strychnine, commonly used to poison dingos, which were considered to be one of the greatest menaces to sheep runs. The man in charge of the Royal Park alpacas in Victoria "was instructed at all times to carry a gun to destroy dogs." PROV, VPRS 2223/P/0000/000001/V2, Acclimatisation Society of Victoria, First Minute Book, 1861–1863, November 6, 1861, 86.

113. My discussion of the various processes of transformation during the lives and afterlives of these seven specimens draws from Martin and Bleichmar (2015, 609); Patchett and Foster (2008); Ryan (2005); and Swinney (2011).

114. "New South Wales Products at the Great Exhibition," *Empire* (Sydney), August 18, 1862.

115. "The Alpacas," *Sydney Morning Herald*, December 21, 1861.

116. At the International Exhibition of 1862 the colony of Victoria also awarded Ledger an Honorable Mention "For his co-operation in the labours of the Society of Acclimatisation of Victoria." (Royal Commission for the International Exhibition [Victoria] 1863, 14). Beside the stuffed specimens, Ledger submitted a pomade that he made from the animals' tallow. He recommended it to perfumers, claiming that he was not an expert in its confection but that in "South America, where the Pomade is much used, the luxuriant and beautiful hair of the ladies is proverbial" (International Exhibition 1861, 75). He received an "Honourable Mention" medal

328 | Notes to Pages 244–250

for his mixture and a second for the alpaca tallow that he submitted (International Exhibition 1863, 12).

117. "Australia," *Times* (London), April 15, 1862.

118. PROV, VPRS 02223/P0000/000002/V2, Minute Book, Acclimatisation Society of Victoria (1858–1861), letter from Charles Ledger to the Acclimatisation Society of Victoria, March 13, 1861. See also PROV, VPRS/3422/P/0000/000001/V2, Cash Books Royal Zoological and Acclimatisation Society (1861–1867), April 24, 1861 and July 17, 1861, 101.

119. SRNSW, NRS8362 (9/2659), letter from Acclimatisation Society of Victoria to Charles Ledger, February 13, 1862.

120. SRNSW, NRS8362 (9/2659), letter from Charles Ledger to Acclimatisation Society of Victoria, March 7, 1862.

121. PROV, VPRS 2223/P/0000/000001/V2, Acclimatisation Society of Victoria, First Minute Book (1861–1863), Minutes, August 21 and August 28, 1861, 59, 61.

122. As it turned out, Duffield completed only one shipment of fewer than two hundred llamas and alpacas. The animals that survived the voyage died in the months following their arrival. PROV, VPRS 02223/P0000/000003, Minute Book of the Zoological Acclimatisation Society, May 27, 1863–April 16, 1867, Minutes, February 9, 1864, 492.

123. PROV, VPRS, 2223/P/0000/000001/V2, Acclimatisation Society of Victoria, First Minute Book (1861–1863), Minutes, April 29, 1862, 170–171.

124. PROV, VPRS, 2223/P/0000/000001/V2, Acclimatisation Society of Victoria, First Minute Book (1861–1863), Minutes, April 29, 1862, 171.

125. "In the Legislative Council Yesterday," *Empire* (Sydney), November 6, 1862.

126. Citizen, "The Alpaca Imposition," *Empire* (Sydney), November 18, 1862.

127. Citizen, "The Alpaca Imposition," *Empire* (Sydney), November 18, 1862.

128. Charles Ledger to the editor, *Empire* (Sydney), January 26, 1863.

129. Charles Ledger to the editor, *Sydney Morning Herald*, October 3, 1863.

130. Charles Ledger to the editor, *Sydney Morning Herald*, October 3, 1863.

131. PROV, VPRS, 2223/P/0000/000001/V2, Acclimatisation Society of Victoria, First Minute Book (1861–1863), March 10, 1863, 346.

132. PROV, VPRS, 2223/P/0000/000001/V2, Acclimatisation Society of Victoria, First Minute Book (1861–1863), telegram from Charles Cowper, colonial secretary of New South Wales, to Acclimatisation Society of Victoria on Ledger's suspension, conveying his opinion that the society's £600 would likely never be returned, August 11, 1862, 226–227.

133. PROV, VPRS, 2223/P/0000/000001/V2, Acclimatisation Society of Victoria, First Minute Book (1861–1863), Sydney, extract of a memorandum from John Robertson, the secretary for lands, sent to chief secretary John O'Shanassy of Victoria from Charles Cowper, October 8, 1862, 261–263.

134. PROV, VPRS, 2223/P/0000/000001/V2, Acclimatisation Society of Victoria, First Minute Book (1861–1863), letter from Charles Ledger to John Robertson, August 14, 1862, 266.

135. Charles Ledger, "The Management of the Alpacas," *Sydney Morning Herald*, March 4, 1864.

136. The government's economic loss from the alpacas was ongoing. Money brought in from the sale of the wool totaled only £146 in 1862 and £200 in 1863 (estimated to be the same in 1864). In contrast, in his capacity as superintendent of

Notes to Pages 244–250 | 329

alpacas, Ledger received an annual salary of £500 in 1863, the overseer was paid £100, and six shepherds received a total of £330 a year. Additional expenses included travel costs, housing, multiple paddocks, a run, sheds, and fencing, bringing the total amount spent for 1863 to £1630. NSW, *VPLA* (1863–1864), vol. 3, "Estimates of the Probable Expenditure of the Government of New South Wales for the Year 1864," 739, 809.

137. John Bowie Wilson, secretary for lands, quoted in "The Alpaca for Australia," *Argus* (Melbourne), March 21, 1864.

138. "The Alpaca for Australia," *Argus* (Melbourne), March 21, 1864.

139. "The Alpacas," *Sydney Morning Herald*, June 28, 1864.

140. ML, CYA886, Sir Henry Parkes Correspondence, vol. 16, letter from Thomas Holt to Henry Parkes, May 23, 1873, 333–334.

141. "Alpacas in Australia," *Courier* (Brisbane), July 14, 1866.

142. On the importance of civility in gentlemanly and scientific etiquette and its role in establishing relationships of trust, see Raj (2007, 102–107) and Shapin (2011).

143. "Mr. Ledger and the Alpacas," *Empire* (Sydney), November 13, 1862.

144. KEW, JEH/1/41—Correspondence: Letters to John Eliot Howard from Charles Ledger: 1877–1883, letter from Charles Ledger to John Eliot Howard, Cachi (Argentina), December 22, 1874; "Mr. Ledger's Alpacas," *Sydney Morning Herald*, April 14, 1875. See also Mitre (1913, 170–171). After the Acclimatisation Society of Victoria broke off negotiations, Ledger informed Cabrera that the venture was off and that Cabrera should get the best deal possible for the alpacas already purchased. KEW, JEH/1/41—Correspondence: Letters to John Eliot Howard from Charles Ledger: 1877–1883, letter from Charles Ledger to John Eliot Howard, Cachi (Argentina), December 22, 1874; "Mr. Ledger's Alpacas," *Sydney Morning Herald*, April 14, 1875; Mitre (1913, 170–171). After learning that Ledger could no longer fund the project, Cabrera sold the flock in Jujuy to the Italian Enrique Vigo, who planned to take the animals to Uruguay for the Acclimatization Society of Montevideo. For more on Vigo, his death, and the Montevideo alpacas, see Alviña (1872); Fauvety (1867, 10–13); and "Une nouvelle industrie dans la rivière de la Plata" (1868).

145. KEW, JEH/1/41—Correspondence: Letters to John Eliot Howard from Charles Ledger: 1877–1883, letter from Charles Ledger to John Eliot Howard, Tucuman, May 5, 1880.

146. KEW, JEH/1/41—Correspondence: Letters to John Eliot Howard from Charles Ledger: 1877–1883, letter from Charles Ledger to John Eliot Howard, Cachi (Argentina), December 22, 1874.

147. New South Wales State Archives, Act-66, January 1, 1860, Agricultural Pest Management.

148. "Mr. Ledger's Alpacas," *Sydney Morning Herald*, April 14, 1875.

Chapter 7. US Camelid Contact Zones in the Twentieth Century

1. See Asma (2001) for the way museums exploit the concept of edutainment (education and entertainment) as a means of attracting visitors to collections.

2. Hillard Gordon, "Newburgh Suffered a Setback," *Newburgh Evening News*, June 15, 1985; Michael Randall, "City's History Cloaked in Strook's," *Record Weekly* (Newburgh/Hudson Valley), December 4, 1997; Newburgh (New York) Historical Society (hereafter cited as NHS), scrapbook item, "Sam Stroock Started in NYC Loft" (n.d.).

3. Hillard Gordon, "Newburgh Suffered a Setback," *Newburgh Evening News*, June 15, 1985. According to long-time employee and plant manager Daniel J. Leo, Stroock

330 | Notes to Pages 258–267

was "one of probably the three finest woolen companies in the world." Michael Randall, "City's History Cloaked in Strook's." *Record Weekly* (Newburgh/Hudson Valley), December 4, 1997.

4. NHS, scrapbook item, "Sam Stroock Started in NYC Loft" (no source, n.d.).

5. Hillard Gordon, "Newburgh Suffered a Setback," *Newburgh Evening News*, June 15, 1985.

6. Sylvan Stroock, president of the company, was one of four recipients of the Neiman-Marcus Award in 1940, a prestigious prize acknowledging prominent figures in the fashion industry. "Four Leaders in Fashion World to get Neiman-Marcus Awards," *Dallas Morning News*, August 18, 1940.

7. As one example, *Stroocks' Tours: Personal Glimpses of Distant Places* (Stroock and Stroock 1964) compiled a series of travel articles promoting tourism. The chapters dedicated to the Andes drew from the couple's visits to the area during the late 1920s. Black-and-white photos enhanced a lively text and showcased the camelids and fiber production.

8. Elsewhere the fabric was described as "[b]orrowed from a sunset . . . the cloud softness, the glowing tones." Historical Annual Reports Collection, S. Stroock & Company, Angelo Bruno Business Library, University of Alabama. "Annual Report to Stockholders for the Year Ended June 30, 1947."

9. NHS, Scrapbook, "Sam Stroock Started in NYC Loft" (no source, n.d.).

10. My discussion on the continuum between nature and culture draws from Alberti (2008).

11. See Livingstone (2007) on talk-as-transformation for the sciences.

12. Although the pushmi-pullyu disappeared from the Doctor Dolittle books, the creature had a celebrated afterlife in the 20th Century Fox film *Dr. Dolittle* (1967), where it was reanimated as a two-headed llama from Tibet, presumably winking at the lama/llama homophone in English. The film was nominated for an Academy Award for Best Costumes and for Best Picture of 1967, winning Best Original Song for "Talk to the Animals" and Best Visual Effects.

13. "Rare Fleece Limits Vicuna Coat-Making," *New York Times*, December 26, 1949. For more on the twentieth-century movement to save vicuñas from the threat of extinction, see Wakild 2020.

14. Although pictured on the cover of *Life* magazine in 1945, the Afghan hound only became popular in the United States in the 1970s. Like the woman in the ad, Afghan hounds are described as independent, beautiful, and aristocratic: "[the hound's] whole appearance one of dignity and aloofness with no trace of plainness or coarseness. He has a straight front, proudly carried head, eyes gazing into the distance as if in memory of ages past." American Kennel Club, https://www.akc.org/dog-breeds/afghan-hound (accessed August 26, 2018).

15. According to Hochswender (1993, 13), "The sartorial influence of the Prince of Wales is repeatedly cited [in *Esquire*]. . . . The prince crops up so much that a caption in April 1936 declared, 'Every third or fourth issue we swear off mentioning the Prince of Wales, getting sicker, if possible, of talking about him than you are of hearing about him.'"

16. I follow Heaney (2010) here, preferring the term "revelation" to "discovery."

17. Heaney (2010) observes that Bingham likely served as a real-life model for Indiana Jones. On the relationship of fashion, advertising, and mountaineering in the Andes, see Logan (2011, 89–113).

Notes to Pages 268–277 | 331

18. On taxidermy and the creation of encounters, see Poliquin (2016, 330–331). Desmond (2002) is key for understanding the relationship between taxidermy and narrative; Nyhart (2004) analyzes how the use of original objects in natural history displays can create a sense of authenticity for the viewer.

19. University of Rochester River Campus Libraries, Hickey-Freeman Company Papers (hereafter cited as UoR H-FCP), D.80, Box 1, Folder 6, Hugo Gemignani, manuscript copy of talk given in the late 1940s, 7.

20. UoR H-FCP, D.80, Box 1, Folder 14, Orientation Packet for Jennifer Tirone, May 1987.

21. UoR H-FCP, D.80, "Behind the Seams: The Hickey-Freeman Quality Story Unfolds," n.d., no pagination (ellipses in original).

22. Yale Beinecke Library, Inge Morath Collection (hereafter YBL IMC), GEN MSS 996, Box 628, II, Papers, Shows, *Mother Jones* Portfolio, 1957–1958, New York/ New York, Inge Morath, "Encounter on Times Square, 1957."

23. John P. Jacob, "A Llama in Times Square (1957)." http://ingemorath.org/a-llama-in-times-square-1957 (May 2, 2010). Lorrain D'Essen's comments elsewhere suggest that the llama was not permitted to ride about town with its head out the car window. Maureen Daly, "Offbeat Pets of the City," *New York Times*, June 16, 1957.

24. Karen Radkai, quoted in Nan Robertson, "Animals Also Are Clicking as Models in Fashion Photography." *New York Times*, November 28, 1958.

25. Irving Penn, quoted in Nan Robertson, "Animals Also Are Clicking as Models in Fashion Photography," *New York Times*, November 28, 1958.

26. Pulitzer-winning photographer Nat Fein captured an image of D'Essen and Llucky one day when on their rounds, portraying the allure of the exotic creature and the public's excitement at seeing the llama out and about: "Woman Walks Llama (December 18, 1954). Lorraine [*sic*] D'Essen and her llama named Lucky [*sic*] on their way to work. Ms. D'Essen rents out large animals from her west side brownstone for stage and television shows" (Vintage Photos, Nat Fein Collection): https://www.vintagephotos.com/Image%2064%20llama.htm (accessed March 15, 2023).

27. Peru, however, was not Llucky's native land; D'Essen described him elsewhere as being a "fourth generation American, born on a Catskill game farm" in upstate New York. Quoted in Val Adams, "TV Specialist: Booker of Talented Animals," *New York Times*, April 11, 1954.

28. "High-Paid Llama in the Big City," *Life*, December 2, 1957.

29. See Peiss (1998), on Revlon and the rise of cosmetics and feminine beauty products following World War II.

30. "Neiman-Marcus Reveals Plans for South American Fortnight," *Dallas Morning News*, January 30, 1959. Neiman Marcus stopped using the hyphenated version of its name in 1988. I only include the hyphen in quotations, repository items, and titles that use it.

31. The nonprofit council was formed in 1951 with an expressed focus on international relations, hoping to "engage residents in global issues and position North Texas as a player on the world stage": https://www.dfwworld.org/who-we-are/our-history (accessed March 15, 2023).

32. Dallas Museum of Art Archives, John and Nora Wise Papers (hereafter cited as DMAA JNWP), Dorothy Hinz, "South American Fortnight," Grace Log, "Dallas' South American Fortnight" issue (November–December 1959).

332 | Notes to Pages 277–279

33. DeGolyer Library, Stanley Marcus Papers (digitized collection), Southern Methodist University (hereafter cited as DGL SMP), "Fortnight to Encompass Many Phases of Art, Entertainment," *Dallas Morning News*, September 20, 1959; DGL SMP, "Neiman-Marcus Announces the South American Fortnight Tour, February 29–March 29, 1960."

34. DMAA JNWP, Dorothy Hinz, "South American Fortnight," *Grace Log*, "Dallas' South American Fortnight" issue (November–December 1959), 13. See also DPLA, Neiman Marcus Box 10-1, "Press Release, Sunday, October 4, 1959," 15.

35. The celebrations originally were planned to honor all thirteen countries of South America but eventually focused only on the Spanish-speaking countries and Brazil.

36. Quoted in Si Dunn, "Fabulous Fortnight '84: The Neiman-Marcus Extravaganza Brings Britain Back to Dallas," *D Magazine* (October 1, 1984): https://www.dmagazine.com/publications/d-magazine/1984/october/fabulous-fortnight-84.

37. Marcus claimed that museums served as an important source of inspiration for the Fortnights (1985, 187–188; 2001).

38. "Fortnight to Encompass Many Phases of Art, Entertainment," *Dallas Morning News*, September 20, 1959.

39. DPLA, Neiman Marcus Box 10-3, Neiman Marcus press release, September 20, 1959, 3.

40. DPLA, Neiman Marcus Box 10-1, Neiman Marcus press release, October 4, 1959. The press release's description of the retablos harks back to the bezoar stone examined in chapter 1. Like the bezoar stone, the retablo's connection with enigmatic Indigenous practices served as a means of piquing the customer's interest and encouraging a sale.

41. DPLA, Neiman Marcus Box 10-1, Neiman Marcus press release, October 4, 1959; DMAA JNWP, Dorothy Hinz, "South American Fortnight," *Grace Log*, "Dallas' South American Fortnight" issue (November–December 1959), 13; Jeanne Barnes, "Décor Re-Created from Colonial Era." *Dallas Morning News*, October 18, 1959.

42. According to Marcus (2001, no pagination), "The Rockefeller pieces alone had a value in excess of $1,000,000, and since they were very fragile, I carried them on my lap on the flight to Dallas." Donors for the gold exhibit included art dealer John Wise from New York, the Cleveland Museum of Art, Paul Tishman, the Rockefellers, and Robert Woods Bliss and Mildred Barnes Bliss. "Fortnight to Encompass Many Phases of Art, Entertainment," *Dallas Morning News*, September 20, 1959.

43. "Fortnight to Encompass Many Phases of Art, Entertainment," *Dallas Morning News*, September 20, 1959; see also Jeanne Barnes, "Décor Re-Created from Colonial Era," *Dallas Morning News*, October 18, 1959; DMAA JNWP, Dorothy Hinz, "South American Fortnight," *Grace Log*, "Dallas' South American Fortnight" issue (November–December 1959), 12.

44. "South American Fortnight: The Folk Art of South America," *Dallas Morning News*, October 19, 1959; see also DMAA JNWP, Dorothy Hinz, "South American Fortnight," *Grace Log*, "Dallas' South American Fortnight" issue (November–December 1959), 12.

45. DPLA, Neiman Marcus Box 10-3, Neiman Marcus press release, October 4, 1959.

46. DPLA, Neiman Marcus Box 10-3, Neiman Marcus press release, October 4, 1959.

Notes to Pages 279–289 | 333

47. Gay Simpson, "Fashions to Mirror South American Life," *Dallas Morning News*, October 18, 1959; see also DMAA JNWP, Dorothy Hinz, "South American Fortnight," *Grace Log*, "Dallas' South American Fortnight" issue (November–December 1959), 12.

48. DMAA JNWP, Dorothy Hinz, "South American Fortnight, *Grace Log*, "Dallas' South American Fortnight" issue (November–December 1959), 12.

49. DMAA JNWP, Dorothy Hinz, "South American Fortnight," *Grace Log*. "Dallas' South American Fortnight" issue (November–December 1959), 12. See also DPLA, Box 10-3, Neiman Marcus press release, September 20, 1959; and DPLA, Neiman Marcus Box 10-1, Neiman Marcus press release, October 4, 1959; "Fortnight to Encompass Many Phases of Art, Entertainment," *Dallas Morning News*, September 20, 1959.

50. DPLA, Neiman Marcus Box 10-1, Neiman Marcus press release, October 4, 1959.

51. DPLA, Folder 7, Sara Marshall to the Press of Dallas, "Schedule of Events for the 'South America Fortnight,'" October 15, 1959.

52. See DPL Photographic Archives.

53. DGL SMP, "Lorrain D'Essen, Llinda Llee Llama, and Stanley Marcus, South American Fortnight, October 1959."

54. DPLA, Neiman Marcus Box 10-6, Ethel Woodby, "A Visit to an Asado: Complete with Llama," *Texas Record-Chronicle* (Denton), n.d.

55. The phrase comes from Majluf's (1997) analysis of the reception of Latin American art in the Paris Universal Exhibition of 1855.

56. DPLA, Neiman Marcus Box 10-4, Stanley Marcus, advertising insert in *Town & Country* (October 1959), "Sunrise in South America."

57. My argument draws from Majluf (1997, 869), who highlights a similar contradiction in the critical reception of Latin American art by the West.

Conclusion. The Afterlives of Camelid Contact Zones

1. Space limitations prevent discussion of other Latin American countries that wanted to import the camelids. Mexico, Colombia, and Uruguay expressed interest in the possibility of implementing camelid acclimatization projects, none of which really got off the ground, primarily due to inability to obtain the stock.

2. Van Dooren (2014, 7; emphasis in the original) argues that extinction stories do not arise from single events. Rather, they reflect "a *distinct* unraveling of ways of life, a distinctive loss and set of changes and challenges that require situated and case-specific attention."

3. The statue's location reminds us of D'Essen's (1959, 169) prescient observation on how the llama, being an animal from a high mountainous region, could serve as an ideal model for "the luxurious roof garden of a hotel."

4. "Llinda Llee Llama Statue Unveil at the Statler Dallas": https://www.youtube .com/watch?v=7LTGCaVholQ; see also https://www.historichotels.org/us/hotels -resorts/the-statler/history-mystery.php (accessed January 22, 2022). On the day of the unveiling, following the lead of the artists and their inventive conception of the star, the online magazine *Papercity* published a tell-all interview with Llinda Llee on her life and celebrated career (December 8, 2017): https://www.papercitymag.com /culture/llinda-llee-llama-hollywood-star-modeling-tasteful-nudes-statler-hotel-dallas -trip. Llinda Llee even maintains a social media presence on Facebook (https://www

334 | Note to Page 289

.facebook.com/LlindaLleeLlama) and Instagram (https://www.instagram.com/llinda
_llee_llama), where she discusses llama-related news and can be direct messaged for
advice on fashion, life, and love (#AskLlindaLlee).

5. My reading of the sculpture of Llinda Llee Llama is informed by Patchett and
Foster's (2008) analysis of the craft of taxidermy.

Works Cited

Abecia, Carlos. 1952. "La provincia 'Sur Lípez.'" *Boletín de la Sociedad Geográfica y de Historia de Potosí* 40.12 (1952): 97–123.

Abercrombie, Thomas A. 1998. *Pathways of Memory and Power: Ethnography and History among an Andean People*. Madison: University of Wisconsin Press.

Acosta, P. José de. (1590) 1962. *Historia natural y moral de las Indias [. . .]*. Edited by Edmundo O'Gorman. 2nd ed. Mexico City: Fondo de Cultura Económica.

Adams, Bluford. 1997. *E Pluribus Barnum: The Making of the Great Showman & U.S. Popular Culture*. Minneapolis: University of Minnesota Press.

Adorno, Rolena. 1990. "The Depiction of Self and Other in Colonial Peru." *Art Journal* 49: 110–118.

Alberti, Samuel J. M. M. 2005. "Objects and the Museum." *Isis* 96: 559–571.

Alberti, Samuel J. M. M. 2008. "Constructing Nature behind Glass." *Museum and Society* 6.2: 73–97.

Alberti, Samuel J. M. M. 2011a. "Introduction: The Dead Ark." In *Afterlives of Animals: A Museum Menagerie*, edited by Samuel J. M. M. Alberti, 1–16. Charlottesville: University of Virginia Press.

Alberti, Samuel J. M. M., ed. 2011b. *Afterlives of Animals: A Museum Menagerie*. Charlottesville: University of Virginia Press.

Alexander, Thomas E. 2009. *Stanley Marcus: The Relentless Reign of a Merchant Prince*. Waco, TX: Eakin Press.

Alfonso Mola, Marina, and Carlos Martínez Shaw. 2003. *Oriente en palacio: Tesoros asiáticos en las colecciones reales españoles* (exhibit catalogue). Madrid: Patrimonio Nacional.

Alfonso X el Sabio. (1250) 1981. *Lapidario (Según el manuscrito escurialense H.I.15)*. Edited by Sagrario Rodríguez M. Montalvo. Madrid: Editorial Gredos.

Algarotti, Francesco. 1769. *Essai sur la peinture, et sur l'Académie de France, établie à Rome*. Translated by M. Pingeron. Paris: Chez Merlin.

"Alpacas for the Great Exhibition: A Great Category." 1861. *Times* (London), November 19.

Al Tifaschi, Ahman ibn Yusuf. (ca. 1243) 1998. *Arab Roots of Gemology: Ahmad ibn Yusuf Al Tifaschi's Best Thoughts on the Best of Stones*. Translated by Samar Najm Abul Huda. Lanham, MD: Scarecrow Press.

Álvarez, Bartolomé. (1588) 1998. *De las costumbres y conversión de los indios del Perú [. . .]*. Edited by María del Carmen Martín Rubio, Juan J. R. Villarías Robles, and Fermín del Pino Díaz. Madrid: Ediciones Polifemo.

Álvarez de Quindos y Baena, Juan Antonio. 1804. *Descripción histórica del Real Bosque y Casa de Aranjuez [. . .]*. Madrid: Imprenta Real.

Alviña, Miguel. 1872. *Alpacas: Su cultivo como elemento principal de riqueza de la República de Bolivia y su aclimatación en otros países*. Buenos Aires: Imprenta de Pablo E. Coni.

Amorós, J. L. 1963. "Notas sobre la historia de la cristalografía y mineralogía III: La

336 | Works Cited

colección del caballero Franco Dávila y el origen del real gabinete de historia natural." *Boletín de la Real Sociedad Española de Historia Natural: Sección Geológica* 61.1: 9–37.

Andrien, Kenneth J. 1998. "The *Noticias secretas de América* and the Construction of a Governing Ideology for the Spanish American Empire." *Colonial Latin American Review* 7.2: 175–192.

Aragón, Santiago. 2005. *El zoológico del museo de ciencias naturales: Mariano de la Paz Graells (1809–1898), la Sociedad de Aclimatación y los animales útiles.* Madrid: Museo Nacional de Ciencias Naturales/Consejo Superior de Investigaciones Científicas.

Arnold, Denise Y. 2004. "Midwife Singers: Llama-Human Obstetrics in Some Songs to the Animals by Andean Women." In *Quechua Verbal Artistry: The Inscription of Andean Voices/Arte expresivo Quechua: La inscripción de voces andinas,* edited by Guillermo Delgado-P. and John M. Schechter, 145–179. Aachen, Germany: Shaker Verlag.

Arnold, Denise Y., and Juan de Dios Yapita. 1998. *Río de vellón, río de canto: Cantar a los animales, una poética andina de la creación.* La Paz: Facultad de Humanidades y Ciencias de la Educación, Carrera de Literatura, UMSA, HISBOL.

Arriaga, Pablo José de. (1621) 1968. "Extirpación de la idolatría del Pirú." In *Crónicas peruanas de interés indígena,* edited by Francisco Esteve Barba, 191–277. Biblioteca de Autores Españoles 209. Madrid: Ediciones Atlas.

Arzadún y Zabala, Juan. 1910. *Albores de la independencia argentina.* Madrid: Imprenta de Eduardo Arias.

Arzáns de Orsúa y Vela, Bartolomé. (1700–1736) 1965. *Historia de la villa imperial de Potosí.* Edited by Lewis Hanke and Gunnar Mendoza. Vol. 1. Providence, RI: Brown University Press.

Asma, Stephen T. 2001. *Stuffed Animals and Pickled Heads: The Culture and Evolution of Natural History Museums.* Oxford: Oxford University Press.

Asúa, Miguel de, and Roger French. 2005. *A New World of Animals: Early Modern Europeans on the Creatures of Iberian America.* Burlington, VT: Ashgate Publishing.

Avenzoar (Abū Marwān 'Abd al-Malik b. Zuhr). (12th c.) 1992. *Kitāb al-agdiya (Tratado de los alimentos).* Edited and translated by Expiración García Sánchez. Madrid: Consejo Superior de Investigaciones Científicas/Instituto de Cooperación con el Mundo Árabe.

Ávila, Francisco de. (1598?) 2009. *Dioses y hombres de Huarochirí: Narración quechua recogida por Francisco de Ávila.* Translated by José María Arguedas. Lima: Universidad Antonio Ruíz de Montoya.

Bader, Thomas M. 1988. "The Roaring Days: Trade and Relations between Chile and Australia, 1849–1860." *Journal of Australian Studies* 12:23: 29–44.

Baker, John. 2006. "Bezoar-Stones, Gall-Stones, and Gem-Stones: A Chapter in the History of the Tort of Deceit." In *Mapping the Law: Essays in Memory of Peter Birks,* edited by Andrew Burrows and Lord Rodger of Earlsferry, 545–559. Oxford: Oxford University Press.

Ballivián, Manuel V., and Eduardo Idiáquez. 1890. *Diccionario geográfico de la república de Bolivia.* Vol. 1. Departamento de La Paz. La Paz: Imprenta y Litografía de "El Nacional" de Isaac V. Vila.

Barnard, Alan. 1961. *Visions and Profits: Studies in the Business Career of Thomas Sutcliffe Mort.* Melbourne: Melbourne University Press.

Works Cited | 337

Barras de Aragón, Francisco de las. 1912. "Una historia del Perú contenida en un cuadro al óleo de 1799." *Boletín de la Real Sociedad Española de Historia Natural* 12: 225–286.

Barrera-Osorio, Antonio. 2006. *Experiencing Nature: The Spanish American Empire and the Early Scientific Revolution.* Austin: University of Texas Press.

Barthélemy-Lapommeraye, Christophe Jérôme. 1847. "Importation en France d'animaux utiles par la voie d'association." *Annales Provençales d'Agriculture Pratique* 20: 204–219.

Barthes, Roland. 1975. *The Pleasure of the Text.* Translated by Richard Miller. New York: Noonday Press.

Bauer, Ralph, and Marcy Norton. 2017. "Introduction: Entangled Trajectories: Indigenous and European Histories." *Colonial Latin American Review* 26.1: 1–17.

Bauer, Rotraud, and Herbert Haupt, eds. 1976. "Das Kunstkammerinventar Kaiser Rudolfs II, 1607–1611." *Jahrbuch der Kunsthistorischen Sammlungen in Wien* 72: 1–191.

Bayers, Peter L. 2003. *Imperial Ascent: Mountaineering, Masculinity, and Empire.* Boulder: University Press of Colorado.

Belhoste, Bruno. 2011. *Paris Savant, Capital of Science in the Age of Enlightenment.* Translated by Susan Emanuel. Oxford: Oxford University Press.

Benize-Daoulas, Régine. 2002. "Voyage en Paulie-Laurencie, essai sur une construction narrative polyphonique." *Boletín del Instituto Francés de Estudios Andinos* 31.2: 183–218.

Bennett, George. 1862. *Acclimatisation: Its Eminent Adaptation to Australia—A Lecture* (delivered in Sydney). Republished by the Acclimatisation Society of Victoria. Melbourne: Goodhugh and Co.

Bermingham, Ann. 2000. *Learning to Draw: Studies in the Cultural History of a Polite and Useful Art.* New Haven, CT: Yale University Press.

Bertonio, Ludovico. (1612) 2006. *Vocabulario de la lengua aymara.* Arequipa, Peru: Ediciones El Lector.

Bertrand, Alejandro. 1885. *Memoria sobre las cordilleras del desierto de Atacama i rejiones limítrofes.* Santiago, Chile: Imprenta Nacional.

Betts, John Richards. 1959. "P. T. Barnum and the Popularization of Natural History." *Journal of the History of Ideas* 20.3: 353–368.

Bigelow, Allison. 2016. "Incorporating Indigenous Knowledge into Extractive Economies: The Science of Colonial Silver." *Extractive Industries and Society* 3: 117–123.

Bleichmar, Daniela. 2005. "Books, Bodies, and Fields: Sixteenth-Century Transatlantic Encounters with New World *Materia Medica.*" In *Colonial Botany: Science, Commerce, and Politics in the Early Modern World,* edited by Londa Schiebinger and Claudia Swan, 83–99. Philadelphia: University of Pennsylvania Press.

Bleichmar, Daniela. 2009. "A Visible and Useful Empire: Visual Culture and Colonial Natural History in the Eighteenth-Century Spanish World." In *Science in the Spanish and Portuguese Empires: 1500–1800,* edited by Daniela Bleichmar, Paula de Vos, Kristin Huffine, and Kevin Sheehan, 290–310. Stanford, CA: Stanford University Press.

Bleichmar, Daniela. 2011. "Peruvian Nature Up Close, Seen from Afar." *RES: Anthropology and Aesthetics* 59–60: 60–73.

Bleichmar, Daniela. 2012. *Visible Empire: Botanical Expeditions & Visual Culture in the Hispanic Enlightenment.* Chicago: University of Chicago Press.

338 | Works Cited

Bleichmar, Daniela. 2017. *Visual Voyages: Images of Latin American Nature from Columbus to Darwin*. New Haven, CT: Yale University Press, in association with the Huntington Library, Art Collections, and Botanical Gardens; and with the assistance of the Getty Foundation.

Bleichmar, Daniela, and Peter C. Mancall, eds. 2011. *Collecting Across Cultures: Material Exchanges in the Early Modern Atlantic World*. Philadelphia: University of Pennsylvania Press.

Blin, Pierre Christian. 1981. "Les écorchés de Fragonard." In *L'autre Fragonard*, edited by Michel Ellenberger, 6. Paris: Jupilles.

Boitard, Pierre. 1835. *Manuel du naturaliste préparateur, ou l'art d'empailler les animaux et de conserver les végétaux et les minéraux*. 3rd ed. Paris: À la Librairie Encyclopédique de Roret.

Boitard, Pierre. 1842. *Le Jardin des Plantes: Description et moeurs des mammifères de la Ménagerie et du Muséum d'Histoire Naturelle*. Paris: J.-J. Dubochet.

Bolívar, Simón. 1983. *Decretos del libertador, 1813–1825*. Vol. 1. Los Teques, Venezuela: Biblioteca de Autores y Temas Mirandinos.

Bollaert, W. 1863. "The Llama, Alpaco, Huanacu, and Vicuña." *Sporting Review* 49: 123–132.

Bonafous, Mathieu. 1847. "Note sur l'acclimatation du lama et autres animaux congénères." *Compte Rendu des Séances de l'Académie des Sciences* 25: 827–828.

Bory de Saint-Vincent, Jean-Baptiste. 1823. *Guide du voyageur en Espagne*. Paris: Louis Janet, Libraire.

Bottiglia, William F. 1958. "The Eldorado Episode in *Candide*." *Papers of the Modern Language Association* 73.4: 339–347.

Bourgoing, Jean-François. 1797. *Tableau de l'Espagne moderne*. 2nd ed. Vol. 3. Paris: by the author.

Bourguet, Marie-Noëlle. 2010. "A Portable World: The Notebooks of European Travellers (Eighteenth to Nineteenth Centuries)." *Intellectual History Review* 20.3: 377–400.

Bouysse-Cassagne, Thérèse, with Philippe Bouysse. 1988. *Lluvias y cenizas: Dos pachacuti en la historia*. La Paz: HISBOL.

Bouysse-Cassagne, Thérèse, and Olivia Harris. 1987. "Pacha: En torno al pensamiento Aymara." In *Tres reflexiones sobre el pensamiento andino*, 11–59. La Paz: HISBOL.

Boxer, C. R. 1963. *Two Pioneers of Tropical Medicine: Garcia d'Orta and Nicolás Monardes*. Lecture Series 1. London: Wellcome Historical Medical Library.

Brack Egg, Antonio. 1987. "Historia del manejo de las vicuñas en el Perú." *Boletín de Lima* 9.50: 61–76.

Bradshaw, Mr. 1858. "The Llamas—Mr. Ledger." *Sydney Morning Herald*, November 30.

Brantz, Dorothee. 2007. "The Domestication of Empire: Human-Animal Relations at the Intersection of Civilization, Evolution, and Acclimatization in the Nineteenth Century." In *A Cultural History of Animals in the Age of Empire*, edited by Kathleen Kete, 73–93. Oxford: Berg, 2007.

Brawern, Heinrich, and Elias Herckemann. *Die fünff und zweyntzigste Schifffahrt Königreich Chili in West Indien*. Frankfurt: Christoph Le Blon, 1649.

Brayer, G. Sheldon. 1999. *A Temple of Fine Tailoring: The Hickey-Freeman Story, a Century of Quality Clothing*. Rochester, NY: Hickey-Freeman Co.

Brenna, Brita. 2013. "The Frames of Specimens: Glass Cases in Bergen Museum around 1900." In *Animals on Display: The Creaturely in Museums, Zoos, and*

Natural History, edited by Liv Emma Thorsen, Karen A. Rader, and Adam Dodd, 37–57. University Park: Pennsylvania State University Press.

Brosseder, Claudia. 2014. *The Power of Huacas: Change and Resistance in the Andean World of Colonial Peru*. Austin: University of Texas Press.

Browman, David L. 1990. "Camelid Pastoralism in the Andes: Llama Caravan Fleteros, and Their Importance in Production and Distribution." In *Nomads in a Changing World*, edited by Carl Salzman and John G. Galaty, 395–437. Naples: Istituto Universitario Orientale, Dipartimento di Studi Asiatici.

Buffon, Georges Louis Leclerc, Comte de. 1761. "Animaux du nouveau monde." In *Histoire naturelle, générale et particulière, avec la description du cabinet du roi*, 84–96. Vol. 9. Paris: Imprimerie Royale.

Buffon, Georges Louis Leclerc, Comte de. 1764. "Description des bézoards orientaux et occidentaux." In *Histoire naturelle, générale e particulière, avec la description du cabinet du roi*, 278–293. Vol. 12. Paris: L'Imprimerie Royale.

Buffon, Georges Louis Leclerc, Comte de. 1765. "Le lama et le paco." In *Histoire naturelle, générale et particulière, avec la description du cabinet du roi*, 16–33. Vol. 13. Paris: L'Imprimerie Royale.

Buffon, Georges Louis Leclerc, Comte de. 1782a. "De la vigogne." In *Supplément à l'histoire naturelle, générale et particulière*, 208–220. Vol. 6. Paris: Imprimerie Royale.

Buffon, Georges Louis Leclerc, Comte de. 1782b. "Du lama." In *Supplément à l'histoire naturelle, générale et particulière*, 204–207. Vol. 6. Paris: Imprimerie Royale.

Burton, Robert. (1621) 1676. *The Anatomy of Melancholy*, 8th ed. London: Printed for Peter Parker.

Bustinza Choque, Víctor. 1989. "Algunas consecuencias de la agresión cultural en la ganadería andina." In *Crianza de llamas y alpacas en los Andes*, 115–120. Puno, Peru: Proyecto Alpacas PAL/Convenio COTESU-INIAA/Proyecto Andino de Tecnologías Campesinas PRATEC.

Cabral Chamorro, Antonio. 1995. "El Jardín Botánico Príncipe de la Paz de Sanlúcar de Barrameda: Una institución ilustrada al servicio de la producción agraria y forestal." *Revista de Estudios Andaluces* 21: 165–188.

Cabrera de Córdoba, Luis. 1857. *Relaciones de las cosas sucedidas en la córte de España, desde 1599 hasta 1614*. Madrid: Imprenta de J. Martín Alegria.

Cajías de la Vega, Fernando. 1975. *La provincia de Atacama, 1825–1842*. La Paz: Empresa Editora "Universo."

Calancha, Fray Antonio de la. (1638) 1974. *Crónica moralizada*. Edited by Ignacio Prado Pastor. 2 vols. Lima: Universidad Nacional Mayor de San Marcos.

Caldas, Francisco José de. 1912. "Memoria sobre la importancia de connaturalizar en el Reino la vicuña del Perú y Chile." In *Obras de Caldas*, edited by Eduardo Posada, 481–493. Bogotá: Imprenta Nacional.

Calderón Jemio, Raúl Javier. 1991. "Conflictos sociales en el altiplano paceño entre 1830 y 1860." *Revista del Instituto de Estudios Andinos y Amazónicos* 1: 145–157.

Callen, Anthea. 1997. "The Body and Difference: Anatomy Training at the École des Beaux-Arts in Paris in the Later Nineteenth Century." *Art History* 20.1: 23–60.

Cañete y Domínguez, Pedro Vicente. (1787) 1952. *Guía de la provincia de Potosí*. Potosí, Bolivia: Editorial "Potosí."

Cañizares-Esguerra, Jorge. 1995. "La utopía de Hipólito Unanue: Comercio, naturaleza, y religión en el Perú." In *Saberes andinos: Ciencia y tecnología en Bolivia,*

340 | Works Cited

Ecuador y Perú, edited by Marcos Cueto, 91–108. Lima: Instituto de Estudios Peruanos, 1995.

Cañizares-Esguerra, Jorge. 2001. *How to Write the History of the New World: Histories, Epistemologies, and Identities in the Eighteenth-Century Atlantic World.* Stanford, CA: Stanford University Press.

Cañizares-Esguerra, Jorge. 2006a. *Nature, Empire, and Nation: Explorations of the History of Science in the Iberian World.* Stanford, CA: Stanford University Press.

Cañizares-Esguerra, Jorge. 2006b. *Puritan Conquistadors: Iberianizing the Atlantic, 1550–1700.* Stanford, CA: Stanford University Press.

Capus, Guillaume. 1883. *Guide du naturaliste préparateur et du voyageur scientifique [. . .].* Edited by A. T. de Rochebrune. 10th ed. Paris: Librairie J.B. Baillière et Fils.

Cárdenas, José de, Bráulio Antón Ramírez, Pablo González de la Peña, and Feliciano Herreros de Tejada. 1879. "Biografía." In *Ensayo sobre las variedades de la vid común que vegetan en Andalucía* by don Simón de Rojas Clemente y Rubio, xiii–xvii. Madrid: Imprenta Estereotipía Perojo/Biblioteca Digital, Real Jardín Botánico.

Carlino, Andrea. 1999. *Books of the Body: Anatomical Ritual and Renaissance Learning.* Translated by John Tedeschi and Anne C. Tedeschi. Chicago: University of Chicago Press.

Caro, Deborah A. 1994. "Incorporation or Resistance? Pastoral Relations of Production in an Export Economy." In *Pastoralists at the Periphery: Herders in a Capitalist World*, edited by Claudia Chang and Harold A. Koster, 23–41. Tucson: University of Arizona Press.

Carter, Christopher, Flora Vilches, and Calogero M. Santoro. 2017. "South American Mummy Trafficking: Captain Duniam's Nineteenth-Century Worldwide Enterprises." *Journal of the History of Collections* 29.3: 395–407.

Carter, Paul. 1988. *The Road to Botany Bay: An Exploration of Landscape and History.* New York: Alfred A. Knopf.

Casas, Bartolomé de las. (1563) 1958. *Los tesoros del Perú.* Translated and edited by Ángel Losada. Madrid: Consejo Superior de Investigaciones Científicas.

Cereceda, Verónica. 1980. "A partir de los colores de un pájaro . . ." *Boletín del Museo Chileno de Arte Precolombino* 4: 57–104.

Chaton, Mireille. 1970. "L'époque alforienne de Claude Bourgelat et la création de l'École Vétérinaire d'Alfort." Dissertation, Interbus, Paris.

Checa Cremades, Fernando. 1997. *Las maravillas de Felipe II.* [Bilbao?:] Banco Bilbao Vizcaya.

Chevallier, Bernard. 1989. *Malmaison: Château et domaine des origines à 1904.* Paris: Ministère de la Culture, de la Communication, du Bicentenaire et des Grands Travaux/Éditions de la Réunion des Musées Nationaux.

Chevallier, Bernard. 2005. "A Short History of Malmaison." Translated by Charles Pearo. In *The Empress Josephine: Art and Royal Identity*, edited by Carol Solomon Kiefer, 87–95. Amherst, MA: Mead Art Museum.

Chevallier, Bernard, and Christophe Pincemaille. 1988. *L'impératrice Joséphine.* Paris: Presses de la Renaissance.

Choque Canqui, Roberto, with Xavier Albó Corrons, Esteban Ticona Alejo, Félix Layme Pairumani, and Astvaldur Astvaldsson. 2003. *Cinco siglos de historia.* La Paz: Plural/CIPCA/Cuadernos de Investigación.

Choque Canqui, Roberto, and Christina Quisbert Quispe. 2010. *Líderes indígenas aymaras: Por la defensa de tierras comunitarias de origen.* La Paz: Unidad de Investigaciones Históricas-Pakaxa.

Works Cited | 341

"Chronique de l'Amérique Latine." 1861. *La Revue du Monde Colonial, Asiatique et Américain*, 265–280.

Cieza de León, Pedro. (1553) 1853. "La crónica del Perú." In *Historiadores primitivos de Indias*, edited by Enrique de Vedia, 349–458. Biblioteca de Autores Españoles 26. Vol. 2. Madrid: M. Rivadeneyra.

Clark, Stuart. 1997. *Thinking with Demons: The Idea of Witchcraft in Early Modern Europe*. Oxford: Clarendon Press.

Clifford, James. 1997. *Routes: Travel and Translation in the Late Twentieth Century*. Cambridge, MA: Harvard University Press.

Cobo, P. Bernabé. (1653) 1956. *Obras del P. Bernabé Cobo de la Compañía de Jesús*. Edited by P. Francisco Mateos. Biblioteca de Autores Españoles 91. Vol. 1. Madrid: Atlas.

Collett, Anne. 1997. "'Sharing a Common Destiny': Censorship, Imperialism and the Stories of Doctor Dolittle." *New Literature Review* 33: 81–93.

The Compact Edition of the Oxford English Dictionary: The Complete Text Reproduced Micrographically. 1971. Vol. 1. Oxford: Oxford University Press.

Contreras y Valverde, Vasco de. (1640) 1965. "Relación de la ciudad del Cuzco, de su fundación, descripción, vidas de los obispos, religiones, y de todo lo demás perteneciente a eclesiástico desde el descubrimiento de este reyno hasta el tiempo presente. In *Relaciones geográficas de Indias: Perú*, edited by Marcos Jiménez de la Espada, 1–15. Biblioteca de Autores Españoles 184. Vol. 2. Madrid: Biblioteca de Autores Españoles.

Cook, Harold J. 2007. *Matters of Exchange: Commerce, Medicine, and Science in the Dutch Golden Age*. New Haven, CT: Yale University Press.

Coote, Anne. 2013. "Science, Fashion, Knowledge and Imagination: Shopfront Natural History in 19th-Century Sydney." *Sydney Journal* 4.1: 1–18.

Cornulier-Lucinière, M. le Comte R. de. 1864. "Rapport adressé a son Exc. le Ministre de la Marine et des Colonies sur les alpacas et lamas transportés de Guayaquil à Brest." *Bulletin de la Société Impériale Zoologique d'Acclimatation*, 2nd series, 1: 393–401.

Cosme Bueno y Alegre, Francisco Antonio. 1764–1778. *Descripción de las provincias de los obispados y arzobispados del virreinato del Perú*. Lima: Impreso en la Oficina de la Calle de la Coca.

Cowie, Helen. 2017a. "From the Andes to the Outback: Acclimatising Alpacas in the British Empire." *Journal of Imperial and Commonwealth History* 45.4: 551–579.

Cowie, Helen. 2017b. *Llama*. London: Reaktion Books.

Cowie, Helen Louise. 2022. *Victims of Fashion: Animal Commodities in Victorian Britain*. Cambridge: Cambridge University Press.

Crosby, Alfred W. 2004. *Ecological Imperialism: The Biological Expansion of Europe, 900–1900*. 2nd ed. Cambridge: Cambridge University Press.

Cuba, Johannes de. ca. 1499–1502. *Ortus sanitatis*. Paris: A. Verard.

Cushman, Gregory T. 2013. *Guano and the Opening of the Pacific World: A Global Ecological History*. Cambridge: Cambridge University Press.

Cuvier, Georges. 1835. *Leçons d'anatomie comparée*. Vol. 4, part 2. 2nd ed. Paris: Crochard et Cie.

Dalence, José María. (1851) 1975. *Bosquejo estadístico de Bolivia*. La Paz: Universidad Boliviana, Universidad Mayor de San Andrés.

Darian-Smith, Kate. 2008. "'Seize the Day': Exhibiting Australia." In *Seize the Day: Exhibitions, Australia and the World*, edited by Kate Darian-Smith, Richard

342 | Works Cited

Gillespie, Caroline Jordan, and Elizabeth Willis, 1.01–1.14. Clayton, Victoria, Australia: Monash University Publishing.

Daston, Lorraine. 2000a. "Introduction. The Coming into Being of Scientific Objects." In *Biographies of Scientific Objects*, edited by Lorraine Daston, 1–14. Chicago: University of Chicago Press.

Daston, Lorraine. 2000b. "Preternatural Philosophy." In *Biographies of Scientific Objects*, edited by Lorraine Daston, 15–41. Chicago: University of Chicago Press.

Daston, Lorraine, and Katharine Park. 2001. *Wonders and the Order of Nature: 1150–1750*. New York: Zone Books.

Dávila, Pedro Franco. 1767. *Catalogue systématique et raisonné des curiosités de la nature et de l'art*. Vol. 1. Paris: Chez Briasson.

Dawson, Gowan, Richard Noakes, and Jonathan R. Topham. "Introduction." 2004. *Science in the Nineteenth-Century Periodical*, edited by Geoffrey Cantor, Gowan Dawson, Graeme Gooday, Richard Noakes, Sally Shuttleworth, and Jonathan R. Topham, 1–34. Cambridge: Cambridge University Press.

Dedenbach-Salazar Sáenz, Sabine. 1990. *Inka Pachaq Llamanpa Willaynin: Uso y crianza de los camélidos en la época incaica*. Bonn: Bonner Amerikanistische Studien.

Degueurce, Christophe. 1999. "Le musée Fragonard, école nationale vétérinaire d'Alfort." *Les musées de médecine: Histoire, patrimoine et grandes figures de la médecine en France*, edited by Gérard Tilles and Daniel Wallach, 91–104. Toulouse: Éditions Privat.

Degueurce, Christophe. 2011. *Fragonard Museum, the Écorchés: The Anatomical Masterworks of Honoré Fragonard*. Translated by Philip Adds. New York: Blast Books.

"De las vicuñas." 1801. *Semanario de Agricultura y Artes Dirigido á los Párrocos* (Madrid) 10.251 (October 22): 262–269.

Delgado-P., Guillermo. 2004. "'¡Katari, Jatariy!' Una revisita al mesianismo y tres *canciones-memoria*." In *Quechua Verbal Artistry: The Inscription of Andean Voices/Arte expresivo Quechua: La inscripción de voces andinas*, edited by Guillermo Delgado-P. and John M. Schechter, 183–235. Aachen, Germany: Shaker Verlag.

Delgado-P., Guillermo. 2005. "Una aproximación filológica para entender las luchas por la autonomía ayllica." In *Conocimiento indígena y globalización*, edited by Ethel Wara Alderete, 35–58. Quito: Ediciones Abya-Yala.

Desmond, Jane. 2002. "Displaying Death, Animating Life: Changing Fictions of 'Liveness' from Taxidermy to Animatronics." In *Representing Animals*, edited by Nigel Rothfels, 159–179. Bloomington: Indiana University Press.

D'Essen, Lorrain. 1959. *Kangaroos in the Kitchen: The Story of Animal Talent Scouts*. New York: David McKay.

Deville, Émile. 1854. "Considérations sur les avantages de la naturalisation en France de l'alpaca." In *Domestication et naturalisation des animaux utiles*, edited by Isidore Geoffroy Saint-Hilaire, 1–16. 3rd ed. Paris: Dusacq/Librairie Agricole de la Maison Rustique.

Diccionario de autoridades. (1726, 1732, 1737) 1963. Facsimile ed. 3 vols. Real Academia Española. Madrid: Editorial Gredos.

Dictionnaire encyclopédique des sciences médicales. 1868. Vol. 9, Bej–Ble. Paris: Victor Masson et Fils/P. Asselin, Sr. de Labé.

Dior, Christian. 1954. *Talking about Fashion*. Translated by Eugenia Sheppard. New York: G. P. Putnam's Sons.

D'Orbigny, Alcide. 2002. *Viaje a la América Meridional*. Translated by Alfredo Cepeda. Vol. 3. La Paz: IFEA-Plural.

Works Cited | 343

Dransart, Penelope. 1996. "Las flores de los rebaños en Isluga: La vida cultural de los ganaderos y camélidos en el norte de Chile." *Nuevo Texto Crítico* 9.18: 29–39.

Dransart, Penelope. 1997. "Cultural Transpositions: Writing about Rites in the Llama Corral." In *Creating Context in Andean Cultures*, edited by Rosaleen Howard-Malverde, 85–98. New York: Oxford University Press.

Dransart, Penelope. 2002. *Earth, Water, Fleece and Fabric: An Ethnography and Archaeology of Andean Camelid Herding*. London: Routledge.

Dransart, Penelope. 2007. "Mysteries of the Cloaked Body: Analogy and Metaphor in Concepts of Weaving and Body Tissues." *Trivium* 37: 161–187.

Duffin, Christopher J. 2013. "Bezoar Stones and Their Mounts." *Jewellery History Today* 16: 3–4.

Duncan, James, and Derek Gregory. 1999. "Introduction." In *Writes of Passage: Reading Travel Writing*, edited by James Duncan and Derek Gregory, 1–13. London: Routledge.

Duviols, Pierre. 1967. "Un inédit de Cristóbal de Albornoz: 'La instrucción para descubrir todas las guacas del Pirú y sus camayos y haziendas.'" *Journal de la Société des Américanistes* 56.1: 7–39.

Duviols, Pierre. 1971. *La lutte contre les religions autochtones dans le Pérou colonial: 'L'extirpation de l'idolâtrie' entre 1532 et 1660*. Lima: Institut Français d'Études Andines.

Dyce, K. M., W. O. Sack, and C. J. G. Wensing. 2002. *Textbook of Veterinary Anatomy*. 3rd ed. Philadelphia: Saunders.

Eamon, William. 1994. *Science and the Secrets of Nature: Books of Secrets in Medieval and Early Modern Culture*. Princeton, NJ: Princeton University Press.

Eamon, William. 2014. "Epilogue: The Difference That Made Spain, the Difference That Spain Made." In *Medical Cultures of the Early Modern Spanish Empire*, edited by John Slater, María Luz López-Terrada, and José Pardo-Tomás, 231–243. Farnham, UK: Ashgate Publishing.

Edmonds, Penelope. 2006. "The Le Souëf Box: Reflections on Imperial Nostalgia, Material Culture and Exhibitionary Practice in Colonial Victoria." *Australian Historical Studies* 37.127: 117–139.

Elferink, Jan G. R. 1999. "The Use of Poison and Malevolent Magic in Criminal Practices among the Incas in Pre-Columbian Peru." *Colonial Latin American Historical Review* 8.3: 339–360.

Elgood, Cyril, trans. 1935. "A Treatise on the Bezoar Stone by the Late Mahmud Bin Masud the Imad-Ul-Din the Physician of Ispahan." *Annals of Medical History* 7.1: 73–80.

Ellenberger, Michel. 1981. "L'autre Fragonard: Essai biographique." In *L'autre Fragonard*, 8–47. Paris: Jupilles.

Escobari de Querejazu, Laura. 2014. *Producción y comercio en la historia de Bolivia colonial: Siglos XVI–XVIII*. La Paz: Instituto de Investigaciones Históricas/Plural Editores.

Esteras Martín, Cristina. 2004. "Acculturation and Innovation in Peruvian Viceregal Silverwork." In *The Colonial Andes: Tapestries and Silverwork, 1530–1830*, edited by Elena Phipps, Johanna Hecht, and Cristina Esteras Martín, 59–71. New York: Metropolitan Museum of Art/New Haven, CT: Yale University Press.

Esteras Martín, Cristina. 2006. "Silver and Silverwork: Wealth and Art in Viceregal America." In *The Arts in Latin America: 1492–1820*, edited by Joseph J. Rishel and Suzanne Stratton-Pruitt, 178–227. Philadelphia: Philadelphia Museum of Art.

344 | Works Cited

"Expérimentation de l'emploi du liama dans les Vosges." 1859. *Bulletin de la Société Régionale d'Acclimatation pour la Zône du Nord-Est* 2–3: 439–441.

Farber, Paul Lawrence. 2000. *Finding Order in Nature: The Naturalist Tradition from Linnaeus to E. O. Wilson.* Baltimore: Johns Hopkins University Press.

Fauvety, Augusto. 1867. *Primera introducción de alpacas y llamas en la República Oriental del Uruguay.* Montevideo: Imprenta tipográfica á vapor.

Fernández de Oviedo y Valdés, Gonzalo. 1851–1852. *Historia general y natural de las Indias, Islas y Tierra-Firme del Mar Océano*, edited by José Amador de los Rios. 2 vols. Madrid: Imprenta de la Real Academia de la Historia.

Férussac, Andre-Étienne, Baron de. 1823. *Coup d'oeil sur l'Andalousie, précédé d'un journal historique du siège de Saragosse.* Paris: Chez Ponthieu, Delaunay, Béchet aîné, Aimé André, Anselin et Pochard, et chez tous les Marchands de Nouveautés.

Feuillée, Louis. 1725. *Journal des observations physiques, mathématiques et botaniques [. . .].* Vol. 3. Paris: Chez Jean Mariette.

Few, Martha, and Zeb Tortorici. "Introduction: Writing Animal Histories." In *Centering Animals in Latin American History*, edited by Martha Few and Zeb Tortorici, 1–27. Durham, NC: Duke University Press.

Figueroa, Marcelo. 2012. "Cuestionarios, instrucciones y circulación de objetos naturales entre España y América (siglos XVI y XVIII)." *Anuario del Centro de Estudios Históricos "Prof. Carlos S.A. Segreti"* 12.12: 121–136.

Fisher, Clemency. 2002a. "The Knowsley Aviary & Menagerie." In *A Passion for Natural History: The Life and Legacy of the 13th Earl of Derby*, edited by Clemency Fisher, 85–95. Liverpool: National Museums and Galleries on Merseyside.

Fisher, Clemency, ed. 2002b. *A Passion for Natural History: The Life and Legacy of the 13th Earl of Derby.* Liverpool: National Museums and Galleries on Merseyside.

Fisher, Clemency, and Christine E. Jackson. 2002. "The 13th Earl of Derby as a Scientist." In *A Passion for Natural History: The Life and Legacy of the 13th Earl of Derby*, edited by Clemency Fisher, 45–51. Liverpool: National Museums and Galleries on Merseyside.

Fletcher, Chrissy. 2002. *Arthursleigh: A History of the Property, 1819 to 1979.* Sydney: University of Sydney.

Flores Galindo, Alberto. 1977. *Arequipa y el sur andino: Ensayo de historia regional (siglos XVIII–XX).* Lima: Editorial Horizonte.

Flores Ochoa, Jorge. 1977. "Enqa, enqaychu, illa y khuya rumi." In *Pastores de puna: Uywamichiq punarunakuna*, edited by Jorge Flores Ochoa, 211–237. Lima: Instituto de Estudios Peruanos.

Flores Ochoa, Jorge. 1988. "Clasificación y nominación de camélidos sudamericanos." In *Llamichos y paqocheros: Pastores de llamas y alpacas*, edited by Jorge Flores Ochoa, 121–137. Cuzco: Centro de Estudios Andinos Cuzco/Consejo Nacional de Ciencia y Tecnología.

Flores Ochoa, Jorge, and Yoshiki Kobayashi, eds. 2000. *Pastoreo altoandino: Realidad, sacralidad y posibilidades.* La Paz: Plural Editores, CID.

Flores Ochoa, Jorge, and Kim MacQuarrie. 1994a. "The Andean Camelids." In *Gold of the Andes: The Llamas, Alpacas, Vicuñas and Guanacos of South America*, translated by Joanna Martinez, 25–35. Vol. 1. Barcelona: Francis O. Patthey and Sons.

Flores Ochoa, Jorge, and Kim MacQuarrie. 1994b. "Man's Relationship with the Camelids." In *Gold of the Andes: The Llamas, Alpacas, Vicuñas and Guanacos of South America*, translated by Joanna Martinez 36–285. Vol. 1. Barcelona: Francis O. Patthey and Sons.

Works Cited | 345

Fouque, Joseph-Gustave. 1872. "Notice sur les llamas du Pérou, livrés en cheptel par la Société zoologique d'acclimatation de Paris, à la Société d'agriculture de la Haute-Garonne, pour tenter l'acclimatation de ces animaux dans les Pyrénées." *Journal d'Agriculture Pratique et d'Économie Rurale pour le Midi de la France*, 3rd series, 23: 29–33.

Frampton, John. (1577) 1925. *Joyfull Newes Out of the Newe Founde Worlde*. 2nd ed. 2 vols. London: Constable/New York: Alfred A. Knopf.

Freedgood, Elaine. 2000. *Victorian Writing about Risk: Imagining a Safe England in a Dangerous World*. Cambridge: Cambridge University Press.

French, Roger. 1999. *Dissection and Vivisection in the European Renaissance*. Aldershot, UK: Routledge.

Frézier, Amédée. 1716. *Relation du voyage de la mer du sud aux côtes du Chily et du Pérou, fait pendant les années 1712, 1713 & 1714*. Paris: Chez Jean-Geoffroy Nyon, Étienne Ganeau, Jacque Quillau.

Fučíková, Eliška, James M. Bradburne, Beket Bukovinska, Jaroslava Hausenblasova, Lumomir Konecny, Ivan Muchka, and Michal Sronek, eds. 1997. *Rudolf II and Prague: The Court and the City*. London: Prague Castle Administration/Thames and Hudson.

Fuentes, Manuel A. 1875. *Compendio del derecho administrativo*. 2nd ed. Lima: Imprenta del Estado.

Gade, Daniel W. 2013. "Llamas and Alpacas as 'Sheep' in the Colonial Andes: Zoogeography Meets Eurocentrism." *Journal of Latin American Geography* 12.2: 221–243.

Galmiche, Charles. 1860. "Note sur un lama employé à divers travaux à Remiremont (Vosges)." *Bulletin de la Société Impériale Zoologique d'Acclimatation* 7: 401–404.

Galmiche, Charles. 1864a. "Rapport sur les lamas introduits dans les Vosges." *Bulletin de la Société Impériale Zoologique d'Acclimatation*, 2nd series, 1: 456–459.

Galmiche, Charles. 1864b. "Rapport sur le troupeau de liamas de la Société régionale d'Acclimatation du Nord-Est." *Bulletin de la Société Régionale d'Acclimatation Fondée à Nancy pour la Zône du Nord-Est* (second trimester): 233–246.

Galmiche, Charles. 1865. "Rapport sur la maladie et la mort du troupeau de Liamas confié par la Société régionale d'Acclimatation de la zône du nord-est." *Bulletin de la Société Régionale d'Acclimatation Fondée à Nancy pour la Zône du Nord-Est* (second trimester): 408–415.

Garcilaso de la Vega, Inca. (1609) 1985. *Comentarios reales de los Incas*, edited by Aurelio Miró Quesada. 2 vols. 2nd ed. Caracas: Fundación Biblioteca Ayacucho.

Geoffroy (le Jeune), Claude-Joseph. 1731. "Observations sur le bézoard, & sur les autres matières qui en approchent." *Histoire de l'Academie Royale des Sciences*, part 1: 199–208.

Geoffroy (le Jeune), Claude-Joseph. 1732. "Observations sur le bézoard, & sur les autres matières qui en approchent." *Histoire de l'Academie Royale des Sciences*, part 2: 235–242.

Geoffroy Saint-Hilaire, Albert. 1864. "Rapport sur les lamas et alpacas récemment amenés en France de la république de l'Équateur." *Bulletin de la Société Impériale Zoologique d'Acclimatation*, 2nd series, 1: 321–326.

Geoffroy Saint-Hilaire, Albert. 1870. "Note sur le transport des animaux vivants." *Bulletin de la Société Impériale Zoologique d'Acclimatation*, 2nd series, 7: 1–18.

Geoffroy Saint-Hilaire, Albert. 1872. "Lettre adressée à M. N. Joly, professeur a la faculté des sciences et délégué de la Société d'Acclimatation à Toulouse, à l'occasion

346 | *Works Cited*

de son rapport sur les lamas confiés à la Société d'Agriculture de la Haute-Garonne." *Bulletin de la Société Impériale Zoologique d'Acclimatation*, 2nd series, 9: 152–155.

Geoffroy Saint-Hilaire, Isidore. (1861) 1986. *Acclimatation et domestication des animaux utiles.* Facsimile, 4th ed. Paris: La Maison Rustique/Flammarion.

Gerbi, Antonello. 1973. *The Dispute of the New World: The History of a Polemic, 1750–1900.* Translated by Jeremy Moyle. Pittsburgh: University of Pittsburgh Press.

Gesner, Conrad. 1560. *Icones animalium quadrupedum viviparorum et oviparorum [. . .].* 2nd ed. Tiguri (Zürich): Excudebat C. Froschoverus.

Gibbs, Fredrick W. 2013. "Specific Form and Poisonous Properties: Understanding Poison in the Fifteenth Century." *Preternature: Critical and Historical Studies on the Preternatural* 2.1: 19–46.

Gil Albarracín, Antonio. 2002. "Vida y obra de Simón de Rojas Clemente Rubio." In *Viaje a Andalucía: "Historia natural del Reino de Granada" (1804–1809)* by Simón de Rojas Clemente y Rubio, 47–82. Barcelona: Griselda Bonet Girabet.

Gilbert, Helen, and Anna Johnston. 2002. "Introduction." In *In Transit: Travel, Text, Empire,* edited by Helen Gilbert and Anna Johnston, 1–20. New York: Peter Lang.

Gillbank, Linden. 1986. "The Origins of the Acclimatisation Society of Victoria: Practical Science in the Wake of the Gold Rush." *Historical Records of Australian Science* 6.3: 359–374.

Gillbank, Linden. 1996a. "A Paradox of Purposes: Acclimatization Origins of the Melbourne Zoo." In *New Worlds, New Animals: From Menagerie to Zoological Park in the Nineteenth Century,* edited by R. J. Hoage and William A. Deiss, 73–85. Baltimore: Johns Hopkins University Press.

Gillbank, Linden. 1996b. "A Tale of Two Animals—Alpaca and Camel: Zoological Shaping of Mueller's Botanic Gardens." *Victorian Historical Journal* 67.1: 83–102.

Gil Montero, Raquel. 2008. *La construcción de Argentina y Bolivia en los Andes Meridionales: Población, tierras y ambiente en el siglo XIX.* Buenos Aires: Prometeo Libros.

Gilpin, William. 1792. *Three Essays: On Picturesque Beauty; On Picturesque Travel; and On Sketching Landscape, to Which Is Added a Poem, on Landscape Painting.* London: Printed for R. Blamire.

Godoy, Manuel. 1836. *Cuenta dada de su vida política por don Manuel Godoy, príncipe de la Paz.* Vol. 3. Madrid: Imprenta de I. Sancha.

Gómez-Centurión Jiménez, Carlos. 2009. "Curiosidades vivas: Los animales de América y Filipinas en la *Ménagerie* real durante el siglo XVIII." *Anuario de Estudios Americanos* 66.2: 181–211.

Gómez López, Susana. 2005. "Natural Collections in the Spanish Renaissance." In *From Private to Public: Natural Collections and Museums,* edited by Marco Beretta, 13–40. Sagamore Beach, MA: Watson Publishing International.

González Enciso, Agustín. 1980. *Estado e industria en el siglo XVIII: La fábrica de Guadalajara.* Madrid: Fundación Universitaria Española.

González Holguín, Diego. (1608) 1989. *Vocabulario de la lengua general de todo el Perú llamada lengua qquichua o del Inca.* Facsimile of the 1952 ed. Lima: Universidad Nacional Mayor de San Marcos.

González-Stephan, Beatriz. 2003. "Showcases of Consumption: Historical Panoramas and Universal Expositions." In *Beyond Imagined Communities: Reading and Writing the Nation in Nineteenth-Century Latin America,* edited by Sara Castro-Klarén and John Charles Chasteen, 225–238. Washington, DC: Woodrow Wilson Center Press/Baltimore: Johns Hopkins University Press.

Works Cited | 347

Gordon, Avery. 1997. *Ghostly Matters: Haunting and the Sociological Imagination.* Minneapolis: University of Minnesota Press.

Gosden, Chris, and Chantal Knowles. 2001. *Collecting Colonialism: Material Culture and Colonial Change.* Oxford: Berg.

Gosse, Philip Henry. 1855. "Sur l'alpaca." *Bulletin de la Société Impériale Zoologique d'Acclimatation* 2: 319–323.

Gould, Stephen Jay. 2000. "Church, Humboldt, and Darwin: The Tension and Harmony of Art and Science." In *Latin American Popular Culture: An Introduction,* edited by William H. Beezley and Linda A. Curcio-Nagy, 27–42. Wilmington, DE: Scholarly Resources.

Gramiccia, Gabriele. 1988. *The Life of Charles Ledger (1818–1905): Alpacas and Quinine.* London: Macmillan.

Grandjean, Serge. 1964. *Inventaire après décès de l'Impératrice Joséphine à Malmaison.* Paris: Réunion des Musées Nationaux; Ministère d'État—Affaires Culturelles.

Greenblatt, Stephen. 1991. *Marvelous Possessions: The Wonder of the New World.* Chicago: University of Chicago Press.

Grew, Nehemiah. 1681. *Musaeum Regalis Societatis.* London: Printed by W. Rawlins, for the Author.

Guaman Poma de Ayala, Felipe. 1615/1616. *Nueva corónica y buen gobierno.* Copenhagen: Det Kongelige Bibliotek, GKS 2232 4°. http://www5.kb.dk/permalink /2006/poma/info/en/frontpage.htm.

Guerra, Francisco. 1961. *Nicolás Bautista Monardes: Su vida y su obra (c. 1493–1588).* Mexico City: Compañía Fundidora de Fierro y Acero de Monterrey.

Guerra, Francisco. 1966. "Drugs from the Indies and the Political Economy of the Sixteenth Century." In *Analecta Medico-Historico: Materia Medica in the XVIth Century,* edited by M. Florkin, 29–54. Oxford: Pergamon Press.

Guybert, Philbert. 1629. *Les tromperies du bézoard decouvertes.* 2nd ed. Paris: n.p.

Hanke, Lewis, and Gunnar Mendoza. (1700–1736) 1965. "Bartolomé Arzáns de Orsúa y Vela: Su vida y obra." In *Bartolomé Arzáns de Orsúa y Vela's History of Potosí,* xxvii–clxxxii. Vol. 1. Providence, RI: Brown University Press.

Haraway, Donna. 1989. *Primate Visions: Gender, Race, and Nature in the World of Modern Science.* New York: Routledge.

Harcourt, Raoul d'. 1950. "L'impératrice Joséphine et les lamas." *Journal de la Société des Américanistes* 39: 259–262.

Harris, Olivia. 1995. "The Sources and Meanings of Money: Beyond the Market Paradigm in an *Ayllu* of Northern Potosí." In *Ethnicity, Markets, and Migration in the Andes: At the Crossroads of History and Anthropology,* edited by Brooke Larson and Olivia Harris, with Enrique Tandeter, 297–328. Durham, NC: Duke University Press.

Harrison, Regina. 1995. "The Language and Rhetoric of Conversion in the Viceroyalty of Peru." *Poetics Today* 16.1: 1–27.

Heaney, Christopher. 2010. *Cradle of Gold: The Story of Hiram Bingham, a Real-Life Indiana Jones, and the Search for Machu Picchu.* New York: Palgrave Macmillan.

Henderson, Peter V. N. 2008. *Gabriel García Moreno and Conservative State Formation in the Andes.* Austin: University of Texas Press.

Hernández Príncipe, Rodrigo (Licenciado). (1621) 1923. "Mitología andina." *Inca* 1.1: 25–68.

Hess, Katherine Paddock. 1958. *Textile Fibers and Their Use.* 6th ed. Chicago: J. B. Lippincott.

348 | Works Cited

Hetherington, Kevin. 2004. "Secondhandedness: Consumption, Disposal, and Absent Presence." *Environment and Planning D: Society and Space* 22: 157–173.

Hochswender, Woody. 1993. *Men in Style: The Golden Age of Fashion from Esquire.* New York: Rizzoli.

Hoffman, Eric. 2001–2002. "Hearst Herd Smaller Influence Than Believed." *Llama Life* 60: 11.

Houdaille, Jacques. 1959. "Gaetan Souchet D'Alvimart, the Alleged Envoy of Napoleon to Mexico, 1807–1809." *Americas* 16.2: 109–131.

Howe, George Frederick. 1936. "García Moreno's Efforts to Unite Ecuador and France." *Hispanic American Historical Review* 16.2: 257–262.

Huanca L., Tomás. 1991. *Jilirinaksan arsüwipa: "Testimonios de nuestros mayores."* La Paz: Taller de Historia Oral Andina.

Hünefeldt, Christine. 1982. *Lucha por la tierra y protesta indígena: Las comunidades indígenas del Perú entre colonia y república, 1800–1830.* Bonn: Bonner Amerikanische Studien/Estudios Americanistas de Bonn.

Hunter, John. 1861. *Essays and Observations on Natural History, Anatomy, Physiology, Psychology, and Geology.* Edited by Richard Owen. Vol. 1. London: John Van Voorst.

International Exhibition. 1861. *Catalogue of the Natural and Industrial Products of New South Wales, Exhibited in the School of Arts by the International Exhibition Commissioners, Sydney, October 1861.* Sydney: Printed by Reading and Wellbank.

International Exhibition. 1863. *Reports of the Juries of the Subjects in the Thirty-Six Classes into Which the Exhibition Was Divided.* London: Society of Arts.

Jacobsen, Nils. 1993. *Mirages of Transition: The Peruvian Altiplano, 1780–1930.* Berkeley: University of California Press.

Jemio Arnez, Kathya R. 2015. "A espaldas vueltas, memorias muertas: La cotidianidad de Cobija, puerto Lamar y las tareas de los prefectos (1864–1871)." PhD dissertation, History, Universidad Nacional de Colombia, Medellín. https://repositorio.unal.edu.co/handle/unal/53067.

Jiménez Díaz, Pablo. 2001. *El coleccionismo manierista de los Austrias entre Felipe II y Rodolfo II.* Madrid: Sociedad Estatal para la Conmemoración de los Centenarios de Felipe II y Carlos V.

Joly, Nicolas. 1854. "Notice sur la naturalisation et la domestication du lama et de l'alpaca en France." In *Domestication et naturalisation des animaux utiles*, edited by Isidore Geoffroy Saint-Hilaire, 1–14. 3rd ed. Paris: Dusacq, Libraire Agricole de la Maison Rustique.

Joly, Nicolas. 1869. *Project d'acclimatation du llama et de l'alpaca du Pérou dans les Pyrénées françaises.* Excerpt from *Journal d'Agriculture Pratique et d'Économie Rurale* (May and June): 1–15. Toulouse: Impr. Douladoure, de Rouget frères et Delahaut.

Joly, Nicolas. 1870. *Rapport sur un project d'acclimatation du llama péruvien dans les Pyrénées françaises.* Excerpt from *Journal d'Agriculture Pratique et d'Économie Rurale* (January): 3–11. Toulouse: Impr. Douladoure, de Rouget frères et Delahaut.

Joly, Nicolas. 1872a. "Rapport adressé à M. le Président de la Société d'Acclimatation de Paris." *Bulletin de la Société Impériale Zoologique d'Acclimatation*, 2nd series, 9: 145–151.

Joly, Nicolas. 1872b. "Rapport adressé à M. le Président de la Société d'Acclimatation de Paris." *Journal d'Agriculture Pratique et d'Économie Rurale pour le Midi de la France*, 3rd series, 23: 34–39.

Jones, Phyllis Mander. 1953. "A Sketch Book Found in Australia." *Revista Interamericana de Bibliografía/Inter-American Review of Bibliography* 3.3: 280–288.

Jones, Robert W. 1997. "'The Sight of Creatures Strange to Our Clime': London Zoo and the Consumption of the Exotic." *Journal of Victorian Culture* 2.1: 1–26.

Jordanova, Ludmilla J. 1985. "Gender, Generation and Science: William Hunter's Obstetrical Atlas." In *William Hunter and the Eighteenth-Century Medical World*, edited by W. F. Bynum and Roy Porter, 385–412. Cambridge: Cambridge University Press.

Jouanin, Christian. 1997a. "La ménagerie." In *L'impératrice Joséphine et les sciences naturelles*, 112–120. Paris: Éditions de la Reúnion des Musées Nationaux.

Jouanin, Christian. 1997b. "La passion de la nature ou Joséphine amateur et mécène des sciences de la nature." In *L'impératrice Joséphine et les sciences naturelles*, 20–34. Paris: Éditions de la Reúnion des Musées Nationaux.

Jouanin, Christian. 1999. "Le zèbre de Joséphine et les representations d'animaux dans sa collection de tableaux." *Bulletin de la Société des Amis de Malmaison* 33: 47–56.

Jouanin, Christian, and Guy Ledoux-Lebard. 1993. "Histoire des troupeaux de mérinos de Joséphine à Malmaison et d'Eugène à la Ferté-Beauharnais." *Bulletin de la Société des Amis de Malmaison*: 48–55.

Jouanin, Christian, and Guy Ledoux-Lebard. 1997. "Les mérinos de Malmaison." In *L'Impératrice Joséphine et les sciences naturelles*, 154–161. Paris: Éditions de la Reúnion des Musées Nationaux.

Juan, Jorge, and Antonio de Ulloa. 1748. *Relación histórica del viage a la América meridional [. . .]*. 2 vols. Madrid: Antonio Marin.

Juan, Jorge and Antonio de Ulloa. 1749. "Discurso y reflexion[s] políticas: Sobre el estado presente de los reynos del Perú." In "Memorias sobre el Perú y Chile por Dn Antonio Ulloa" (1749), 181–858. Archivo del Museo Naval (Madrid), MS 483.

Ju-kua, Chau. (1783) 1911. *Chau Ju-kua: His Work on the Chinese and Arab Trade in the Twelfth and Thirteenth Centuries [. . .]*. Translated and annotated by Friedrick Hirth and W. W. Rockhill. St. Petersburg: Imperial Academy of Sciences.

Julien, Catherine J. 1999. "History and Art in Translation: The *Paños* and Other Objects Collected by Francisco de Toledo." *Colonial Latin American Review* 8.1: 61–89.

Julien, Pierre. 1968. "Les curieuses collections du château d'Ambras et leur interêt pour l'histoire de la médecine et de la pharmacie." *Revue d'Histoire de la Pharmacie* 19.196: 27–30 (including plate 5).

Kavey, Allison. 2007. *Books of Secrets: Natural Philosophy in England, 1550–1600*. Urbana: University of Illinois Press.

Kingston, Beverley. 1988. *The Oxford History of Australia, 1860–1900: Glad, Confident Morning*. Vol. 3. Oxford: Oxford University Press.

Kociumbas, Jan. 1992. *The Oxford History of Australia, 1770–1860: Possessions*. Vol. 2. Oxford: Oxford University Press.

Lacépède, Bernard-Germain-Étienne de, and Georges Cuvier. 1801. *La ménagerie du Muséum National d'Histoire Naturelle [. . .]*. Paris: Miger.

Lacépède, Bernard-Germain-Étienne de, Georges Cuvier, and Étienne Geoffroy Saint-Hilaire. 1804. "Le LAMA: Camelus Llacma. Linn." In *La ménagerie du Muséum National d'Histoire Naturelle*, 156–176. Vol. 2. Paris: C. F. Patris, Impr. de la Cour de Justice Criminelle.

Lafuente, Antonio. 2000. "Enlightenment in an Imperial Context: Local Science in the Late-Eighteenth-Century Hispanic World." *Osiris*, 2nd series, 15: 155–173.

350 | Works Cited

Laker, Jerry. 2001. "Wildlife or Livestock? Divergent Paths for the Vicuña as Priorities Change in the Pursuit of Sustainable Development." https://www.researchgate.net /profile/Jerry-Laker/research.

Laker, Jerry, Jorge Baldo, Yanina Arzamendia, and Hugo Yacobaccio. 2006. "La vicuña en los Andes." In *Investigación, conservación, y manejo de vicuñas*, edited by Bibiana L. Vilá, 37–50. Buenos Aires: Proyecto MACS.

Landes, Joan B. 2012. "Animal Subjects: Between Nature and Invention in Buffon's Natural History Illustrations." In *Gorgeous Beasts: Animal Bodies in Historical Perspective*, edited by Joan B. Landes, Paula Young Lee, and Paul Youngquist, 21–40. University Park: Pennsylvania State University Press.

Langer, Erick. 2004. "Indian Trade and Ethnic Communities in the Andes, 1780–1880." *Estudios Interdisciplinarios de América Latina y el Caribe* 15.1: 9–33.

Langlois, N.-G., and J.-F.-O. Lévesque. 1804. *Notice descriptive de l'École Vétérinaire d'Alfort*. Paris: de l'Imprimerie de Marchant, Collège d'Harcourt.

Lara, A. Darío. 1986a. "Del Chimborazo a los campos Elíseos." *El Comercio* (Quito), December 4.

Lara, A. Darío. 1986b. "Una lección de ciencias naturales." *El Comercio* (Quito), December 10.

Larsen, Anne. 1996. "Equipment for the Field." In *Cultures of Natural History*, edited by N. Jardine, J. A. Secord, and E. C. Spary, 358–377. Cambridge: Cambridge University Press.

Larson, Brooke. 2004. *Trials of Nation Making: Liberalism, Race, and Ethnicity in the Andes, 1810–1910*. Cambridge: Cambridge University Press.

Lasteyrie, Charles Philibert de. 1834. "Histoire naturelle et économique du lama." In *Histoire naturelle et économique du chameau, du dromadaire, du renne, du lama, et de la vigogne*, 54–61. Paris: Rue Taranne.

Layard, E. L. 1865. "Report upon the Subject of the Acclimatisation of Animals in Connection with the Production and Capabilities of the Cape of Good Hope." In *The Fourth Annual Report of the Acclimatisation Society of New South Wales, and the Amended Rules and Proceedings of the Society during the Past Year*, 65–74. Sydney: Joseph Cook.

"Le Chimborazo: Ascensions diverses." 1851. *Magasin Pittoresque* (19th year): 109–111.

Lecoq, Patrice. 1997. "Algunos apuntes sobre la importancia de las caravanas de camélidos en el desarrollo de la ciudad de Potosí (Comienzo del período colonial)." *Yachay* 14.26: 175–203.

Lecoq, Patrice, and Sergio Fidel M. 2000. "Algunos aspectos de la vida y de los ritos ganaderos en Ventilla, una comunidad pastoral del sud de Potosí, Bolivia." In *Pastoreo altoandino: Realidad, sacralidad y posibilidades*, edited by Jorge A. Flores Ochoa and Yoshiki Kobayashi, 149–187. La Paz: Plural Editores/CID.

Ledger, Charles. 1859. "An Account of the Llama and Alpaca with Notes of a Journey from the Bolivian and Argentine Provinces into Chili with a Flock of These Animals." *Sydney Magazine of Science and Art* 2: 150–156, 182–185, 190–196, 221–222.

Ledger, Charles. 1860a. "Lettre de M. Ledger à M. B. Poucel." *Bulletin de la Société Impériale Zoologique d'Acclimatation* 7: 260–262.

Ledger, Charles. 1860b. "The Peruvian Government and the Alpacas." *Sydney Morning Herald*, September 10.

Works Cited | 351

Ledger, Charles. 1860c. "Sur un troupeau d'alpacas introduit en Australie." *Bulletin de la Société Impériale Zoologique d'Acclimatation* 7: 457–461.

Ledger, Charles. 1861. "Acclimatisation of the Alpaca and Vicuña in Australia." *Journal of the Society of Arts* 9 (June 14): 547–548.

Ledger, Charles. 1864a. "Address to the Acclimatisation Society of New South Wales." In *The Third Annual Report of the Acclimatisation Society of New South Wales [. . .]*, 90–100. Sydney: Printed by Joseph Cook.

Ledger, Charles. 1864b. "Documents sur les alpacas." *Bulletin de la Société Impériale Zoologique d'Acclimatation*, 2nd series, 1: 623–630.

Ledger, George. 1860–1861. "The Alpaca: Its Introduction into Australia and the Probabilities of Its Acclimatisation There." *Journal of the Society of Arts* 9.431: 212–224.

Le Goux (Legoux) de Flaix, Alexandre. 1804. "De la lana y ganado lanar de Cachemira" (extract from the memoir of Alexandre Le Goux de Flaix, 210–216). *Semanario de Agricultura y Artes Dirigido á los Párrocos* (Madrid) 15.379 (April 5): 210–216.

Lemire, Michel. 1990. *Artistes et mortels*. Paris: Éditions Raymond Chabaud.

Lemon, Robert. 1828. "Warrant of Indemnity and Discharge to Lionel Earl of Middlesex, Lord High Treasurer, and to the Other Commissioners of the Jewels, for Having Delivered Certain Jewels to King James the First, Which Were Sent by His Majesty into Spain, to the Prince of Wales and Duke of Buckingham, dated July 7, 1623" (communicated by Robert Lemon, Esq., in a letter to Henry Ellis, Esq. FRS secretary). *Archaeologia: or, Miscellaneous Tracts Relating to Antiquity* 21: 148–157.

Lévêque, A. 1864. "Rapport adressé à M. le Président de la Société Impériale d'Acclimatation sur les lamas et alpacas transportés du Pérou à Toulon." *Bulletin de la Société Impériale Zoologique d'Acclimatation*, 2nd series, 1: 397–401.

Lever, Christopher. 1992. *They Dined on Eland: The Story of the Acclimatisation Societies*. London: Quiller Press.

Levey, Martin. 1966. "Medieval Arabic Toxicology: The *Book on Poisons* of Ibn Wahshīya and Its Relation to Early Indian and Greek Texts." *Transactions of the American Philosophical Society* 56.7: 1–130.

Lightman, Bernard. 2000. "The Story of Nature: Victorian Popularizers and Scientific Narrative." *Victorian Review* 25.2: 1–29.

Livingstone, David N. 2003. *Putting Science in Its Place: Geographies of Scientific Knowledge*. Chicago: University of Chicago Press.

Livingstone, David N. 2007. "Science, Site and Speech: Scientific Knowledge and the Spaces of Rhetoric." *History of the Human Sciences* 20.2: 71–98.

Lofting, Hugh. 1948. *The Story of Doctor Dolittle* (1920). 51st impression. Philadelphia: J. B. Lippincott.

Logan, Joy. 2011. *Aconcagua: The Invention of Mountaineering on America's Highest Peak*. Tucson: University of Arizona Press.

Lohmann Villena, Guillermo, and María Justina Sarabia Viejo, eds. 1986–1989. *Francisco de Toledo: Disposiciones gubernativas para el virreinato del Perú, 1569–1574*. 2 vols. Seville: Escuela de Estudios Hispano-Americanos.

Long, Pamela O. 2002. "Objects of Art/Objects of Nature: Visual Representation and the Investigation of Nature." In *Merchants & Marvels: Commerce, Science, and Art in Early Modern Europe*, edited by Pamela H. Smith and Paula Findlen, 63–82. New York: Routledge.

Loor, Wilfrido, ed. 1954. *Cartas de Gabriel García Moreno (1862–1867)*. Vol. 3. Quito: La Prensa Católica.

352 | Works Cited

López Baralt, Mercedes. 1988. *Icono y conquista: Guamán Poma de Ayala*. Madrid: Hiperión.

López Piñero, José María. 1990. "Las 'nuevas medicinas' americanas en la obra (1565–1574) de Nicolás Monardes." *Asclepio: Archivo Iberoamericano de Historia de la Medicina y Antropología Médica* 42: 3–68.

Maccagno, Luis. 1932. *Los auquénidos peruanos*. Lima: Ministerio de Fomento, Dirección de Agricultura y Ganadería, Sección de Propaganda.

MacCormack, Sabine. 1988. "Pachacuti: Miracles, Punishments, and Last Judgement: Visionary Past and Prophetic Future in Early Colonial Peru." *American Historical Review* 93.4: 960–1006.

MacCormack, Sabine. 1991a. "Demons, Imagination, and the Incas." *Representations* 33: 121–146.

MacCormack, Sabine. 1991b. *Religion in the Andes: Vision and Imagination in Early Colonial Peru*. Princeton, NJ: Princeton University Press.

Macé, C. 1859. "Voyage de M. Roehn, dans les Cordillères, à la recherche des rhunas-llamas." *L'Illustration: Journal Universel* 33 (January–June): 234–236.

MacLeod, Roy M. 1988. "Introduction." In *Disease, Medicine, and Empire: Perspectives on Western Medicine and the Experience of European Expansion*, edited by Roy M. MacLeod and Milton J. Lewis, 1–18. London: Routledge.

Maiguashca, Juan. 2005. "El proyecto garciano de modernidad católica republicana en Ecuador, 1830–1875." In *La mirada esquiva: Reflexiones históricas sobre la interacción del estado y la ciudadanía en los Andes (Bolivia, Ecuador y Perú), siglo XIX*, edited by Marta Irurozqui Victoriano, 233–259. Madrid: Consejo Superior de Investigaciones Científicas.

Maimonides, Moses. (1198) 1997. *Selected Medical Writings of Moses Maimonides*. Translated and edited by Suessman Muntner and Fred Rosner. New York: Classics of Medicine Library, Division of Gryphon Editions.

Majluf, Natalia. 1997. "'Ce n'es pas le Pérou,' or, the Failure of Authenticity: Marginal Cosmopolitans at the Paris University Exhibition of 1855." *Critical Inquiry* 23.4: 868–893.

Malcom, Corey. 1998. "Bezoar Stones." *Navigator: Newsletter of the Mel Fisher Maritime Heritage Society* 13.6: no pagination. https://www.yumpu.com/en/document/view/10157915/bezoar-stones-mel-fisher-maritime-museum.

Manrique, Nelson. 1983. "Los arrieros de la sierra central durante el siglo XIX." *Allpanchis: Revista del Instituto de Pastoral Andina* 18: 27–46.

Manthorne, Katherine Emma. 1989. *Tropical Renaissance: North American Artists Exploring Latin America, 1839–1879*. Washington, DC: Smithsonian Institution Press.

Marcus, Stanley. 1985. *Quest for the Best*. New York: McGraw-Hill.

Marcus, Stanley. 2001. *Minding the Store: A Memoir*. Facsimile e-book edition (published for the ninetieth anniversary of Neiman Marcus). Denton: University of North Texas Press.

Marsh, Bill "Swampy." 2007. *Great Australian Shearing Stories*. Sydney: ABC Books.

Martín, Luis. 2001. *La conquista intelectual del Perú: El Colegio Jesuita de San Pablo, 1568–1767*. Barcelona: Editorial Casiopea.

Martin, Meredith, and Daniela Bleichmar. 2015. "Introduction: Objects in Motion in the Early Modern World." *Art History* 38.4: 604–619.

Martin de Moussy, Victor. 1860. *Description géographique et statistique de la Confédération Argentine*. Vol. 2. Paris: Librairie de Firmin Ditot.

Works Cited | 353

Martínez de Leyua, Miguel. 1597. *Remedios, preservativos, y cvrativos, para en tiempo de la peste*. Madrid: En la Imprenta Real por Iuan Flamenco.

Martín Polo, Fernando. 2010. "Simón de Rojas Clemente y Rubio: Vida y obra, el compromiso ilustrado." Thesis, University of Barcelona.

Marvin, Garry. 2006. "Perpetuating Polar Bears: The Cultural Life of Dead Animals." In *Nanoq: Flat Out and Bluesome, a Cultural Life of Polar Bears*, edited by Bryndís Snæöjrnsdóttir and Mark Wilson, 156–167. London: Black Dog Publishing.

Mason, Peter. 2009. *Before Disenchantment: Images of Exotic Animals and Plants in the Early Modern World*. London: Reaktion Books.

Matienzo, Juan de. (1567) 1910. *Gobierno del Perú*. Buenos Aires: Compañía Sud-Americana de Billetes de Banco.

Mazzitelli Mastricchio, Malena. 2015. "Geografías en disputa: Los cambios en los discursos geográficos de la Argentina (1852–1905)." *Journal of Latin American Geography* 14.3: 67–90.

McClellan, James E., III. 1992. *Colonialism and Science: Saint Domingue in the Old Regime*. Baltimore: Johns Hopkins University Press, 1992.

Medinaceli G., Ximena. 2010. *Sariri: Los llameros y la construcción de la sociedad colonial*. Lima: Instituto Francés de Estudios Andinos/La Paz: Plural Editores.

Meléndez, Mariselle. 2011. *Deviant and Useful Citizens: The Cultural Production of the Female Body in Eighteenth-Century Peru*. Nashville: Vanderbilt University Press, 2011.

Meléndez, Mariselle, and Karen Stolley. 2015. "Introduction: Enlightenments in Ibero-America." *Colonial Latin American Review* 24.1: 1–16.

Mello Pereira, Magnus Roberto de. 2013. "'Las cosas singulares de piedras, animales, plantas': La formación y el funcionamiento de la red imperial española de remesas científicas en el Virreinato del Río de la Plata." *Annais do Museu Paulista* 21.1: 91–138.

Melville, Elinor G. K. 1994. *A Plague of Sheep: Environmental Consequences of the Conquest of Mexico*. Cambridge: Cambridge University Press.

Mercado, Melchor María. 1991. *Albúm de paisajes, tipos humanos y costumbres de Bolivia (1841–1869)*. La Paz: Banco Central de Bolivia/Archivo Nacional de Bolivia/Biblioteca Nacional de Bolivia.

Midelfort, H. C. Erik. 1994. *Mad Princes of Renaissance Germany*. Charlottesville: University of Virginia Press.

Miller, Arthur. 1986. "Introduction." In *Portraits*, by Inge Morath, 6–7. New York: Aperture.

Miller, George Robert. 1979. "An Introduction to the Ethnoarchaeology of the Andean Camelids." PhD dissertation, University of California, Berkeley.

Millones, Luis, ed. 1971. "Las informaciones de Cristóbal de Albornoz: Documentos para el estudio del Taki Onqoy." Special issue: *Sondeos* 79.

Mills, Kenneth. 1997. *Idolatry and Its Enemies: Colonial Andean Religion and Extirpation, 1640–1750*. Princeton, NJ: Princeton University Press.

Minard, Peter Maxwell. 2021. *All Things Harmless, Useful, and Ornamental: Environmental Transformation through Species Acclimatization, from Colonial Australia to the World*. Chapel Hill: University of North Carolina Press.

Mitchell, Jessie. 2010. "Alpacas in Colonial Australia: Acclimatisation, Evolution, and Empire." *Journal of Australian Colonial History* 12: 55–76.

Mitre, Bartolomé. 1913. *Archivo del General Mitre: Presidencia de la República (Continuación), años 1862–1868*. Vol. 26. Buenos Aires: Biblioteca de la Nación.

354 | Works Cited

Molina, Juan Ignacio. 1788. *Compendio de la historia geográfica, natural y civil del reyno de Chile.* Translated by Domingo Joseph de Arquellada Mendoza. Vol. 1. Madrid: Don Antonio de Sancha.

Monardes, Nicolás. 1565. *Dos libros [. . .].* Seville: Impr. en casa de S. Trugillo.

Monardes, Nicolás. 1571. *Segunda parte del libro de las cosas que se traen de nuestras Indias Occidentales.* Seville: Impr. En casa de Alonso Escriuano.

Monardes, Nicolás. 1574. *Primera y segunda y tercera partes de la historia medicinal de las cosas que se traen de nuestras Indias Occidentales que sirven en medicina.* Seville: En casa de Alonso Escriuano.

Montesinos, Fernando. (1605) 1906. *Anales del Perú.* Vol. 2. Madrid: Imprenta de Gabriel L. y del Horno.

Moore, Katherine M. 1989. "Hunting and the Origins of Herding in Peru." PhD dissertation, University of Michigan.

Moore, Katherine M. 2016. "Early Domesticated Camelids in the Andes." In *The Archaeology of Andean Pastoralism,* edited by José M. Capriles and Nicholas Tripcevich, 17–38. Albuquerque: University of New Mexico Press.

Moore, Wendy. 2005. *The Knife Man: The Extraordinary Life and Times of John Hunter, Father of Modern Surgery.* London: Bantam Press.

Morales, Gaspar de. 1605. *Libro de las virtudes y propiedades marauillosas de las piedras preciosas.* Madrid: Luys Sánchez.

Mort, Thomas S. 1850. "The Alpaca or Peruvian Sheep." Offprint, *Proceedings of the Australian Society.* Sydney: n.p.

"Mr. Charles Ledger." 1859. *Illustrated News of the World,* September 17, 1859.

Muir, Barry Richard. 1989. *Jack Howe: The Man and the Legend.* 2nd ed. Blackall, Queensland: B. and J. Muir.

Murphy, Elsie M. 1952. *Wool and Superwool.* New York: S. Stroock.

Murúa, Fray Martín de. (ca. 1611) 2001. *Historia general del Perú.* Edited by Manuel Ballesteros Gaibrois. Reprint. Madrid: Dastin.

Musselman, Elizabeth Green. 2009. "Indigenous Knowledge and Contact Zones: The Case of the Cold Bokkeveld Meteorite, Cape Colony, 1838." *Itinerario* 33.1: 31–44.

Narborough, John, Captain Jasmen Tasman, Captain John Wood, and Frederick Marten of Hamburgh. 1694. *An Account of Several Late Voyages & Discoveries to the South and North towards the Streights of Magellan, the South Seas, the Vast Tracts of Land beyond Hollandia Nova, &c.* London: Printed for Sam Smith and Benj. Walford, Printers to the Royal Society.

"Necrología: Simón de Rojas Clemente." 1827. *Gaceta de Madrid* 37 (March 27): 146–148.

Nélis, (Corneille-François) l'Abbé de. 1780. "Mémoires sur la possibilité et les avantages de naturaliser dans nos provinces différentes espèces d'animaux étrangers." *Mémoires de l'Académie Impériale et Royale des Sciences et Belles-Letres de Bruxelles* 1: 43–58.

Noonan, Meg Lukens. 2013. *The Coat Route: Craft, Luxury & Obsession on the Trail of a $50,000 Coat.* New York: Spiegel and Grau.

Núñez, Ignacio. 1898. *Noticias históricas de la república Argentina.* 2nd ed. Buenos Aires: Litografía, Imprenta y Encuadernación de Guillermo Kraft.

Nyhart, Lynn K. 2004. "Science, Art, and Authenticity in Natural History Displays." In *Models: The Third Dimension of Science,* edited by Soraya de Chadarevian and Nick Hopwood, 307–335. Stanford, CA: Stanford University Press.

Ocaña, Fray Diego de. (1605?) 1969. *Un viaje fascinante por la América Hispana del siglo XVI.* Madrid: STVDIVM Ediciones.

Works Cited | 355

Orlove, Benjamin S. 1977. *Alpacas, Sheep, and Men: The Wool Export Economy and Regional Society in Southern Peru*. New York: Academic Press.

Orta, Garcia da. (1563) 1895. *Coloquios dos simples e drogas da India*. Edited by Conde de Ficalho. Vol. 2. Lisbon: Imprensa Nacional.

Osborne, Michael A. 1994. *Nature, the Exotic, and the Science of French Colonialism*. Bloomington: Indiana University Press.

Osborne, Michael A. 2000. "Acclimatizing the World: A History of the Paradigmatic Colonial Science." *Osiris*, 2nd series, 15: 135–151.

Pagden, Anthony. 1993. *European Encounters with the New World: From Renaissance to Romanticism*. New Haven, CT: Yale University Press.

Pardo Tomás, José. 2002. *Oviedo, Monardes, Hernández: El tesoro natural de América, colonialismo y ciencia en el siglo XVI*. Madrid: Nivola.

Parker, Merryl. 2007. "The Cunning Dingo." *Society and Animals* 15: 69–78.

Patchett, Merle, and Kate Foster. 2008. "Repair Work: Surfacing the Geographies of Dead Animals." *Museum and Society* 6.2: 98–122.

Patchett, Merle, Kate Foster, and Hayden Lorimer. 2011. "The Biogeographies of a Hollow-Eyed Harrier." In *Afterlives of Animals: A Museum Menagerie*, edited by Samuel J. M. M. Alberti, 110–133. Charlottesville: University of Virginia Press.

Patterson, Kay. 1994. "The History and Philosophy of the Patterson Breeding Program and the Industry It Founded." *Llama Life* 31: 6, 8–9.

Peiss, Kathy. 1998. *Hope in a Jar: The Making of America's Beauty Culture*. New York: Metropolitan Books.

Pentland, Joseph Barclay. 1974. "Report on Bolivia, 1827." In *Camden Miscellany*, edited by J. Valerie Fifer, 170–267. Camden Fourth Series. Vol. 25. London: Office of the Royal Historical Society.

Peralta Ruiz, Víctor. 2006. "La frontera amazónica en el Perú del siglo XVIII: Una representación desde la ilustración." *Brocar* 30: 139–158.

Pérez de Tudela, Almudena, and Annemarie Jordan Gschwend. 2001. "Luxury Goods for Royal Collectors: Exotica, Princely Gifts and Rare Animals Exchanged between the Iberian Courts and Central Europe in the Renaissance (1560–1612)." *Jahrbuch des Kunsthistorischen Museums Wien* 3: 1–127.

Peyer, Johann Konrad. 1685. *Merycologia sive de Ruminantibus et Ruminatione Commentarius*. Basel, Switzerland: Apud Joh. Ludovicum Koenig et Joh. Brandmyllerum.

Peyrebonne, Nathalie. 2011. "Le vin-poison dans la littérature espagnole du siècle d'or." In *Poison et antidote dans l'Europe des XVIe et XVIIe siècles*, edited by Sarah Voinier and Guillaume Winter, 49–56. Paris: Artois Presses Université.

Piel, Jean. 1973. "Rebeliones agrarias y supervivencias coloniales en el Perú del siglo XIX." *Revista del Museo Nacional* 39: 301–314.

Pimentel, Juan. 1999. "La monarquía hispánica y la ciencia donde no se ponía el sol." In *Madrid, ciencia y corte*, edited by Antonio Lafuente and Javier Moscoso, 41–61. Madrid: Consejería de Educación y Cultura.

Pitt, Robert. 1702. *The Craft and Frauds of Physick Expos'd*. London: Tim. Childe.

Platt, Tristan. 1982. *Estado boliviano y ayllu andino: Tierra y tributo en el norte de Potosí*. Lima: Instituto de Estudios Peruanos.

Platt, Tristan. 1993. "Simón Bolívar, the Sun of Justice and the Amerindian Virgin: Andean Conceptions of the *Patria* in Nineteenth-Century Potosí." *Journal of Latin American Studies* 25.1: 159–185.

Platt, Tristan. 1995. "Ethnic Calendars and Market Interventions among the *Ayllus*

356 | Works Cited

of Lipes during the Nineteenth Century." In *Ethnicity, Markets, and Migration in the Andes: At the Crossroads of History and Anthropology*, edited by Brooke Larson and Olivia Harris with Enrique Tandeter, 259–296. Durham, NC: Duke University Press.

Platt, Tristan, Thérèse Bouysse-Cassagne, and Olivia Harris, with Thierry Saignes, eds. 2006. *Qaraqara-Charka: Mallku, inka y rey en la provincia de Charcas (siglos XV–XVII): Historia antropológica de una confederación aymara.* Lima Instituto Francés de Estudios Andinos/St. Andrews, Scotland: University of St. Andrews/La Paz: Plural editores.

Poliquin, Rachel. 2008. "The Matter and Meaning of Museum Taxidermy." *Museum and Society* 6.2: 123–134.

Poliquin, Rachel. 2012. *The Breathless Zoo: Taxidermy and the Cultures of Longing.* University Park: Pennsylvania State University Press.

Poliquin, Rachel. 2016. "Taxidermy and a Poetics of Strangeness." Keynote lecture for Taxidermy, Art, and the Animal Question: A Symposium (February 27 to 28). https://www.youtube.com/watch?v=_68hDnsVXr4.

Pólit Laso, Manuel María, ed. 1923. *Escritos y discursos de Gabriel García Moreno.* 2nd ed. Vol. 2. Quito: Tip. y Encuadernación Salesianas.

Pomata, Gianna. 2011. "Observation Rising: Birth of an Epistemic Genre, 1500–1650." In *Histories of Scientific Observation*, edited by Lorraine Daston and Elizabeth Lunbeck, 45–80. Chicago: University of Chicago Press.

Pomet, Pierre. 1694. *Histoire générale des drogues.* Paris: Chez Jean-Baptiste Loyson and Augustin Pillon.

Poole, Deborah. 1997. *Vision, Race, and Modernity: A Visual Economy of the Andean Image World.* Princeton, NJ: Princeton University Press.

Poole, Deborah. 1998. "Landscape and the Imperial Subject: U.S. Images of the Andes, 1859–1930." In *Close Encounters of Empire: Writing the Cultural History of U.S.–Latin American Relations*, edited by Gilbert M. Joseph, Catherine C. LeGrand, and Ricardo D. Salvatore, 106–138. Durham, NC: Duke University Press, 1998.

Porta, John Baptista (Giambattista della Porta) (1558, 1559) 1669. *Natural Magick in Twenty Books Wherein Are Set Forth All the Riches and Delights of the Natural Sciences.* London: Printed for John Wright.

Portús, Javier. 1994. "Europe and the Andean Camelids: Words and Pictures Tell a Story of Cultural Integration." In *Gold of the Andes: The Llamas, Alpacas, Vicuñas and Guanacos of South America*, translated by Joanna Martinez, 8–99. Vol. 2. Barcelona: Francis O. Patthey and Sons.

Potter, M. David, and Bernard P. Corbman. 1959. *Fiber to Fabric.* 3rd ed. New York: McGraw-Hill.

Poucel, Benjamin. 1858. "Sur un project d'introduction et d'acclimatation du lama, de l'alpaca et de la vigogne dans l'Australie et sur les travaux entrepris a cet effet par M. Ledger: Extrait d'une lettre adressée à M. le docteur Vavasseur." *Bulletin de la Société Impériale Zoologique d'Acclimatation* 5: 177–184.

Poucel, Benjamin. 1860. "Sur les lamas, alpacas et vigognes transportés en Australie par M. Ledger." *Bulletin de la Société Impériale Zoologique d'Acclimatation* 7: 255–260.

Poucel, Benjamin. 1861. *La tente du berger des Cordilières.* Marseille: Barlatier-Feissat et Demonchy.

Works Cited | 357

Poucel, Benjamin. 1864a. "La province de Catamarca." *Bulletin de la Société de Géographie* 7 (January–June): 161–176, 267–279.

Poucel, Benjamin. 1864b. "La province de Catamarca." *Bulletin de la Société de Géographie* 8 (July–December): 31–51.

Poynter, F. N. L. 1963. "Foreword." In *Two Pioneers of Tropical Medicine: Garcia d'Orta and Nicolás Monardes*, edited by C. R. Boxer, 3–4. Lecture Series No. 1. London: Wellcome Historical Medical Library.

Pratt, Mary Louise. 1992. *Imperial Eyes: Travel Writing and Transculturation*. London: Routledge.

Price, Uvedale. 1796. *An Essay on the Picturesque, as Compared with the Sublime and the Beautiful [. . .]*. Vol. 1. London: J. Robson.

Primerose, James. 1651. *Popular Errours, or, the Errours of the People in Physick [. . .]*. Translated by Robert Wittie. London: Printed by W. Wilson for Nicholas Bourne.

Qaddumi, Ghada Hijjawi. 1990. "A Medieval Islamic Book of Gifts and Treasures: Translation, Annotation, and Commentary on the Kitab al-Hadava wa al-Tuhaf." PhD dissertation, Harvard University.

Raftery, Frances. 1939. *Stroock's Animal Kingdom*. New York: S. Stroock.

Railliet, Alcide Louis Joseph, and Léon Théophile Moulé. 1908. *Histoire de l'École d'Alfort*. Paris: Asselin and Houzeau.

Raj, Kapil. 2007. *Relocating Modern Science: Circulation and the Construction of Knowledge in South Asia and Europe, 1650–1900*. New York: Palgrave Macmillan.

Raj, Kapil. 2010. "Introduction: Circulation and Locality in Early Modern Science." *British Journal for the History of Science* 43.4: 513–517.

Ramos Gavilán, Alonso. (1621) 1988. *Historia del santuario de nuestra señora de Copacabana*. Lima: Edición Ignacio Prado Pastor.

Reidy, Michael S. 2015. "Mountaineering, Masculinity, and the Male Body in Mid-Victorian Britain." *Osiris* 30: 158–181.

Religiosos Agustinos. (1560) 1918. "Relación de la religión y ritos del Perú hecha por los primeros religiosos agustinos que allí pasaron para la conversión de los naturales." In *Colección de libros y documentos referentes a la historia del Perú*, edited by Horacio H. Urteaga, 3–56. Lima: Imprenta y Librería Sanmartí y Compañía.

Rennie, James. 1829. *The Menageries: Quadrupeds, Described and Drawn from Living Subjects*. Vol. 1. London: Charles Knight. Google Books.

Ridder de Zemboraín, Maud de. 1998. "Vicuñas para una emperatriz." *Todo Es Historia* 32.376: 38–47.

Ritvo, Harriet. 1987. *The Animal Estate: The English and Other Creatures in the Victorian Age*. Cambridge, MA: Harvard University Press.

Ritvo, Harriet. 1997. *The Platypus and the Mermaid and Other Figments of the Classifying Imagination*. Cambridge, MA: Harvard University Press.

Rivera Cusicanqui, Silvia. 1993. "La raíz: Colonizadores y colonizados." In *Violencias encubiertas en Bolivia*, edited by Silvia Rivera C. and Raúl Barrios. Vol. 1: *Cultura y política*, 25–139. General editors: Xavier Albó and Raúl Barrios. La Paz: CIPCA-Aruwiyiri.

Rivera Cusicanqui, Silvia. 2012. "Ch'ixinakax utxiwa: A Reflection on the Practices and Discourses of Decolonization." *South Atlantic Quarterly* 111.1: 95–109.

Robbins, Louise E. 2002. *Elephant Slaves & Pampered Parrots: Exotic Animals in Eighteenth-Century Paris*. Baltimore: Johns Hopkins University Press.

358 | *Works Cited*

Roberts, K. B., and J. D. W. Tomlinson. 1992. *The Fabric of the Body: European Traditions of Anatomical Illustration.* Oxford: Clarendon Press.

Roehn, Eugène. 1855. "Descriptive Account of Part of the Province of Panama." *Panama Star and Herald*, August 11, 1855.

Roehn, Eugène. 1859. "Mémoire sur les lamas (*rhuna-llamas*) et congénères de la chaine des Andes de l'Amérique du Sud (extrait)." *Bulletin de la Société Impériale Zoologique d'Acclimatation* 6: 132–140.

Roehn, Eugène. 1860. "Sur l'expédition du troupeau d'alpacas et de lamas destiné à la Société Impériale d'Acclimatation." *Bulletin de la Société Impériale Zoologique d'Acclimatation* 7: 497–503.

Roehn, Eugène, and Christophe Jérôme Barthélemy-Lapommeraye. 1848a. *Mémoire sur l'introduction en France de la race des alpacas et llamas de l'Amérique du Sud, par la voie d'association départementale.* Paris: Imprimerie Lacour.

Roehn, Eugène, and Christophe Jérôme Barthélemy-Lapommeraye. 1848b. "Notice sur l'alpaca des Andes du Pérou (*Camelus paco*, de Buffon)." In *Recueil Industriel ou de la Société Polytechnique*, 1–11. Paris: Guiraudet et Jouaust.

Rosa Olmos, Ramón. 1970. *Benjamin Poucel, un viajero francés que visitó Catamarca a mediados del siglo XIX.* Catamarca, Argentina: Editorial "La Unión."

Ross, Corey. 2017. *Ecology and Power in the Age of Empire: Europe and the Transformation of the Tropical World.* Oxford: Oxford University Press.

Royal Commission for the International Exhibition (Victoria). 1863. *International Exhibition, 1862: Victoria.* Melbourne: Government Printer.

Rufz de Lavison, Étienne. 1864. "Note sur les différentes tentatives d'introduction et d'acclimatation des lamas et alpacas qui ont eu lieu en Europe." *Bulletin de la Société Impériale Zoologique d'Acclimatation*, 2nd series, 1: 327–337.

Ryan, James R. 2005. "'Hunting with the Camera': Photography, Wildlife and Colonialism in Africa." In *Animal Spaces, Beastly Places: New Geographies of Human-Animal Relations*, edited by Chris Philo and Chris Wilbert, 205–222. London: Routledge.

Safier, Neil. 2010a. "Global Knowledge on the Move: Itineraries, Amerindian Narratives, and Deep Histories of Science." *Isis* 101.1: 133–145.

Safier, Neil. 2010b. "Itineraries of Atlantic Science: New Questions, New Approaches, New Directions." *Atlantic Studies* 7.4: 357–364.

Salomon, Frank. 2004. "Andean Opulence: Indigenous Ideas about Wealth in Colonial Peru." In *The Colonial Andes: Tapestries and Silverwork, 1530–1830*, edited by Elena Phipps, Johanna Hecht, and Cristina Esteras Martín, 115–124. New York: Metropolitan Museum of Art/Yale University Press.

Salomon, Frank, Jorge Urioste, and Francisco de Ávila. 1991. *The Huarochirí Manuscript: A Testament of Ancient and Colonial Andean Religion.* Austin: University of Texas Press.

Salvatore, Ricardo. 2002. "The Early Visions of a Hemispheric Market in South America." In *Transnational America: The Fading of Borders in the Western Hemisphere*, edited by Berndt Ostendorf, 45–64. New York: Barnes and Noble.

Sameiro Barroso, Maria do. 2014. "The Bezoar Stone: A Princely Antidote, the Távora Sequeira Pinto Collection-Oporto." *Acta Medico-Historica Adriatica* 12.1: 77–98.

Sánchez Cantón, F. J., ed. 1958. *Inventarios reales: Bienes muebles que pertenecieron a Felipe II.* 2 vols. Madrid: Imprenta y Editorial Maestre.

Sanford, Herb. 1976. *Ladies and Gentlemen, the Garry Moore Show: Behind the Scenes When TV Was New.* New York: Stein and Day.

Works Cited | 359

Savary des Bruslons, Jacques. 1741. *Dictionnaire universel de commerce: Contenant tout ce qui concerne le commerce qui se fait dans les quatre parties du monde [. . .]*. 3 vols. Paris: Chez la Veuve Estienne.

Sawday, Jonathan. 1995. *The Body Emblazoned: Dissection and the Human Body in Renaissance Culture*. London: Routledge.

Schell, Patience A. 2013. *The Sociable Sciences: Darwin and His Contemporaries in Chile*. New York: Palgrave Macmillan.

Serulnikov, Sergio. 2013. *Revolution in the Andes: The Age of Túpac Amaru*. Translated by David Frye. Durham, NC: Duke University Press, 2013.

Shapin, Steven. 2011. *A Social History of Truth: Civility and Science in Seventeenth-Century England*. Chicago: University of Chicago Press.

"Shearing the Alpacas." 1859. *Sydney Morning Herald*, November 7, 1859.

Simon, Jonathan. 2002. "The Theater of Anatomy: The Anatomical Preparations of Honoré Fragonard." *Eighteenth-Century Studies* 36.1: 63–79.

Simon, Jonathan. 2008. "Honoré Fragonard, Anatomical Virtuoso." In *Science and Spectacle in the European Enlightenment*, edited by Bernadette Bensaude-Vincent and Christine Blondel, 141–158. Aldershot, UK: Ashgate, 2008.

Sivasundaram, Sujit. 2010. "Sciences and the Global: On Methods, Questions, and Theory." *Isis* 101.1: 146–158.

Smith, Pamela H., and Paula Findlen. 2002a. "Introduction: Commerce and the Representation of Nature in Art and Science." In *Merchants and Marvels: Commerce, Science, and Art in Early Modern Europe*, edited by Pamela H. Smith and Paula Findlen, 1–25. New York: Routledge.

Smith, Pamela H., and Paula Findlen, eds. 2002b. *Merchants and Marvels: Commerce, Science, and Art in Early Modern Europe*. New York: Routledge.

"Sobre la necesidad de domesticar á la vicuña para que no se extermine su especie: Providencias que se podrian tomar para conseguirlo y medio de fomentar los rebaños de Alpacas blancas." 1803. *Semanario de Agricultura, Industria, y Comercio* (Buenos Aires) 1.33 (May 4): 257–264.

"Sobre la posibilidad de domesticar á la vicuña, cruzar su casta con las de la llama, la oveja, la alpaca y el guanaco, y medios que debían tentarse para conseguirlo." 1804–1805. *Semanario de Agricultura, Industria, y Comercio* (Buenos Aires) 3: 283–287, 309–312, 319.

Socolow, Susan Migden. 2007. "2007 CLAH Luncheon Address: History and the Goddess Fortune: The Case of Santiago de Liniers." *Americas* 64.1: 1–9.

Solórzano y Pereira, Juan de. (1648) 1972. *Política indiana*. Vol. 4. Madrid: Compañía Ibero-Americana de Publicaciones.

Sonter, Sharyn Louise. 1997. "The Museum and the Department Store." MA thesis, University of Western Sydney, Nepean.

Soubeiran, J. León. 1864. "Rapport annuel sur les travaux de la Société d'Acclimatation." *Bulletin de la Société Impériale Zoologique d'Acclimatation*, 2nd series, 1: xii–xliii.

Soule, Emily Berquist. 2014. *The Bishop's Utopia: Envisioning Improvement in Colonial Peru*. Philadelphia: University of Pennsylvania Press.

Sournia, Jean-Charles. 1981. "L'anatomie du tragique." In *L'autre Fragonard*, edited by Michel Ellenberger, 4–5. Paris: Jupilles.

S. Stroock & Co. 1939. *Fine Men's Wear Fabrics*. New York: S. Stroock.

S. Stroock & Co. 1948. *America's Most Distinguished Woolens* (fabric book). New York City: F. Eugene Ackerman Associates.

360 | Works Cited

Stafford, Barbara Maria. 1984. *Voyage into Substance: Art, Science, Nature, and the Illustrated Travel Account, 1760–1840.* Cambridge, MA: MIT Press.

Stafford, Barbara Maria. 1991. *Body Criticism: Imaging the Unseen in Enlightenment Art and Medicine.* Cambridge, MA: MIT Press.

Stark, Marnie. 2003–2004. "Mounted Bezoar Stones, Seychelles Nuts, and Rhinoceros Horns: Decorative Objects as Antidotes in Early Modern Europe." *Studies in the Decorative Arts* 11.1: 63–94.

Stephenson, Marcia. 2023. "Hybridity and the Domestication of Wildness: Creating the Paco-vicuña in Early Nineteenth-Century Peru." *Hispanic American Historical Review* 103.4 (forthcoming).

Stroock, Margaret, and Bert Stroock. 1964. *Stroocks' Tours: Personal Glimpses of Distant Places.* 2 vols. Newtown, CT: Margaret and Bert Stroock.

Stroock, Sylvan I. 1937a. *Llamas and Llamaland.* New York: S. Stroock.

Stroock, Sylvan I. 1937b. *The Story of Vicuna: The World's Finest Fabric.* New York: S. Stroock.

Subrahmanyam, Sanjay. 1997. "Connected Histories: Notes Towards a Reconfiguration of Early Modern Eurasia." *Modern Asian Studies* 31: 735–762.

"Sur les llamas ou liamas." 1859. *Société Régionale d'Acclimatation Fondée à Nancy pour la Zône du Nord-Est: Bulletin du Second Trimestre*: 327–332.

Swinglehurst, Henry. 1893. *Silver Mines and Incidents of Travel: Letters and Notes on Sea and Land.* Kendal, UK: T. Wilson, Printer.

Swinney, Geoffrey N. 2011. "An Afterword on Afterlife." In *Afterlives of Animals: A Museum Menagerie*, edited by Samuel J. M. M. Alberti, 219–233. Charlottesville: University of Virginia Press.

Tandeter, Enrique, Vilma Milletich, María Matilde Ollier, and Beatríz Ruibal. 1995. "Indians in Late Colonial Markets: Sources and Numbers." In *Ethnicity, Markets, and Migration in the Andes: At the Crossroads of History and Anthropology*, edited by Brooke Larson and Olivia Harris with Enrique Tandeter, 196–223. Durham, NC: Duke University Press.

Taylor-Leduc, Susan. 2013. "Josephine as Shepherdess: Estate Management at Malmaison." In *Of Elephants & Roses: French Natural History, 1790–1830*, edited by Sue Ann Prince, 44–57. Philadelphia: American Philosophical Society Museum.

Taylor-Leduc, Susan. 2019. "Joséphine at Malmaison: Acclimatizing Self and Other in the Garden." *Journal 18* 8: no pagination.

Terrall, Mary. 1998. "Heroic Narratives of Quest and Discovery." *Configurations* 6.2: 223–242.

Theran, Francisco de. 1821. "Primeiro ensaio, feito em Hespanha para domesticar, e aclimatar as Vigonhas, e para aclimatar igualmente os outros animaes da sua especie, conhecidos pelos nomes de Lhamas e Alpacos." *Annaes das Sciencias, das Artes, e das Letras* 14 (part 2, year 4, October, Paris): 16–24.

Thomson, Sinclair. 2002. *We Alone Will Rule: Native Andean Politics in the Age of Insurgency.* Madison: University of Wisconsin Press.

Tirado Bramen, Carrie. 2002. "A Transatlantic History of the Picturesque: An Introductory Essay." *Nineteenth-Century Prose* 29.2: 1–19.

Tomoeda, Hiroyasu. 1996. "El discurso indígena en las crónicas de Felipe Guaman Poma de Ayala y Juan Santa Cruz Pachacuti Yamqui Salcamaygua." *Nuevo Texto Crítico* 9.18: 65–73.

Toribio Medina, José. 1908. *El veneciano Sebastián Caboto al servicio de España [. . .]*. Vol. 1. Santiago de Chile: Imprenta y Encuadernación Universitaria.

Trnek, Helmut, and Nuno Vassallo e Silva, eds. 2001. *Exotica: The Portuguese Discoveries and the Renaissance Kunstkammer*. Lisbon: Fundação Calouste Gulbenkian/Vienna: Kunsthistorisches Museum.

Tschudi, Johann Jakob von. 1847. *Travels in Peru, during the Years 1838–1842 [. . .]*. Translated by Thomasina Ross. London: David Bogue.

Turgot, Étienne-François. 1758. *Mémoire instructif sur la manière de rassembler, de préparer, de conserver, et d'envoyer les diverses curiosités d'histoire naturelle*. Paris: Chez Jean Marie Bruyset.

Turner, Brian. 1981. "When Llamas Came to New South Wales." *Geo: Australasia's Geographical Magazine* 3.2: 110–123.

Uhl, Max. 1906. "Las llamitas de piedra del Cuzco." *Revista Histórica* 1: 388–392.

"Une nouvelle industrie dans la rivière de la Plata." 1868. *Bulletin de la Société Impériale Zoologique d'Acclimatation*, 2nd series, vol. 5: 363–366.

Valdivieso, Enrique, ed. 1998. *Zurbarán: IV centenario de nacimiento*. Seville: Museo de Bellas Artes de Sevilla/Junta de Andalucía, Consejería de Cultura.

Valdizán, Hermilio, and Angel Maldonado. 1922. *La medicina popular peruana: Documentos ilustrativos*. Vol. 3. Lima: Imprenta Torres Aguirre.

Valenzuela González, Álvaro. 1968. "Historia de la sociedad científica de Valparaíso." *Anales del Museo de Historia Natural de Valparaíso* 1: 27–47.

Van Aken, Mark J. 1989. *King of the Night: Juan José Flores and Ecuador, 1824–1864*. Berkeley: University of California Press.

Van den Abbeele, Georges. 1992. *Travel as Metaphor: From Montaigne to Rousseau*. Minneapolis: University of Minnesota Press.

Van Dooren, Thom. 2014. *Flight Ways: Life and Loss at the Edge of Extinction*. New York: Columbia University Press.

Viennot. 1862. "L'acclimatation en Australie." *Bulletin de la Société Impériale Zoologique d'Acclimatation* 9: 827–829.

Vietmeyer, Noel D. 1978. "Incredible Odyssey of a Visionary Victorian Peddler: Charles Ledger Smuggled Quinine and Alpacas from South America, But the World Was Not Ready for Him." *Smithsonian* 9.5 (August): 91–108.

Vilá, Bibiana, ed. 2006. *Investigación, conservación, y manejo de vicuñas*. Buenos Aires: Proyecto MACS–Universidad Nacional de Luján.

Villalba F., Jorge, ed. 1976. *Epistolario diplomático del presidente Gabriel García Moreno, 1859–1869*. Quito: Artes Gráficas.

Voltaire. (1759) 1968. *Candide or Optimism*. Translated by John Butt. Baltimore: Penguin Books.

Von Bergen, Werner, ed. 1963. *Wool Handbook*, 3rd ed. Vol. 1. New York: Interscience Publishers.

Wakild, Emily. 2020. "Saving the Vicuña: The Political, Biophysical, and Cultural History of Wild Animal Conservation in Peru, 1964–2000." *American Historical Review* 125.1: 54–88.

Walton, William. 1811. *An Historical and Descriptive Account of the Four Species of Peruvian Sheep, Called* Carneros de la Tierra. London: Longman, Hurst, Rees, Orme, and Brown.

Walton, William. 1844. *The Alpaca: Its Naturalization in the British Isles Considered*

362 | Works Cited

as a National Benefit and as an Object of Immediate Utility to the Farmer and Man-ufacturer. Edinburgh: William Blackwood and Sons.

Weddell, Hugh A. 1853. *Voyage dans le nord de la Bolivie et dans les parties voisines du Pérou ou visite au district aurifère de Tipuani.* Paris: Chez P. Bertrand/Chez H. Baillière.

Wells, Kristina. 1996. "Woolen Mill's Retail Store Begun in the 1920s." *Mid Hudson Times* (November).

Whatmore, Sarah. 2002. *Hybrid Geographies: Natures, Cultures, Spaces.* London: Sage Publications.

Wheeler, Jane C. 2005a. "Pre-Conquest Alpaca and Llama Breeding." *Camelid Quarterly* (December): 1–5.

Wheeler, Jane C. 2005b. "The Question of Alpaca Origins." *Camelid Quarterly* (September): 1–3.

Wheeler, Jane C. 2012. "South American Camelids—Past, Present and Future." *Journal of Camelid Science* 5 (2012): 1–24.

Wheeler, Jane C., A. J. F. Russel, and Hilary Redden. 1995. "Llamas and Alpacas: Pre-Conquest Breeds and Post-Conquest Hybrids." *Journal of Archaeological Science* 22: 833–840.

White, Hayden. 1978. "The Forms of Wildness: Archaeology of an Idea." In *Tropics of Discourse: Essays in Cultural Criticism*, 150–182. Baltimore: Johns Hopkins University Press.

Wilson, Edward. 1862. "Acclimatisation." Letter to the editor of the *Times* (London), June 26, 1862.

Wisse, Sebastian. 1849. "Notice sur le lama." *Comptes Rendus Hebdomadaires des Séances de la Académie des Sciences* 29: 217–222.

Withers, Charles W. J. 2007. *Placing the Enlightenment: Thinking Geographically about the Age of Reason.* Chicago: University of Chicago Press.

Witt, Heinrich. 1992. *Diario 1824–1890: Un testimonio personal sobre el Perú del siglo XIX, Volumen II (1843–1847).* Translated by Gladys Flórez-Estrada Garland. Lima: Banco Mercantil.

Wonders, Karen. 2005. "Hunting Narratives of the Age of Empires: A Gender Reading of Their Iconography." *Environment and History* 11: 269–291.

Wood, Ian. 2005. *Argyle Agricultural & Horticultural Society (1857–1873). A Collection of Facts.* Melba, Australian Capital Territory: Ian Wood.

Yapita, Juan de Dios, Denise Y. Arnold, and Elvira Espejo Ayca. 2014. *Los términos textiles aymaras de la región Asanaque: Vocabulario semántico según la cadena productiva.* La Paz: ILCA.

Yocabaccio, Hugo. 2009. "The Historical Relationship between People and the Vicuña." In *The Vicuña: The Theory and Practice of Community Based Wildlife Management*, edited by Iain J. Gordon, 7–20. Boston: Springer-Verlag.

Young, Linda. 1983. "Wool, Wheat and Alpacas?" *Journal of the Royal Australian Historical Society* 69.2: 109–117.

Index

NOTE: Page numbers in italic type indicate information contained in images or image captions.

Abercrombie, Thomas A., 62, 67, 306n21

Académie Royale de Peinture et de Sculpture, Paris, 84

Acclimatisation Society of Victoria, 236, 239–240, 246–247, 249–251

acclimatization: in Australia, 213–215; background and history of in Europe, 125–129; Buffon in support of, 75; camelids, focus on, 14; case studies overview, 127–129; definition, 125–126; development of successful transport model, 148–153; early debate on relocation and adaptation, 91–93; paradox of adaptability, 312n3; of plants, 11, 91, 106, 120, 129, 255. *See also* Paris Acclimatization Society (Société Zoologique d'Acclimatation)

Acclimatization Society of Montevideo, 329n144

Acclimatization Society of Paris. *See* Paris Acclimatization Society (Société Zoologique d'Acclimatation)

Acclimatization Society of the Alps, 142

Aconcagua Valley, Chile, 115

Acosta, P. José de, 42

Adams, William Pitt, 172

Adorno, Rolena, 66

Adorno, Theodor, 209

ageism, 177–178

Alarcón, Manuel, 179

Albornoz, Cristóbal de, 42, 51–52

Alexander, Thomas E., 277

Alfort/Maisons-Alfort (Paris suburb). *See* National Veterinary School of Alfort (École Nationale Vétérinaire d'Alfort)

Alfort Veterinary School. *See* National

Veterinary School of Alfort (École Nationale Vétérinaire d'Alfort)

Algeria, 130, 131, 314n35

Allocamelus (mythical creature, possibly mistaken camelid), 79, 101, 279n8

alpacas (*Vicugna pacos*), 98, *240*; Buffon's focus on, 77, 103; concession (Peru) allowing export of, 241, 246–247; domestication and use, 2–3, 97; fleece quality, 3, 226; habitat overviews, 2, 112; interest in for fabric production, 100, 123, 154; law (Peru) prohibiting export of (1845), 169, 212; meat of, 239–241; medal for successful introduction in Europe, 130–131; physical and behavioral descriptions of, 230, 242–243; preserved specimens of, 217, 237–239; seen as "pest" species, 254; shearing of, 225–226; white wool demand, impact of, 100. *See also* Australia, Ledger's alpaca extraction venture to; Ecuadorian extraction project; Empress Josephine Bonaparte (Empress of the French); Roehn, Eugène

"Alpacas' Remonstrance, The" (IDU-MEA), 223–224

Alps as proposed habitat, 101, 128, 142

Álvarez de Quindos y Baena, Juan Antonio, 100

amaru (legendary Andean serpent, Quechua lang.), 45, 48–49

Amat y Junyent, Manuel de, 99

anatomical study of camelids: convergence of science and colonialism in, 67–68, 70–74, 76, 308n42; Feuillée's study of guanaco digestive tract, 70–73; Fragonard llama (*écorché*

364 | Index

specimen), 80–87; Lacépède and Cuvier volume illustrations, 107–108; Monardes's early description of (1574), 57–61; penis configuration of camelids, 76–77; scientific study overview, 57–61; specimen collection and preparation guidelines, 73–74

Andean cosmology and cultural practices: around bezoar stones, 29, 45–46, 50; augury through dissection, 64–65; ceremonial and revered items, 50–53; cutting and marking practices, 62; sacrifice ritual, 3, 19, 37–38, 60, 62–67; serpents, imagery and mythology of, 45, 48–49. *See also* bundles of sacred/ceremonial objects (*señalu q'epi*, Quechua lang.)

angora goats, 120, 142

Animal Talent Scouts Enterprises, 273

anthropomorphization of animals: in colonial artistic representations, 10–11, 12, 79–80, 198–199; Doctor Dolittle story, 263–264; and Ledger's heroic narrative, 223–224; in marketing, 262–263, 281. *See also* "Llinda Llee Llama"

Aranjuez, Spain, 99, 100–101

Argus (newspaper), 225, 235

Argyle Agricultural Society, 237

Arica, Chile, 112, 138–139, 172

Arnold, Denise Y., 47–48

Arriaga, Julián de, 99

Arriaga, Pablo José de, 44, 302n33

Arthursleigh (Holt estate), 229, 251

Asian (oriental) bezoar stones, 19, 28, 31, 32, 35–36, 40. *See also* bezoar stones (Peruvian, occidental)

Atkinson, James Henry, 224, 238

Atlas Mountains as proposed habitat, 130

Atocha (*Nuestra Señora de Atocha*, Spanish treasure ship), 44

Aucapitaine, Henri, 130

Australia: earlier camelid extractions to, 211–215; economic boom in (1850s), 212; geographical similarity to Andean landscapes, 220–221. *See also* Australia, Ledger's alpaca extraction venture to; New South Wales (NSW) colony, Australia; Victoria colony, Australia

Australia, Ledger's alpaca extraction venture to: arrival in Sydney, 215; conflict with Indigenous locals, 175–178; financial support for, 187, 203–204; Ledger's accrued debt from, 204; Ledger's journal and book project, 183, 184, 186; overview, 207–211; reconnaissance and outfitting for, 173, 212; recuperation and rest at Laguna Blanca, 182–183, 189–191; shepherds return to South America, 229, 233; smuggling of flock from Bolivia to Argentina, 178–182; "superintendent of alpacas" position, 208, 209–210, 228, 237, 250; testimonial award raised by his supporters, 322n39; trek from Copiapó to port of departure, 204–205; trek from Laguna Blanca to Copiapó, 197–202. *See also* Australia, Ledger's post-arrival endeavors; Savage, Santiago

Australia, Ledger's post-arrival endeavors: assignment to assess interior of colony for pasturage, 219–221; attempted collaboration with Acclimatisation Society of Victoria, 234–237, 249–251; criticisms and denunciation of Ledger, 247–251, 254–255; NSW offer and conditions for sale, 217–219; offering of flock for sale, 216–218; orders to relocate flock, 227–230. *See also* Australia, Ledger's alpaca extraction venture to

Australian Alpaca Association, 144

Australian Horticultural and Agricultural Society, 217

Australian Museum, Sydney, 217

Australian Mutual Provident Society of Sydney, 236

autopsy/autopsia, definitions, 12, 19, 57. *See also* anatomical study of camelids

"autoptic imagination," 59

Ávila, James Alexander, 231, 232

Azara, Félix de, 104

Barbey, Th., 154–155, 314n36
Barnum, P. T., 248, 260, 261
Barthélemy-Lapommeraye, Christophe Jérôme, 131–133
Bass, George, 212
Beauharnais, Eugène de, 106, 108
Beliardy, Alessandro (Agostino), 102, 103–104
Beltrán, Luis (San Luis Beltrán), 43–44
Belzú, Manuel Isidoro, 174–175, 178
Benbow, George F., 327n110
Bermingham, Ann, 86
bernegal (drinking vessel), 43–44
Bertonio, Ludovico, 45, 51
Besançon, France, 154
Bexon, Gabriel-Léopold-Charles-Amé, 102, 103–104
bezoar stones (Peruvian, occidental): commodification of, 27, 39, 49–53; counterfeits of, 36, 300n21; curative properties of (alleged), 26, 27, 29, 31–32, 34–40, 42–44, 46; debunking of healing properties, 54–55; etymology of, 31–32, 299n12; formation of, 32–34, 299n15; historical European interest in, 25–28; hunting of and decimation of camelid populations, 2, 15, 19, 28–29, 37–40; Indigenous cultural value of, 19, 27–29, 37–38, 46–50, 54; location of inside body, 69–70; overviews, 1–2; as symbol of idolatry, 28, 34, 40–42, 49, 50–55. *See also* Asian (oriental) bezoar stones
Bigelow, Allison, 285
Bingham, Hiram, 267, 283
"biogeographies," 4, 5, 108
Black, John, 228
"Blanchette" (female llama in Vosges project), 157, 160
Bleichmar, Daniela, 9, 59, 97, 98, 186
Bois de Boulogne acclimatization gardens, 140–141, 147
boleadoras (slings), 191
Bolivia: Ledger's smuggling of camelids from, 166, 174, 179–182, 203, 254; quinine seeds smuggled from, 254; relations with Peru, 137, 138–139,

173; Roehn's smuggling of camelids from, 137–140
Bonaparte, Joseph, 122
Bonaparte, Josephine (Empress). *See* Empress Josephine Bonaparte (Empress of the French)
Bonaparte, Napoleon (Napoleon I), 105, 109, 118. *See also* Napoleonic Wars
Bonaparte, Napoleon (Napoleon III), 128, 143, 144–146
Bory de Saint-Vincent, Jean-Baptiste, 122
Bourbon Reform period ideologies, 58, 93
Bourgelat, Claude, 80–81, 306–307n24
Bourgoing, Jean-François, 100–101
Boxer, C. R., 303–304n47
Brad Oldham Sculpture, 288–289
Braniff International Airways, 277, 280–281
Brawern, Heinrich, 11. *See also* Brawern-Herckemann expedition "camel-sheep" engraving
Brawern-Herckemann expedition "camel-sheep" engraving, 9–13, 16–18
breeding and crossbreeding: in Ecuadorian flock, 152; for fleece color and quality, 3, 100, 121, 189–190, 195, 249; hybridization and taxonomic understanding, 2, 11, 18, 76, 121; to improve hardiness, 125; indiscriminate by Spanish, 3–4; Ledger's experiments in crossbreeding, 189–192, 196, 218, 241–242; in Victoria colony, 234–235
Buenos Aires, Argentina, 91, 103, 111–112, 113–118
Buffon, Comte de (Georges-Louis Leclerc), 61, 74–80, 91, 101–104, 299n15
Bulletin de la Société Zoologique d'Acclimatation, 129, 145, 148–149, 159, 161, 196–197, 241
bundles of sacred/ceremonial objects (*señalu q'epi*, Quechua lang.), 46–48, 50, 61–62. *See also illas* (sacred/ceremonial objects)

366 | Index

Cabrera, Juan Pablo (priest), 189–190, 195

Cabrera, Pedro (guide), 173, 179, 229, 232, 254, 329n144

Cádiz, Spain, 113, 118–123

Calancha, Fray Antonio de la, 44, 49, 301–302n29

Calchaquí Valleys, Argentina, 181, 185, 189

Caldera, Chile, 204, 207

Callao, Peru, 113, 148, 150–151

Camacho, José, 110

camel hair fabric, 258

camels, 75, 77, 130, 245, 258

"camel-sheep," 9–12, 17

Candide (Voltaire), 89–91, 123

Cañete y Domínguez, Pedro Vicente, 94–96

Cañizares-Esguerra, Jorge, 42–43, 72

Cantal department of Auvergne-Rhône-Alpes region, 142

carache (skin disease, usually scabies/mange), 52. *See also* skin diseases of camelids

Carangas area of Bolivia, 112, 116, 175

Carlos III (king of Spain), 94, 130–131

Carlos IV (king of Spain), 111, 114, 120

Carmen Cuevas Conjunto (musical troupe), 280

carneros (term used for camelids, also rams), 51

Caro, Deborah A., 171

Cartagena (Colombia), 108–109

Carter, Paul, 86

Casa de las Vacas, Aranjuez, Spain, 99, 100

cashmere, 109, 246, 258

Castelnau, Francis de, 127

Catamarca, Argentina, 166, 196. *See also* Laguna Blanca, Argentina (Catamarca)

Catskill Game Farm, 16, 273, 274

"caveat emptor" principle, 300n21

"celebrity" llamas, 15, 16–18, 156–160, 288–289. *See also* "Llinda Llee Llama"

chacos (vicuña hunts), 3, 94, 98, 112, *190*, 191–192, *193*

Chanorier, Jean, 105–106

cheptel (lease system), 154

Chile Musical Conservatory of Guitar and Folklore, 280

ch'illa form of sacrifice, 63–64, 305nn10–11

Chimborazo volcano, 134–136

Christianity: conversion, religious, 38–39, 41, 43–44, 63; Darwinism as threat to, 243; and sacrifice, 63–66. *See also* idolatry

Chulluncayani (Ledger hacienda in Bolivia), 170, 210

Church, Fredric, 135

cinchona plants, 170, 316n9. *See also* quinine (and cinchona plant)

Ciruelo, Pedro, 300n19

Cisneros, Baltasar Hidalgo de, 118–119

Clark, Stuart, 40–41

classification (taxonomic) speculations and challenges, 11, 20, 75–77, 87, 98, 121, 141

Clayton, Thomas, 244

Clemente, Simón de Rojas, 109

climate and weather: considerations for camelid adaptation, 91, 96, 99, 101; dangers of extraction journeys, 90, 174, 180, 198–199; shipboard conditions, 152; winds and gales, 198, 318n30

Cobelle, Charles, 261–262, 271, 289

Cobo, Bernabé, 28–29, 50, 301n29

Colegio de San Pablo, Lima, 300–301n24

colla (medicinal philter or lethal poison, Aymara lang.), etymology and derivatives of, 45

Collasuyo, Inca territory, 45

Collège Royal de Chirurgie, Paris, 84

colonialism: coloniality of picturesque aesthetics, 86; and commodification of resources, 12–13, 27, 30–31, 39, 49–53, 73–74; conquest tropes, 103, 262; and decimation of camelid populations, 3–4; and empire overreach, 210; impacts and legacies of extractions, 7–9, 285–288; poetry as colonialist narrative, 223–224, 262–263.

See also convergence of science and colonialism; losses of animals

color: in anatomical specimen preservation, 84–86; in Andean culture, 62; in bezoar stones, 33, 49; of camelid wool, 3, 90, 99–100, 141

Colque, Benito, 201

Colt, Alvin, 277

Coltrin, Christy, 288–289

Columbus, Christopher, 38

commodification of resources, 9, 12–13, 27, 30–31, 39, 49–53, 73–74

comparative anatomy studies, 57. *See also* anatomical study of camelids

condors, 180–181, 201

conopas (small stone camelid figures), 46, 51, 302n33

Consejo Real de Indias (Council of the Indies), 30

contact zones (sites of intercultural encounter), 8–15, 285–289. *See also* ecological concerns in contact zones

Contreras y Valverde, Vasco de, 300–301n24

convergence of science and colonialism: and Age of Enlightenment, 57–59, 71, 76, 91–92, 97; in anatomical studies, 67–68, 70–74, 76, 308n42; and explorer-traveler heroic narrative, 67–68, 136–138, 167, 219–221, 239, 242

conversion, religious, 38–39, 41, 44, 63

Cook, Harold J., 59

Cooma, NSW, Australia, 221

Copiapó, Chile, 173, 202, 203

Córdoba, Argentina, 111

Cornélie (ship), 148, 149–150

Cornulier-Lucinière, René de, 148–149, 150

Correa Morales, Joaquín, 116–117

costumbrista/costumbrismo (imagery depicting local everyday culture), 184, 187, 191, 282

Cowper, Charles, 239

creoles, roles in extraction efforts, 8, 121, 128, 166

crossbreeding. *See* breeding and crossbreeding

Cuba, Johannes de, 31

curiosity and discovery dynamic, 11–13, 54–55, 102, 111, 161

Cuvier, Georges, 72, 107–108

d'Alvimart, Gaëtan Souchet, 106

Darwinism, 243

Dauberton, Louis-Jean-Marie, 299n15

Davidson, Gilbert, 226–227

Dávila, Pedro Franco, 304n48

Davin, Frédéric, 140

De Blois, Samuel W., 173

Dedenbach-Salazar Sáenz, Sabine, 63

deer and bezoar stone myths, 32–33

Degueurce, Christophe, 83, 86–87, 307n36

Delgado-P., Guillermo, 48–50

de Sève, Jacques, 77–80, 82, 97

D'Essen, Bernard and Lorrain, 16–18, 271, 273–276, 280–281

Deville, Émile, 127

Diccionario de autoridades (Real Academia Española), 63

Dictionnaire encyclopédique des sciences médicales (Amédée Dechambre, ed.), 54

Dictionnaire universel de commerce (Savary des Bruslons), 101

dietary needs. *See* feed/fodder for extracted camelids; water needs of camelids

Dior, Christian, 259

dioramas in marketing, 257, 258, 268, 270, 278, 286

Discovery of America, The (Straet and Galle), 9

Disposiciones gubernativas (Toledo), 52

dissection of camelids. *See* anatomical study of camelids

dogs and dingos, 108, 116, 191, 192, 243

Dolittle, Doctor, 263–264

domestication and relocation programs, 127, 170, 191–196

donkeys, comparison to llamas as working animals, 156

dragons, imagery and mythology of, 45. *See also* serpents, imagery and mythology of

Dransart, Penelope, 305n6

368 | Index

Dr. Dolittle (film), 330n12
Drouyn de Lhuys, Édouard, 146, 147, 148
drugs and medicines. *See* medicinal products from New World
Duffield, Alexander James, 246–247
Duniam, George, 172, 316n12
Duviols, Pierre, 44, 52–53
dyeing camelid wool, 99–100

École Nationale Vétérinaire d'Alfort. *See* National Veterinary School of Alfort (École Nationale Vétérinaire d'Alfort)
ecological concerns in contact zones, 3, 13, 21, 60, 286. *See also* neo-ecological imperialism
écorché (anatomical figure with the skin removed), 61, 80–87
Ecuadorian extraction project: arrival in France and analysis of shipboard practices, 148–152; García Moreno's plans and motivations for, 144–148; overview, 128; upheld as optimal transportation model, 152–153
El Ambato (Catamarca newspaper), 196
eland dinner in London (1860), 239
Eldorado, symbolic significance of, 89–91
Ellenberger, Michel, 83
Embling, Thomas, 212–213, 216
Emperor Napoleon. *See* Napoleon I (emperor); Napoleon III (emperor)
Empire (Sydney), 233–234, 248
Empress Josephine Bonaparte (Empress of the French): interest in natural history, 104–106; Malmaison llamas and menagerie, 20, 102, 104, 106–109; negotiating camelid acquisition, 20–21, 109–118; routing of flock to Spain, 118–119
Enlightenment, Age of, 57–59, 71, 76, 91–92, 97. *See also* convergence of science and colonialism
enqa/enqay (vital life force), 47–49
Épinal, France, 155, 159
Era (newspaper), 222–223

Escobari de Querejazu, Laura, 117–118
Escobedo, Mariano, 169
escuerzonera plant, 31
Esquire magazine, 269
exceptionalism, 170–171, 209. *See also* neo-ecological imperialism
exotica: European fascination with, 2, 28, 39, 54, 106–107; and picturesque aesthetics, 79, 85; in product marketing strategies, 16–18, 258, 268–269, 273–274, 282–283
explorer-traveler tradition, 137, 219–221. *See also* convergence of science and colonialism; heroic paradigm narratives
extinction stories, 333n2
extractivism and global improvement ideologies, 202–203. *See also* neo-ecological imperialism
eyewitness reporting, value of, 12, 59, 69–70, 197

Fabre, Amédée, 147–148
fabrics from camelid wool, 15–16, 99–100, 267–270. *See also* S. Stroock & Co.
fashion, 109, *110. See also* fabrics from camelid wool
feed/fodder for extracted camelids: debated adaptability/acceptance of new sources, 96–97, 152; shortages of during extraction journeys, 119, 139, 144, 169, 174, 181; starvation incidents, 90, 229–230; *ycho*, need for, 103, 221
Fein, Nat, 331n26
Felipe II (king of Spain), 25, 26, 36, 54
Felipe III (king of Spain), 25
Fernández de Oviedo y Valdés, Gonzalo "Oviedo," 299n13, 308n2
fertility: of crossbred offspring/hybrids, 2, 121, 191, 244; rituals and traditions, 47–49, 61–62, 87. *See also* breeding and crossbreeding
Férussac, André de, 122
Feuillée, Louis, 60–61, 70–74
Few, Martha, 5

fiber from camelids. *See* fleece/wool of
camelids
Fine Men's Wear Fabrics (S. Stroock&
Co.), 259
Fitzpatrick, Michael, 228
Fitzroy, Charles, 208
Flandrin, Pierre, 81, 306–307n24
fleece/wool of camelids: characteristics
of, 3; counterfeit, 94; crossbreeding
for color and quality, 3, 100, 121,
189–190, 195, 249; quality concerns
due to relocation, 96–97, 103; results
of crossbreeding experiments, 121;
staple length in wool processing,
315n3, 323n55; symbolic associations
with Indigenous culture, 61–62;
value of, 65, 95, 265, 318n42; weight
of alpaca fleece, 226. *See also* fabrics
from camelid wool; shearing; *individual species*
Flores, Antonio, 145–146, 147
Flores, General Juan José, 146
Flores Ochoa, Jorge, 47
Folie, M. de la, 102, 103
Fortnight (Neiman Marcus event
campaigns), 276–277. *See also* South
America Fortnight (Neiman Marcus
event campaign)
Foster, Kate, 4, 269
Fourcroy, Antoine-François, 108
Fragonard, Honoré, 61, 80–87
Fragonard, Jean-Honoré, 81
Fragonard llama (*écorché* specimen), 61,
80–87
Fragonard Museum (Musée Fragonard
d'Alfort), 80–87
Frampton, John, 29
Francastel, Adrien, 106, 110–111
France's camelid strategies: disburse-
ment plan, 153–154; efforts to
acquire camelids, 101–104, 203,
218; Jura mountains placement proj-
ect, 154, 161; Pyrenees placement
project, 154, 161–163;
Vosges mountains placement, 142,
154–161
Freedgood, Elaine, 209

French Academy of Sciences (Académie
des sciences), 90
French Acclimatization Society. *See*
Paris Acclimatization Society (Société
Zoologique d'Acclimatation)
Frézier, Amédée-François, 71, 79
frostbite, 174, 254
Fugger family of Germany, sixteenth
century, 30–31

Galatée (ship), 148–149, 150, 151
Galenic concept of anatomy, 57
Galle, Theodoor, 9
Galmiche, Charles, and Vosges place-
ment project, 154–161, 315n41
Gálvez, José de, 102
Garay, Martín de, 118
García, Julián, 113–119, 121, 123–124,
287, 288
García de León y Pizarro, Ramón, 112
García Moreno, Gabriel, 15, 128,
144–148
Garcilaso de la Vega, Inca, 39, 63, 64, 71
garden theory in art, 85
Garry Moore Show, The, 274
Gee, Benjamin, 214–215, 312n8
Gemignani, Hugo, 269
gender: and colonialist compartmental-
ization, 9, 137, 177–178; and heroic
masculinity narrative, 167, 177–178,
225–226. *See also* women (Indige-
nous)
genetic diversity and selective breeding
programs, 3–4, 100
Geoffroy Saint-Hilaire, Albert, 147, 148,
149, 152, 153, 162, 197
Geoffroy Saint-Hilaire, Isidore, 126, 127,
131, 141–142, 143
Gesner, Conrad, 79, 101, 279n8
Gilbert, Helen, 210
goats: angora, 120, 142; cashmere, 109,
246, 258
Godin, Louis, 93
Godoy, Manuel, 106, 120
Goethe, Johann Wolfgang von, 57
gold (South American), 51, 52, 212, 279
González Holguín, Diego, 45, 49, 50–51

370 | Index

Grace, J. Peter, 277
Grace Line (Grace Shipping), 277, 280
Gramiccia, Gabriele, 218, 230
Granja Azul (restaurant), 279
Greenblatt, Stephen, 13, 38–39
Grew, Nehemiah, 33
Grey, Thomas, 187–188
Guaman Poma de Ayala, Felipe, 60, 64–67, 85, 303n41
guanacos, wild (*Lama guanicoe*): anatomization of by Feuillée, 70–74; crossbreeds in Ecuadorian flock, 152; extractions of, 100–101; as false vicuña fleece, 94; misconceptions around taxonomy, 77; physical and behavioral descriptions of, 98; taxonomy and habitat overviews, 2, 97
guano industry, 168–169
Guayaquil, Ecuador, 145, 146
Guerra, Francisco, 304n47

Haraway, Donna, 269
Harris, Olivia, 177
haunting, concepts of, 308n48
Haute-Garonne Agriculture Society, 154, 161
Haute Garonne Pyrenees, 154, 161–162
Havana (Cuba), 131, 133
hayntilla (large bezoar stones, Aymara lang.), 51
Hearst, William Randolph, 16
Heart of the Andes (Church), 135
Heesen, Anke te, 87
Hénon, Jacques-Marie, 307n36
Herckemann, Elias, 11. *See also* Brawern-Herckemann expedition "camel-sheep" engraving
Hernández Príncipe, Rodrigo, 41
heroic paradigm narratives: and contact zone encounters, 14–15; and convergence of science and colonialism, 67–68, 136–138, 167, 219–221, 239, 242; and gender, 167, 177–178, 225–226; moralizing in, 203, 209; Roehn, Eugène, in, 135–138. *See also under* Ledger, Charles
Herring, J., 216

Hetherington, Kevin, 308n48
Hickey-Freeman Company, 267–270, 283
hihua colla (poisonous food, Aymara lang.), 45
Histoire naturelle, générale et particulière (Leclerc/Buffon), 75, 102, 104
Historia medicinal (Monardes): and autoptic narratives, 59; on bezoar stones, 27, 28, 31–35, 39–40, 41–42; on camelid anatomy, 67–70; publication and introduction of, 29–31, 41
Hochswender, Woody, 269
Holt, Thomas, 229, 251
Horkheimer, Max, 209
Howard, John Eliot, 253
Howe, Jackie and Jack, 226–227
huacas (sacred sites, beings or objects), 28, 46, 51–54
human anatomy specimens, preserved, 82
Humboldt, Alexander von, 123, 135
Hunter, John, 74, 84–85, 304n1
Hunter, William, 84
Hunterian Museum, London, 304n49
hunting camelids: for bezoar stones, 2, 15, 19, 28–29, 37–40; *chacos* (vicuña hunts), 3, 94, 98, 112, 190, 191–193; hunting and skinning *v.* live capture and shearing, 3, 94–96, 260, 264; restrictions imposed on, 94–95
hybridization and taxonomic understanding, 11, 18, 76, 125. *See also* breeding and crossbreeding; classification (taxonomic) speculations and challenges

Ibernégaray, Miguel, 171–172
ichu. See ycho (native Andean grass)
idolatry: bezoars as symbol of, 28, 34, 40–42, 50–55; condemnation of in service to commodification, 49–53; as poison, 42–49; and sacrifice, 63–67
illas (sacred/ceremonial objects), 47–49, 50–52. *See also* bundles of sacred/ceremonial objects (*señalu q'epi*, Quechua lang.)
illas-llamas (*conopas*), 51–52

Illustrated London News, 214, 238, *240*, 243

imperialism, 8, 209, 210, 220, 239, 242, 261. *See also* Indigenous Andeans; neo-ecological imperialism

Inca culture: art and designs used in marketing, 279–280; cultural and economic relationship with camelids, 3, 258; early *chacos*, 94; messianic ideology, 48–49; as signifier in marketing strategies, 258–259, 265–267, 279

Indiana Jones (character), 330n17

Indigenous Andeans: clashes with European economic culture, 176–177; cultural and economic relationship with camelids, 4, 46, 66–67, 171; and cultural value of bezoar stones, 19, 27–29, 37–38, 46–50, 54; denigration of, 50, 52, 170, 245; marginalization and decontextualization of, 8–9, 49–53, 73, 74, 266, 286; resistance to extraction and refusal to sell, 8, 137–138, 169–172, 175–178, 287; stereotyping of, 9, 66, 137, 177–178, 262. *See also* Andean cosmology and cultural practices; Inca culture; shepherds/caretakers, Indigenous; women (Indigenous)

Inge Morath Foundation, 271

"*Instrucción*" (Albornoz), 51, 52

insurance policy dispute in Victoria venture, 236–237, 246

intercultural encounter, sites of, 8. *See also* contact zones (sites of intercultural encounter)

Iriarte, Domingo de, 116

Isabella II (queen of Spain), 145

Jacob, John P., 271

Jacquemart, Frédéric, 142

Jardin d'Acclimatation (Paris), 147, 148. *See also* Bois de Boulogne acclimatization gardens

Jardín de Aclimatación (Cádiz), 118. *See also* Sanlúcar de Barrameda acclimatization garden

Jesuits in Peru, 300–301n24

"jigsaw-puzzle" beast concept, 11

Johnston, Anna, 210

Joly, Nicolas, 127, 154, 161–163

Josephine, Empress. *See* Empress Josephine Bonaparte (Empress of the French)

Joyfull Newes Out of the Newe Founde Worlde (Frampton), 29

Juan, Jorge, 91, 93–96, 103

Julia (ship), 172, 212

Jura mountains placement project, 154, 161

katari (legendary Andean serpent, Aymara lang.), 48–49

Kew Gardens, London, 126

King, Philip Gidley, 212

knowledge-as-possession concept, 20, 58, 71, 86, 87. *See also* commodification of resources; knowledge production

knowledge production: and Andean ritual practices, 64; of collective experience with camelids, 146–147; and Enlightenment era conceptions, 58–59; through artistic representations/imagery, 11–13, 97–99, 287; through record keeping, sharing, and analysis, 148–153; through study of colonial extractive industries, 8, 285–288; and value of collaborative relationships, 128, 133, 148, 153, 154, 167–168, 188, 210–211, 231

Kociumbas, Jan, 219

Lacépède, Bernard-Germain-Étienne, 107–108

La Condamine, Charles-Marie de, 93

Lafuente, Antonio, 58

Laguna Blanca, Argentina (Catamarca), 166, 167–168, 181–184, 187–189, 196–197

Lake Titicaca region, 138, 168

"*lama*" v. "*llama*," confusion between, 156, 330n12

Landes, Joan B., 79

landscape art, 84–86, 135–137

language: and convergence of science and colonialism, 41, 67–68, 137;

372 | Index

etymology of "bezoar," 31–32; experiments for acceptable translations of Spanish "*llama*," 156–157; and identity dilemmas, 185; Ledger's facility with, 168, 171, 253; "linguistic-discursive" analytical method, 285; "llama language," 67; research resources, 27; Westernized translations of Andean concepts, 49–53

La Paz, Bolivia, 111, 116, 137

Lara, A. Darío, 136–137

Laredo, Jaime, 280

Larson, Brooke, 176

Las Casas, Bartolomé de, 53

Leclerc, Georges-Louis (Comte de Buffon), 61, 74. *See also* Buffon, Comte de (Georges-Louis Leclerc)

Leçons d'anatomie comparée (Cuvier), 72

Ledger, Charles: 1851 failed smuggling attempt, 172; 1862 London International Exhibition, 237–245; arrests and escape of, 179–180; background and early years in Peru, 168; development of flocks at Chulluncayani (Ledger hacienda), 169–172, 173; on future of alpaca industry, 244–245; heroic paradigm narrative, 167, 172, 180, 202, 205, 219–224, 249; intercultural relationship with shepherds, 167–168, 188, 211, 230–234, 249, 252–254; journal and book project, 183, 184–187; medals and awards, 130, 237, 241, 244, 327–328n116; media campaigns by, 223–224, 232, 233–234; medical treatment of Bolivian mayor's wife, 179; overview, 165–168; return to South American, 210; and taxidermy specimen in Paris, 6–7; vicuña domestication experiment, 191–196. *See also* Australia, Ledger's alpaca extraction venture to; Australia, Ledger's post-arrival endeavors

Ledger, George, 168, 202–203, 220–221

Léon de Wailly, Armand François, 107

"Leo" the MGM lion, 273

Lequanda, José Ignacio, 97, 98

Lévêque, A., 148, 150, 151–152

liama (male llama), *liame* (female llama), *liameau* (young llama), 157

liberalism and culture clashes, 176–177, 245

Life magazine, 271

L'Illustration (weekly, Paris), 135–137

Lima, Peru, 111, 113, 168

"Lima" (female llama in Vosges project), 157, 160

Linares, José María, 137, 138

Lindemann, Roland, 16, 273

"linguistic-discursive method," 285

Liniers, Santiago, 117

Linnaeus, Carl, 75

liver fluke parasite (*unca*), 181

Livingstone, David (explorer), 165, 208, 219, 248

Livingstone, David N. (contemporary scholar), 108, 205

"Llama in Times Square, A" (Morath), 271, 289

"llama king," 16

"llama language," 67

llamando (beckoning, calling), 267

"Llamando" line of menswear, 267–270

llamas (*Llama glama*), 98, 240; Buffon's study of, 75–80; domestication and use, 2–3, 97; early study of, 60–61, 71–72; ears, piercing/cutting and decoration of, 62, 86–87; Empress Josephine's menagerie, 20, 102, 104, 106–109; physical and behavioral descriptions of, 76–77, 107–108, 194–195; preserved specimens of, 5–7, 61, 80–87, 270; sacrifice of, 62–67; shearing of, 226–227; US flocks, 16–18, 273–274; as wet-nurses in vicuña domestication experiment, 22, 193–195. *See also* "celebrity" llamas; Roehn, Eugène; Vosges (mountains) project

Llamas and Llamaland (Stroock, S.), 258–259

Llaullacasu (*conopas*), 51

"Llinda Llee Llama": as advertising model, 16–18, 274–276; background, 273–274; and Neiman Marcus marketing campaign, 276–283; sculptural tribute to, 288–289; Times Square photograph of, 271–273

Lloyd, George A., 214, 223, 226

"Llucky" llama, 16–18, 273–274

Lofting, Hugh, 263–264

Lorimer, Hayden, 4

Lorraine Friends of Art Society, 158

losses of animals: 1842 *Sir Charles Napier* venture, 169; Cádiz flock, 119; Ecuador project, 148, 151; entire Vosges flock, 160–161; impacts overview, 286; Ledger's ventures, 166, 180, 181, 200, 201–202, 215, 229; and quest for bezoar stones, 2, 15, 19, 28–29, 37–40; Roehn's expedition, 139, 140, 142; and survival rates overviews, 15, 153. *See also* hunting camelids

Louis XIV (king of France), 70

Louis XVI (king of France), 102

lunatic asylums, camelids in, 251

Macarthur, John, 183, 208, 215, 223

Macarthur, William, 237

MacCormack, Sabine, 300n19

Macé, C., 135–136

Machu Picchu, 267, 279

Maimonides, Moses, 32

Majluf, Natalia, 187, 282

Malmaison (Empress Josephine's chateau), 20, 105–106

Malmaison llamas and menagerie, 20, 102, 104, 106–109

Mamani, Manuel Incra, 184, 316n9

Mamani, Santiago (Manuel's son), 185, 188, 254

Manchester Times, 140

Maneroo area, Australia, 220, 221, 227–228, 229

manure as fertilizer and fuel, 2–3, 156, 316–317n17

Mapuche couple of 1649 engraving, 9, 12, 17

Marchand, Édouard, 139

Marcus, Edward, 281

Marcus, Stanley, 276, 278, 281, 282

María Luisa (queen of Spain), 111

Martin de Moussy, Victor, 197

Martínez de Compañón, Baltasar Jaime, 97

Martínez de Leyua, Miguel, 299n8, 301n27

Marvin, Garry, 297n6

material remains, studies of, 5–7

Mazzitelli Mastricchio, Malena, 197

meat of camelids, 3, 97, 98, 161, 238–241, 243, 308n2

medals and awards for contributors to extraction projects: Barbey, 314n36; early Paris Acclimatization Society recognitions, 129–131; Galmiche, 315n41; Ledger, *130*, 237, 241, 244, 327–328n116; Northeast Regional Acclimatization Society, 159; Roehn, 134, 143, 153

media/press: coverage of Ledger's undertakings, 196–197, 208, 210, 217, 247–249; and Ledger's hero narrative, 183, 222–224, 230–231

medicinal products from New World, 29–31, 45. *See also under* bezoar stones (Peruvian, occidental); *Historia medicinal* (Monardes); poisons; quinine (and cinchona plant)

Melbourne Botanical and Zoological Gardens, 234–235

Meléndez, Mariselle, 194–195

Mémorial Universel: Journal du Cercle des Arts, 123

menageries/zoos, notable: Doctor Dolittle, 263–264; Malmaison llamas (and menagerie), 20, 102, 104, 106–109; Melbourne Botanical and Zoological Gardens, 234–235; National Museum of Natural History, Paris, 7, 107–108, 126, 307n34; National Veterinary School of Alfort, 75

Mendoza, Argentina, 113–115

merino sheep, 105–106, 110, 123, 183, 207, 245

"Mexico" (male llama bred in Vosges project), 157–158, 159

Milagro (ship for Empress Josephine's camelids), 113

Miller, Arthur, 273

Miller, George Robert, 305nn10–11

374 | Index

Miller, Henry, 304n49
mining industry, 3, 39, 71, 97
mita (forced labor) system, colonial, 3
Mitchell, Jessie, 239
Mitchell Library, Sydney, Australia, 166, 183
Moens and Marriott (merchants), 169
Monardes, Nicolás: background and overview, 27, 29–30; on convergence of science and colonialism, 67–70; criticism of, 54, 303–304n47; introduction to bezoar stones, 34–35; and Osma's bezoar account, 35–40; on Osma's letter and package, 68–69; writing style, 59. *See also Historia medicinal* (Monardes)
Moore, Wendy, 304n1
Morales, Gaspar de, 33–34
moralizing in heroic narrative paradigm, 203, 209
Morath, Inge, 271–273, 289
Moreno, Gabriel, 178–179
Morro de Sama, Peru, 139
Mort, Thomas Sutcliffe, 212, 237
Mort and Brown (NSW company), 172
Mueller, Ferdinand, 220, 235, 250
Murphy, Elsie, 260
Murúa, Fray Martín de, 45
Musée Fragonard d'Alfort, 80–87
Muséum National d'Histoire Naturelle, Paris. *See* National Museum of Natural History, Paris
Museum of Natural History, Marseille, 131
Museum of Natural History, Paris. *See* National Museum of Natural History, Paris

Nancy, France, 154
ñandús (rheas), 191, *192*
Napoleon I (emperor), 105, 109, 118. *See also* Napoleonic Wars
Napoleon III (emperor), 128, 143, 144–146
Napoleonic Wars, 111, 117, 119, 120
Narborough, John, 306n17
National Museum of Natural History, Paris, 5, 7, 107–108, 126, 307n34

National Veterinary School of Alfort (École Nationale Vétérinaire d'Alfort), 57, 61, 75, 80–87
Natural History (Pliny), 31
natural history, Enlightenment era interest in, 58–59, 70–71, 75, 104–106
naturalization. *See* acclimatization
Naylor's Kendall & Co. (Peru), 168
negocio (enterprise, business), 38
Neiman Marcus, Dallas, 16–18, 22, 276–283
Neiman-Marcus Award, 330n6
neo-ecological imperialism, 22, 126, 131, 167, 170–171, 298n17. *See also* convergence of science and colonialism
Nesle, Marquis de (Louis Charles de Mailly), 77
New South Wales Acclimatisation Society, 319n5
New South Wales (NSW) colony, Australia, 173, 183. *See also* Australia, Ledger's alpaca extraction venture to; Sydney, Australia
New York City, 16, 133, 214, 258, 271, 273
Nicholson, William, 235
"non/ne plus ultra" concept, 195–196, 305n12
Noonan, Meg Lukens, 264
Northeast Regional Acclimatization Society (Société Régionale d'Acclimatation pour la Zône du Nord-Est), 154–155, 156–157, 158, 159
Novaes, Guiomar, 280
NSW colony. *See* New South Wales (NSW) colony, Australia
Nuestra Señora de Atocha (Spanish treasure ship), 44
Nueva corónica y buen gobierno (Guaman Poma), 64
Nugent, George Hodges, 172

Obando (intermediary to acquire alpacas for Ledger), 175–176, 177, 180
Oldham, Brad, 288–289
Olliver, Charlotte (Ledger's second wife), 210

Index | 375

Orta, Garcia da, 299n12, 303–304n47
Ortiz, Candelaria (Ledger's first wife), 168, 212, 319n4
Ortiz, Major (Ledger's brother-in-law), 173, 212, 220
Osborne, Michael A., 8, 163
O'Shanassy, John, 216
Osma, Pedro de (Spanish soldier), 35–40, 41, 44–45, 46, 60, 68–69
ovejas (used for camelids, also ewes), 303n40
Oviedo y Valdés, Fernández de. *See* Fernández de Oviedo y Valdés, Gonzalo "Oviedo"

pachacuti concept, 45–46, 54
paco (alpaca). *See* alpacas (*Vicugna pacos*)
Padgen, Anthony, 59
Palmer, James Samuel, 327n110
Palmer v. Ledger, 327n110
Panama, 132, 139
Pan American–Grace Airways, 277, 280
Pan-Americanism, 259, 276–277
Pardo de Zela, F., 264
Pardo Tomás, José, 30, 299n9, 300n20
Paris, France. *See* National Museum of Natural History, Paris; National Veterinary School of Alfort (École Nationale Vétérinaire d'Alfort); Paris Acclimatization Society (Société Zoologique d'Acclimatation)
Paris Acclimatization Society (Société Zoologique d'Acclimatation), 14, 21, 126–127, 129–131, 241. *See also Bulletin de la Société Zoologique d'Acclimatation*; Ecuadorian extraction project; Roehn's 1859 extraction expedition; Vosges (mountains) project
Parker, Merryl, 243
Parkes, Henry, 251
Patchett, Merle, 4, 269
Peace of Basel treaties (1795), 106
penis configuration of camelids, 76–77
Penn, Irving, 273
Pepe (unidentified hapless shepherd boy), 185, *186*, 198, *199*, 287

"Pérou" (male llama in Vosges project), 155–156, 157, 160
Peru: as camelid habitat, 2; concession to export of camelids, 241, 246–247; conflict with Ecuador, 145; law prohibiting camelid exports, 169, 212; war/conflict with Bolivia, 137, 173
Peyer, Johan Conrad, 73
Phifer, Volney, 273
Philosophical Institute of Victoria, 219, 220
picturesque aesthetics and traditions, 84–86, 184, 187, 282
Pimentel, Juan, 196
Pinondel de la Bertoche, H., 154, 161
Pitt, Robert, 300n21
Pitt Adams, William, 172
Pizarro, Francisco, 282
plants, Andean native: artistic representation of, 97–98, 125–126; commodification of, 27, 29, 31; poisonous, 32, 44, 45; relocation and acclimatization of, 11, 91, 106, 120, 129, 255; study and classification of, 75. *See also* feed/fodder for extracted camelids; quinine (and cinchona plant)
Platt, Tristan, 177
Pliny the Elder (Gaius Plinius Secundus), 31
"plus ultra" concept, 196, 305n12
poetry as colonialist narrative, 223–224, 262–263
poisons: bezoar as antidote for, 26, 28, 31–34, 42–44, 46; idolatry as, 44; Indigenous use of, 44–46
Polinquin, Rachel, 5, 82
politics and science, and imperial control. *See* convergence of science and colonialism
Pomet, Pierre, 33, 42
Poopó area of Bolivia, 112, 116
Portugal, bezoar stones acquired by, 28, 34, 35, 40
Potosí, Bolivia, 3, 39, 111
Poucel, Benjamin, 182, 183, 190–191, 193, 196–197
Pratt, Mary Louise, 8–9
preserved camelid specimens: Frago-

nard llama (*écorché* specimen), 61, 80–87; for Great London Exposition, 238, 243–244; Ledger to Australia Museum in Sydney, 217; as narrative of material culture, 5–6, 83, 87, 287; skeletal, 163, 217, 287; as trophies of empire, 244. *See also* taxidermy specimens

price of fiber products. *See under* fleece/ wool of camelids

prizes and medals. *See* medals and awards for contributors to extraction projects

Purdue University College of Veterinary Medicine, 1

pushmi-pullyu, 263–264

Pyrenees: placement project in, 154, 161–163; as proposed habitat, 96, 101, 128

Qaqachaka, Bolivia, 47–48, 61–62

Quadro de historia natural (Thiebaut and Lequanda), 97–99

quinine (and cinchona plant), 170, 253–254, 316n9

quinto real ("royal fifth" tax), 52–53

"Quito" (male llama sent to Vosges project), 160

racialization and colonialist compartmentalization, 9, 137, 262. *See also* Indigenous Andeans

Rafferty, Frances, 261

Rambouillet merino sheep, 105. *See also* merino sheep

Real Fábrica de Guadalajara (Royal Factory of Guadalajara, Spain), 99–100

realia, 268, 278–280, 286–287. *See also* *costumbrista/costumbrismo* (imagery depicting local everyday culture)

Redden, Hilary, 3–4

regulation of camelid extraction and export. *See under individual species*

religion. *See* Christianity

Remiremont, France, 154, 158

reproduction (of camelid herds). *See* breeding and crossbreeding; fertility

Revlon, 274–275

rheas (*ñandús*), 191, 192

Ridder de Zemboraín, Maud de, 105

Río de la Plata, Viceroyalty of, 94, 100, 103, 111, 113, 117

risk-reward concepts, 209, 322n45

Rivera, José V., 178

Robbins, Louise E., 92

Roberts, Tom, 225

Robertson, John, 205, 218, 219, 220, 224, 227, 232, 238

Roehn, Eugène, 171; 1840s extraction proposal to France, 132–133; education and early projects, 131–132; extractions to New World locations, 133, 214; final attempted extraction project, 143; medals and awards, 134, 143, 153; overviews, 14, 127–128, 152, 153; as represented in heroic narrative/imagery, 135–138. *See also* Roehn's 1859 extraction expedition

Roehn's 1859 extraction expedition: extraction and voyage to France, 137–140; female from sent to Vosges, 157; health issues after arrival, 140–142; proposal from France, 133–135; results and impacts of, 142–144

Rojas Clemente, Simón de, 120–121

romanticization and "re-discovery" of South America. *See* tourism, promotion of

Rothschild, James de, 142

routes of extraction: advantages *v.* risks of, 91, 103, 108–109, 112, 114, 115, 132–133; map of, *x*

Royal Botanical Garden, Madrid, 109

Royal Society of Victoria, 235

royalty imagery as marketing strategy, 265–267, 283

Royal Veterinary School of Alfort, Paris (École Nationale Vétérinaire d'Alfort), 57. *See also* National Veterinary School of Alfort (École Nationale Vétérinaire d'Alfort)

Rubottom, Roy Richard, 277

Rufz de Lavison, Étienne, 147

ruminant digestion, evaluation of, 72–74

Russel, A. J. F., 3–4

sacrifice, Indigenous ritual, 3, 19, 37–38, 60, 62–67
Safier, Neil, 137, 139, 231
Saint-Domingue (later Haiti), 106, 108
Saint-Mont community, 155, 156, 158, 160
Salomon, Frank, 29, 48, 50–51
Salt, Titus, 249, 315n3, 323n55
Salta, Argentina, 111, 116–117, 173
Salvadora (ship), 203, 205
Sanford, Herb, 274
San Lorenzo pharmacy (royal palace, Spain), 25
Sanlúcar de Barrameda acclimatization garden, 20, 118, 119, 120–123
San Luis Beltrán, 43–44
San Román, Miguel de, 143
Savage, Santiago: departure of from group, 204; identity of, 185; Ledger excursion, 180–181, 183, 184–189, 198–200; Ledger's breeding experiments, 189–195, 196; and Ledger's heroic narrative, 166; value of in knowledge production, 210, 287
Savary des Bruslons, Jacques, 101
Sawday, Jonathan, 59–60, 66, 67
scabies (*Sarcoptes scabiei/Psoroptes communis*), 3. See also skin diseases of camelids
Schell, Patience A., 167
scholarship on Andean camelids, 4–5
Scholastic Magazine, 274
science and colonialism, intersection of. See convergence of science and colonialism
Scientific and Literary Society of Valparaíso, 183, 203
Scotland, extraction projects, 132
"secrets of nature" concept, 41–42, 301n26
Seidenbach's (department store), 265, 266
Semanario de Agricultura, Industria y Comercio (*Agriculture, Industry and Commerce Weekly*), 100, 109
señalu q'epi (sacred bundles, Quechua lang.), 46–48
serpents, imagery and mythology of, 32–34, 44, 45, 48–49

Seventeen magazine, 275
shearers, Australian, 225–227
shearing: of Australian flock, 224–227; and skin disease treatment, 142; traditional methods and schedules, 315n3; *v.* hunting and skinning, 3, 94–96, 260, 264
Shearing the Rams (Roberts), 225
sheep: camelids likened/compared to, 9, 89–91, 141, 212; "camel-sheep," 9–12, 17; merino sheep, 105–106, 110, 123, 207, 245
shepherds/caretakers, Indigenous: follow-up of Ledger's crew, 253–254; importance of in extraction projects, 123; Ledger's contradictory perspectives on, 211, 216, 230–234, 249, 252–254; Ledger's ethos of trust and collaboration, 167–168, 188, 253; marginalization of, 13, 16, 109, 123–124, 128, 287, 288; and questions of Savage's identity, 185; Roehn's expedition, 142, 143; as scapegoats for animal health issues, 13, 163
shipboard conditions, 148–153
silver mining, 31, 39, 217, 274, 285
Sir Charles Napier (ship), 168–169
skeletal museum specimens, 163, 217, 287. See also Fragonard llama (*écorché* specimen)
skin diseases of camelids: and bezoar alleged preventive qualities, 52; Joly's Pyrenees flock, 161–162; lack of in Ecuadorian transport flock, 150, 153; Roehn's flock, 140, 142, 150, 157; scabies organism, 3; treatments for, 115, 142, 230; in Vosges flock, 157, 160–161
skins (hides) of camelids: in foster-mothering programs, 195; skin as fabric metaphor, 305n6; skinning *v.* live shearing, 94–96, 260, 264. See also under fleece/wool of camelids; *individual species*
snakes. See serpents, imagery and mythology of
snow and ice, 174, 180, 198–199
Sobremonte, Rafael de, 111, 112, 116

378 | Index

Sociedad Real de Fomento (Royal Development Society, Havana), 131
Société Régionale d'Acclimatation pour la Zône du Nord-Est (Northeast Regional Acclimatization Society), 154
Société Zoologique d'Acclimatation. *See* Paris Acclimatization Society (Société Zoologique d'Acclimatation)
Society of Arts, London, 241
Solórzano y Pereira, Juan de, 53–54
Sophienburg (Atkinson estate), 224–225, 238, 239, *240*
Sosa, Pablo ("servant"), 173, 175, 254
Soult, Jean-de-Dieu, 122
South America Fortnight (Neiman Marcus event campaign), 22, 276–283
Spanish War of Independence (Peninsular War), 120
spitting by camelids, 77, 107, 194, 227
squatters, 212, 213
S. Stroock & Co.: advertising strategies, overviews, 257, 258–259, 283; background and history of, 15–16, 258; and conservation of vicuñas, 264–265; "edutainment" theme in marketing strategies, 257–259; fabric quality, importance of, 259; imagery and illustration in marketing, 261–263; labeling strategies as marketing device, 259–260; poetry in marketing, 262–263
Stafford, Barbara Maria, 57–58, 85
starvation losses, 90, 229–230
Statler Hilton Dallas, The, 281, 288–289
status symbols, camelid products as, 2, 260, 265, 268–269
storefront displays, 258, 268–269. *See also* dioramas in marketing
Story of Doctor Dolittle, The (Lofting), 263–264
Story of Vicuna, The (Stroock, S.), 258–259
Straet, Jan van der ("Stradanus"), 9
Stroock, Samuel, 158
Stroock, Sylvan I., 259, 261, 330n6
Stroock's Animal Kingdom (Rafferty), 261, 262

Subrahmanyam, Sanjay, 231
Sue, Jean-Joseph, 84, 86
Suri alpacas, 261
Swinglehurst, Henry: on friendship between Ledger and Savage, 186, 187, 204–205; on Ledger's achievements, 165–166, 167; Ledger's gift of Savage's artwork to, 181, 187
Swinney, Geoffrey N., 5
Sydney, Australia, 173, 207–208, 212, 215–216, 235, 238–240
Sydney Morning Herald, 202, 222, 223, 232, 316n12

Tacna, Peru, 112, 138–139, 168
Taqui Onqoy movement, 45–46
taxidermy specimens: Ledger's donations, 217, 240, 241–242; as narrative of material culture, 5–6, 7; in product marketing displays, 258, 268, 269, 270, 273, 286
taxonomy. *See* classification (taxonomic) speculations and challenges
Taylor-Leduc, Susan, 91, 105
Terán, Francisco (Theran), 119, 120–123
terra nullius doctrine, 213
Tessier, Henri Alexandre, 123
Textbook of Veterinary Anatomy (Dyce, Sack, and Wensing), 57
textile industry. *See* fabrics from camelid wool
textile wrapping/unwrapping metaphor, 48, 61–62
theatricality in retail marketing, 278, 282–283, 286–287
Thiebaut, Luis, 97, 98
Thouvenel, Édouard Antoine de, 145–146
Times (London), 213, 214, 238
Toledo, Francisco de (viceroy of Peru/Bolivia), 25, 52–53
Tomoeda, Hiroyasu, 50
Torres, Marcos, 116
Tortorici, Zeb, 5
Toulouse, France, 127, 162, 163
tourism, promotion of, 259, 262, 276, 280, 282

Town & Country Magazine, 277
Trece Monedas (restaurant), 279
tributes (taxes), 95
Trujillo of Peru (Martínez de Compañón), 97, 99
Tupak Amaru (Inca leader), 48–49
Tupak Katari (Inca leader), 48–49
tupaq (resplendent leader), 49

Ulloa, Antonio de, 91, 93–96, 103
Ulloa, Pedro Sórez de, 301–302n29
unca (liver fluke parasite), 181, 189
urination orientation in camelids, 76–77
Uspallata Pass, Chile, 115

Valparaíso, Chile, 113–115, 147, 173, 174, 180, 203–204
value of camelid wool. See under fleece/wool of camelids
Van Dooren, Thom, 170, 333n2
Vega, Julián, 113
Venegas, Francisco Javier, 122
Vespucci, Amerigo, 9
Victoria colony, Australia: Burke and Wills expedition, 219; early efforts to acquire camelids, 212–213; Ledger's dealings with, 216, 217, 234–237, 246–247, 249–251; rivalry with NSW colony, 209, 215, 217–218, 244, 250; Wilson-Westgarth camelid venture, 213–215, 234–235
Vicuña Mackenna, Benjamin, 197n7
vicuñas (Vicugna vicugna): Buffon's study of, 61, 75–80, 101; chacos (vicuña hunts), 3, 94, 98, 112, 190, 191–192, 193; conservation and regulation of, 93–97, 264–265; extraction speculation and attempts, 99, 102–104, 109–118; hunting and skinning v. live capture and shearing, 94–96, 260, 264; Ledger's domestication experiment, 22, 191–196; physical and behavioral descriptions of, 77–79, 98, 107, 194–195; preserved specimens, 80; taxonomic speculation and understanding, 2, 77, 103–104. See also S. Stroock & Co.

Vilca Pujio, Bolivia, 175, 176
Vocabulario (Bertonio, Aymara lang.), 45
Vocabulario (González Holguín, Quechua lang.), 45
Voltaire (François-Marie Arouet), 89–91
Vosges (mountains) project, 15, 21–22, 128, 142, 154–161

Waddington, Joshua, 187, 218
Waddington, Templeman & Co., 203–204
Wailly, Léon de, 107
Warwick Examiner and Times, 226–227
water needs of camelids: anecdotal assumptions, 77; quality issues, 152, 181; shortage of during extraction journeys, 139, 144, 174, 181, 200–201
wax injection preservation method, 81
weather. See climate and weather
Weber, Max, 209
Welser family of Germany, sixteenth century, 30–31
Westgarth, William, 213–215
Wheeler, Jane C., 3–4
white camelids, demand for, 3, 100
Wilkie, David E., 219
William II and III of Netherlands, 7
Wilson, Edward, 213–215, 219, 242, 245
Wilson-Westgarth camelid venture, 214, 215, 216, 234–235
winds and gales, 198, 318n30
Wingello Park, 251
Winthrop, Theodore, 135
women (Indigenous): colonialist compartmentalization of, 9, 137, 177–178; and fertility rituals, 47–48, 61–62; indignation over extraction of flocks, 175, 176, 177–178, 287; shearing by, 225
wool animals. See fleece/wool of camelids; goats; merino sheep
wool industry in Australia, 172, 212, 217, 222. See also merino sheep
Worms, Jules, 136–137
wrapping/unwrapping as cultural metaphors, 48, 61–62. See also bundles

of sacred/ceremonial objects (*señalu q'epi*, Quechua lang.)

Württemberg king, gift of llama to, 108, 109

Yale Peruvian Archaeological Expedition, 267

ycho (native Andean grass), 103, 221

ylla/illa and derivatives (Spanish translations of, Aymara and Quechua lang.), 50–51. *See also illas* (sacred/ceremonial objects)

yllarik (resplendent thing, Quechua lang.), 49

yllarini (to blaze, shine, Quechua lang.), 49

Yocabaccio, Hugo, 95

Young, John, 218, 239

Zea, Francisco, 109

Zoological Society of Victoria, 217

zoos. *See* menageries/zoos, notable

Zurbarán, Francisco de, 43–44